REVELATION

This book is the first of its kind: an innovative socio-rhetorical commentary on the book of Revelation. Without sacrificing scholarly perspective or academic rigor, it is written to be accessible for a wide audience – including pastors, scholars, teachers, seminarians, and interested laypeople. A "Suggested Reading" list – a feature of all volumes in the New Cambridge Bible Commentary – will serve as a point of entry for the new serious student of Revelation and as a helpful annotated bibliography for all readers. Frequent "Closer Look" sections examine key elements of the Roman-Greco world that bear on the text's meaning, while "Bridging the Horizons" articles connect this world with the cultural, political, and religious environments of today. The entire NRSV translation is provided throughout the text as a convenience to the reader. Award-winning author Ben Witherington III brings a New Testament scholar's insight and successful clergyman's lucidity to the often opaque passages of the last book of the New Testament.

Ben Witherington III is a leading New Testament scholar and author of twenty-one books, including *The Jesus Quest: The Third Search for the Jew of Nazareth* (1995) and *Grace in Galatia* (1998).

NEW CAMBRIDGE BIBLE COMMENTARY

GENERAL EDITOR: Ben Witherington III

HEBREW BIBLE/OLD TESTAMENT EDITOR: Bill T. Arnold

The New Cambridge Bible Commentary (NCBC) aims to elucidate the Hebrew and Christian Scriptures for a wide range of intellectually curious individuals. While building on the work and reputation of the Cambridge Bible Commentary popular in the 1960s and 1970s, the NCBC takes advantage of many of the rewards provided by scholarly research over the last four decades. Volumes utilize recent gains in rhetorical criticism, social scientific study of the Scriptures, narrative criticism, and other developing disciplines to exploit the growing edges in biblical studies. Accessible, jargon-free commentary, an annotated "Suggested Reading" list, and the entire New Revised Standard Version (NRSV) text under discussion are the hallmarks of all volumes in the series.

FORTHCOMING VOLUMES
Genesis, Bill T. Arnold
Exodus, Carol Meyers
Deuteronomy, Brent Strawn
Judges and Ruth, Victor H. Matthews
1–2 Chronicles, William Schniedewind
Isaiah 1–39, David Baer
Jeremiah, Baruch Halpern
Hosea, Joel, and Amos, J. J. M. Roberts
The Gospel of Matthew, Craig A. Evans
The Gospel of John, Jerome H. Neyrey
Paul's Letters to the Corinthians, Craig S. Keener
The Letters of James and Jude, William F. Brosend
The Letters of John, Duane F. Watson

Revelation

Ben Witherington III
Asbury Theological Seminary

PUBLISHED BY THE PRESS SYNDICATE OF THE UNIVERSITY OF CAMBRIDGE
The Pitt Building, Trumpington Street, Cambridge, United Kingdom

CAMBRIDGE UNIVERSITY PRESS
The Edinburgh Building, Cambridge CB2 2RU, UK
40 West 20th Street, New York, NY 10011-4211, USA
477 Williamstown Road, Port Melbourne, VIC 3207, Australia
Ruiz de Alarcón 13, 28014 Madrid, Spain
Dock House, The Waterfront, Cape Town 8001, South Africa

http://www.cambridge.org

First published   2003

Printed in the United States of America

Typeface Minion 10/12 pt.   *System* LATEX 2$_\varepsilon$ [TB]

A catalog record for this book is available from the British Library.

Library of Congress Cataloging in Publication Data
Witherington, Ben, 1951–
Revelation / Ben Witherington III.
    p.   cm. – (New Cambridge Bible commentary)
Includes bibliographical references and index.
ISBN 0-521-80609-7 – ISBN 0-521-00068-8 (pbk.)
1. Bible. N.T. Revelation – Commentaries.   2. Bible. N.T. Revelation – Socio-rhetorical criticism.
I. Title.   II. Series.
BS2825.53.W58   2003
228′.077 – dc21   2002041245

ISBN 0 521 80609 7 hardback
ISBN 0 521 00068 8 paperback

Contents

Preface

For many years the book of Revelation has been to most of the Christian world like a terra incognita – an unknown land. After all, what do multiheaded beasts and warriors in blood-drenched robes have to do with the modern condition of the church or of the world? Even if one concludes that Revelation is historically referential in nature, there is no unanimity on what particular historical figures and events the book has in view. Indeed if one is a student of the history of the interpretation of Revelation, one recognizes a near 100 percent failure rate when matching up images and events in Revelation with particular historical figures.

It is not surprising that some of the Protestant Reformers were reticent to make pronouncements about Revelation. Calvin, the great exegete, decided that this was the one New Testament (NT) book on which he would not do a commentary. Luther, when he wasn't busy saying he didn't understand Revelation, in his first preface to the book expressed serious doubts about its apostolicity and prophetic character, but in his second preface he became enthusiastic about the book, seeing it as chronicling church history (including his own period). John Wesley, in his *Explanatory Notes on the New Testament*, simply passed along the views of earlier exegetes, in particular Johannes Bengel, with the disclaimer that he didn't necessarily think Bengel was correct but that what he had to offer was better than the alternatives. To say that some of the major founding fathers of Protestantism did not know what to do with this book is an understatement.[1] Yet the plethora of modern interpreters and modern works on Revelation suggests a rebirth

---

[1] Yet there were others who found the book illuminating and fascinating. Richard Bauckham has pointed out to me in private correspondence, "It was a great age of commentaries on Revelation, because everyone (RC and Protestant) had an apocalyptic sense of a crisis of history and turned to Revelation (as well as Daniel, etc.) to understand it. Its relevance was strongly felt by the Marian martyrs in England, and Heinrich Bullinger's immensely popular commentary brought this out. John Foxe's *Book of Martyrs* also popularized this reading of Revelation." See Bauckham's *Tudor Apocalypse* (Abingdon, Oxford: Sutton Courtney Press, 1978).

of hope in making some sense of this complex and challenging masterpiece. Perhaps now as we move into the twenty-first century and the third millennium of church history John's Revelation will give up some of its secrets. In any event it is a propitious time to attempt a more adequate interpretation of the work. "Let the reader understand" that what lies herein is but one reading of a complex and fascinating work.

A thank you to Craig Koester for reading the manuscript and making various helpful suggestions while he also was working on a Revelation commentary. A special thank you to Darlene Hyatt who proofed the entire manuscript, saving me from various blunders and infelicities of style and grammar. This work is dedicated to two scholars who are also good friends from whom I have learned much about Revelation – Richard Bauckham and Craig Keener. Their fingerprints are all over this manuscript, even though the ink is mine.

Christmas 2002

A Word about Citations

All volumes in the New Cambridge Bible Commentary (NCBC) include foot-notes, with full bibliographical citations included in the note when a source text is first mentioned. Subsequent citations include the author's initial or initials, full last name, abbreviated title for the work, and date of publication. Most readers prefer this citation system to endnotes that require searching through pages at the back of the book.

The Suggested Reading lists, also included in all NCBC volumes after the Introduction, are not a part of this citation apparatus. Annotated and orga-nized by publication type, the self-contained Suggested Reading list is intended to introduce and briefly to review some of the most well-known and helpful literature on the biblical text under discussion.

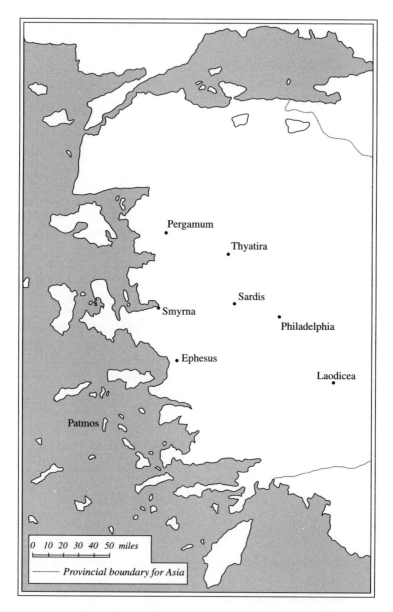

MAP OF WESTERN ASIA MINOR AND THE ISLAND OF PATMOS

Roman Emperors

The following list of Roman emperors will be useful for reference:

Augustus	27 B.C.–A.D. 14
Tiberius	A.D. 14–37
Caligula	A.D. 37–41
Claudius	A.D. 41–54
Nero	A.D. 54–68
Galba	A.D. 68–69
Otho	A.D. 69
Vitellius	A.D. 69
Vespasian	A.D. 69–79
Titus	A.D. 79–81
Domitian	A.D. 81–96

Abbreviations

ABD   D. N. Freedman, ed., *Anchor Bible Dictionary*, 4 vols. (New York: Doubleday, 1992)

ANRW   *Aufstieg und Niedergang der römischen Welt*

AUSS   *Andrews University Seminary Studies*

BA   *Biblical Archaeologist*

BAR   *Biblical Archaeology Review*

BETL   Bibliotheca Ephemeridum Theologicarum Lovaniensium

Bib. Sac. *Bibliotheca Sacra*

BJRL   *Bulletin of the John Rylands Library*

CBQ   *Catholic Biblical Quarterly*

CT   *Christianity Today*

ExpT   *Expository Times*

HTR   *Harvard Theological Review*

Interp. *Interpretation*

JB   Jerusalem Bible

JBL   *Journal of Biblical Literature*

JETS   *Journal of the Evangelical Theological Society*

JSJ   *Journal for the Study of Judaism in the Persian, Hellenistic, and Roman Period*

JSNT   *Journal for the Study of the New Testament*

JSP   *Journal for the Study of the Pseudepigrapha*

JTS   *Journal of Theological Studies*

KJV   King James Version (or Authorized Version)

LXX   Septuagint

NCBC   New Cambridge Bible Commentary

NEB   New English Bible

NIV   New International Version

NovT   *Novum Testamentum*

NRSV   New Revised Standard Version

NT   New Testament

NTS	*New Testament Studies*
OT	Old Testament
PC	Proclamation Commentaries
ProtoBib	*Protokolle zur Bibel*
QJS	*Quarterly Journal of Speech*
RevBib	*Revue Biblique*
SBL Seminar Papers	*Society of Biblical Literature Seminar Papers*
SNTS	Society of New Testament Studies
TEV	Today's English Version
TynB	*Tyndale Bulletin*
TZ	*Theologische Zeitschrift*
WTJ	*Westminster Theological Journal*
ZNW	*Zeitschrift für die Neutestamentliche Wissenschaft*
ZTK	*Zeitschrift für Theologie und Kirche*

I. Introduction

❦

As the majority of scholars recognize, Revelation is not a pseudonymous document. Its author identifies himself at the beginning as someone named John. But which John? Is it a John we know from elsewhere in the NT, say, for example, John the son of Zebedee or, as J. M. Ford conjectured in her Anchor Bible commentary, John the Baptist? Could this John be John Mark or perhaps some heretofore unknown John? Later Christian tradition identified the author as John the son of Zebedee, but it must be borne in mind that this notion dates at least a half century after Revelation was written (the earliest possible witnesses are Justin Martyr and Irenaeus from the mid- and late second century A.D. respectively – Justin, *Dial.* 81.4; Irenaeus, *Adv. Haer.* 4.20.11) and during an era when connecting sacred documents to apostolic witnesses was considered crucial, especially if such documents were to be recognized as having some sort of canonical status.

How does the author identify himself? He calls himself John the servant of Christ (1.2) who testified to certain things based on what Christ showed him through an angelic mediator. In other words John is claiming to be a visionary and a testifier, and if the term "servant" has the fuller resonance it does sometimes in the Old Testament (OT) prophetic corpus, in the Pauline writings, and elsewhere, he is claiming to be a prophet. In Rev. 22.9 the author clearly classes himself as among the prophets, and other chapters in the work (e.g., Rev. 10) make it apparent that this is the way the author chiefly views himself. In short the author is John the seer who offers up prophetic testimonies and proclamations. He does not identify himself as an apostle, nor does he call himself the Beloved Disciple or, for that matter, the Elder (see 2 and 3 John).

The discussion of which John has been complicated by attempts to figure out the interrelationships between the Gospel, Epistles, and Revelation that came to be associated with John's name. Unlike the Gospel and the Epistles, which do not state the name of the author within the text itself, Revelation states that it is

1

written by one John the seer. We must consider some of the particulars of these texts to further sort out the issue of authorship.

Linguistic study of the Johannine Gospel, Epistles, and Revelation makes it unlikely that these five documents were written by the same person. Differences were noticed as early as the mid-third century A.D. by Dionysius of Alexandria, who is quoted favorably by Eusebius. Almost a century ago, R. H. Charles laid out the linguistic evidence in some detail, and here I will simply offer some highlights.[1] (1) While it is possible to argue that Revelation reflects Semitic interference (i.e., the Greek of an author who thinks in a Semitic language and struggles to translate) and even that the author is deliberately archaizing (in this case Semitizing)[2] because of the nature of this document, which stands in part in the tradition of Jewish apocalyptic, these suggestions do not adequately explain all the differences in grammatical habits between Revelation and the other Johannine writings.[3] (2) In Revelation *axios* (worthy) is followed by the infinitive, while in the Gospel it is followed by *hina* (in order that). (3) In the Gospel we find *mn* used with the participle eleven times and with the genitive absolute frequently, but the author of Revelation uses neither, when there were opportunities to do so. (4) The author of Revelation frequently uses different words than the Gospel writer does to refer to the same concept. Thus *arnion* is used for lamb some twenty-nine times by the former but not at all by the latter, where *amnos* is used (twice). (5) Jerusalem is spelled *Ierosalem* in Revelation but *Ierosoluma* in the Gospel. (6) For exclamations Revelation uses *idou* some twenty-six times, but the Gospel uses *ide*. 7) To refer to what something is called or named Revelation always has *kaleo*, and the Gospel always has *lego* (cf. Rev. 16.16; John 19.13). (7) Even more striking is when the writers of these documents use the same word to mean very different things. Thus, for example, *alethinos* means true as opposed to false in Revelation but means authentic or genuine in the Gospel. (8) *Ethnos/ethne* means Gentiles or all nations in Revelation, but it refers exclusively to the Jews (five times) in the Gospel. (9) *Kosmos* in Revelation means the created world, while in the Gospel it means the world of humanity. (10) *Laos* means Gentiles or Christians in Revelation, but it means Jews in the Gospel of John, except perhaps in one case. (11) *Proskunein* with the

---

[1] R. H. Charles, *A Critical and Exegetical Commentary on the Revelation of St. John*, vol. 1 (Edinburgh: T + T Clark, 1920), pp. xxii ff.

[2] But see the following analysis. This hypothesis is unlikely considering that the author finds it natural to use the Hebrew OT as his major external resource.

[3] For arguments against so-called Semitic Greek and against biblical Hebrew being John's first language and in favor of his knowing Palestinian Aramaic or possibly later (Mishnaic-style) Hebrew, see G. Horsley et al., eds., *New Documents Illustrating Early Christianity*, vol. 5 (Grand Rapids, Mich.: Eerdmans, 1981), pp. 5–35, especially pp. 34–35. These arguments are mainly against the sort of treatment of Revelation found in S. Thompson, *The Apocalypse and Semitic Syntax* (Cambridge: Cambridge University Press, 1985).

dative means to worship in Revelation while with the accusative it means to do homage. This is the reverse of the usage in the Gospel.

These differences in diction rather strongly favor the conclusion that the person who produced the final form of Revelation did not also produce the final form of the Gospel of John (or the Johannine Epistles, which are similar in diction and grammar to the Gospels). Yet there are terms such as ***logos*** that are applied to Christ only in the Fourth Gospel and in Revelation. There are also passages where there is similarity of diction and usage between the two works (cf. Rev. 2.2 to John 16.2; Rev. 20.6 to John 13.8; Rev. 22.15 to John 3.21; Rev. 22.17 to John 7.37). The question then is how to explain the similarities as well as the differences between these works. While style does evolve, a total change in style and usage is most unlikely. Furthermore the Gospel is written in rather plain and simple Koine Greek, whereas in Revelation the vocabulary is much more complex and the grammar is often prolix.[4] For example, one out of eight words in Revelation is a ***hapax legomenon***. While some of this can be explained by different subject matter in the two works, not all of it can be.[5] On the whole this internal evidence strongly favors the conclusion that the person who wrote Revelation did not also write the Fourth Gospel or the Epistles, yet John the seer has some sort of relationship with those who wrote the rest of the Johannine corpus or with their communities or with both.

In my view John the seer is a prophet from the Johannine community operating at a time when there is apparently no apostolic presence left in that community (see Rev. 22.14, which views apostles as a foundation of the church, apparently in the past). Were he John the son of Zebedee it is passing strange that he does not identify himself as an apostle or as an original disciple of Jesus in the letter portion of Revelation, where credentials were important and would have contributed to the rhetorical establishment of the author's authority in relationship to the audience. Nor does he identify himself as "the elder/old man" as the author of the Epistles does. In fact there is nothing in Revelation establishing John's *personal* authority. His vision has the authority of a revelation from Jesus for which John is the mouthpiece, which is to say he reflects the derived authority of a prophet.

In regard to the date of this work there have been really only two major possibilities that scholars have explored – a date at the end of or just after the reign of Nero or a date considerably later than that, during the reign of Domitian. The arguments for a Neronian date need to be given their due, as

---

[4] See the discussion by S. E. Porter, "The Language of the Apocalypse in Recent Discussion," *NTS* 35 (1989), pp. 582–603. On whether John is being deliberately idiosyncratic in his use of the Greek, perhaps to make a protest against the dominant culture, see A. D. Callahan, "The Language of the Apocalypse," *HTR* 88 (1995), pp. 453–70.

[5] Nor can this phenomenon be adequately explained by the numerous echoes and allusions to OT texts in Revelation.

they have some merit.[6] The first organized Roman persecution of Christians took place under the reign of Nero in the wake of the fire in A.D. 64.[7] The antagonistic attitude toward Roman government coupled with the references to persecution or suffering in Revelation could certainly reflect fresh memories of what had happened in the mid-sixties A.D. (cf. Rev. 2.3, 10, 13; 3.8; 6.9–11; 13.1 ff; 17.1 ff.). Yet one needs to keep in mind that Revelation is not written to an audience in Rome, and we have no clear evidence that the persecution in the sixties was anything but local. What we are looking for is a social situation affecting the churches in Asia.[8]

There are certain key internal factors that seem to favor a date from late in the first century.

1) The epistolary part of Revelation appears to reflect a knowledge of the Pauline corpus or at least some of Paul's letters, in particular of the form of those letters.

2) There is evidence of knowledge of some of the sayings of the historical Jesus. Yet if Revelation is written at or around A.D. 69–70, none of the Gospels were likely yet extant.

3) Rome is clearly identified as Babylon in Revelation, an identification that makes better sense after, rather than before, the destruction of Jerusalem by Titus. The same applies to the description of Jerusalem being like two previously destroyed cities – Sodom and Gomorrah.[9]

4) The condition of the churches in Asia that John addresses seems to reflect that they have existed for a considerable period of time, enough time to suffer various trials and defections, and a loss of zeal.

5) The lack of apostolic presence and, by contrast, the presence of powerful prophets (both John and those he calls false prophets) seem to reflect a time after the apostles had died off late in the first century A.D. (cf. the Didache).

6) All things being equal, the allusions to the emperor cult and its dangers for Christians seems to suit better the time of Domitian than the time of Nero.

[6] See J. C. Wilson, "The Problem with the Domitianic Date of Revelation," *NTS* 39 (1993), pp. 587–605.

[7] See my discussion in *New Testament History* (Grand Rapids, Mich.: Baker Books, 2001), pp. 333–55.

[8] In regard to the state of the text of Revelation, see D. Aune, *Revelation*, 3 vols. (Dallas: Word, 1997; Nashville, Tenn.: Nelson, 1998), cliv–clix and throughout the beginning translation sections of each of his divisions of the work. We have some 287 Greek manuscripts from various centuries of part or all of Revelation. Fortunately over half of the verses of Revelation are variant free. There were only two early papyri of Revelation until recently. Some new relatively early (third–fourth century) evidence has been found in the form of p115. See D. C. Parker, "A New Oxyrhnchus Papyrus: p115 (P. Oxy. 4499)," *NTS* 46 (2000), pp. 159–74.

[9] Although it would already make good sense in Rome after the fire in 64 and before 70, when the Christians were being persecuted, and 1 Pet. may reflect this Sitz im Leben.

7) The Christological references that counterbalance Christ against the lord-ship and deity of the Emperor best suit a post-Neronian period of NT history. This does not appear to be a major concern for Paul during his day.

Thus on the whole a date during the reign of Domitian seems more plausible than one during or just after the reign of Nero.

But what was the reign of Domitian actually like? There has been an effort by some NT scholars (e.g., A. Yarbro Collins, L. Thompson) to rehabilitate Domitian, and they suggest that he was not the maniacal tyrant that later Roman historians depicted him to be. It is perhaps true that the Roman historians, from the time of Trajan on, overdid the use of black in their portraits of Domitian. There are, however, severe problems with the arguments suggesting that it is unlikely there was any persecution of Christians under Domitian's reign. We will dialogue with the case Thompson makes as he presents the fullest form of these sorts of arguments.

First, Thompson is arguing against not only the most important primary his-torical sources we have on this subject (Tacitus, Suetonius, Dio Cassius) but also against the judgment of Domitian by the majority of Roman historians in our own era. Thompson realizes that these standard sources paint Domitian as evil "almost without qualification. Suetonius, the most generous among the sources, says that Domitian began his reign with 'some leniency and self-restraint' but that those qualities 'were not destined to continue long, although he turned to cruelty somewhat more speedily than to avarice" (*Dom.* 10.11).[10] The portrait in Dio Cassius is even more bleak. To rehabilitate Domitian, Thompson turns to sources contemporary with Domitian, such as Martial, Statius, and Quintilian. Unfortunately they do not really support his case. There are some positive re-marks by these authors about Domitian, mainly about his military exploits (see, e.g., Quintilian's *Inst. Or.* 10.1.9.1). But frankly, Domitian had very few successful military exploits, and so one must expect that some of this positive verbiage is gratuitous, aimed at keeping the authors in the Emperor's good graces. Both Quintilian and Statius were close to the throne at the end of Domitian's reign.

Thompson tries to make the case that Domitian was not called *dominus* and *deus* during his reign, even though he recognizes that Martial in *Epigrams*, Book 5, does so, and Statius also shows Domitian addressed as dominus (*Silv.* 1.6.84). In striking contrast to the conclusions of Thompson are the remarks of Roman historian M. Griffin, who, having evaluated the pertinent evidence, states,

The most striking departure from the senatorial ideal of a *princeps* who was one of them was Domitian's encouragement of the flattering mode of address "dominus et deus." . . . What was at issue was the way the *princeps* was *addressed*, not only orally but in writing. . . .

---

[10] L. Thompson, *The Book of Revelation: Apocalypse and Empire* (Oxford: Oxford University Press, 1990), p. 97.

Domitian, in a more than passive way, abandoned the practice of "good" emperors who deliberately discouraged or rejected "dominus" as a form of address, aligning himself instead with Caligula. The addition of "deus" to "dominus" only made the salutation more offensive. . . . It was the way that Domitian used it of himself, combined it with "deus" and encouraged that form of address by others which, added to his own manifest intention to behave as a "dominus," created the resentment that still echoes in the ancient texts.[11]

Griffin demonstrates at length the tyranny that Domitian engaged in, particularly during the last years of his reign. After citing various examples, Griffin stresses, "Domitian's reign was characterized, not by exceptional efficiency nor by an increased concern for justice and welfare, but by the censoriousness of a disciplinarian."[12] Domitian believed in reviving the old Augustinian laws about sexual misconduct (particularly homosexuality) and about preserving the traditional and state religion. It was precisely on these latter grounds that Domitian would have approved of persecuting Christians, who were deemed atheists because they refused to honor the traditional gods or the Emperor. We know that Domitian followed in the footsteps of his father, Vespasian, in continuing to exact the tax on the Jews, paid to the Temple of Jupiter instead of the then defunct temple in Jerusalem. This went to such extremes in Domitian's day that persons were examined to see if they were circumcised when they were suspected of being Jewish and had avoided paying the tax (Suetonius, *Dom.* 12.2; Suetonius was an eyewitness of this practice in the provinces).

But it is not true to say that we have no evidence of the persecution of Christians during the reign of Domitian. Even if we omit the evidence in Revelation, we still must reckon with evidence from the second century A.D. that favors such a conclusion. For example, Melito of Sardis writing in the mid-second century to Emperor Marcus Aurelius says that Domitian, like Nero, was persuaded to slander Christian teaching and to instigate the practice of falsely accusing Christians (see Eusebius, *Hist. Eccl.* 4.26.9). Thus, even if Domitian did not initiate an empire-wide persecution (and the evidence does not suggest that he did), it is plausible that he created a climate where local persecution not only could, but from time to time did, happen.

Pliny reported to Trajan that a practice of interrogation and flogging or worse of Christians and of forcing them to venerate an image of the Emperor had been ongoing in the province (Bithynia), where he was governing for some time, dating back to the reign of Domitian. He was now consulting with Trajan to seek his advice about dealing with such Christians. In his *Epistle* 10, written about A.D. 112, we find the following elements: (1) Pliny knows full well that Christians had been investigated before when complaints were brought to Roman officials, though he himself had not previously participated in such investigations. He says, "In investigations of Christians I have never taken part: hence I do not know

---

[11] M. Griffin, "The Flavians," *Cambridge Ancient History* 11 (2000), pp. 81–82.
[12] Ibid., p. 79.

how the crime *is usually punished.*" Notice his assumption that being a professed Christian is indeed a crime, for it is usually punished. (2) What punishment did Pliny think fit if a person who came before him persisted in confessing to be a Christian? He says, "If they kept to it, I ordered them for execution." (3) Pliny notes that this "superstition" has spread to even the upper echelon of society. He says, "There were others of the like insanity: but as these were Roman citizens, I noted them down to be sent to Rome." (4) Pliny goes on to explain that some of those who were brought before him had renounced Christ some twenty years previous, or in other words during the reign of Domitian. But under what circumstances would they have made such a public renunciation? Surely it would have been under the same sort of circumstances being chronicled in *Epistle* 10. Certain citizens or residents of a provincial town, whether pagans or Jews, had made complaints to the governing officials about Christians, who had been brought before those officials and asked whether it was true that they were Christians and refused to venerate the Emperor. True enough, this persecution was not instigated by Roman officials, but it was carried out by them since they reserved the use of force to themselves. Trajan did not encourage the seeking out of Christians for persecution but did endorse the practice followed by Pliny if they were so accused at the public tribunal. (5) Finally, Pliny notes that Christianity is very widespread in his province, in towns, villages, and the countryside, involves all ranks of society, and has led to the neglect of the worship and animal sacrifices in the traditional pagan temples. This surely did not happen overnight, and it seems plausible that what we witness in Revelation is evidence that the spread of Christianity had produced similar persecution and suffering for Christians during the reign of Domitian. T. B. Slater and S. R. F. Price are right to point out that there is sufficient evidence of enthusiastic promotion of the imperial cult in Asia and simultaneous repression of nonsupporters of this cult to make plausible the argument that Christians, especially the higher-status ones, were under significant social pressure to conform during and after the reign of Domitian.[13]

We must take seriously the evidence in Rev. 2–3 that it is a document addressed to actual particular congregations with which John had contact, congregations on the western edge of the province of Asia. All of these congregations are on the main road or on roads out of Ephesus that connect this region. Early Christianity was a urban phenomenon by and large at this juncture, a fact to which Revelation bears witness. If we probe more closely about the social situation of some or most of these Christians, then we need to keep in mind that only two letters, those to Smyrna (2.8–11) and Pergamum (2.9–10), address the relationship of the church to a social reality outside itself. In both cases

---

[13] T. B. Slater, "On the Social Setting of the Revelation," *NTS* 44 (1998), p. 238; S. R. Price, *Rituals and Power: The Roman Imperial Cult in Asia Minor* (Cambridge: Cambridge University Press, 1984), pp. 123–26, 197–98.

we discover that "the only references to the wider Roman Asian milieu are to the repression of Christians,"[14] including the martyrdom of someone named Antipas. To this may be added the unremittingly negative portrait of the powers-that-be, including the Emperor, in various parts of Revelation that follow these letters. We cannot say that we have no evidence of a systematic persecution of Christians by Roman officials in this period because we do have clear evidence of suffering, oppression, repression, suppression, and occasional martyrdom. On the whole it appears Slater is on target when he concludes, "I propose a socio-religious setting for the Revelation of John in which Asian Christians experienced local harassment, ridicule, discrimination and oppression in the early 90s for their religious beliefs and customs."[15] Thus it is not possible to agree with those who believe that Revelation reflects merely the fear of persecution rather than the actual social crisis for early Christians.[16] Furthermore a careful examination of the use of the term *martus* in Revelation shows that in each occurrence (five – 1.5; 3.14 [of Jesus]; 2.13; 11.3; 17.6) there is reference to the violent death of someone who was a faithful witness. Indeed the term *pistos* (faithful) in 2.10 and 2.13 and perhaps also in 1.5 seems to mean faithful unto death. This does not mean that *martus* in Revelation is already a technical term for martyr for Rev. 15.5 shows it can be used simply for a witness; rather it means that it regularly carries the connotation of a witness who is faithful even unto a violent death.[17]

---

[14] T. B. Slater, "Social Setting" (1998), p. 241.

[15] Ibid., p. 254.

[16] Some care needs to be taken in how one frames this discussion. In private correspondence Bauckam has remarked to me, "On Domitian and persecution, I would say the evidence for emphasis on the emperor cult is more important than evidence of persecution. But one should remember that the impetus for the emperor cult largely did not come from the centre but spontaneously from the local elites in the cities of the east, and Revelation in fact accurately reflects that in the figure of the second beast/false prophet. Nor was persecution an initiative from the centre, but depended much on local dynamics, as is clear from Pliny (Pliny's actions are very dependent on locals actually denouncing Christians – hence in Rev. the fury against the Jews who are in effect betraying Christians to the authorities). In other words, I would dissociate myself from the many older scholars who thought there was a widespread, centrally organized persecution under Domitian. That the historical evidence doesn't support that seems to me to concur with Revelation, rather than require Thompson's line. Revelation, of course, is not concerned with whether Domitian is a good emperor in some of the terms that mattered to his fellow Romans (was he successful in war? – the more he was, the worse he would be in Christian eyes, the better in Roman), so one must be careful about the classical scholars' discussion as to what aspects of Domitian are actually relevant to a negative assessment of him by Christians, but remember that Revelation has a generally negative assessment of the imperial institution as such – all seven heads (all the emperors) are heads of the beast! Domitian needn't be worse than others. Nero, on the other hand, was – and for Revelation that matters."

[17] The technical sense of martyr and martyrdom is found for *martus* and its cognates already in the late second century A.D. in *The Martyrdom of Polycarp* (see especially 2.iii.397). On this whole matter, see A. A. Trites, "*Martus* and Martyrdom in the Apocalypse," *NovT* 15 (1973), pp. 72–80.

What does this signify about the particular circumstances of John himself? Domitian, like other emperors and with the aid of those who served him, regularly used the form of punishment known as relegation, which could take one of two forms: *relegatio in insulam* or *deportatio ad insulam*. The former meant confinement within an island, the latter deportation to an island after which one had freedom within the island context. In either case banishment for life was involved. This was indeed, under any normal circumstances, a permanent ban of someone from where they had previously lived. It is very possible that John was suffering such a lifetime ban from the western coast of Asia Minor, hence the urgency to write to his converts. Note that he nowhere states that he hopes to come to them soon. Indeed he only speaks of Jesus coming quickly.

Patmos was indeed no prize to live on. Like other islands, it was probably used as a penal colony by the Romans. It is not clear from our text whether John was merely deported or whether he was also confined and subjected to hard labor while on Patmos, but in either case he could not hope to visit his converts again. In light of this one can see Revelation as an attempt to provide the whole apocalyptic picture to the Johannine audience in one effort, since John himself would be unable to come and explain these matters to these churches through conversations over a period of time. It is possible that John was among the social elite, since the elite tended to be exiled for their crimes, whereas the nonelites of society were simply executed (see Eusebius, *His. Eccl.* 3.17– 20; 4.27–9). Certainly he is literate, and his knowledge of the OT and other literature suggests that, at least in a specific and limited range of subjects, he is learned.

If it is true that John had suffered banishment from Asia Minor, from a sociological point of view this strongly suggests he was someone important not only in a general sense as I have just suggested but also as a leader in the churches in Asia Minor, and not merely as a peripheral prophet. This would explain why he takes it upon himself to exhort these various churches – he has some intimate knowledge of their spiritual and social conditions. Writing before the time of the monarchial bishops but probably after the time when the apostles were present in the region, John sought to assert his prophetic authority to help these churches get through a dark period of oppression and suppression that sometimes led to martyrdom.[18]

---

[18] See A. Boesak, *Comfort and Protest: The Apocalypse from a South African Perspective* (Philadelphia: Westminster, 1986), p. 19: "Because of their political perception and challenge in such dangerous times, these books could not be written in the 'normal' way. Any person who has ever lived under political oppression, where every move is watched and every word carefully weighed and where every other person could be an informer, knows this. Therefore these books were written in a way that only the initiated could really understand and draw encouragement from. These books were, in the real sense of the word, underground protest literature."

J. R. Michaels is right to urge that John was dealing with a situation of real social trauma for himself and his audience.

Some of us may know individuals in our own time who lead quiet and peaceful lives in prosperous suburban communities, yet who talk constantly of "spiritual warfare," "attacks of Satan," "demonic oppression" and the like, but we are reluctant to think of John as such a person. We prefer to believe he has solid grounds in the real world for his perceptions of the great conflict between God and the devil. When the Revelation is stripped of actual historical references we are tempted to conclude that it is merely an expression of a mood or an eccentric worldview and is not "about" anything.[19]

That temptation should be resisted.

THE RESOURCES, RHETORIC, AND RESTRUCTURING OF REVELATION

The textual history of Revelation is in various ways different from most of the rest of the NT corpus. For one thing some of our major witnesses do not include Revelation at all. Codex Vaticanus breaks off at Heb. 9.14. Neither of the manscripts labeled D include Revelation.[20] Indeed there really is no Western text of Revelation, unlike a book such as Acts, though there are a few Latin, Syriac, Coptic, and Armenian versions of Revelation. Both Codex Sinaiticus and Codex Alexandrinus do include Revelation, as does Codex C, and there are two important papyri, p47 and p115. As Michaels points out, "The reason for the very different textual history of the book is the fact that its canonicity was rejected by some segments of the ancient church, so that it was often not copied either with the Gospels or the letters of Paul, or even with then disputed 'general epistles,' of Peter, Jude, James, and John."[21] Most of the textual issues in this book boil down to whether one is going to follow the later readings found in the majority text, which provided the basis for the King James Version (KJV, or Authorized Version), or the earlier witnesses. The differences are not inconsequential at several points in the text. For example, at Rev. 13.1 should we translate "I stood" following the majority text, or should we translate "he stood" (referring to the dragon) with p47, Aleph, A, C, and other early witnesses? The latter reading is probably to be preferred, and thereby Rev. 12 and 13 are more closely linked. The dragon is frustrated in his attempt to kill Christ (12.17) and so takes out his anger on Christ's offspring (12.17). I will discuss

---

[19] J. R. Michaels, *Interpreting the Book of Revelation* (Grand Rapids, Mich.: Baker Books, 1992), p. 49.

[20] The Western text called D has more than one copy, or recension, and even though there are some differences, they are of the same tradition and text type.

[21] J. R. Michaels, *Interpreting* (1992), p. 79.

some of the other variants at the appropriate junctures in the text.[22] Here it is important to stress a few facts: (1) Only six papyri contain parts of Revelation, the earliest from the second century, which proves the document was already in circulation by the early second century.[23] (2) There are basically four text types in Revelation, and they differ from the text types in the rest of the NT.[24] (3) Only eleven uncials include Revelation, and a few later manuscripts that do have Revelation show that it was added by a later hand. This fact and the absence of Revelation from the the earliest lectionaries reveal clearly how controversial this book was in the early church and how its inclusion in the canon did not happen without considerable dispute. It was belatedly accepted in various parts of the church, particularly in the East.

That Revelation is full of allusions to and partial quotations of the OT is well known. Usually it is maintained that John used the OT and other early Jewish (and Greco-Roman) sources rather like the way a miner goes after gold, digging around looking without much regard for the setting in which the precious material was originally found. It is also argued that in this reappropriation of earlier material John shows little interest in the significance or meaning that a verse or an image or an idea originally had. This view has of late been challenged.[25] R. Bauckham and J. Fekkes have both argued that John engaged in meticulous exegesis of his source material, largely the OT prophetic books. The full-length monograph on this subject by Fekkes deserves our attention.[26]

Fekkes, following the earlier conclusions of Charles, rightly stresses that John the prophet draws his materials directly from the Hebrew or Aramaic prophecies in the OT, not from the Septuagint (hereafter LXX, so known because of its translation by seventy people).[27] This is an important point, and it suggests that while Revelation may not be an example of translation Greek, it may well be one of second language Greek; the author's primary language is a

---

[22] On some of the grammatical infelicities of the book, see ibid., pp. 85–94. While some have wanted to call John's Greek Semitic or Semitized, the larger question is whether or not it is translation Greek.

[23] P98 is from Cairo, and one must allow for time for this document to have reached Egypt from Asia Minor and been copied there.

[24] See J. K. Elliot, "The Distinctiveness of the Greek Manuscripts of the Book of Revelation," *JTS* 48 (1997), pp. 116–24.

[25] A useful survey of the entire discussion for and against these issues can be found in G. K. Beale, *John's Use of the Old Testament in Revelation* (Sheffield, UK: Sheffield Academic Press, 1998), with a helpful critique of those such as J. P. Ruiz and S. Moyise, who do not see John as sensitive to the literary context of the OT material he uses.

[26] One should also see R. Bauckham, *The Climax of Prophecy* (Edinburgh: T + T. Clark, 1993) especially pp. 38–91.

[27] J. Fekkes, *Isaiah and the Prophetic Traditions in the Book of Revelation: Visionary Antecedents and Their Developments* (Sheffield, UK: Sheffield Academic Press, 1994), p. 17.

Semitic one.[28] Fekkes furthermore urges that sometimes too much stress has
been placed on John's use of apocalyptic traditions and not enough on his
self-understanding as a prophet.[29] This is a matter of proper balancing, and
as I stress John's text needs to be seen as a work of prophetic apocalyptic or
perhaps better said apocalyptic prophecy. The apocalyptic symbols and ideas
serve the cause of prophetic interpretation of numerous OT texts, and as Fekkes
stresses, the OT is John's primary nonvisionary source of material. John believes wholeheartedly that he and his audience live in an age when various of the
prophecies have come and are coming true, and so there is a definite concern
on his part about the relationship between promise/prophecy and fulfillment,
though he approaches the matter somewhat differently than the First or Third
Evangelists.

Instead of pretending to be an ancient luminary, while actually writing
"history" in the guise of prophecy, John grounds his work in his own historical
situation. He begins by addressing particular congregations dealing with specific issues. The "attachment of a epistolary format to the visions, along with the
personal identification of John, lifts the book out of the realm of the pseudonymous apocalypses and places it within the context of real churches with specific
problems in a fairly limited local setting."[30] John knows his audience and their
issues, and he reflects a detailed knowledge of their geographical, historical,
political, and religious circumstances.[31] But what we find in this book should
hardly be called mere prophetic letters. The epistolary form that frames this
work involves too little of the document to be seen as its defining feature. No,
John wishes to unveil some of the revelation, in particular the revelatory visions,
he has received from God and to do so in a manner that exhorts and comforts his
audience. I tend to agree with Fekkes that the initial phrase "revelation of Jesus
Christ" is not some technical term for the genre of the work or the manner of the
revelation or some specific sort of vision experience, but rather an indication
that all that follows ultimately comes from God and is divine revelation.[32]

It is no accident that Revelation is the only book in the NT that, as we
often find in OT prophetic works, includes first-person oracles in the name of

[28] This places in doubt the suggestion that the author's Greek style is deliberately prolix
because of his apocalyptic subject matter. John's interest is in unsealing the seals. His
concern is revelation not deliberate obfuscation. The arguments of Bauckham and Fekkes
also clash with arguments such as one finds in Callahan, "Language of the Apocalypse,"
pp. 453–54, which incorrectly assumes John is drawing on the LXX. Callahan, however,
may be right that John is deliberately idiosyncratic in the way he uses Greek, reflecting
his own unique style.

[29] J. Fekkes, *Isaiah* (1994), p. 38.

[30] Ibid., p. 39.

[31] See C. Hemer, *The Letters to the Seven Churches of Asia* (Sheffield, UK: JSOT Press, 1986);
cf. R. H. Worth, *The Seven Cities of the Apocalypse and Roman Culture* and *The Seven
Cities of the Apocalypse and Greco-Asian Culture* (Mahwah, N.J.: Paulist Press, 1999).

[32] J. Fekkes, *Isaiah* (1994), p. 48.

the deity. John sees himself like many another prophet as God's mouthpiece and would repudiate the notion that what he unveils is *his* prophecy. It is the revelation of Jesus Christ that this book contains. This is why John stresses the inviolability of these prophecies (Rev. 22.18–19). John is talking about a sort of prophecy that does not require sifting and weighing unlike some other NT prophecy referred to by Paul (in 1 Cor. 14, cf. 1 Thess. 5.21), but rather is by and large meant to be received and applied, like the prophecies in the OT. "John not only takes up *where* the Prophets left off – he also takes over *what* they left behind. He is not only part of a prophetic circle, but stands in a prophetic continuum which carries on and brings to final revelation the living words of God entrusted to the care of the brotherhood (Rev. 10.7)."[33] It is in this context that one must evaluate John's use of the OT, especially its prophetic portions.

Perhaps John does not quote the OT very frequently because he approaches that material not as a scribe, sage, or apostle, but as a prophet. "He does not commend his visions on the basis of apostolic authority conferred by the *earthly* Jesus. Nor is his book a personal word of exhortation which derives its authority from quoting divine revelation. . . . His commission gives birth to a new prophecy – a fresh revelation – which is authorized simultaneously by God, the *risen* Christ, and the divine Spirit."[34] This new revelation can entail quoting the OT, but since John sees himself on par with OT prophets, or among their number, he does not often feel the need to quote it (but cf., e.g., Rev. 2.26b–27 to Ps 2.8a, 9). The vast array of allusions to and quotes of the OT (at least 278 allusions in the 404 verses in the book) serves a variety of purposes, one of which is to bolster the authority of the entire work and the ethos of the speaker, John.

John speaks like the prophets of old in the use of both prophetic diction and the first-person style, but also in the use of prophetic phrases, images, and ideas. John does not borrow OT material merely for its poetic effect or metaphorical force; rather he "wants the readers to appreciate the prophetic foundation of his statements."[35] Fekkes shows in great detail how most of John's use of an OT text goes beyond similarities of language and imagery to a similar use of themes, and the correspondence even extends "to the setting and purpose of the original biblical passage" when compared to its reuse in Revelation. John seems to choose his texts on the basis of theme and the issue he wishes to address rather than on the basis of canonical source, though clearly he favors apocalyptic material such as found in Ezekiel, Daniel, and Zechariah, as well as material in 2 Isaiah, Jeremiah, and Joel. "Special books do not appear to play as important a role as special themes."[36] It is untrue that John "simply uses the OT as a religious

[33] Ibid., p. 58.
[34] Ibid., p. 66.
[35] Ibid., p. 69.
[36] Ibid., p. 103.

thesaurus to pad his visions with conventional symbolism and rhetoric."[37] It is, however, accurate that John feels free to meld and mold various apocalyptic images from the OT to make his own, often Christological, points.

Fekkes goes on to demonstrate, using examples from Isaiah, that John uses the Hebrew Scriptures not in an *ad hoc* manner but in accord with known early Jewish hermeneutical procedures.[38] As it turns out, John is interested in exegesis and being faithful to the thrust of various OT prophetic texts, and he handles them in conventional ways. "By means of a Revelation of Jesus, John became the 'high priest' and prophet who handled them, interpreted them, and delivered their message to the expectant community."[39]

Fekkes is also helpful in formulating how the book of Revelation may have come to be composed. He recognizes that John had actual visionary experiences but that this work is not a mere transcript of such experiences but the literary repristination of them. One must also take into account John's previsionary influences, as well as his postvisionary redaction of his source material. It is neither a purely literary product nor a mere exercise in exegesis of the OT texts, but some combination of revelation, reflection, and literary composition.[40] "For all that Revelation is visionary, it is not *ad hoc*. And for all that its use of Scripture is implicit, it is not superficial."[41]

But what are the rhetorical aims and results of John's assembling of this document? About what is John seeking to persuade his audiences? One of the keys to understanding this matter is that John has deliberately begun his document with three things: (1) an introduction indicating that this is visionary and prophetic material, (2) a prophetic commissioning/visioning report, and (3) brief letters to the churches. The letters are clearly presented as being generated out of the visionary encounter (cf. Rev. 2.1, 8, 12). The epistolary form is used because the author is at a distance from his audiences and perhaps also because these congregations are quite used to receiving letters from Christian authorities – in some cases perhaps from both the Beloved Disciple and from Paul. The judicial or forensic tone of Revelation has often been noted, preoccupied as it is with issues of justice and vindication for the saints. It is then not surprising that the schematized brief letters found in Rev. 2–3 have this tone. They consist of a brief exordium establishing the ethos and authority of the one who is ultimately speaking (namely Christ, the judge of the churches), followed by a litany of complaints about past sins as well as praises of some good deeds, which makes up in each case the *narratio*. This is followed by a series of exhortations, varying from church to church, and by a schematized command to listen to what the

---

[37] Ibid., p. 288.
[38] Ibid., pp. 191–278.
[39] Ibid., p. 289.
[40] Ibid., pp. 289–90. On this matter, see the discussion that follows.
[41] Ibid., p. 290.

Spirit is saying to the churches (plural; cf., e.g., 2.7, 11, 17; 3.6, 13, 22). This last exhortation refers not to what is said within each individual letter but to the contents of the rest of the work beginning with Rev. 4.

If the letters are a particularized preamble, then Rev. 4–22 makes up the apocalyptic prophecies the Spirit is addressing to all the churches. These prophecies, including the visionary material constituting what we would call the *logoi* or arguments presented by the seer, are meant to persuade the audiences to heed the exhortations in the letters. Basically John is offering an eschatological and otherworldly sanction for those exhortations, showing what the rewards are for faithfulness and for "conquering," and what the punishments are for failing to do so. John reveals what is happening above and what will happen beyond the present (see Rev. 4.1), not merely a preview of coming attractions to comfort the faithful, though it serves that purpose as well. The "rhetorical function of these assertions is to change the audience's mind in the present."[42]

This entire schema fits well within the parameters of forensic rhetoric, even though there are also elements of deliberative and epidectic rhetoric (e.g., the worship scenes) in the document as well. E. Schüssler Fiorenza puts the matter well:

All three modes of rhetoric – deliberative, forensic, and ceremonial – appear to have shaped parts of Revelation. Revelation and its epistolary framework and its calls to deliberation and decision function as deliberative rhetoric in the assembly of the community. Its indictments, warnings, and narrative symbolization of divine judgments, as well as its promises and depictions of reward and punishment, qualify it as forensic rhetoric; whereas its visionary depictions of the heavenly "liturgy" and its hymnic praises identify it as ceremonial rhetoric. To decide for one over and against the other would not enhance but diminish our readings.[43]

Nevertheless the dominant form of rhetoric in this document is forensic rhetoric. The author is not just trying to comfort his audience with the truth that God is in heaven and that all will one day be right with the world. He is calling them to repent, believe, and behave in light of the coming redemptive judgment. He is also trying to re-vision the world, taking into account the divine actions above, within, and beneath the surface of history's tapestry. The regular topics of forensic rhetoric center, of course, on the issue of justice. According to *Rhetorica ad Herrennium* 3.3.4,

We shall be using the topics of Justice . . . if we show that it is proper to repay the well-deserving with gratitude . . . if we urge that faith [*fidem*] ought zealously to be kept . . . if we contend that alliances and friendships should scrupulously be honored; if we make it clear that the duty imposed by nature towards parents, gods, and the fatherland must

---

[42] R. Royalty, *The Streets of Heaven: The Ideology of Wealth in the Apocalypse of John* (Macon, Ga.: Mercer University Press, 1998), p. 128.

[43] E. Fiorenza, *Revelation: Vision of a Just World* (Minneapolis : Fortress, 1991), p. 26

be religiously observed; if we maintain that ties of hospitality, clientage, kinship, and relationship by marriage must inviolably be cherished if we show that neither reward nor favor nor peril nor animosity ought to lead us astray from the right path.

The book of Revelation is urging that God be properly honored and served at the expense of other claimants, such as the Emperor. It also reassures that justice will be done by this God.

Consistent with forensic rhetoric there is a great deal of rhetorical hyperbole both in the images and in the verbiage of this work.[44] Forensic rhetoric of the first century A.D. often involved caricature. Such is the stuff of polemics. It is important to bear in mind, however, that these are polemics about real persons and entities. While the language is not descriptive in any literal sense, it is nonetheless referential, which is also in keeping with the apocalyptic prophecy in this work.

One of the more helpful treatments of the rhetoric of Revelation is by R. Royalty, who stresses the performative character of the work; that is, he emphasizes that this is a work meant to be heard by the audience, by those who have ears to hear.[45] He reminds us that in forensic rhetoric external proofs, such as the testimony of witnesses or court documents, are crucial. In John's context, where there is a fundamental trust in sacred Scripture as well as in the living prophetic word, John chooses to draw on both the OT and the living voice of Jesus, perhaps the two highest authorities he could appeal to, to persuade his audience to heed his exhortations. Christ is obviously the most compelling living witness, but notice how John also appeals to other witnesses, including other prophetic figures in Rev. 11.[46] His audience stands before the heavenly court and hears compelling testimonies (including from the martyrs), which reminds them that earthly courts and judgments do not have the last word on their lives. Official documents are at the heart of the revelations in Rev. 4–21, which is only appropriate in a forensic setting, and it is in court that they are unsealed and read. The audience is comforted because the divine verdict is a foregone conclusion – the faithful will one day conquer and the wicked will one day be judged – but in the meantime the audience must remain faithful and must repent of their sin and lethargy and cowardice. The unsealing of the official scrolls that chronicle the coming redemptive judgments are meant to facilitate this outcome.

The performative character of this work has also been stressed by A. D. Callahan, who urges,

The auditors who came together to hear the Apocalypse were summoned to a transformative experience. Those first ancient auditors of the Apocalypse came together not

---

[44] Amplification was by no means characteristic of only epideictic rhetoric; one could find it in the other two species of rhetoric as well.

[45] R. Royalty, *Streets of Heaven*, p. 127.

[46] Ibid., p. 132; "The function of the visions in Revelation [is] as external proofs ..."

merely to be informed, but to be transformed, to undergo a collective change in consciousness, an aspiration that makes modern individual and group reading practices trivial by comparison, with the possible exception of the reading of wills. Reading the Apocalypse aloud, and hearing the Apocalypse read aloud, was effectual: through exhortations and exclamations, threat and thunder, the reading of the Apocalypse moved its hearers, affected them; the text *did* something to them.[47]

Revelation clearly follows the basic rhetorical pattern for persuasion. The speaker's authority is first established with the audience (in the introduction the report of the commissioning vision, and in the letters, which demonstrate he has the authority to address these audiences), then the authority of his arguments in the form of visions is confirmed through making clear that they come from ultimate authorities – the living Word and the written Word. Finally there is the authority of the emotional appeal at the end, where pathos comes into play. Redemption is finally unveiled to the audience, which is under duress and crisis, and a promise of the end of disease, decay and death, suffering and sorrow is made (see Rev. 20–22). Ethos, logos, and pathos are all found in rhetorically appropriate places in Revelation. Furthermore we have clear evidence in Revelation of John's use of particular rhetorical techniques, such as the use of overlap or chain link construction of transitional material. As B. W. Longenecker has made clear, Rev. 22.6–9 manifests this technique where one introduces the next topic before concluding the first one and then concludes the former argument or presentation. We see this technique also in Rev. 3.21–22, where the content of Rev. 4–5 is introduced and then the discussion in Rev. 3 is concluded. Quintilian advises the use of this sort of technique in *Inst. Or.* 9.4.129–30.[48] D. De Silva has also shown at some length that part of John's rhetorical strategy is to use honor discourse both to encourage those who are praiseworthy and are overcoming and to shame those who are more concerned with conforming to this world's honor codes than with honoring God in their living and dying.[49] There is, in addition, a great deal of appeal throughout this work to the primary or "pathetic" emotions of fear and anger and also of trust and love. Yet these forms of rhetorical analysis do not tell us in detail about the carefully laid out macrostructure of the book, which we turn to now.[50]

---

[47] A. D. Callahan, "Language of the Apocalypse," *HTR* 88 (1995), p. 460.

[48] See B. W. Longenecker, "'Linked like a Chain': Rev. 22.6–9 in Light of Ancient Transition Technique," *NTS* 47 (2001), pp. 105–17. For comparison to Quintilian, see Lucian, *How to Write History*, Loeb Classical Library Editions (Cambridge, Mass.: Harvard University Press), p. 55.

[49] D. de Silva, "Honor Discourse and the Rhetorical Strategy of the Apocalypse of John," *JSNT* 71 (1998), pp. 79–110.

[50] John's use of rhetoric is particularly in evidence in the letters in Rev. 2–3 and in the overall way that ethos, logos, and pathos are manifested in the correct parts of the discourse. Further, having chosen to focus on matters forensic, John uses the appropriate images, ideas, and approach for such a focus. This book is about official documents, witnesses, judgments, and the like. Furthermore there are examples of John using particular rhetorical techniques, such as interlocking structure. But it is not possible to derive a detailed

How has our author structured or, better said, restructured his source material? This is one of the most debated issues in the scholarly study of Revelation. Is the main section of this book intended to be a chronological account of the events leading up to the end of the world, or is the arrangement of materials topical or thematic? First, as Fiorenza, Bauckham, and others have urged, this document manifests a unity, for its major symbols and themes are used consistently throughout. Furthermore the letters in Rev. 2–3 are introduced by the vision in Rev. 1, and some scholars, such as L. Hurtado and G. R. Beasley-Murray, think the vision in Rev. 4–5 introduces the main body of Revelation.

The storm center of the debate about the work centers on Rev. 6–19. Is this a continuous chronological series of revelations, or does it represent a two- or threefold repetition of the same sequence? Put another way, are the seven seals, the seven trumpets, and the seven bowls or cups describing the same reality, perhaps with some variation? One can compare 11.15 ff. and 16.17 and argue that both of these visions seem to climax at the end of the age. Yet, on first blush, it appears that the seventh seal is opened in order to usher in the events heralded by the seven trumpets. Against this, however, is that the opening of the sixth seal in 6.12 ff. seems to involve a graphic description of the end of the world. The subsequent set of seven judgments do not merely repeat what has been said in the previous set of seven judgments. They evolve from and expand upon them. They then could be seen as increasingly precise or intense disclosures of the same reality, like a photographer getting a wider and at the same time more detailed focus on the same scene. Or, better, one could say these sets of sevens overlap, with the second set beginning before the end of the first and then carrying things further, and the third picking up in the midst of the second set and carrying things even further.[51]

Another of the major points in the debate about the structure of Revelation revolves around the scenes of heavenly worship in Rev. 7 and in 10.1–11.13. There is an inherent problem with seeing these sections as pregnant pauses, or

---

rhetorical outline of John's arguments, unlike of Paul's letters, in part because he is taking a narrative approach and in part because he is using apocalyptic prophecy, which dictates a good deal of how he presents his material. Thus rhetorical analysis of Revelation requires a certain amount of balance, taking into account other factors that have also shaped this material.

[51] To use a mundane analogy, it's rather like the old refrain used in singing at summer camp, where the song leader said, "Second verse, same as the first, a little bit louder and a little bit worse." J. L. Resseguie, *Revelation Unsealed: A Narrative Critical Approach to John's Apocalypse* (Leiden: Brill, 1998), pp. 160–66, makes clear that the recapitulation theory has some serious weaknesses. In particular, 15.1 indicates that this set of seven judgments is the last, as distinguished from the two sets that have come before. Furthermore, the silence in heaven after the seventh seal is opened does not signal the end, for the silence allows the saints' prayers to be heard. Resseguie also stresses that John wants to show that God exhausts every possible avenue before final judgment. This theology is better expressed by a series of preliminary judgments, giving time for repentance before a final set of judgments.

interludes, in the chronological account much less as diversions. The hymns clearly comment on and complement the visions and auditions of the book, and Fiorenza has suggested that they serve rather like a Greek chorus. It might be better to say they function as a sort of divine commentary, rather like a court reporter putting things in perspective. In fact there are many more hymns than those in Rev. 7 and 10–11. One may also compare Rev. 12.10; 14.1–5; 15.2–4; 19.1–9, and 20.4–6. These hymns not only serve as commentary but as praise of the apocalyptic actions being taken.

Perhaps because of Revelation's complex structure some have sought overly simplistic answers to structural questions. For example, some have suggested that Rev. 1.9–3.22 is about the things that are and that Rev. 4.1–22.5 is about the things that are to come. This is not wholly satisfactory not only because of the threefold pattern of seven judgments and overlapping figures and ideas found in Rev. 3–4 but also because the author seems to be discussing a past event – the destruction of the Temple – in Rev. 11. Notice too that the first trumpet voice at 4.2 is the same as the voice like a trumpet in 1.10–12.

Fiorenza has suggested a chiastic structure, making Rev. 10.1–15.4 the central section of the book: A – 1.1–8; B – 1.9–3.22; C – 4.1–9.21, 11.15–19; D – 10.1–15.4; C′ – 15.1, 5–19.10; B′ – 19.11–22.9; A′ – 22.10–21.[52] The artificiality of this is evident because C in fact involves two sections of the book, not one, and C′ skips some material as well. Fiorenza, however, has rightly put her finger on this book's use of parallelism and to some degree of recapitulation. One of the more compelling demonstrations of John's use of parallelism in general has been offered by C. H. Giblin, who shows that Rev. 17.1–19.10 needs to be seen as parallel to 21.9–22.11, dealing with mirror opposite great cities, one wicked, one wonderful.[53] But this particular example of parallelism or recapitulation of a structure does not indicate duplication. These two passages are not alternate discussions of the same reality.

Perhaps the most helpful discussion of the structure and composition of Revelation is that of Bauckham.[54] It is the most helpful not least because he shows how both scholars who stress recapitulation and those who stress progression in the central section of Rev. 6–19 are partially correct. Bauckham stresses that the structure of the book, which is crucial to understanding its meaning, must have been recognizable in oral performance (1.3),[55] which requires clear linguistic markers; that is, it requires repetition of certain key terms and phrases. In Bauckham's view the key to interpreting the book's structure is the phrase "in the Spirit" found in 1.10; 4.2; 17.3; 21.10. Rev. 4.2 is an exact reproduction of

---

[52] On this matter, compare and contrast her earlier work, *The Book of Revelation: Justice and Judgment* (Philadelphia: Fortress, 1985), pp. 159–80, to her later work *Revelation* (1991), pp. 27–37, though she retains the chiastic suggestion (pp. 35–36).

[53] C. H. Giblin, "Recapitulation and John's Apocalypse," *CBQ* 56 (1994), pp. 81–95.

[54] See R. Bauckham, *Climax of Prophecy* (1993), pp. 1–37.

[55] Ibid., pp. 1–2.

1.10 ("I was in the Spirit"), whereas the latter two references are basically the same in form, "[the angel] carried me away in the Spirit." Rev. 1.9–10 begins the inaugural vision; 4.2 provides a second beginning of the visionary experience; 17.3 and 21.9–10 introduce the two final parallel visionary experiences.[56] Rev. 17.11–19.10 and 21.9–22.9 present the visions of the two cities portrayed as women. The entire book has been pressing forward toward the conclusion, revealed in these two sections involving the destruction of Babylon and its replacement by the New Jerusalem. "The intimate connection between the two parallel sections is further indicated by the announcement of the Lamb's marriage to his bride at the end of the rejoicing over the fall of Babylon (19.7–9a)."[57] Bauckham goes on to argue that 22.6–9 is a transitional passage that concludes the last major section and introduces the epilogue. Recognition of the two parallel passages in Rev. 17 and 21 means that the material between these two sections (19.11–21.8) must necessarily be about the transition from the demise of Babylon to the descent of the New Jerusalem.[58] It cannot be about the time before the demise of Babylon.[59]

Bauckham also demonstrates the interlocking nature of the book's motifs. For example, the voice heard in 1.10–11 is the same as the voice in 4.1, and the angel introducing John to the visions beginning in 17.1 and 21.9 is one of the seven angels who pours judgments out the bowl or cup in Rev. 6–16.[60] Furthermore he provides extra foundation for the conclusion that the threefold "seven" judgments are basically describing one reality (though perhaps in progressively more intense or complete ways) for they all conclude with the same final judgment. This is demonstrated by the repeated use of the terms "thunder," "lightning," "earthquake," and "heavy hail" in varying order at 4.5; 8.5; 11.19, and 16.18–21. This phrase is an echo of Exod. 19.16: "The seven seal-openings are linked to the seven trumpets by the technique of overlapping or interweaving."[61] For Bauckham the whole sequence of bowls is a development of the seventh trumpet, and the three woes are identical to the judgments inaugurated by the last three trumpets.

Yet another of the intricacies of the structure that Bauckham notes is that "all parts of Chapters 6–11 [are linked] into the vision of heaven in chapter 4–5. The

---

[56] Ibid., pp. 3–4.
[57] Ibid., p. 5.
[58] Ibid.
[59] This in turn means that if one takes Babylon as a multivalent symbol not merely referring to Rome (though in the first instance that is its referent) but referring more universally to humanity organized against God, then the suggestion of Augustine and others after him of an amillennial reading of 19.11–21.8 simply would not work. John was indeed a millenarian prophet, which is one of reasons folk such as Eusebius had such an allergic reaction to Revelation. They had grown weary of the "chiliasts," as Eusebius calls them.
[60] R. Bauckham, *Climax of Prophecy* (1993), pp. 6–7.
[61] Ibid., pp. 8–9.

two series of sevens – the seal-openings and the trumpets – develop sequentially out of the vision of the Lamb and the scroll in chapter 5. . . . [and] both series at their climactic conclusions (8.5; 11.19) are linked back to the vision of the divine throne in chapter 4 (4.5)."[62]

One of the great structural puzzles of Revelation lies in Rev. 12–14, which is a section that begins abruptly. Bauckham rightly indicates that the fresh start was needed because this section involves a flashback to a time chronologically earlier than anything up to Rev. 12. The series of seven bowls then becomes a continuation of the narrative begun in Rev. 12. The seven bowls are a fuller version of the seventh trumpet. There is a provisional conclusion at the end of the seven bowls sequence with a further conclusion in 19.11–21.8.[63] Put another way, "the seventh of each series portrays the final act of judgment in which evil is destroyed and God's kingdom arrives. But the three series are so connected that the seventh seal-opening includes the seven bowls. Thus each series reaches the same end, but from starting-points progressively closer to the end. This is why the three series of judgments are of progressive severity."[64] These conclusions lead Bauckham to see the following as the structure of the work:

1.1–8	Prologue
1.9–3.22	Inaugural vision of Christ and seven messages to churches
4.1–5.14	Inaugural vision of heaven leading to three series of sevens and two intercalations
6.1–8.1; 8.3–5	Seven seals
8.2; 8.6–11.19	Seven trumpets
12.1–14.20; 15.2–4	The story of God's people in conflict with evil
15.1; 15.5–16.21	Seven bowls
17.1–19.10	Babylon the harlot
19.11–21.8	Transition from Babylon to New Jerusalem
21.9–22.5	The New Jerusalem, the bride
22.6–21	Epilogue[65]

One further feature of Bauckham's analysis deserves comment. He notes how carefully the sevens have been structured into the text, with seven representing completion. Thus there is a complete set of judgments and a full set of the title Lord God Almighty (1.8; 4.8; 11.17; 15.3; 16.7; 19.6; 21.22), but there is also a complete set of beatitudes, and as Bauckham says, the seven beatitudes provide a sort of summary of Revelation's positive message to believers and also encapsulate an appropriate response to the prophecies (cf. 1.3; 14.13; 16.15; 19.9; 20.6; 22.7,14). We will see that the majority of these beatitudes cluster at the end of the work,

---

[62] Ibid., p. 14.
[63] Ibid., p. 16.
[64] R. Bauckham, *The Theology of the Book of Revelation* (Cambridge: Cambridge University Press, 1993), p. 40.
[65] Ibid., pp. 21–22.

where the events of final redemption are recounted. If the believers are characterized by hearing and keeping faithfulness and readiness, they will obtain the fullness of these blessings (rest from labors, invitation to Lamb's supper, participation in the first resurrection, sharing in the tree of life, and entry into New Jerusalem).[66]

REVELATION IN ITS SOCIAL SETTING IN WESTERN ASIA MINOR

We have already had occasion to say some things about the Emperor and the sort of crises the Christians in Western Asia Minor may have been facing, but here is the place where we need to comment on the general social milieu and structure as it existed toward the end of the first century A.D. A little of the social history is required in order to understand Revelation in context.

In the first place, it is a mistake to see the situation of the residents in western Asia Minor as having the same mental outlook on Rome and its Empire as the Jewish residents in Judea and Galilee did in the first century A.D. Unlike the Syrian province, there were no legions stationed in western Asia Minor, and unlike Jews in the Holy Land, the residents of western Asia Minor did not consider themselves as having been occupied or subjugated by Rome. This was in part because the province of Asia was incorporated into the Roman structure of things by the granting of territory by King Attalus of Pergamum to Rome in about 133 B.C. There was only one brief period, from 88 to 86 B.C., when one local king resisted Roman rule and expelled Roman authorities. Once Augustus basically put an end to civil wars in the southern part of the Empire about 30 B.C. (until the Jewish one flared up in the A.D. sixties), there was little social unrest in the regions that bordered the Mediterranean, including in the province of Asia. Difficulties with Christians in Asia in the last few decades of the first century constituted a minor irritation compared to the Jewish war. In other words, the view among most residents in Asia who were not part of the minority sect of Christians would have been that there was not a significant social crisis involving repression and injustice in the region, though there were periodic economic crises to handle[67] "Despite the growth of urban and semi-urban settlements throughout the Empire . . . by far and away the greater population dwelt in the country and engaged in rural activities. The Empire's economy was firmly linked with agriculture. . . . The primacy of land both as a measure of status and a form of investment was never doubted in the ancient world."[68]

---

[66] Ibid., pp. 29–30.

[67] It may well be the case that Christians in Asia Minor, unaccustomed to having a bunker mentality, may have been extremely traumatized by any persecution at all, for they had not been conditioned to expect such a response to their beliefs and behavior, especially if most of them were Gentile Christians in these congregations.

[68] J. Wacher, *The Roman World* (London: Routledge, 1987), p. 8.

Augustus had canceled all the province's debt to Rome, and the imperial policy toward this very valuable province involved retaining the existing provincial elite in authority. However, there were not so subtle changes made to suit the fact that Asia was now part of an empire. For example, the *boule*, or Hellenistic council, was modified in structure so that it supported an elitist rather than a democratic way of doing things. The honorable families became members for life on this council, and a property qualification for membership was instituted. In short, upon the advent of Empire, Asian society became more highly stratified and hierarchial in relation to politics and also wealth.[69] From the time of Augustus the elite in Asia could hold dual citizenship, both in their cities and as citizens of Rome. In addition the Empire pursued a policy of urbanization, even though the economy was agrarian based and dependent on the crops (especially corn and wheat) to maintain social stability. It was the Flavians, especially Vespasian, who pursued the agenda of urbanization, and this added further tension to the socioeconomic situation for cities, of course, consumed far more than they were able to produce. "The cities were only viable because of Rome's transfer of food from the countryside to the cities."[70] And we are not talking about just any sort of cities for Ephesus (about 200,000 residents), Pergamum (120,000), Sardis (100,000), and Smyrna (75,000), according to R. Stark, were the third, sixth, seventh, and fourteenth largest cities in the Roman Empire in the late first century.[71] John is writing to churches in perhaps the most urbanized and crucial region of the Empire, outside of Rome and perhaps Alexandria.

In this situation the cities mentioned in Revelation competed with one another for recognition, honor, and beneficences bestowed by the Emperor. One form this took was the building of temples for the sake of furthering the emperor cult. Since the Emperor was seen as the ultimate benefactor, protector, and provider of peace and order in society, there needed to be a way in a reciprocity culture for the residents to repay the Emperor. This was largely accomplished through the deference, loyalty, and even worship offered through the emperor cult. Because the Emperor seldom toured the provinces (no Emperor visited Asia in the first century) and because most residents seldom if ever went to Rome, the chief way to have contact with and to know their Emperor was through the emperor cult, which involved temples, statues, public festivals, honor columns, inscriptions, coins, and holidays.

Temples were the banks of antiquity, not merely because they provided storage for valuable property, but they also loaned money at interest, provided mortgages, and the like. In temples one saw the convergence of political, economic, and religious life, especially in temples dedicated to the Emperor. Asia

---

[69] See W. Howard-Brook and A. Gwyther, *Unveiling Empire: Reading Revelation Then and Now* (Maryknoll, N.Y.: Orbis, 1999), pp. 88–92.
[70] Ibid., p. 98.
[71] R. Stark, *The Rise of Christianity* (Princeton: Princeton University Press, 1996), pp. 131–32.

was perhaps the first province to generate an emperor cult, with Pergamum building a temple to Rome in 29 B.C. and Smyrna doing so only four years after Augustus pacified the Empire (27 B.C.). The temple in Pergamum was the meeting place of the provincial assembly of Asia and where decrees and letters from Rome would be read out. It is possible that John, knowing full well about Pergamum, conceives of heaven as the Christians' assembly hall where the divine decrees would be read out and justice would finally be done by Christ, who is truly "our Lord and our God," in contradistinction to the Emperor Domitian.[72] If so, his high Christology (on which see the next section) is hardly just a religious statement; it is a political one as well. This explains why Christians are warned to expect stern reprisals for their allegiance to a very different Lord than Caesar. Their exclusivistic faith would be seen as dangerous and unpatriotic, for Christians would not participate in the emperor cult.

"The imperial cult was a *religio* in that it bound the residents of the cities together in the broader context of empire. All members were expected to participate in the imperial cult. . . . there was a social expectation that one would voluntarily participate as a demonstration of one's 'faith' in the empire."[73] This is why eating meat sacrificed to idols is such an issue in Revelation, as well as in 1 Cor. and Acts 15. To fail to fellowship with one's neighbors in the temple feasts was antisocial and, indeed, if it was an emperor cult feast, unpatriotic. The following chart provided by W. Howard-Brook and A. Gwyther[74] shows how pervasive the influence of the imperial cult would have been in the cities to which John wrote.

Asian City	Imperial Cult	Imperial Altar	Imperial Priest
Ephesus	X	X	X
Smyrna	X	X	X
Pergamum	X	X	X
Thyatira		X	X
Sardis	X	X	X
Philadelphia	X		X
Laodicea		X	

There had been an increase in imperial cult visibility and activity during the reign of Domitian. In the eighties various wealthy families from a variety of cities and towns in Asia banded together to build a new temple to the Flavian Emperor. Approval was granted for this construction, even though there were already two

---

[72] See, e.g., R. Royalty, *Streets of Heaven* (1998), p. 242: "the introduction (Rev. 1.1–20) challenges Roman authority and power by casting God and Christ as the wealthy patrons of the Christian communities with more power and status than Caesar." "[O]pposition to the dominant culture in the Apocalypse is not an attempt to redeem that culture but rather an attempt to replace it with a Christianized version of the same thing" (p. 246).

[73] Howard-Brook and Gwyther, *Unveiling Empire*, p. 103.

[74] Ibid., p. 104.

provincial cults in the region (in Pergamum to Augustus and Rome and in Smyrna to Tiberius, Livia, and the Senate), both existing since 26 B.C. "No other province is known to have had more than one provincial cult of the emperors at this time, and several provinces appear to have had none. Clearly, Asia was on the cutting edge of imperial cult activity. And John was denouncing the entire institution as coming from the devil."[75] John's revelation comes to him at a time when the imperial cult was increasingly being used as the social glue to bind each major Asian city, but also the province, together. "John's vision excoriated this system. It declared invalid the increasingly successful social contract of late-first century Asia. That contract, according to Revelation, was based on blasphemy, maintained by violence and dedicated to the destruction of those who sought to live a godly life. To those of like mind, John's visions were prophetic. To most of the inhabitants of Asia, however, they would have seemed like sedition."[76] Texts such as Rev. 13.4; 15–16; 14.9–11; 15.2; 16.2; 19.20; 20.4, which refer or allude to worship of the Beast, likely reflect the impact of the emperor cult on John and other early Christians.

These observations raise important questions about how particularistic John's Revelation really was intended to be. Are his symbols really multivalent (or universal) in character, or are they particularistic? Or do they involve the use of universal symbols in a particular way? It is my view that in fact the lattermost option is the case. John's Revelation is on target for his Asian audience, but the symbols he uses are flexible enough that they could and would be appropriately used to address many another situation of crisis in church life.

The search for particular allusions in Revelation to local social phenomena was initially championed by W. Ramsay and has been carried forward by a variety of scholars, particularly C. Hemer in his detailed study of the letters portion of the work.[77] A couple of examples will suffice. Hemer argues that Rev. 6.6 alludes to an edict of Domitian in A.D. 92 restricting provincial planting of vineyards. In fact the edict ordered half the vineyards in Asia and other provinces to be destroyed. The opposition to this law was so severe in Asia that the edict was rescinded before it was even enforced, but apparently the edict was ordered because there were major grain shortages, and Domitian needed grain crops to be planted, not grapevines, to ease social tensions in Rome and elsewhere. Hunger and starvation were happening in various parts of the Empire due to the grain shortage, and many were clamoring for relief. However, cities

---

[75] S. Friesen, "Ephesus: Key to a Vision in Revelation," *BAR* (May/June 1993), p. 34.

[76] Ibid., p. 37.

[77] Hemer, *Letters*. Hemer does not follow Ramsay uncritically; indeed he is critical of the apologetical stances Ramsay's later work took. For a critique of Hemer, see S. J. Freisen, "Revelation, Realia, and Religion: Archaeology in the Interpretation of the Apocalypse," *HTR* 88 (1995), pp. 291–314.

like Philadelphia that depended on viticulture for economic survival would have strongly resisted this edict, and Rev. 6.6, though something of a carica-ture, could represent the sentiments of the elite in the region who owned the vineyards.[78]

Hemer also points to Rev. 3.15–18 where Hierapolis was noted for its hot springs and Colossae for its pure, clear, cold water, but Laodicea had no such good water supply. Water had to be brought to the city by aqueduct and even then was not very potable. Hemer suggests,

the affluent society was far from the sources of its life-giving water, and when by its own resources it had sought to remedy the deficiency, the resulting supply was bad, both tepid and emetic. The effect of their conduct upon Christ was like the effect of their own water: no other church was condemned in terms so strong. Rev. 3.17 is seen against the background that Laodicea was a wealthy city and after the earthquake in the early 60s, she had refused Roman aide and done the reconstruction on her own. Then too the references to maladies and eyesalve could be a reference to Laodicea's famous medical school and its practices of healing.[79]

These allusions are more or less convincing depending on which one we are con-sidering, but since the point of these letters has to do with the spiritual condition of the various congregations, despite these possible particular allusions, there is a more general or multivalent character to the complaints and exhortations.

Modern social scientific theories have also been applied to the book of Revela-tion, and some of these efforts have been illuminating. For example, millenarian sect theory has been used quite frequently and relatively successfully, but theo-ries about cognitive dissonance, status inconsistency, cultural dislocation, and introversion have also been applied to Revelation.[80] Millenarian sect theory in essence suggests that the worldview of John, and perhaps also of his audience, is colored by eschatological beliefs. This theory suggests that a tightly knit group held "the acute expectation of the End; cosmic catastrophe; a division of time into set periods accompanied by a close connection between previous history and the end-time; angelogy and demonology; a new salvation beyond the catas-trophe; a savior figure; and so on."[81] The difficulty with suggesting that such an outlook characterizes John's audience is that Revelation in the main reflects John's own outlook. We do not in fact know that his eschatology is shared with even the majority of his audience. Indeed one could argue that John is trying to interject future eschatology into a group of communities not noted for such beliefs (to judge from the rest of the Johannine corpus) to help them cope with the pressure and persecution they seem to be experiencing. Nevertheless John

[78] Hemer, *Letters*, pp. 158–59.
[79] Ibid., pp. 192–97.
[80] See the discussion by P. Esler, "Political Oppression in Jewish Apocalyptic Literature: A Social Scientific Approach," *Listening: Journal of Religion and Culture* 28 (1993), pp. 181–99.
[81] Ibid., p. 185.

himself seems clearly to be a millenarian and about the business of trying to inculcate such beliefs in his audience.

It is a reasonable suggestion that some, if not much, of John's audience seems to be compromising too much, in John's view, with the larger culture's values. Revelation thus could be an attempt to interject some cognitive dissonance into a situation where some have become far too comfortable with the compromises they have been making to fit into their Greco-Roman communities. In other words, John wants more cultural dislocation not less. And lastly introversion might be emerging as a problem due to pressure and persecution. But John seems clearly enough to recognize he is part of an evangelistic minority religious group. Yet equally clearly he is concerned about protecting his communities from apostasy and related dangers. His outlook seems far more inward looking and protective than, for instance, the approach of Luke in Luke-Acts, not least because he sees the Roman Emperor and his minions as demonic in character and action, unlike Luke. It appears to me that the application of some of the social scientific theories to Revelation are more helpful than others. It is a far surer thing to concentrate on social history rather than to try to process this complex piece of ancient literature through abstract modern social categories.

THE CHRISTOLOGY OF REVELATION

Revelation is presented from the outset as a "revelation of Jesus Christ," which among other things reminds us that Christology is the heart of the matter for John when it comes to theology. It is Christ's vision that John conveys, and the vision is about Christ, in whose hands are all the scrolls that are to be unsealed and all the truths to be revealed. Christ is the one who sets in motion the eschatological judgments and provides the final redemption. It thus behooves us to consider carefully John's reflections on the Christ as that is a key to understanding the work as a whole.

There is a plethora of primitive ideas and images and also some highly polished ones about Christ in this book.[82] Since Revelation is a document meant to address Christians in physical and spiritual danger, we should not be surprised if it concentrates on images and ideas of Christ that would help address that situation. It is natural for the author to stress the sovereignty of God, the power of Christ, and Christ's judgment of the wicked for the saints and the like. In short, it is natural for the author to stress forensic images of Christ both as judge and as redeemer of the faithful from judgment (as the Lamb of God). It is not surprising that we do not find a gentle Jesus meek and mild in this book but rather one who sits on the judgment seat with his Father, one who rides forth

---

[82] What follows is found in a somewhat different form in my *The Many Faces of the Christ* (New York: Crossroad, 1998).

in judgment with a sword proceeding from his mouth, one who even when he can be seen as a Lamb can also be seen as a Lion. Here is a mighty and fearsome Christ indeed, with most of the emphasis on what Christ in heaven now is (an exalted Lord) or will be for believers when he returns. There is little attention to the ministry of Jesus or the merely human side of Jesus except to emphasize his death and its benefits.

A rapid survey of the various titles applied to Christ in Revelation reveals the following: Christ appears only seven times, Son of God once, Son of Man twice (but in each case as part of an analogy not as a title), Logos or Word once, but Lord twenty-three times (and also used interchangeably with God and with Christ), and Lamb twenty-eight times. In this work none of the human titles of Jesus, such as teacher, rabbi, servant, prophet, or man, are used. It is equally interesting that some of the more Hellenistic titles, such as Savior or God, are also notably absent. In terms of terminology and titles, this book is very different from John's Gospel, where Son of God and Son of Man dominate the landscape, and from the Epistles, where Christ and Son of God are prominent. The extreme Jewishness of this document and its different Christological terms make one suspect that it was not written by the same person who wrote either the Gospel or the Epistles or both, an opinion reinforced when one notes the very different sort of Greek in this document compared to the rest of the Johannine corpus. Revelation has a high Christology stressing Christ's heavenly exaltation and roles since and because of his death and resurrection.

The Christological tone for the whole book is set in the first chapter with the first Christological vision of John of Patmos. The book begins with the assertion that this is "the revelation of Jesus Christ," and it is probably no accident that it is only in this chapter that we have the title Jesus Christ (three times). "The first Christian readers would need to be led from Jesus Christ to the Lamb, the name which dominates the second part of the book."[83] Jesus is the faithful witness, the first born from the dead, the ruler of the kings of the earth (1.5), and also the one who will come on the clouds in the future for judgment (1.7). Rev. 1.5 also mentions Jesus' redemptive death and blood and the first of only two references in this book to Jesus as one like a Son of Man, only here his garb makes clear his divinity. The author begins here a trend that will continue throughout the work of applying OT images and names formerly used of Yahweh but now applied to Christ or to both the Father and Christ. It was the Ancient of days in Dan. 7 that has such raiment, whereas here it is Christ who is both divine and one like a Son of Man (1.13). It is not clear whether the person referred to as Alpha and Omega in Rev. 1.8 is God or Christ (cf. also Rev. 21.6), though it is probably God, but more clearly at 1.17–18 Christ is referred to as the First and Last (and at Rev. 22.13 he is the Alpha and Omega), the one who was dead but is now alive forever and has in his hands the keys of Death and Hades. He also holds the

---

[83] See D. Guthrie, "The Christology of Revelation," in *Jesus of Nazareth: Lord and Christ*, ed. J. B. Green et al. (Grand Rapids, Mich.: Eerdmans, 1994), p. 398.

churches in the palm of his hand, something a Christian under fire might find comforting. From this lofty Christological height the book never descends.

It is worthwhile to consider the significance of calling both God and Christ the Alpha and Omega. Bauckham is likely correct in suggesting that it conveys the idea that the person in question "precedes and originates all things, as their Creator, and he will bring all things to their eschatological fulfillment. The titles cannot mean anything else when they are used of Christ in 22:13."[84] Furthermore when Jesus is called the First and the Last, this seems to be grounded in Isa. 44.6 and 48.12, where it is a divine self-designation of Yahweh. Not only so but it is used in a context where it aids in stressing the exclusive monotheistic proposition "besides me there is no God." Here in Revelation, First and Last probably does not mean anything very different from Alpha and Omega.

This interpretation comports with Rev. 3.14, where Christ is called "the origin [*arche*] of God's creation," which likely does not mean he is the first created being or the first-born from the dead (for which John uses other terminology) but rather is another way of saying about Christ what is said clearly in Rev. 22.13. In other words Christ, as in the Logos hymn in John 1, is seen as preceding all things and as, in part, the source or Creator of all things, along with the Father. By Omega or Last, we are probably meant to think of Christ's assumption of the role of the coming final judge on the eschatological Day of the Lord (see Rev. 19). Bauckham concludes about this First and Last/Alpha and Omega language that "as a way of stating unambiguously that Jesus belongs to the fullness of the eternal being of God, this surpasses anything in the [rest of the] New Testament."[85] It is not surprising that in Revelation, perhaps more than in any other NT book, Jesus is the object of worship and adoration, which in this same book is said not to be appropriate of mere angelic supernatural beings (cf. 19.10 and 22.8–9).

Because Jesus is included in John of Patmos's definition of God, he is seen as an appropriate object of worship. In Rev. 5 we are introduced to the image of Christ as the Lamb, which becomes the dominant image in the book thereafter. Notice, for example, how in Rev. 5.8 the Lamb, who has triumphed through his death and resurrection, is the focus of the circle of worship in heaven that includes the worship of the living creatures and the elders, the representatives of all creatures both animal and human (cf. 5.6 and 7.17).[86] It is precisely as a slain lamb that this Lamb conquers and then judges with righteous wrath (6.16). The worship of the Lamb is not separate or distinct from the worship of

---

[84] R. Bauckham, *Theology of the Book of Revelation* (1993), p. 55. In the next few paragraphs I shall be echoing and amplifying various of Bauckham's arguments with which I am in agreement.

[85] Ibid., p. 57.

[86] Even as Lamb, Christ is seen not as weak but rather as powerful and fully capable of overthrowing enemies not unlike the lamb symbol in the Testament of Joseph. There is perhaps some indebtedness of John to the author of this work, for in Test. of Jos. 19.8–9 we hear of the twofold Messiah who is presented as both Lion and Lamb.

God but is seen as a part of it in 5.13. If a doxology is a clear indication of the object of worship, then the one offered to Christ alone in Rev. 1.5–6 indicates he is approached as deity. This doxology should be compared to two other such doxologies offered to Christ alone at 2 Tim. 4.8 and 2 Pet. 3.18, suggesting that the practices described in Revelation of worshiping Christ were not abberations but rather were widespread in a variety of Christian communities.[87]

It is perhaps right to note that John of Patmos does not, as is the case in the Fourth Gospel, choose to use the concept of the Wisdom of God to be able to include Christ in the godhead. Indebtedness to Wisdom of Solomon seems apparent at one crucial point however (19.11 ff.), where the conquering warrior is called the Word of God. To this we must compare Wisd. of Sol. 18.16 ff., where the Word leaps from heaven with a sharp sword.

John stresses that Christ shares the names, the throne, the work, and the worship of God. While it is true that for Christians, because Christ functioned as God – namely as creator, redeemer, present Lord, and coming future judge – he was thus worshiped, this is probably to say too little. At the end of the day, John believes that only God can perform what Christ performs, and thus there is at least an implicit assertion of Christ's divine nature in all this material. Consider what it means to say that the slaughtered lamb is seen on the throne and is worshipped for his overcoming through death and resurrection the powers of this world. It must include the notion that God was in Christ reconciling the world to himself, but more to the point that God rules the world by and in the slaughtered and exalted Lamb. Christ's suffering and death are seen as the act of an eternal being. Thus they are seen as having eternal efficacy and making evident how God has chosen to overcome evil and rule the world. Only God saves, and he has done this as the Lamb.

The one who is called ruler of God's creation in Rev. 3.14 is also in that same chapter called the one who holds the key of David (3.7) and thus is the Jewish Messiah. Just because John thinks he is more than the Jewish Messiah does not mean he takes this notion as unimportant. In Rev. 5.5 Jesus is seen as Lion of the tribe of Judah and also the Root of David. The Lamb image is, of course, also thoroughly Jewish, and a slaughtered lamb the ultimate symbol of atonement for sins in a Jewish context. But John has transformed this image to speak not only of a lamb slain but of something else no early Jew who was not a Christian spoke of – a lamb once slain but now glorified and powerful. Here the story of Jesus has transformed this Jewish image into something unexpected, paradoxical, new. It is no surprise that the slain-lamb image arises repeatedly in a document written to Christians who are being persecuted. They too are lambs for the slaughter, but, like Jesus, they in the end will have victory over death and their human tormentors.

[87] Does it say anything to us that these three texts may all be addressed to Christians in Asia Minor in areas where emperor worship was prevalent?

Another image transferred from God to Christ is that of Jesus being the one who has the book of life and also the one who opens the scrolls that disclose God's future plan and will. Only he is worthy enough to open not only the scroll but all the seals upon it (Rev. 5). We see here the notion of Christ as the implementer of divine justice upon the earth. The concept of redemptive-judgment may seem foreign, but it is a prevalent concept in the OT, especially in Joshua and Judges. God redeems his oppressed people by judging their enemies. Thus our author is not saying anything novel by predicating both judgment and redemption of his deity; the only novelty is that Christ is said to be assuming these divine roles. He is both savior of the saved and judge of the wicked. The end result of the battle of good and evil will be and indeed in John's view already is "the kingdom of the world has become the kingdom of our Lord and of his Christ, and he will reign forever and ever" (11.15). Lord here refers to God rather than to Christ, and Christ is used in its titular and Jewish sense. Our author is not guilty of Christomonism, though he clearly includes Christ within his description of God alongside the Father. This way of putting things in 11.15 suggests John was in touch with the earliest Jewish Christian ways of confessing their monotheism, such as can be seen in 1 Cor. 8.6.[88]

Thus the Lamb will triumph and one day invite his own to a wedding feast (19.9). He will also come as the pale rider, grim reaper, or executioner spoken of in Rev. 19. The Lamb is also the Lion. As Christ he will reign for a thousand years with his martyrs (Rev. 20.4 ff.). This may refer to his present reign in heaven with the martyrs already there, but in view of the discussion of resurrection in John 20, it probably refers to a future reign on earth at the close of the age. Christ is the one who began and will bring to a close God's plan for humanity.

We are told in Rev. 21 that Christ and the Lord God (here the Father) will be the temple and glory of God's people and that they will dwell together forever – beyond disease, decay, death, sin, suffering, sorrow, tears, or torment. For now our author sees Christ as one who stands at the door of human hearts and knocks, but one day he shall burst on the human scene as a ravaging Lion destroying or at least judging the wicked and thereby rescuing the righteous. Thus believers are urged at the close of the book to plead for him – the one who is Daystar dawning on history's horizon – to come. Both horizontal and vertical eschatology fuse in the final vision such that heaven and earth in effect merge. The New Jerusalem descends from above, making a new earth to go along with a new heaven. The one who lies at the center of this vision, indeed the one who turns this vision into reality, is, according to John, none other than Jesus, who is at once Lamb, Lion, and Lord. We should have expected this Christocentric and theocentric conclusion because we were told at the outset of the book that this is "the revelation of (and about) Jesus Christ."

---

[88] See p. 32.

We need to ask in what ways John of Patmos is indebted to the Christology we find in the other Johannine documents. In some ways this is an easy question to answer. We may point to texts such as Rev. 7.17, where we see Christ as Shepherd leading his people to springs of living water. This parallels what we find in John 10 (cf. John 21), where Christ claims to be the Good Shepherd. However, when we try to examine how our author uses the term **Logos** in the form "the Word of God" in Rev. 19.13 compared to what we find in John 1, the context is very different. Here the Word, as in Wisdom of Solomon, is involved in judgment, but in John 1 the image is used to speak of a role in creation and redemption. Or again we may explore the differences between the Lamb in John 1.29, 32 and in Revelation, immediately noting that a different Greek term for lamb is used in each (**amnos** in the Gospel, **arnion** in Revelation). In the Gospel the Lamb is seen as a purely redemptive one who takes away sin, whereas in Revelation the Lamb's role involves both redemption and judgment. In John 10.7 Jesus is said to be the gate, while in Rev. 3.20 he stands outside it and knocks. In the Fourth Gospel Son of Man is an important title with a cluster of key ideas surrounding it. In Revelation it is simply part of an allusion to the analogy found in Dan. 7.

Overall it appears that John of Patmos knows Johannine Christology, but he is not interested in slavishly imitating it or simply passing it along. Rather, he deliberately varies or modifies what he knows of it to suit the message he wants to convey. There is, on the whole, a much more varied scope of images and ideas in Revelation than in the other Johannine documents, but then the other documents are not apocalyptic literature and do not really use pictographic language. What all of the Johannine corpus does share is a strong emphasis on the importance of Jesus' death and an equally strong stress on both the true humanity and the divinity of Christ. It is repeatedly the Christ of glory, the exalted one, who appears in these documents, even in the account of the ministry in the Fourth Gospel. These documents have no problem using the various names and titles of God for Jesus Christ, nor do they have any problem offering worship to Christ as God. They all seem prepared to redefine Jewish monotheism to accommodate what they wish to say about Christ. Thus we may say that certainly some of the highest Christology in the NT can be found in Revelation, but this is not surprising if this document comes from the same circles that produced the Gospel of John.[89]

THE GENRE OF REVELATION

The debate about the genre of Revelation continues to rage on, with most scholars now convinced that Revelation is some sort of apocalyptic literature. The question is, What sort? I have argued elsewhere that apocalyptic is a type

[89] For the debate on just how Christian and Christological the book of Revelation really is, see E. Lohse, "Wie christlich ist die Offenbarung des Johannes?" *NTS* 34 (1988), pp. 321–38.

of hybrid literature that reflects the confluence of the Jewish prophetic and sapiential traditions, and this is as true of a book like Daniel as it is of Revelation.[90] But Revelation, in view of its audience, must also be set in the context of Greco-Roman prophecy as well. It is in order then to discuss this matter of genre before we begin the commentary proper.

Hebrew protoapocalyptic and apocalyptic literature was highly synthetic in character; indeed it was rather like a vortex taking in materials from all directions, including from Greco-Roman sources from the Hellenistic era onward. It is no surprise to one who has studied the history and trajectory of apocalyptic literature that we find echoes of the non-Jewish combat myth in Rev. 12. But, of course, Jewish and Jewish Christian writers were bound to transform their source material to be compatible with their monotheistic faith. Certain social factors affected the development of apocalyptic literature, the chief of which seems to have been the social dislocation caused first by the exile, then by life under occupation in the Holy Land, by the loss of the Jewish war in the A.D. sixties, and perhaps lastly by the loss of the Bar Kokhba rebellion. For Jewish Christians like John, there were compensatory factors that changed the character of their apocalypse, in particular the impact of the Christ event. But for John, as well as for his Jewish predecessors, the primary stimuli for his work are the Hebrew prophetic tradition and to a lesser degree the sapiential tradition. Greco-Roman sources are less influential, and with John we must also take into account the early Christian epistolary tradition as well as the Jesus tradition. Again we must ask, How does one define such a hybrid sort of literature?

The Society of Biblical Literature definition, arising out of its Seminar on Apocalyptic Literature, is as good a starting point as any. It says that an apocalypse is "a genre of revelatory literature with a narrative framework, in which a revelation is mediated by an otherworldly being to a human recipient, disclosing a transcendent reality which is both temporal, insofar as it envisages eschatological salvation, and spatial insofar as it involves another, supernatural world."[91] Present, mundane reality is interpreted in light of both the supernatural world and the future. For the book of Revelation this entails beginning with the present experiences of the churches and trying to help them interpret and endure those experiences given John's visions of what is above and beyond. This is clearly minority literature written in a somewhat coded way for persons enduring some sort of crisis.

Eschatological ideas are not necessarily the heart of what apocalyptic is all about, for such ideas are found in many types of early Jewish and Christian literature, and there are apocalypses that do not really focus on the final form the future will take. Apocalyptic then is primarily a matter of the use of a

---

[90] B. Witherington, *Jesus the Seer* (1999), pp. 216–45.

[91] J. J. Collins, ed., *Apocalypse: The Morphology of a Genre, Semeia* 14 (1979), p. 9. To this definition D. Helholm added that it is literature intended for a group in crisis with the intent of exhortation or consolation by means of divine authority.

distinctive form – visions with often bizarre and hyperbolic metaphors and images. Some apocalypses focus almost entirely on otherworldly journeys without saying much about the end of human history. In other words historical apocalypses are not the pattern for the whole genre.

The very heart of apocalyptic is the unveiling of secrets and truths about God's perspective on a variety of subjects, including justice and the problem of evil, and what God proposes to do about such matters. This literature is the dominant form of prophecy in Jewish contexts from the second century B.C. to the second century A.D., and it reflects the authors' belief that they lived in the age when earlier prophecies were being fulfilled, and, therefore, it was right to contemplate what God's final answer and solution would be to the human dilemma. This dominance of apocalyptic also reflects the deeply held conviction that God's people lived in dark times when God's hand in matters and God's will for believers were not perfectly evident. God's plan had to be revealed like a secret for matters in human history were mysterious and complex.

It is my view that the major cause of the shift from traditional prophecy to apocalyptic during the era mentioned was not the absence of traditional-style oracular and sign prophets abroad (e.g., John the Baptist) but the conviction that God's people were living at the dawn of or actually in the eschatological age. The final things had already been set in motion, and under such circumstances it was appropriate to talk about the end of the end times. It is no accident that the historical apocalypses begin to disappear from Jewish literature after A.D. 70 and from Christian literature in the second and third centuries A.D. Otherworldly journeys, such as we find in Dante's *Divine Comedy*, take their place. Future eschatology came largely to be replaced by otherworldly eschatology and mysticism the closer one gets to the Middle Ages. The grip of imminentist eschatology on believers gradually loosened after the first century A.D. This is as true of Jewish as of Christian literature. A futurist eschatological outlook explains much about Jesus, about the earliest Christian's belief system, and about the belief system of the author of Revelation.[92]

When one delves into Greek and Roman literature, one quickly learns that there was a widespread belief in the pagan world that dreams and visions were real means by which gods and demigods could reveal truths to and instruct human beings.[93] But not just dreams and visions are pertinent to the discussion of how John's audience would hear Revelation. There is also the oracular tradition in the Greco-Roman world about the succession of emperors and empires. We find this sort of material in the Sibylline Oracles. One example will suffice from the Eighth Sibylline Oracle, which seems to see the terminus of things

---

[92] One can begin to recognize the sea change in eschatology when one compares and contrasts Revelation with Hermas. See my *Jesus the Seer* (1999), pp. 371–78.

[93] Ibid., pp. 353–57.

in the reign of Hadrian and so comes from within twenty years of the date of Revelation:

When the sixth generation of Latin kings will complete its last life and leave its scepter, another king of this race will reign, who will rule over the entire earth, and hold power over the scepter; and he will rule well in accord with the command of the great god; the children and generation of children of this man will be safe from violation according to the prophecy of the cyclic time of years.

When there will have been fifteen kings of Egypt, then, when the phoenix of the fifth span of years will have come ... there will arise a race of destructive people, a race without laws, the race of the Hebrews. Then Ares will plunder Ares, and he will destroy the insolent boast of the Romans, for at time the luxuriant rule of the Romans will be destroyed, ancient queen over conquered cities. The plain of fertile Rome will no longer be victorious when rising to power from Asia, together with Ares, he comes. He will arise arranging all these things in the city from top to bottom. You will fill out three times three hundreds and forty and eight cycling years when an evil, violent, fate will come upon you, filling out your name (Sib. Or. 8.131–150; trans. D. Potter).[94]

The sixth generation of Latin kings in all likelihood refers to the Flavians, with Nero being the sixth Caesar, who is in turn a part of the sixth generation (cf. the number 666 of the Neronian anti-Christ figure in Revelation). I refer to this example to show that the character of Revelation would not necessarily have seemed so foreign to the Gentile mind, which was well familiar with the notions of revelatory dreams, visions, and oracles about human history. A detailed knowledge of the Jewish practice of gematria would not be required to realize that various of the numbers in Revelation had symbolic significance. Jewish apocalyptic imagery offered a new twist, but the story was still about political matters and the rise and fall of rulers and realms and their times and seasons. This larger Greco-Roman context also makes clear that it would be unlikely for John's audience to see his work as not historically referential. Rather, it would be viewed as some sort of symbolic but nonetheless prophetic material involving the history of the period leading into the final future of humankind, unveiling the overarching and underlying supernatural forces involved in the human drama.

One of the major points I have made in my earlier study of prophecy is that it is important to distinguish between prophetic experience, prophetic expression, and prophetic tradition. The book of Revelation is certainly not simply a transcript of a prophetic experience, as its epistolary framework makes clear. Rather the seer has incorporated into a complex literary whole a report of his vision or visions reflected upon in light of the Hebrew Scriptures and a variety of other sources. John had visions and then fashioned an apocalyptic

---

[94] D. Potter, *Prophets and Emperors* (Cambridge, Mass. Harvard University Press, 1994), p. 104.

prophetic work to express not merely what he had seen but what bearing that vision had on his audiences. This means we might well not have an apocalypse at all had John not been some distance from his audiences. Rather he might have just shared most of the visions orally with his churches as they came, without resorting to a literary creation.

We probably should not imagine John on Patmos poring over Hebrew Scripture scrolls and then creating a literary patchwork quilt. The visions that came to John came to a Scripture-saturated mind and to a mind well acquainted with popular and mythical images of the larger Greco-Roman world. What John heard he may have transcribed almost verbatim, but what he saw he had to describe and thus draw on his existing mental resources. When one sees images and symbols in odd combinations, one must grope for analogies to describe the experience (hence the repeated use of the phrase "it was like . . ."). One must resort to aspective, metaphorical, mythological, and sometimes multivalent language. One must turn to somewhat universal symbols, which explains why such works have been able to communicate across time and helps explain why these works were preserved. But paradoxically it is also true that apocalyptic prophecy always requires interpretation or explanation. It is indeed a somewhat coded form of language, and those not knowing that universe of discourse will be in the dark.

It is plausible to imagine an extended process such as J. Crenshaw has suggested for the composition of works of prophecy, involving (1) putative revelatory moment, (2) reflection, (3) articulation, (4) refinement of word by poetry, (5) addition of supporting arguments, and (6) performance. But this process might be telescoped considerably in an apocalyptic work like Revelation.[95]

First, the prophetic experience may have involved hearing poetry, perhaps in the form of songs (cf. Rev. 4.8–11; 5.9–14). Second, at least in the case of Revelation, the seer himself did not perform this work in part or in toto so far as one can tell, though it is likely his messenger or some other Christian did. In view of all that has been seen in this study of prophetic materials it would seem that various prophets and seers experienced their revelations as poetry. Poetry was not necessarily the later refinement of an inchoate word. But what one finds in Revelation is not just a transcript of experience. Whatever the content of these pneumatic experiences ("I was in the Spirit on the Lord's day . . ." Rev. 1.10), the book as it now exists is a literary attempt to use such materials to persuade and exhort several groups of Christians who were apparently badly in need of some reassurance, encouragement, and instruction. The rhetorical dimensions and function of the book must not be overlooked.

---

[95] What follows here is found in a somewhat different form in my *Jesus the Seer* (1999), pp. 359–71. See J. Crenshaw, "Transmitting Prophecy across Generations" (paper presented at the annual meeting of the SBL, Orlando, Fla., Nov. 23, 1998).

Bearing these genre considerations in mind, it is time to take a brief tour of the contours (general shape) and content of Revelation. On the one hand, while it is true that there are various examples of otherwordly visions in Revelation, this work is not just about what is transpiring in heaven. The seer is not simply a mystic, like other early Jewish or Christian mystics. A historical and eschatological dimension to this book is found not only in the opening letters but also in the descriptions of destruction followed by a new earth as well as a new heaven. The seer is concerned about both a heaven that is spatially near and events that are thought to be at least possibly temporally near. His focus is not just up there but also out there. It is perhaps a product of modern tendencies to separate the social and the spiritual or the mundane and the supernatural that one finds the notions of traffic between heaven and earth, or of an open heaven and an influenced earth, or indeed of a merger between heaven and earth (Rev. 21–22) somewhat off-putting. John has not substituted an otherworldly view of eternity for an earlier, more temporal, historical, eschatological one. Rather, the two are intertwined. A quick comparison with the Shepherd of Hermas or even better Dante's *Divine Comedy* will show just how eschatological John's Revelation actually is.[96]

On the other hand, one cannot assume that John himself believed he was simply using mythical images to describe all too mundane realities. John believed not merely in God and Christ and angels but in their regular interaction with humankind on earth. The angels, for instance, are not symbols or figures of human beings. One should not be misled by the hyperbolic nature and rhetorical dimensions of various apocalyptic images into thinking that this material is not intended to be referential. Indeed it is, but the references are sometimes to human figures and sometimes to superhuman ones.

That this material uses universal metaphorical symbols and is not literally descriptive should not lead one to assume that it is not referring to some reality John believed existed. John focuses, like most biblical writers, on the redemption and judgments of God in space and time. As such, he shares an essential kinship with other prophets and seers in the Jewish and Christian traditions who are concerned about the future of God's people not merely in heaven but on earth. This is one of the things that distinguishes John from those who simply have mystical visions of heaven or go on ecstatic otherworldly tours of heaven and its occupants and activities. Indeed it could be disputed that John had an otherworldly tour in the Spirit. It appears more likely that John's experience was a matter of receiving certain revelations seriatim. His account does not read like Enoch's tour of heaven. One must allow John to have his say about the historical future and indeed about the conclusion of human history at the return of Christ,

---

[96] See C. Rowland, *The Open Heaven: A Study of Apocalyptic in Judaism and Early Christianity* (New York: Crossroad, 1982), on the otherwordly aspect of the book.

however wrong some may think he is not only about the timing but also about the substance of his predictions.

Fiorenza's conclusion is worth pondering at this point: "Early Christian prophecy is expressed in apocalyptic form and early Christian apocalyptic is carried on by early Christian prophets. Early Christian prophecy is an ecstatic experience in the Spirit . . . and the revelation of divine mysteries."[97] What is not so apt about this is the assumption that all early Christian prophecy took this form or was an expression of apocalyptic, or that apocalyptic is the mother genre and prophecy a subset under it. But this much is absolutely correct – apocalypses like that of John are not purely literary products of tradents. They are generated by prophets and grounded in prophetic experience of an apocalyptic sort. Fiorenza is also quite right that Revelation shares with early Christian prophecy the following – it is an eschatological revelation of or about Jesus Christ that has as a main purpose exhortation and strengthening of communities and is meant to be read aloud or performed in Christian worship, for unlike much of Greco-Roman prophecy, it is not individual but rather communal in nature. Christian prophecy and apocalyptic were not in general matters or products of private consultation.

It cannot be stressed enough that one of the rhetorical functions of a work like Revelation is to give early Christians perspective, especially in regard to the matters of good and evil, redemption, and judgment. Revelation seeks to reveal to the audience the supernatural forces at work behind the scenes that are affecting what is going on at the human level. In short a certain limited dualism is evident in this literature. The message is often, "though it appears that evil is triumphing, God is still in his heaven and all in due course will be right with the world." The goal of life is ultimately beyond death in either the afterlife or the afterworld on earth or both. There is also usually a strong sense of alienation and loss of power in these documents and thus major emphases on God's sovereignty and divine intervention in human affairs and on transcendent solutions to human dilemmas, though human efforts have not been rendered either meaningless or pointless.

Here is a good place to say a bit more about the use of multivalent symbols in Revelation. It is true that the wounded beast in Rev. 13 and 17 probably does allude to Nero, but with the help of mythological imagery Nero is portrayed as but a representative example of a higher supernatural evil – the anti-Christ figure. The author knows that Nero does not exhaust the meaning of the beast, but he certainly exemplifies it. There could be other such figures as well, for the author is dealing with types. These symbols are plastic, flexible, and on the order of character analysis rather than literal descriptions. Christ can be depicted in Revelation as the blood-drenched warrior or a lamb who was slain, or a lion,

---

[97]   E. Fiorenza, *Book of Revelation* (1985), p. 149.

or an old man with snow-white hair. All these descriptions are meant to reveal some aspect of his character and activity. In this respect, these symbols are very much like some modern political cartoons.

Apocalyptic literature is basically minority literature, and often even sectarian literature, the product of a subset of a subculture in the Greco-Roman world. While it is not always true that such literature is written in a time of crisis or for a people experiencing crisis or persecution at that specific point, it is certainly written for people who feel vulnerable in a world that largely does not concur with their own worldview. In the case of Revelation, there is probably enough internal evidence to suggest that there had been some persecution and even martyrdom and more was expected.

It is not surprising then that apocalyptic prophecy often has a political dimension, dealing with the dominant human powers that appear to be shaping the destiny of God's people. Whether it is Revelation portraying Rome as a modern-day Babylon or Daniel portraying a succession of beastly empires, there is frequent discussion of these matters in such literature but always under the veil of apocalyptic symbols and images. One must be an insider to sense the referents and the drift of the polemic and promises. This aspect of apocalyptic literature grows directly out of the classical Jewish prophetic material in which nations and rulers, including Israel's, are critiqued, but here the critique is by "outsiders" (those who do not have controlling access to the political process) using "insiders" language.

It is not just the loss of the monarchy that changed Jewish prophecy and prophets, but its replacement by a hostile and anti-Semitic foreign power. All Jewish or Christian prophets in such a situation are peripheral prophets and often must resort to coded language to express their message. From a psychological point of view, one might wish to consider that having been cut off from their spiritual center in Jerusalem (or in John's case in the Christian communities in western Asia Minor), revelation was expected to come to God's people in less clear and more enigmatic ways for they were farther from the perceived central locale of the divine presence.

There is a great fascination in apocalyptic literature with symbolic numbers and so something more must be said about gematria. There are, of course, the oft repeated numbers of four, seven, ten, twelve, and their multiples. Knowing that seven means completion or perfection helps one to understand not only why there are the number of seals that one has in Revelation (a complete and comprehensive set of judgments) but also why the anti-Christ figure is numbered 666, which signifies chaos and incompletion. There is also a tendency in this literature to speak of time elusively or elliptically – such as Daniel's "a time, a time and a half, and a time" or his famous interpretation of Jeremiah's seventy weeks. Yet it is rare to find in either Jewish or Christian apocalypses any sort of precise calculations about how many days or years are left before the end. Scholars have often puzzled over the two different numbers, apparently referring to the same time period, in Dan. 12.11–12, but it need not be a case of recalculation or later editorial emendation. If the numbers are symbolic in nature (e.g., multiples of seven, or one-half of seven), they should probably not be taken as attempts, much less failed attempts, at precise calculation. Such numbers suggest when they describe periods of time that matters are determined or fixed already by God, and thus God is still in control so that evil and suffering will at some point in time cease. The message of such numbers is that "this too will pass" or "this too will come to pass." They were not meant to encourage ancient or modern chronological forecasting.

But what if justice is indeed deferred or is not seen to be done in a reasonably short period of time? One of the major impetuses producing apocalyptic literature is this sense of justice deferred for the minority group, which has led to a robust emphasis on vindication both in the afterlife and, more important, in the end times. It is not an accident that apocalypses often manifest interest in justice and political issues on the one hand and in the otherworld and the afterlife on the other. If there is no life to come, then many of the wrongs done in this life will never be rectified, and God's justice will be called into question.

Apocalyptic literature, especially apocalyptic prophecy, often attempts to deal with theodicy. For instance, Revelation reassures the saints not only about personal individual vindication in the afterlife but about justice for God's people in the end. Indeed it is at the point where cosmology and history meet, when heaven comes down to earth in the form of the Messiah and the New Jerusalem, that there is finally both resolution and reward for the saints, and a solution to the human dilemma caused by suffering and evil. Suffering and death are overcome by resurrection and everlasting life, and evil is overcome by the last judgment. The persuasiveness of this schema depends on the audience's belief in not only a transcendent world but also a God who cares enough to intervene in human history and set things right once and for all.

But that this sort of information is only conveyed through visions and dreams and oracles makes clear that without revelation, without the unveiling of divine secrets and mysteries, humans would be in the dark about such matters. It is the message of apocalyptic literature that the meaning and purpose of human history cannot be discovered simply by empirical study or analysis of that history. This does not mean that the author has given up on history, as is sometimes asserted, but rather he places his trust in what God can finally make of history rather than in what humans can accomplish in history.

A BRIEF TOUR OF THE BOOK OF REVELATION

At this juncture, it will be well to analyze closely some core samplings from Revelation. As D. Aune has demonstrated at some length, while Revelation contains oracles, it is not just like a classical collection of oracles such as that found in Amos. For example, embedded within the narrative of John's commissioning experiences, one finds quotations of God's direct words to the seer in Rev. 1.8, "I am the Alpha and Omega," or at 1.17b–20, "Do not be afraid; I am the first and the last, and the living one. I was dead and see I am alive forever and ever; and I have the keys of Death and Hades. Now write what you have seen what is, and what is to take place after this. . . ." It is no accident that at the inception of this remarkable book John says that when he was in a pneumatic state he first heard something and then saw something (1.10–11). Though this is mostly a visionary work, it has its aural and oracular dimensions, and the visionary material is set within the context of the interpreting oracles.

In Rev. 1.17b–20, the revealer is the exalted Christ, who identifies himself as one who was once dead but is now alive. In short he speaks appropriately according to the time in which John lives. There is nothing here that suggests that sayings of the risen Lord that would be appropriate to place on the lips of the historical Jesus were conveyed in this way. Indeed a saying such as Rev. 1.17b–20 would not have been appropriate if found on Jesus' lips before he died. The same may be said about the oracle in Rev. 16.15, where we hear, "Behold I am coming like a thief . . ." (cf. Rev. 22.7, 12–14), an oracle that is appropriate from the exalted Christ but different from the one by the historical Jesus, who refers to a future coming of the Son of Man in the third person. One could also point to other examples of oracular speech in Rev. 13.9–10, 14.13, 18.21–24 (words of an angel), 19.9, 21.3–4, 5–8, 22.18–20, and there is a concentration of such oracles at the beginning and end of the book, making clear the prophetic character of the work.[98]

To such oracles one could add the clearly demarcated prophetic character of the oracles to the seven churches in Rev. 2–3, all of which have a shared prophetic pattern involving (1) introductory commissioning word, (2) middle portion, and (3) double conclusion with a call for vigilance and a saying about conquering. In each case John is commanded to write to each of these churches, which due to his exile is "a functional equivalent to the sending of prophetic messengers in the OT."[99]

Notice that in each case there is a citation formula, here "thus says" (*tade legei*), after which the exalted Christ speaks. Of course, the content of each oracle after the citation formula in the central or middle "I know" part of the oracle varies according to the situation of each church. The exhortative nature of the central section of these prophecies is clear, and the often strongly negative tone reminds us that Christian prophets and seers like John saw themselves having a similar role to OT prophets as "guardians and preservers of Christian behavior, beliefs, and customs."[100] They too could be prosecutors of the covenant lawsuit, only

---

[98] D. E. Aune, *Prophecy in Early Christianity and the Ancient Mediterranean World* (Grand Rapids, Mich.: Eerdmans, 1983), pp. 280–88.

[99] Ibid., p. 275

[100] Ibid., p. 277.

in this case it is the new covenant lawsuit. One may conjecture as Aune does that there must have been a dearth of leadership in these churches that in turn necessitated prophetic intervention by John. Prophets and seers could be seen as crisis intervention specialists, especially when there was a power or leadership vacuum.

Let us consider a specific sample of visionary material from Revelation to get a sense of its character. Scrutiny will be given to two consecutive sections – Rev. 11, which presents the tale of the two witnesses, and Rev. 12, the story of the woman and the dragon. It is possible to see Rev. 11 as a continuation of Rev. 10, but this may be debated. There is no debate about the indebtedness of Rev. 11 to Ezek. 40–48. In the vision John is given a staff and told to rise and measure the temple of God and its surroundings. There have been at least four suggestions as to what this measuring means.

1) It is the preliminary to rebuilding and restoring the temple. This is true of Ezek. 40–48, and it is understandable how an exiled Jewish Christian prophet after A.D. 70 might see himself as being in the same position as Ezekiel. How then would this square with John seeming to see the church as the new temple of God such that any restoration of the old temple would be superfluous?
2) The temple is being sized up for destruction. This makes good sense if this book was written in the sixties rather than in the nineties, as is usually thought, and if our author was familiar with the Jesus tradition on this subject (see Mark 13). On the whole the arguments for a date in the sixties do not convince.
3) The measurements are taken to indicate the parts to be protected from physical harm. This does not seem to fit with the theme found earlier in Revelation of partial judgments even on God's people.
4) Measuring refers to protection from spiritual rather than physical harm.

One clue to unraveling this mystery is found at 11.14, where one discovers that what is recounted as happening to the temple and to its worshippers (the latter being a point against this being a retrospective remark about A.D. 70) is said to be the second woe, not the last woe. This event is clearly identified as happening in Jerusalem for there is mention of the place where the Lord was crucified.

One must now broach the subject of the two witnesses. It is clear that they are presented here as being at least like Moses and Elijah, the two witnesses who stood with Jesus on the Mount of Transfiguration according to the Synoptic tradition found in Mark 9 and par. These witnesses bring the fire-breathing Word of God to earth, including plagues and the like, but they are also taken back up into heaven. If this is a prophecy of Jerusalem's fall, why has it been placed in this locale in Revelation and called the second woe? If this is a prophecy about the final preservation of the Jewish people, why then are the witnesses identified with the figure used in the letters to identify the church? A more probable explanation is that this is about the universal church and its task of witnessing or, more specifically, about the churches at Smyrna and Philadelphia that were undergoing persecution and perhaps enduring instances of martyrdom, as John wrote. This would explain why there are two witnesses here rather than the earlier seven of all the churches John is addressing.

Some have seen here an allusion to Deut. 19.15, where it is said that the verification of the truth of anything requires the validating testimony of two witnesses. But if John believed this was still true, would this not imply the need of a second witness to validate his own testimony, something this prophet doesn't appear to think he needs? His words appear to have independent authority for the seven churches, and he expects them to be unchallenged. It is surely easier to see here a reference to two of John's churches undergoing persecution. This fits with the reference to the lampstands (cf. Rev. 2–3). If John could cast his own role in the light of the prophet Ezekiel, there is no reason why he could not cast the role of two of his churches in the light of the experiences of Elijah and Moses.[101] This implies that not only the life of but that of his churches bear prophetic witness to God's revelation or truth. The idea of outward harm and even physical death is meant to suggest that even such extreme persecution cannot harm such witnesses spiritually.

The witnesses are called olive trees for they carry within them the fuel needed to light their candlesticks. The reference to Daniel's three and one-half years suggests the church will go through such persecution, not be raptured out of it. One must also see the reference to Sodom and Egypt as a statement about the spiritual status of Jerusalem – a city occupied and trampled under foot by Gentiles in the last decade of the first century. In other words, it is a place of oppression, slavery, and immorality. That the bodies of the witnesses are not allowed to be buried was considered one of the utmost indignities or crimes against a people in the ancient near east (ANE) (cf. Ps. Sol. 2.30 ff).

Again, Ezekiel is drawn upon in Rev. 11.11 to speak of the two witnesses' resurrection, possibly alluding to the resurrection of the martyrs referred to in Rev. 20.2. According to vs. 13, once the witnesses were vindicated by being taken to heaven, judgment fell upon a tenth part of the unholy city, during a supernaturally induced upheaval, and 7,000 were said to be killed. Perhaps not coincidentally this would have been about a tenth of the nonfestival season population of Jerusalem. John is suggesting the Jews, symbolized by Jerusalem, are the persecuting agents troubling the churches in this case. There is here a coded message of great relevance to the present and future situation of at least two of John's churches, offering them future hope of vindication despite present difficulties.

Of a similar sort and with a similar point is the much controverted revelation about the woman and the dragon in Rev. 12, a classic case where the author has

[101] See D. E. Aune, *Revelation 1–5* (1997), p. 600.

drawn on various sources including pagan myths to make a Christian point. One gets the feeling in apocalyptic, especially when one's audience is largely Gentile, that any and all sources are fair game for raw material, so long as they can be Christianized. A. Y. Collins has spent considerable time in a book-length treatment of this material demonstrating that the story line in this chapter is based in part on the ancient combat myth, probably in its Babylonian form.[102] The myth in its basic form involves a dragon threatening the reigning gods or the supreme god. Sometimes the supreme god is even killed, which results in the dragon reigning in chaos for a time. Finally the dragon is defeated by the god who had ruled before or one of his allies.

Perhaps the closest form of the myth to the text of Revelation is the Greek version, which involves the birth of the god Apollo from the goddess Leto. One form of this tale speaks of the great dragon Python who pursued Leto because he learned that she would bear a child who would kill him. Leto was carried off to Poseidon, the god of the sea, who placed her on a remote island and then sank the island beneath the sea for good measure. After a vain search, Python went away to Parnassus, and Leto's island was brought back up to the surface of the sea. When the infant Apollo was born, he immediately gained full strength and within four days went and slew Python at Mt. Parnassus. An even more primitive version of this story, this time from Babylonia, speaks of war between Tiamat, the seven-headed sea monster, and the gods of heaven. Tiamat's flaunting of these gods was ended by Marduk, a young god of light, who hewed the sea monster in pieces. In the war with Tiamat, a third of the stars were thrown from the sky. Marduk's mother is portrayed in similar fashion to the way the woman is depicted in Rev. 12. One may also point to the Egyptian story about Osiris, whose wife, Isis, gives birth to the sun god, Horus. Isis is portrayed with the sun on her head. The dragon, Typhon, is red (but is sometimes represented as a crocodile or a serpent). In this Egyptian myth, the dragon slays Osiris and pursues Isis, who is about to give birth. In a miraculous manner, she does give birth and escapes to an island in a papyrus boat. The son, Horus, eventually overcomes the dragon, which is destroyed through fire (cf. Rev. 20.1 ff).

The parallels between these various myths and the visionary materials in Rev. 12 are too striking to be accidental and, in most forms, too early to be derived from Revelation. Rather John has freely drawn on elements of these myths, adding certain components to conform the tale to the Christian story about the Savior. John's audience probably would have been familiar with at least one if not more forms of this myth and would recognize what the seer was doing. The implication in part would be that in Christ all the primal myths and the truths they enshrine come true. He proves to be the archetype of which all these others are mere types or fictional copies.

---

[102] A. Y. Collins, *The Combat Myth in the Book of Revelation* (Missoula, Mont.: Scholars Press, 1976).

Yet there is a more ominous undercurrent here for various emperors saw these myths as being about themselves (being the incarnation of divine Apollo, for example). It is probable that the woman in our chapter is portrayed as the queen of heaven. On Roman coins, the emperor and his wife were portrayed as the sun and the moon. Roma, the patron goddess, was represented as the queen of the gods and mother of the savior, the emperor. Here then in Rev. 12 we find a counterclaim. Jesus, the male child, is the real conqueror, not the emperor, and the woman from whom he comes, either the people of God or Mary, is the real queen of heaven, the real mother of the savior instead of Roma. This is an antiestablishment story borrowing from classical myths but is also grounded in the story of Christ in the Hebrew Scriptures (e.g., in Dan. 7).

One of the keys to understanding this and other texts in Revelation is the notion of the intertwined nature of things heavenly and earthly. Thus I must disagree with G. B. Caird that John is simply describing earthly realities and struggles using mythical or heavenly symbols.[103] Rather John believed he was describing supernatural as well as earthly realities though freely using metaphorical and mythical language. John is not describing a sort of heavenly parallel universe to earth so that war in heaven mirrors war on earth. Rather, in his view, there is but one struggle, both heavenly and earthly, both supernatural and natural, both divine and human, and these forces interact with each other.

Chapter 12 begins by saying that the seer saw a great portent or sign in the heavens, the normal place where such portents were expected to appear (cf., e.g., Matt. 2). We hear of a woman clothed with the sun, with the moon under her feet, and a crown with twelve stars. Some have suggested this crown might represent the constellations or, more to the point, the twelve signs of the zodiac. If so, the point would seem to be that in this woman lies the whole destiny or fate of the race, drawing on the notion that stars controlled one's future (but cf. below) Though it is possible we have a reference to Mary here, it is more probable that we do not for several reasons: (1) notice in vs. 17 that one hears about the rest of her offspring, who are unlikely to be Jesus' actual brothers and sisters. It is far more likely to refer to Christ's brothers and sisters in the faith who are being addressed in this book, especially those facing or even enduring persecution; (2) the echoes of Isa. 66.6–9 here are loud, which means echoes of the mother Zion tradition. Paul in Gal. 4.26 refers to the new heavenly Jerusalem as "our mother." What is likely in view here is the community of God's people, portrayed as a woman (cf. Rev. 21.9–14). There is an implied continuity between the OT and NT people of God at least in the sense that Jesus came forth from the Jewish people of God, and his brothers and sisters did likewise.

The woman is depicted as being in anguish to give birth. The red or fiery (or bloody) dragon is said to be a second portent in the sky or heavens. That he has

---

[103] G. B. Caird, *The Revelation of St. John the Divine* (Peabody, Mass: Hendrickson, 1966), pp. 147 ff.

ten horns suggests one of awesome strength, and clearly the imagery of Dan. 7–8 is drawn on here, though in Daniel the reference is to beastly empires and their rulers. That the dragon has seven crowns may suggest he has usurped all power, but his crowns are called *diademata* while that of mother Zion's is called a *stephanos* (the laurel wreath crown of those who are victors). The twelve stars in the woman's crown are likely to refer to the twelve tribes of Israel and thus are a symbol that one is dealing with a community – the whole people of God.

This apocalyptic vision involves more than just predictive prophecy for it describes an event that had already transpired – the birth of the male child or savior. Vs. 4b depicts the dragon as almost hovering in front of the woman who is about to give birth so that it can devour the child as soon as it is born. Drawing on Ps. 2, the male child is depicted as destined to be a shepherd who would rule the nations with an iron hand or, as the text says, an iron rod. The image conveys his absolute power over the nations and perhaps also his power to judge. The text goes on to say that at the crucial moment the child was seized by God and carried off to his throne. John has skipped from the savior's birth to his death, ascension, and exaltation. The point for Christians under pressure or persecution is that what the powers of darkness may have seen as the end of Jesus, and as intended for evil, God used for good, indeed used to give the male child more power over the forces of darkness. What might have been thought to diminish the power of the male child actually further empowered him. By his being taken away from earth by God, he was enthroned in heaven.

In vs. 6, the woman flees into the desert and, since she represents the people of God, we hear echoes of the exodus here (note how exodus imagery crops up again in vs. 13 ff.). In the desert this woman is nurtured just as the Israelites were by God during their wilderness wandering period. It is not said that the church is raptured into heaven. Rather it is protected from the wrath of the dragon while on earth. The woman is put in a place prepared by God and made to stay there a definite period of time – Daniel's three and one-half years (1,260 days). In view of Rev. 13.5 and 11.1–13, what is probably meant here is the great tribulation when Satan is viewed as trying to crush the church out of existence.[104]

At vs. 7, the scene shifts to war in heaven. While we might expect this war to be waged by Christ versus the dragon, Michael, the archangel, leads the fighting for the saints. Again this author is adopting and adapting traditional material. In Test. of Dan. 6.2, Michael is a mediator between God and humankind. In the canonical Daniel, Michael is the guardian angel of Israel fighting against the angelic leaders of the Gentile nations (10.13 ff; 12.1). Here in Rev. 12, his task is to take on the adversary of the people of God. In general Michael prevails and the Devil and his minions are cast down to earth. There is in fact a threefold fall of

---

[104] See G. R. Beasley-Murray, *Revelation* (London: Marshall, Morgan and Scott, 1974), p. 191 ff.

Satan in Revelation: (1) from heaven to earth (12.9), (2) from earth to the abyss (20.2), and (3) from the abyss to the lake of fire (20.10).

Satan is not just seen as a prosecuting attorney or the accuser of the people of God. Rather he has lost his role in the heavenly court and now, in vs. 9, he is seen as the deceiver of the whole *oikomene*, a term for the civilized or human world. At vs. 10, a song is sung in heaven, and salvation, kingship, and power come when Satan is cast down to earth. The "our brothers" in vs. 10 may be those who have already been martyred (cf. 6.9–11). The accuser is no longer allowed to accuse because of the atoning death of the Lamb and because of the word of his testimony. The author seems to suggest that the casting down of Satan took place at the death of Christ or immediately thereafter when the benefits of his death began to accrue for God's people. Vs. 12 makes clear that Satan's days are numbered, and he knows it as a result of Christ's death. Some have seen John 12.13 ff. or the saying of Jesus about seeing Satan fall like lightning from the sky as a possible source of some of this imagery as useful commentaries on this text.

Notice, however, that Satan is not prevented from pursuing the woman but that she is aided in her flight by the wings of eagles given to her (cf. Exod. 19.4). Vs. 15 says that Satan produces a river to flush the woman out of the wilderness or desert, another possible allusion to the Exodus/Sinai events. Since in the primal myth the sea monster is the evil one, it is not surprising that here water is his modus operandi to try and do in the woman. Yet, unable to destroy the church collectively, Satan contents himself with attacking individual Christians – the ones keeping God's commandments and bearing the testimony of Christ. The section concludes with the sea monster or dragon standing next to his native element, the sea (often a symbol of chaos and the locus of evil things and creatures in the Hebrew tradition).

In Rev. 11–12 there is a rich intertextual feast with echoes of both biblical and nonbiblical, both Jewish and Gentile traditions. The author hears oracles and songs, and sees visions, but he chooses to relate these visions in language his mostly Gentile audience can understand and apply to themselves. The language is definitely referential, though it is also symbolic and metaphorical and even mythic in character. It cannot be taken literally, but it must be taken seriously, for the author believes he is depicting in apocalyptic language some truths and realities his audience needs to know about. This is not merely heavenly language with an earthly meaning, but rather apocalyptic language about the interplay of heaven and earth, time and eternity, history and the supernatural. If one turns to Rev. 19–22, one sees that our author can indeed offer predictions about the future in apocalyptic form, as well as descriptions of the past and present in that same visionary form. The eschatological as well as the otherwordly and horizontal as well as the vertical dimensions of this author's vision of the final solution are prominent throughout.

Should we see the inscribing of such visions as we find in Rev. 12 into a literary work that we call Revelation as in and of itself a prophetic activity? It need not be because one could use a scribe to accomplish that aim. It is unlikely that we should see Revelation as a purely literary exercise unlike various of the pseudonymous apocalypses, and the presence of actual prophecy (not merely of the *ex eventu* variety) raises again the question of this work's actual genre. I would suggest once more that we recognize this as a work of apocalyptic prophecy by a known and named author – John. As such, it fits the SBL definition of an apocalypse, but that definition was made sufficiently broad to include both pseudonymous and nonpseudonymous works, both works with and without ex eventu prophecy.

At the end of the day, it is best to stick with the phrase apocalyptic prophecy when it comes to the book of Revelation. It stands firmly in the prophetic tradition in its later Jewish and early Christian apocalyptic forms, and it has stood the test of time, being one of the great masterpieces of early Christian literature. It is promulgated not on the basis of a supposed connection with dead Jewish saints but rather on the basis of a connection with the living Lamb and Lion and Lord. Long ago H. B. Swete put things well when he observed,

The Apocalypse of John is in many ways a new departure. (1) The Jewish apocalypses are without exception pseudepigraphical; the Christian apocalypse bears the author's name. This abandonment of a long-established tradition is significant; by it John claims for himself the position of a prophet who, conscious that he draws his inspiration from Christ or His angel and not at second hand, had no need to seek shelter under the name of a Biblical saint. (2) How hard it is to determine the date and provenance of Jewish apocalypses is clear from the wide differences which divide the best scholars on these points.... The Apocalypse of John, on the contrary makes no secret of its origin and destination; it is the work of a Christian undergoing exile in one destination; it is the work of a Christian undergoing exile in one of the islands of the Aegean; and it is addressed to the Christian congregations in seven of the chief cities of the adjacent continent.... Whatever view may be taken of his indebtedness to Jewish sources, there can be no doubt that he has produced a book which, taken as a whole, is profoundly Christian, and widely removed from the field in which Jewish apocalyptic occupied itself. The narrow sphere of Jewish national hopes has been exchanged for the life and aims of a society whose field is the world and whose goal is the conquest of the human race. The Jewish Messiah, an uncertain and unrealized idea, has given place to the historical, personal Christ, and the Christ of the Christian apocalypse is already victorious, ascended, and glorified.[105]

A final word is in order to make very clear before we commence the commentary proper about the nature of the book of Revelation. John Collins in his landmark study on the apocalyptic imagination says the following: "The language of the apocalypses is not descriptive, referential, newspaper language but the expressive language of poetry, which uses symbols and imagery to articulate a sense or feeling about the world. Their abiding value does not lie in

---

[105] H. B. Swete, *Commentary on Revelation* (Grand Rapids, Mich.: Kregel, 1977), pp. xxviii–xxix.

the pseudo-information they provide about cosmology or future history, but in their affirmation of a transcendent world."[106] Collins is right in some of what he affirms, but wrong in much of what he denies, at least as it applies to the book of Revelation. He is wrong because the book of Revelation is indeed a work of prophecy, apocalyptic prophecy to be sure, but nonetheless prophecy, and not the pseudoprophecy of the *ex eventu* sort that one finds in pseudonymous apocalypses. As prophecy the material in Revelation is meant to be referential, whether we can ferret out what the references are or agree with them. To take but one example, Babylon is quite clearly Rome in the book of Revelation. What one can say, however, is that this highly imagaic and poetic language uses universal metaphors and symbols and so is capable of being used to interpret a variety of historical persons and events.

Collins is also mistaken that Revelation is purely about the transcendent. It is rather about providing a transcendent perspective on the interface between the transcendent realm and the historical realm, showing the underlying and overarching supernatural forces at work in human history, guiding and goading human beings and human institutions. There is in this work a passionate concern about how history will ultimately turn out, and the earliest recorded reflections by second- and third-century Christian commentators took the book as referential and historically focused in nature. For example, it was assumed that Rev. 20 was speaking about a millennial kingdom of Christ coming upon the earth at or near the end of human history (see, e.g., the commentary of Victorinus of Pettau).

Thus due attention must be given to the referential nature of John's symbols. He seems to have fervently believed that justice and redemption would not both be finally accomplished nor be seen to be accomplished unless such matters were finalized in space and time, "when the kingdoms of this world shall become the kingdoms of our Lord and of his Christ." None of us are in the position to say that John was wrong about the final climax of human history since we have not arrived there thus far in 2,000 plus years of church history. His language of imminence is a clarion call to be prepared for that end, whenever it may come. The church is called to be the church expectant, prepared for "what will yet come." Like the saints under the altar in Rev. 6, it is more appropriate for the church to cry out "how long O Lord" than to simply wish to join those saints in their present location. By this I mean this book does not encourage us to have a purely otherworldly view of eternal life, it does not encourage us to focus on heaven rather than on history as the final goal or terminus of Christian life, it does not encourage us to abandon the eschatology of the earliest Christians such as Paul. The saints in heaven are impatient for the end of history and final vindication; they are not basking in everlasting peace believing they have reached the end.

---

[106] John Collins, *The Apocalyptic Imagination: An Introduction to the Jewish Matrix of Christianity* (New York: Crossroad, 1984), p. 214.

The book of Revelation has much to tell us about "what was, and is, and is to come." It is our job to have ears capable of hearing what John says on all of these matters. If we do so, we will learn that God's yes to life is louder than evil's and death's no to it, that justice and redemption will one day prevail on earth, and that this is Good News coming in the form of a "revelation from Jesus Christ," which is to say coming from one who both experienced death and triumphed over it. It is Christ who knows what is above and beyond our present mundane historical concerns and situation. He alone is worthy and is able to reveal such profound truths. Bearing these things in mind, we must now take up the challenge of working through the text of Revelation itself, praying that the scales will fall from our eyes as the seals are opened and that we will understand something more about the vision glorious.

II. Suggested Reading on Revelation

◆

*T*his reading list – by annotations, rubrics, and guideposts – is intended to serve as a point of entry for the new student of Revelation. In addition, for all levels of readers it should serve as an up-to-date, annotated bibliography of *some* of the most helpful literature on this complex book; it is meant to be "reader friendly" instead of exhaustive. For a fuller bibliography on particular passages and issues, the reader is encouraged to consult D. Aune's three-volume work on *Revelation* (see commentaries listed below).

For a general introduction to the interpretation of Revelation, see J. Ramsey Michaels, *Interpreting the Book of Revelation* (Grand Rapids, Mich.: Baker Books, 1992), but it covers the literature on the subject only written by 1991. If one is looking for a brief introductory reading of the whole work, one could turn to C. H. Talbert, *The Apocalypse: A Reading of the Revelation of John* (Louisville, Ky.: Westminster/J. Knox, 1994) or P. Barnett, *Apocalypse Now and Then: Reading Revelation Today* (Sydney: Aquila Press, 1989). J. M. Court, *Revelation* (Sheffield, UK: JSOT Press, 1994), presents a largely European discussion of the Apocalypse. Because of its helpful charts and basic level of discussion, J.-P. Prevost's *How to Read the Apocalypse* (New York: Crossroad, 1993) is a fine brief introduction to Revelation. The most recent introduction that is also in most ways the most helpful is C. Koester's *Revelation and the End of All Things* (Grand Rapids, Mich.: Eerdmans, 2001).

THE GENRE OF REVELATION

Most scholars see the book of Revelation as some kind of apocalypse or a work of apocalyptic prophecy within an epistolary framework. On apocalyptic literature the best introduction is still John Collins, *The Apocalyptic Imagination* (New York: Crossroad, 1984). Two collections of essays especially helpful in dealing with this literature are *Apocalypticism in the Mediterranean World and the Near East*, ed. D. Hellholm, 2d ed. (Tübingen, Ger.: Mohr, 1989) and *The Encyclopedia of Apocalyticism*, Vol. 1, ed. J. J. Collins (New York: Continuum, 1998). There are in addition some special studies on this genre of literature that are helpful. C. Rowland, *The Open Heaven* (New York: Crossroad, 1982), emphasizes that apocalyptic often focuses on otherworldly mysteries, and M. Himmelfarb, *Tours of Hell* (Minneapolis: Fortress, 1983), stresses that many such works involve tours of the otherworld. Most scholars recognize that Revelation is some sort of visionary prophecy since it does not involve pseudonymity or *ex eventu* "predictions." Two studies help the reader assess Revelation within the context of Jewish and Christian prophecy as well as of apocalyptic: D. Aune, *Prophecy in Early Christianity and the Ancient Mediterranean World* (Grand Rapids, Mich.: Eerdmans, 1983), and B. Witherington III, *Jesus the Seer: The Progress of Prophecy* (Peabody, Mass.: Hendrickson, 1999). Helpful on the Greco-Roman views of prophecy is D. Potter, *Prophets and Emperors* (Cambridge, Mass.: Harvard University Press, 1994). F. D. Mazzaferri deals with the bearing of sources on the genre question (i.e., does John use preexisting visionary material) in *The Genre of the Book of Revelation from a Source-Critical Perspective* (Berlin: W. de Gruyter, 1989).

COMMENTARIES

Revelation has become in recent years a focal point for study and commentary in the wake of the Seminars on Apocalyptic Literature held both by the Society of Biblical Literature (SBL) and the SNTS. There is also a wide variety of older commentaries that are still useful, including some from the early part of the twentieth century (e.g., R. H. Charles, I. T. Beckwith, H. B. Swete). Of the larger full-scale works there is now no commentary that more fully deals with the wealth of relevant extrabiblical literature than D. Aune, *Revelation*, Vol. 1 (Dallas: Word, 1997), and Vols. 2–3 (Nashville, Tenn.: Nelson, 1998). This commentary, however, has its deficiencies, not the least of which is its inadequate treatment of the theological substance of the work. For a detailed examination of OT allusions and echoes in Revelation, there is no equal to G. K. Beale's *The Book of Revelation* (Grand Rapids, Mich.: Eerdmans, 1999). Besides the massive technical tomes, there are the helpful midlevel commentaries, such as the classic exposition by G. B. Caird, *The Revelation of Saint John the Divine* (Peabody, Mass.: Henrickson, 1998) and the challenging short rhetorical commentary by E. Schüssler Fiorenza, *Revelation: Vision of a Just World* (Minneapolis: Fortress, 1991). The following commentaries all make significant contributions to the discussion:

G. R. Beasley-Murray, *Revelation*, rev. ed. (London: Marshall, Morgan and Scott, 1978).
I. T. Beckwith, *The Apocalypse of John* (New York: Macmillan, 1919).
A. Boesak, *Comfort and Protest: The Apocalypse from a South African Perspective* (Philadelphia: Westminster, 1986).
M. E. Boring, *Revelation* (Louisville, Ky.: Westminster/J.Knox, 1989).
R. H. Charles, *A Critical and Exegetical Commentary on the Revelation of St. John*, 2 vols. (Edinburgh: T+T Clark, 1920).
E. Delebecque, *L'Apocalypse de Jean* (Paris: Mame, 1992).

C. H. Giblin, *The Book of Revelation: The Open Book of Prophecy* (Collegeville, Minn.: Liturgical Press, 1991).

H. Giesen, *Johannes-Apokalypse*, 2d ed. (Stuttgart, Ger.: Katholisches Bibelwerk, 1989). *Die Offenbarung des Johannes* (Regensburg, Ger.: Pustet, 1997).

T. F. Glasson, *The Revelation of John* (Cambridge: Cambridge University Press, 1965).

W. J. Harrington, *Revelation* (Collegeville, Minn.: Liturgical Press, 1993).

C. Keener, *Revelation: The NIV Application Bible Commentary* (Grand Rapids, Mich.: Zondervan, 2002).

H. Kraft, *Die Offenbarung des Johannes* (Tübingen, Ger.: Mohr-Siebeck, 1974).

G. A. Krodel, *Revelation* (Minneapolis: Augsburg, 1989).

G. E. Ladd, *A Commentary on the Revelation of John* (Grand Rapids, Mich.: Eerdmans, 1972).

E. Lohmeyer, *Die Offenbarung des Johannes* (Tübingen, Ger.: Mohr-Siebeck, 1970).

E. Lohse, *Die Offenbarung des Johannes* (Göttingen, Ger.: Vandenhoeck and Ruprecht, 1976).

J. R. Michaels, *Revelation* (Downers Grove, Ill.: InterVarsity Press, 1997).

R. H. Mounce, *The Book of Revelation* (Grand Rapids, Mich.: Eerdmans, 1977).

M. R. Mulholland, *Revelation: Holy Living in a Unholy World* (Grand Rapids, Mich.: Francis Asbury Press, 1990).

U. B. Muller, *Die Offenbarung des Johannes* (Gutersloh, Ger.: Mohn, 1984).

P. Prigent, *L'Apocalypse de Saint Jean* (Geneva: Labor et Fides, 1988).

M. Reddish, *Revelation* (Macon, Ga.: Smith and Helwys, 2001).

J. Roloff, *The Revelation of John* (Minneapolis: Fortress, 1993).

C. Rowland, *Revelation* (London: Epworth Press, 1993).

J. P. M. Sweet, *The Apocalypse of John*, 3d ed. (London: Macmillan, 1908).

A. Wikenhauser, *Die Offenbarung Johannes*, 3d ed. (Regensburg, Ger.: Pustet, 1959).

RHETORICAL STUDIES

The study of the rhetoric of Revelation is still in its nascent stages, and different studies offer differing levels of sophistication. One must also distinguish between examinations of Revelation by means of the ancient canons of Greco-Roman rhetoric and those of the modern socio-rhetorical approach pioneered by V. Robbins (see, e.g., his *Exploring the Texture of Texts* [Valley Forge, Pa.: Trinity Press, 1996]), the latter seeming to have more in common with various forms of literary and narrative criticism than with Greco-Roman rhetoric. I have placed an asterisk beside works that chiefly, if not exclusively, follow the approach of Robbins; the other works listed basically draw on the ancient forms of rhetorical analysis.

D. E. Aune, "The Form and Function of the Proclamations to the Seven Churches (Revelation 2–3)," *NTS* 36 (1990), pp. 182–204.

G. Carey, "Attention Seeking Behavior: Rhetoric, Resistance, and Authority in the Book of Revelation" (Ph.D. diss., Vanderbilt University, Nashville, Tenn., 1995).

*D. A. de Silva, "Honor Discourse and the Rhetorical Strategy of the Apocalypse of John," *JSNT* 71 (1998), pp. 79–110.

E. Schüssler Fiorenza, *The Book of Revelation: Justice and Judgment* (Philadelphia: Fortress, 1985), chap. 7 (also appears as "The Followers of the Lamb: Visionary Rhetoric and Social-Political Situation," in *Discipleship in the New Testament*, ed. F. Segovia [Philadelphia: Fortress, 1985], pp. 144–65; and in *Semeia* 36 (1986) 123–46.
   "The Followers of the Lamb: Visionary Rhetoric and Social-Political Situation," *Semeia* 36 (1986), pp. 123–46.
   Revelation: Vision of a Just World, Proclamation Commentaries (Minneapolis: Fortress, 1991).
W. Foerster, "Bemerkungen zur Bildsprache der Offenbarung Johannis," *Verborum veritas: Festschrift für Gustav Stählin*, ed. O. Böcher (Wuppertal, Ger.: Theologischer Verlag Brockhaus, 1970), pp. 225–36.
R. G. Hall, "Arguing Like an Apocalypse: Galatians and an Ancient *Topos* outside the Greco-Roman Rhetorical Tradition," *NTS* 42 (1996), pp. 434–53.
J. T. Kirby, "The Rhetorical Situations of Revelation 1–3," *NTS* 34 (1988), pp. 197–207.
B. W. Longenecker, " 'Linked Like a Chain': Rev. 22.6–9 in Light of Ancient Transition Technique," *NTS* 47, no. 1 (2001), pp. 105–17.
*S. D. O'Leary, "A Dramatistic Theory of Apocalyptic Rhetoric," *QJS* 79 (1993), pp. 385–426.
   Arguing the Apocalypse: A Theory of Millennial Rhetoric (Oxford: Oxford University Press, 1994).
T. Pippin, *Death and Desire: The Rhetoric of Gender in the Apocalypse of John* (Louisville, Ky.: Westminster/J. Knox, 1992).
*R. F. Reid, "Apocalypticism and Typology: Rhetorical Dimensions of a Symbolic Reality," *QJS* 69 (1983), pp. 229–48.
*R. Royalty, "The Rhetoric of Revelation," in *SBL Seminar Papers 1997* (Atlanta: Scholars Press, 1997), pp. 596–617.
   The Streets of Heaven: The Ideology of Wealth in the Apocalypse of John (Macon, Ga.: Mercer University Press, 1998).
W. A. Shea, "Chiasm in Theme and by Form in Revelation 18," *AUSS* 20 (1982), pp. 249–56.
   "Revelation 5 and 19 as Literary Reciprocals," *AUSS* 22 (1984), pp. 249–57.
   "The Parallel Literary Structure of Revelation 12 and 20," *AUSS* 23 (1985), pp. 37–54.
K. A. Strand, "Chiastic Structure and Some Motifs in the Book of Revelation," *AUSS* 16 (1978), pp. 401–8.

SOCIOLOGICAL AND ANTHROPOLOGICAL APPROACHES

There are now two relatively brief commentaries that take an approach to Revelation grounded in the social sciences: B. J. Malina and J. J. Pilch, *Social-Science Commentary on the Book of Revelation* (Minneapolis: Fortress, 2000), and L. Thompson, *Revelation* (Nashville, Tenn.: Abingdon, 1998). The latter is grounded in his fuller study, *The Book of Revelation: Apocalypse and Empire* (Oxford: Oxford University Press, 1990). There is much to be gained from these studies, but unfortunately they are also grounded in some faulty assumptions about the social matrix of first-century society out of which Revelation arose. In Thompson's case this includes some erroneous conclusions about the nature of the reign of Domitian and the likelihood of Christians' persecution during his reign. In the case of Malina and Pilch the failure to distinguish between ancient speculation about the stars and John's theology of heaven prevents the authors from correctly perceiving John's vision of the otherworld and the afterlife. Much more helpful on the latter is R. Bauckham, *The Fate of the Dead: Studies on the Jewish and Christian Apocalypses* (Leiden, Netherlands: Brill, 1998), especially when coupled with his *Climax of Prophecy*, which can be contrasted with B. J. Malina, *On the Genre and Message of Revelation* (Peabody, Mass.: Hendrickson, 1995).

There are several socio-historical studies that are particularly useful. Pride of place goes to the original work of C. Hemer (which was grounded in the earlier studies of W. Ramsay) entitled *The Letters to the Seven Churches of Asia* (Sheffield, UK: JSOT Press, 1986). R. H. Worth presents us with two different studies that are helpful in regard to the social milieu: *The Seven Cities of the Apocalypse and Roman Culture* and *The Seven Cities of the Apocalypse and Greco-Asian Culture* (Mahwah, N.J.: Paulist Press, 1999). A helpful collection of essays on the region and especially on Ephesus can be found in *Ephesos: Metropolis of Asia*, ed. H. Koester (Valley Forge, Pa.: Trinity Press, 1995). On the imperial cult in western Asia during the relevant period, see J. N. Kraybill, *Imperial Cult and Commerce in John's Apocalypse* (Sheffield, UK: Sheffield Academic Press, 1996); K. Scott, *The Imperial Cult under the Flavians* (New York: Arno, 1975); and S. R. F. Price, *Rituals and Power: The Roman Imperial Cult in Asia Minor* (Cambridge: Cambridge University Press, 1984). One may also wish to consult the somewhat dated but still useful work by P. Touilleux, *L'Apocalypse et les cultes de Domitien et de Cybele* (Paris: P. Geuthner, 1935). Also helpful is W. Howard-Brook and A. Gwyther, *Unveiling Empire: Reading Revelation Then and Now* (Maryknoll, N.Y.: Orbis, 1999), and R. Stark, *The Rise of Christianity* (Princeton, N.J.: Princeton University Press, 1996). On the Jewish presence in Asia Minor, see P. R. Trebilco, *Jewish Communities in Asia Minor* (Cambridge: Cambridge University Press, 1991).

CLASSICAL AND ARCHAEOLOGICAL RESOURCES

There is indeed a wealth of material by classics scholars and by experts in Roman history and in the province of Asia, which is of relevance to the discussion of Revelation at various points. The difficulty is that NT scholars not trained in these fields tend to sound byte this material to prove their own points instead of really listening to the scope of dialogue about the nature of the reign of Nero or Domitian, or about the imperial cult and other matters of concern for evaluating Revelation. A good place to start is with *The Cambridge Ancient History*, Vols. 10–11, ed. A. K. Bowman et al. (Cambridge: Cambridge University Press, 1999, 2000). Both volumes are in new editions, with helpful further discussion. Particularly helpful is M. Griffin's discussion of the Flavians, which makes clear that the "perceived crisis" view of what Revelation reflects (put forward by Yarbro Collins, Thompson, and others) is unlikely to be a fair reading of the situation. See D. Cuss, *Imperial Cult and Honorary Terms in the New*

Testament (Fribourg, Switzerland: University Press, 1974). There is something to be gained from reading R. MacMullen's *Enemies of the Roman Order* (Cambridge, Mass.: Harvard University Press, 1966), and D. Magie's *Roman Rule in Asia Minor* (Princeton, N.J.: Princeton University Press, 1950) although the latter now needs updating. Other standard works are F. Millar, *The Emperor in the Roman World* (Ithaca, N.Y.: Cornell University Press, 1977), and J. Wacher, *The Roman World* (London: Routledge, 1987). The series of volumes published by Macquarrie University (New South Wales, Australia) and now Eerdmans Publishing Co. entitled *New Documents Illustrating Early Christianity*, ed. G. Horsley et al. (1981–) is especially helpful in the way it relates the wealth of epigraphical and numismatic data to NT texts. On slavery, see S. Bartchy, *First-Century Slavery and the Interpretation of 1 Cor. 7.21* (Missoula, Mont.: Scholars Press, 1973), and T. Wiedemann, *Greek and Roman Slavery* (Baltimore: Johns Hopkins University Press, 1981).

HISTORY OF INTERPRETATION

There are several interesting chronicles of how Revelation has been interpreted through the ages, none of which are comprehensive. For an introductory study that looks at various ancient and modern interpretations of the text, including some radical ones such as that of David Koresh and the Branch Davidians, see K. G. C. Newport, *Apocalypse and Millennium* (Cambridge: Cambridge University Press, 2000). For the period 1700–1834, see C. Burdon, *The Apocalypse in England: Revelation Unraveling, 1700–1834* (London: Macmillan, 1997). A further interesting study of English interpreters of Revelation is R. Bauckham's *Tudor Apocalypse* (Oxford: Sutton Courtney Press, 1978). To this one may add the diachronic study of apocalyptic ways of thinking found in S. D. O'Leary, *Arguing the Apocalypse: A Theory of Millennial Rhetoric* (Oxford: Oxford University Press, 1994). He theorizes that apocalyptic functions as a symbolic theodicy providing a sort of rhetorical resolution of the problem of evil "through discursive construction of temporality" (p. 14). Time, evil, and authority are seen as the principle subjects of such literature. For discussion of how the book was interpreted throughout church history, see A. W. Wainwright, *Mysterious Apocalypse: Interpreting the Book of Revelation* (Nashville, Tenn.: Abingdon, 1993). On the issue of the millennium, see my *Jesus, Paul, and the End of the World* (Downers Grove, Ill.: Inter Varsity Press, 1992); R. G. Clouse, ed., *The Meaning of the Millennium: Four Views* (Downers Grove, Ill.: Inter Varsity Press, 1977); and more recently, S. J. Grenz, *The Millennial Maze: Sorting Out Evangelical Options* (Downers Grove, Ill.: Inter Varsity Press, 1992).

THEOLOGY

The most useful small study on this issue is R. Bauckham, *The Theology of the Book of Revelation* (Cambridge: Cambridge University Press, 1993). Bauckham also has a lot more to offer on this subject, including his masterful study *The Climax of Prophecy* (Edinburgh: T+T Clark, 1993), which addresses many of the interpretive problems in a helpful way. A very interesting socio-historical study of certain Christological ideas and images in Revelation is found in T. B. Slater, *Christ and Community: A Socio-Historical Study of the Christology of Revelation* (Sheffield, UK: Sheffield Academic Press, 1999). The most helpful monograph on the use of the OT in Revelation for Christological and other purposes is J. Fekkes, *Isaiah and Prophetic Traditions in the Book of Revelation: Visionary Antecedents and Their Developments* (Sheffield, UK: Sheffield Academic Press, 1994). Other very useful studies are S. Moyise, *The Old Testament in the Book of Revelation* (Sheffield, UK: Sheffield Academic Press, 1995), and G. K. Beale, *John's Use of the Old Testament in Revelation* (Sheffield, UK: Sheffield Academic Press, 1998). For a more specifically Christologically focused monograph, see J. Comblin, *Le Christ dans l'Apocalpyse* (Paris: Desclee, 1965).

IMPORTANT MONOGRAPHS

J. L. Resseguie offers a helpful literary and narrative critical study of Revelation entitled *Revelation Unsealed: A Narrative Critical Approach to John's Apocalypse* (Leiden, Netherlands: Brill, 1998). B. R. Rossing, *The Choice between Two Cities: Whore, Bride, and Empire in the Apocalypse* (Harrisburg, Pa.: Trinity Press, 1999), analyzes the function of the two cities of Revelation. Increasingly there are feminist readings available about Revelation, and while Rossing's work somewhat fits into this category, T. Pippin, *Apocalyptic Bodies: The Biblical End of the World in Text and Image* (New York: Routledge, 1999), presents a more thorough treatment along such lines. W. Howard-Brook and A. Gwyther offer a different sort of postcolonial liberationist reading in *Reading Revelation Then and Now* (Maryknoll, N.Y.: Orbis, 1999). One will also want to consult E. Schüssler Fiorenza's influential study *The Book of Revelation: Justice and Judgment* (Philadelphia: Fortress, 1985), now available in a second edition (1998) with minor updating and a more extensive bibliography, as well as D. Aukerman's *Reckoning with Apocalypse: Terminal Politics and Christian Hope* (New York: Crossroad, 1993). G. Theissen, *The Religion of the Earliest Churches* (Minneapolis: Fortress, 1999), is helpful in these matters as well.

For the intended effect of the apocalyptic language of John, see A. Yarbro Collins's *Crisis and Catharsis: The Power of the Apocalypse* (Philadelphia: Westminster, 1984). Both Collins and J. M. Court have made contributions to the discussion of John's use of mythological images and ideas. See Court's *Myth and History in the Book of Revelation* (London: SPCK, 1979). This work is in fact more useful than his more recent attempt to discuss the trajectory of the apocalyptic tradition beyond the time of Revelation in *The Book of Revelation and the Johannine Apocalyptic Tradition* (Sheffield, UK: Sheffield Academic Press, 2000). He does not convince us that the later works in question (e.g., 2d

Apocalypse of John) really deserve to be compared with or seen as standing in the line of Revelation. A useful collection of articles can be found in *L'Apocalypse johannique et l'Apocalyptique dans le Nouveau Testament*, ed. J. Lambrecht. BETL 53 (Louvain, Belg.: University Press, 1980).

There are not many extended studies on the author of Revelation, but a very helpful one is A. Culpepper's *John: The Son of Zebedee: The Life of a Legend* (Minneapolis: Fortress, 2000). In regard to the language and syntax of Revelation, S. Thompson's monograph *The Apocalypse and Semitic Syntax* (Cambridge: Cambridge University Press, 1985) needs to be consulted, as does G. Mussies's *The Morphology of Koine Greek as Used in the Apocalypse of St. John: A Study in Bilingualism* (Leiden, Netherlands: Brill, 1971). Also helpful is G. K. Beale, *John's Use of the Old Testament in Revelation* (Sheffield, UK: Sheffield Academic Press, 1998), and on the subject of intertextuality and Revelation, see J. Fekkes, *Isaiah and the Prophetic Traditions in the Book of Revelation: Visionary Antecedents and Their Developments* (Sheffield, UK: Sheffield Academic Press, 1994). For dealing with the spiritual substance of Revelation, E. Peterson's *Reversed Thunder* (San Francisco: Harper and Row, 1988) is unsurpassed, and on the issue of suffering, see J. Christian Beker, *Suffering and Hope: The Biblical Vision and the Human Predicament* (Grand Rapids, Mich.: Eerdmans, 1994). On angel worship, see L.T. Stuckenbruck, *Angel Veneration and Christology* (Tübingen, Ger.: Mohr, 1995).

ARTICLES OF INTEREST

There are literally thousands of helpful articles on Revelation, but here are some that I have found most useful because they either offer fresh insights into the text or helpful summaries of the major issues or themes in Revelation:

D. E. Aune, "The Social Matrix of the Apocalypse of John," *Biblical Research* 26 (1981), pp. 16–32.
  "The Influence of Roman Imperial Court Ceremonial on the Apocalypse of John," *Biblical Research* 28 (1983), pp. 5–26.
  "The Apocalypse of John and Greco-Roman Revelatory Magic," *NTS* 33 (1987), pp. 481–501.
  "The Prophetic Circle of John of Patmos and the Exegesis of Revelation 22.16," *JSNT* 37 (1989), pp. 103–16.
  "The Form and Function of the Proclamations to the Seven Churches (Revelation 2–3)," *NTS* 36 (1990), pp. 182–204.
M. Bachmann, "Der erste apoklyptische Reiter und die Anlage des letzen Buches der Bibel," *Biblica* 67 (1986), pp. 240–75.
  "Die apokalyptischen Reiter," *ZTK* 86 (1989), pp. 33–58.
  "Himmlisch: Der 'Tempel Gottes' von Apok. 11.1," *NTS* 40 (1994), pp. 474–80.
J. W. Bailey, "The Temporary Messianic Reign in the Literature of Early Judaism," *JBL* 53 (1934), pp. 170–87.

W. G. Baines, "The Number of the Beast in Revelation 13.18," *Heythrop Journal* 16 (1975), pp. 195–96.

D. Balch, "Two Apologetic *Encomia* Dionysius on Rome and Josephus on the Jews," *JSJ* 13 (1982), pp. 102–22.

L. W. Barnard, "Clement of Rome and the Persecution of Domitian," *NTS* 10 (1964), pp. 251–60.

D. L. Barr, "The Apocalypse as a Symbolic Transformation of the World: A Literary Analysis," *Interp.* 38 (1984), pp. 39–50.

"The Apocalypse as Oral Enactment," *Interp.* 38 (1984), pp. 39–50.

R. J. Bauckham, "The Martyrdom of Enoch and Elijah: Jewish or Christian?" *JBL* 95 (1976), pp. 447–58.

"The Lord's Day," in *From Sabbath to Lord's Day*, ed. D. A. Carson (Grand Rapids, Mich.: Zondervan, 1982), pp. 197–220.

"The List of the Tribes in Revelation 7 Again," *JSNT* 42 (1991), pp. 99–115.

G. K. Beale, "The Danielic Background for Revelation 13.18 and 17.9," *TynB* 31 (1980), pp. 163–70.

"The Influence of Daniel upon the Structure and Theology of John's Apocalypse," *JETS* 27 (1984), pp. 413–23.

"The Origin of the Title 'King of Kings and Lord of Lords,'" *NTS* 31 (1985), pp. 618–20.

"The Interpretive Problem of Rev. 1.19," *NovT* 34 (1992), pp. 360–87.

"The Old Testament Background of Rev. 3.14," *NTS* 42 (1996), pp. 133–52.

R. Beauvery, "L'Apocalypse au eisque de la numismatique: Babylone, la grande Prostituée et le sixième roi Vespasien et la déesse Rome," *RevBib* 90 (April 1983), pp. 243–60.

A. A. Bell, "The Date of John's Apocalypse: The Evidence of Some Roman Historians Reconsidered," *NTS* 25 (1979), pp. 93–102.

H. D. Betz, "Zum Problem des religionsgeschichtlichen Verstandnisses der Apokalyptik," *ZTK* 63 (1966), pp. 391–406.

H. Bietenhard, "The Millennial Hope in the Early Church," *Scottish Journal of Theology* 6 (1953), pp. 12–30.

M. Black, "The Chi-Rho Sign – Christogram and/or Staurogram?" in *Apostolic History and the Gospel: Biblical and Historical Essays Presented to F. F. Bruce*, ed. W. W. Gasque and R. P. Martin (Grand Rapids, Mich.: Eerdmans, 1970), pp. 319–27.

"The Christological Use of the Old Testament in the New Testament," *NTS* 18 (1971–72), pp. 1–14.

"The Two Witnesses of Rev. 11.3 f. in Jewish and Christian Apocalyptic Tradition," in *Donum Gentilicium: New Testament Studies in Honour of David Daube*, ed. E. Bammel, C. K. Barrett, and W. D. Davies (Oxford: Clarendon Press, 1978), pp. 225–37.

B. K. Blount, "Reading Revelation Today: Witness as Active Resistance," *Interp.* 54 (2000), pp. 398–415.

G. Bohak, "Greek-Hebrew Gematrias in 3 Baruch and in Revelation," *JSP* 7 (1990), pp. 119–21.

M.-E. Boismard, "Notes sur l'Apokalypse," *RevBib* 59 (1952), pp. 161–81.

P. J. J. Botha, "God, Emperor, Worship, and Society: Contemporary Experiences and the Book of Revelation," *Neotestamentica* 22 (1988), pp. 87–102.

W. H. Brownlee, "The Priestly Character of the Church in the Apocalypse," *NTS* 5 (1958–59), pp. 224–25.

F. F. Bruce, "The Spirit in the Apocalypse," in *Christ and the Spirit in the New Testament,* ed. B. Lindars and S. S. Smalley (Cambridge: Cambridge University Press, 1973), pp. 333–44.

C. F. Burney, "Christ as the ΑΡΧΗ of Creation (Prov. Viii.22; Col. I.15–18; Rev. iii. 14)," *JTS* (1925–26), pp. 160–77.

G. Biguzzi, "Ephesus, Its Artemision, Its Temple to the Flavian Emperors, and Idolatry in Revelation," *NovT* 40 (1998), pp. 276–90.

G. B. Caird, "On Deciphering the Book of Revelation," *ExpT* 74 (1962–63), pp. 13–15, 51–53, 82–84, 103–5.

A. D. Callahan, "The Language of the Apocalypse," *HTR* 88 (1995), pp. 453–57.

J. Cambier, "Les images de l'Ancien Testament dans l'Apocalypse de Saint Jean," *Nouvelle Revue Theologique* 77 (1955), pp. 113–22.

D. R. Carnegie, "Worthy Is the Lamb: The Hymns in Revelation," in *Christ the Lord: Studies Presented to D. Guthrie,* ed. H. H. Rowden (Downers Grove, Ill.: Inter Varsity Press, 1982), pp. 243–56.

J. H. Charlesworth, "The Jewish Roots of Christology: The Discovery of the Hypostatic Voice," *Scottish Journal of Theology* 39 (1986), pp. 19–41.

A. Y. Collins, "Numerical Symbolism in Jewish and Early Christian Apocalyptic Literature," *ANRW* Part II, vol. 2, no. 21 (1984), pp. 1221–87.

"Reading the Book of Revelation in the Twentieth Century," *Interp.* 40 (1986), pp. 229–42.

"Eschatology in the Book of Revelation," *Ex Auditu* 6 (1990), pp. 63–72.

John Collins, "Apocalyptic Eschatology as the Transcendence of Death," *CBQ* 36 (1974), pp. 21–43.

"The Political Perspective of the Revelation of John," *JBL* 96 (1977), pp. 241–56.

"The Son of Man in First Century Judaism," *NTS* 38 (1992), pp. 448–66.

J. Crenshaw, "Transmitting Prophecy across Generations" (paper presented at the SBL meeting, Orlando, Fla., 1998).

L. V. Crutchfield, "The Apostle John and Asia Minor as a Source of Premillennialism in the Early Church Fathers," *JETS* 31 (1988), pp. 411–27.

D. R. Davies, "The Relationship between the Seals, Trumpets, and Bowls in the Book of Revelation," *JETS* 16 (1973), pp. 149–58.

J. S. Deere, "Premillennialism in Revelation 20.4–6," *Bibliotheca Sacra* 135 (1978), pp. 58–73.

D. A. de Silva, "The Social Setting of the Revelation to John: Conflicts Within, Fears Without," *WTJ* 54 (1992), pp. 273–302.

"Honor Discourse and the Rhetorical Strategy of the Apocalypse of John," *JSNT* 71 (1998), pp. 79–110.

"A Socio-Rhetorical Interpretation of Revelation 14.6–13," *Bulletin for Biblical Research* 9 (1999), pp. 65–117.

"Final Topics: The Rhetorical Function of Intertexture in Revelation 14.14–16.21" (unpublished paper).

C. Deutsch, "Transformation of Symbols: The New Jerusalem in Rv. 21.1–22.5," *ZNW* 78 (1987), pp. 106–26.

F. G. Downing, "Pliny's Prosecutions of Christians," *JSNT* 34 (1988), pp. 105–23.

J. A. Draper, "The Heavenly Feast of Tabernacles: Revelation 7.1–17," *JSNT* 19 (1983), pp. 133–47.

W. Dunphy, "Maranatha: Development in Early Christianity," *Irish Theological Quarterly* 37 (1970), pp. 294–309.

J. K. Elliot, "The Distinctiveness of the Greek Manuscripts of the Book of Revelation," *JTS* 48 (1997), pp. 116–24.

A. M. Enroth, "The Hearing Formula in the Book of Revelation," *NTS* 36 (1990), pp. 598–608.

P. Esler, "Political Oppression in Jewish Apocalyptic Literature: A Social Scientific Approach," *Listening: Journal of Religion and Culture* 28 (1993), pp. 181–99.

J. Fekkes, " 'His Bride Has Prepared Herself': Revelation 12–21 and Isaian Nuptial Imagery," *JBL* 109 (1990), pp. 269–87.

A. Feuillet, "Le premier cavalier de l'Apocalypse (Apc. 6.1–8)," *ZNW* 57 (1966), pp. 229–59.
"Les 144,000 Israelites marques d'un sceau," *NovT* 9 (1967), pp. 191–224.
"Les martyrs de l'humanité et l'Agneau égorge: Une interpretation nouvelle de la prière des égorges en Ap. 6.9–11," *Nouvelle Revue Théologique* 99 (1977), pp. 189–207.

E. Schüssler Fiorenza, "The Followers of the Lamb: Visionary Rhetoric and Social-Political Situation," *Semeia* 36 (1986), pp. 123–46.

S. Friesen, "Ephesus: Key to a Vision in Revelation," *BAR* 19 (1993), pp. 24–37.
"Revelation, Realia, and Religion: Archaeology in the Interpretation of the Apocalypse," *HTR* 88 (1995), pp. 291–314.

A. Geyser, "The Twelve Tribes in Revelation: Judean and Judeo-Christian Apocalypticism," *NTS* 28 (1982), pp. 388–99.

C. H. Giblin, "Revelation 11.1–13: Its Form, Function and Contextual Integration," *NTS* 30 (1984), pp. 433–59.
"Recapitulation and Literary Coherence of John's Apocalypse," *CBQ* 56 (1994), pp. 81–95.
"The Millennium (Rev. 20.4–6) as Heaven," *NTS* 45 (1999), pp. 553–70.

T. F. Glasson, "The Order of Jewels in Revelation XXI.19–20: A Theory Eliminated," *JTS* 26 (1975), pp. 95–100.

S. Goranson, "The Text of Revelation 22.14," *NTS* 43 (1997), pp. 154–57.

M. Gourgues, "The Thousand-Year Reign (Rev. 20.1–6): Terrestrial or Celestial?" *CBQ* 47 (1985), pp. 676–81.

S. Grenz, "The Deeper Significance of the Millennium Debate," *Southwestern Journal of Theology* 36 (1994), pp. 14–21.

R. H. Gundry, "The New Jerusalem: People, Not Place," *NovT* 29 (1987), pp. 254–64.
"Angelomorphic Christology in the Book of Revelation," in *SBL Seminar Papers, 1994* ed. E. H. Lovering (Atlanta: Scholars Press, 1994), pp. 662–78.

J. J. Gunther, "The Elder John, Author of Revelation," *JSNT* 11 (1981), pp. 3–20.

D. Guthrie, "The Christology of Revelation," in *Jesus of Nazareth: Lord and Christ*, ed. J. B. Green et al. (Grand Rapids, Mich.: Eerdmans, 1994), pp. 397–409.

R. G. Hall, "Living Creatures in the Midst of the Throne: Another Look at Revelation 4.6," *NTS* 36 (1990), pp. 609–13.

P. A. Harland, "Honouring the Emperor or Assailing the Beast," *JSNT* 77 (2000), pp. 99–121.

J. P. Heil, "The Fifth Seal (Rev. 6.9–11) as a Key to Revelation," *Biblica* 74 (1993), pp. 220–43.

C. J. Hemer, "The Sardis Letter and the Croesus Tradition (Rev. 2.8–11.3.2–3)," *NTS* 19 (1972), pp. 94–97.

"Unto the Angel of the Churches," *Buried History* 11 (1975), pp. 4–27, 56–83, 110–35, 164–90.

J. Herzer, "Der erste apokalyptischer Reiter und der Konig der Konige: Ein Beitrag zur Christologie der Johannesapokalypse," *NTS* 45 (1999), pp. 230–49.

M. Hopkins, "The Historical Perspective of Apocalypse 1–11," *CBQ* 27 (1965), pp. 42–47.

W. Horbury, "The Benediction of the Minim and Early Jewish-Christian Controversy," *JTS* 33 (1982), pp. 19–61.

L. W. Hurtado, "Revelation 4–5 in Light of Jewish Apocalyptic Analogies," *JSNT* 25 (1985), pp. 105–24.

E. P. Janzen, "The Jesus of the Apocalypse Wears the Emperor's Clothes," in *SBL Seminar Papers 1994*, ed. L. H. Lovering (Atlanta: Scholars Press, 1994), pp. 637–61.

R. L. Jeske, "Spirit and Community in the Johannine Apocalypse," *NTS* 31 (1985), pp. 452–66.

L. T. Johnson, "The New Testament's Anti-Semitic Slander and Conventions of Ancient Rhetoric," *JBL* 108 (1989), pp. 419–41.

E. A. Judge, "The Mark of the Beast," *TynB* 42 (1991), pp. 158–60.

R. A. Kearsley, "Angels in Asia Minor: The Cult of Hosios and Dikaios," in *New Documents Illustrating Early Christianity*, vol. 6, ed. G. Horsley et al. (Grand Rapids, Mich.: Eerdmans, 1981), pp. 206–9.

A. Kerkeslager, "Apollo, Greco-Roman Prophecy, and the Rider on the White Horse in Rev. 6.2," *JBL* 112 (1993), pp. 116–21.

G. W. H. Lampe, "The Testimony of Jesus Is the Spirit of Prophecy (Rev. 19:10)," in *The New Testament Age: Essays in Honor of Bo Reike*, ed. W. C. Weinrich (Macon, Ga.: Mercer University Press, 1980), pp. 245–58.

H. K. LaRondelle, "The Biblical Concept of Armageddon," *JETS* 28 (1985), pp. 21–31.

"The Etymology of Har-Magedon (Rev. 16.16)," *AUSS* 27 (1989), pp. 69–73.

R. E. Loasby, "'Har-Magedon' according to the Hebrew in the Setting of the Seven Last Plagues of Revelation 16," *AUSS* 27 (1989), pp. 129–32.

E. Lohse, "Wie christlich ist die Offenbarung des Johannes?" *NTS* 34 (1988), pp. 321–38.

T. E. McComiskey, "Alteration of OT Imagery in the Book of Revelation: Its Hermeneutical and Theological Significance," *JETS* 36 (1993), pp. 307–16.

A. McNicol, "Revelation 11.1–14 and the Structure of the Apocalypse," *Restoration Quarterly* 22 (1979), pp. 193–202.

M. Marty, "M.E.M.O.: A Revelation," *Christian Century* 114, no. 16 (14 May 1997), p. 495.

J. R. Michaels, "Revelation 1.19 and the Narrative Voices of the Apocalypse," *NTS* 37 (1991), pp. 604–20.

P. S. Minear, "Far as the Curse Is Found: The Point of Rev. 12.15–16," *NovT* 33 (1991), pp. 71–77.

D. G. Mitten, "A New Look at Sardis," *BA* 24 (1966), pp. 38–68.

R. B. Moberly, "When Was Revelation Conceived?" *Biblica* 73 (1992), pp. 376–93.

C. F. D. Moule, "A Reconsideration of the Context of Maranatha," *NTS* 8 (1962), pp. 307–10.

L. Mowry, "Revelation 4–5 and Early Christian Usage," *JBL* 71 (1952), pp. 75–84.

S. Moyise, "Intertextuality and the Book of Revelation," *ExpT* 104 (1993), pp. 295–98.

G. Mussies, "Antipas (Rev. 2.13b)," *NovT* 7 (1964), pp. 242–44.

"The Greek of the Book of Revelation," in *L'Apocalypse johannique et l'Apocalyptique dans le Nouveau Testament,* ed. J. Lambrecht (Louvain, Belg.: University Press, 1980), pp. 167–77.

K. G. C. Newport, "Semitic Influence on the Use of Some Prepositions in the Book of Revelation," *Bible Translator* 37 (1986), pp. 328–34.

"The Use of EK in Revelation: Evidence of Semitic Influence," *AUSS* 24 (1986), pp. 223–30.

"Semitic Influence in Revelation: Some Further Evidence," *AUSS* 25 (1987), pp. 249–56.

D. C. Olson, "'Those Who Have Not Defiled Themselves with Women': Revelation 14.4 and the Book of Enoch," *CBQ* 59 (1997), pp. 492–510.

J. J. O'Rourke, "The Hymns of the Apocalypse," *CBQ* 39 (1968), pp. 399–409.

C. G. Ozanne, "The Language of the Apocalypse," *TynB* 16 (1965), pp. 3–9.

S. H. T. Page, "Revelation 20 and Pauline Eschatology," *JETS* 23 (1980), pp. 31–43.

D. C. Parker, "A New Oxyrhynchus Papyrus p 115 (P. Oxy. 4499)," *NTS* 46 (2000), pp. 159–74.

D. Pezzoli-Oligati, "Images of Cities in Ancient Religions: Some Methodological Considerations," in *SBL Seminar Papers 2000* (Atlanta: SBL, 2000), pp. 80–102.

M. Philonenko, "Dehors les Chiens (Apocalypse 22.16 et 4QMMTB 58–62)," *NTS* 43 (1997), pp. 445–50.

S. E. Porter, "Why the Laodiceans Received Lukewarm Water," *TynB* 38 (1987), pp. 143–49.

"The Language of the Apocalypse in Recent Discussion," *NTS* 35 (1989), pp. 582–603.

W. W. Reader, "The Twelve Jewels of Revelation 21.19–20," *JBL* 100 (1981), pp. 433–57.

M. Rissi, "Rider on the White Horse: A Study of Revelation 6.1–2," *Interp.* 18 (1964), pp. 407–18.

"Die Erscheinung Christi nach Off. 19.11–16," *TZ* 21 (1965), pp. 81–95.

C. Rowland, "The Vision of the Risen Christ in Rev. 1.13 ff.: The Debt of an Early Christology to an Aspect of Jewish Angelology," *JTS* 31 (1980), pp. 1–11.

J. R. Royse, "Their Fifteen Enemies: The Text of Rev. xi.12 in P47 and 1611," *JTS* 31 (1980), pp. 78–80.

E. Russel, "A Roman Law Parallel to Revelation Five," *Bib. Sac.* 115 (1958), pp. 258–64.

S. J. Scherer, "Signs and Wonders in the Imperial Cult: A New Look at the Roman Religious Institution in the Light of Rev. 13.13–15," *JBL* 103 (1984), pp. 599–610.

D. D. Schmidt, "Semitisms and Septuagintalisms in the Book of Revelation," *NTS* 37 (1991), pp. 592–603.

C. H. H. Scobie, "Local References in the Letters to the Seven Churches," *NTS* 39 (1993), pp. 606–24.

W. H. Shea, "The Location and Significance of Armageddon in Rev. 16.16," *AUSS* 18 (1980), pp. 157–62.

"Revelation 5 and 19 as Literary Reciprocals," *AUSS* 22 (1984), pp. 249–57.

T. B. Slater, "King of Kings and Lord of Lords Revisited," *NTS* 39 (1993), pp. 159–60.

"One Like a Son of Man in First-Century CE Judaism," *NTS* 41 (1995), pp. 183–98.

"On the Social Setting of the Revelation," *NTS* 44 (1998), pp. 232–56.

S. S. Smalley, "John's Revelation and John's Community," *BJRL* 69 (1987), pp. 549–71.

C. R. Smith, "The Portrayal of the Church as the New Israel in the Names and Order of the Tribes in Revelation 7.5–8," *JSNT* 39 (1990), pp. 111–18.

"Reclaiming the Social Justice Message in Revelation: Materialism, Imperialism, and Divine Judgement in Revelation 18," *Transformation* 7 (1990), pp. 28–33.

"Revelation 1.19: An Eschatologically Escalated Prophetic Convention," *JETS* 33 (1990), pp. 461–66.

"The Structure of the Book of Revelation in Light of Apocalyptic Literary Conventions," *NovT* 36 (1994), pp. 373–93.

G. M. Stevenson, "Conceptual Background to Golden Crown Imagery in the Apocalypse of John," *JBL* 114 (1995), pp. 257–72.

K. A. Strand, "Another Look at the Lord's Day in the Early Church and in Revelation 1.10," *NTS* 13 (1967), pp. 174–81.

"The Two Witnesses of Rev. 11.3–12," *AUSS* 19 (1981), pp. 127–35.

"The Eight Basic Visions in the Book of Revelation," *AUSS* 25 (1987), pp. 107–21.

R. V. G. Tasker, "The Chester Beatty Papyrus of the Apocalypse of John," *JTS* 50 (1949), pp. 60–68.

C. P. Thiede, "Papyrus Magdalen Greek 17 (Gregory-Aland p64): A Reappraisal," *TynB* 46 (1995), pp. 29–42.

R. L. Thomas, "The Spiritual Gift of Prophecy in Rev. 22.18," *JETS* 32 (1989), pp. 201–16.

L. L. Thompson, "Cult and Eschatology in the Apocalypse of John," *Journal of Religion* 49 (1969), pp. 330–50.

"Lamentation for Christ as a Hero: Revelation 1.7," *JBL* 119 (2000), pp. 683–703.

M. M. Thompson, "Worship in the Book of Revelation," *Ex Auditu* 8 (1992), pp. 45–54.

A. A. Trites, "'Martus' and Martyrdom in the Apocalypse: A Semantic Study," *NovT* 15 (1973), pp. 72–80.

J. H. Ulrichsen, "Die sieben Haupter und die zehn Horner: Zur Datierung der Offenbarung des Johannes," *Studia Theologica* 39 (1985), pp. 1–20.

W. C. Van Unnik, "A Formula Describing Prophecy," *NTS* 9 (1962–63), pp. 86–94.

W. S. Vorster, "Genre and the Revelation of John: A Study in Text, Context, and Intertext," *Neotestamentica* 22 (1988), pp. 103–23.

D. Warden, "Imperial Persecution and the Dating of 1 Peter and Revelation," *JETS* 34 (1991), pp. 203–12.

P. Whale, "The Lamb of John: Some Myths about the Vocabulary of the Johannine Literature," *JBL* 106 (1987), pp. 289–95.

P. Wick, "There Was Silence in Heaven (Revelation 8.1): Annotation to Israel Knohl's 'Between Voice and Silence,' " *SBL* 117 (1998), pp. 512–14.

A. Wikenhauser, "Weltwoche und tausendjahrige Reich," *Tubinger Theologische Quartalschrift* 127 (1947), pp. 399–417.

J. C. Wilson, "The Problem of the Domitianic Dating of Revelation," *NTS* 39 (1993), pp. 587–605.

R. E. Winkle, "Another Look at the List of the Tribes in Revelation," *AUSS* 27 (1989), pp. 53–67.

F. Winter, "Aspekte der Bescreibung des himmelischen Jerusalem auf dem Hintergrund der antiken Architektur- und Verfassungs-theories," *ProtoBib* 8, part 2 (1999), pp. 85–102.

B. Witherington III, "Not So Idle Thoughts about Eidolothuton," *TynB* 44 (1993), pp. 237–54.

III. Commentary

⚜

REVELATION 1.1–1.3 – VISIONARY MATERIAL: HANDLE CAREFULLY

NRSV Revelation 1.1 The revelation of Jesus Christ, which God gave him to show his servants what must soon take place; he made it known by sending his angel to his servant John,
2 who testified to the Word of God and to the testimony of Jesus Christ, even to all that he saw.
3 Blessed is the one who reads aloud the words of the prophecy, and blessed are those who hear and who keep what is written in it; for the time is near.

*M*uch has been and ought to be made of the fact that the Apocalypse, after the brief introductory remarks, starts and ends with epistolary elements. E. Schüssler Fiorenza has especially highlighted the parallels with the Pauline corpus. Notice that even the introductory phrase *apocalypsis Iesou Christou* is found in Paul's writings in various places (cf. 1 Cor. 1.7 to 2 Thess. 1.7), where it refers to the Parousia. But in what is probably Paul's earliest letter (see Gal. 1.12, 16) reference is made to an appearance of Jesus Christ to Paul in a vision, possibly alluding to his Damascus Road experience. Fiorenza thus is likely right to suggest that our author characterizes his experience as a prophetic visionary experience, not unlike Paul's.[1] Notice too that like Paul the author never directly calls himself a prophet, but rather a *doulos*, a term used in the Hebrew Scriptures to refer to servant-prophets (cf. Amos 3.7). But there may be an implicit claim of authority in the use of this term, as there seems to be in the Pauline usage. If one is a servant of Jesus, one has a position of authority. At least in part John is writing to an area where Paul spent a considerable amount of time, though

---

[1] E. Schüssler Fiorenza, *Revelation: Vision of a Just World* (Minneapolis: Fortress, 1991), pp. 39–40.

perhaps not in all these particular communities. It should not then be surprising if the Pauline Gospel and theology had affected John of Patmos. It was William Ramsay's conjecture that, by the end of the first century A.D., the primary locus of the Christian movement was in Asia Minor. This might explain the intensified hostility of pagans in the area.

The initial question to be asked about the phrase *apocalypsis Iesou Christou* is, Do we have an objective or subjective genitive? Usually the question is asked, Is this a revelation by or about Jesus? It could of course be both. If the phrase is used as it is in Galatians, this favors the view that it is a vision of and about Jesus Christ that comes from God and is delivered by an angel to John. Then the "him" in question would be John rather than Jesus. But "him" is more naturally taken to refer to Jesus. Thus it appears that John is claiming this to be a revelation that comes from Jesus, though it is mediated through an angel. This claim helps establish the authority of this work. The word *apocalypsis* probably does not refer to a literary genre here, unless one considers visions a genre of literature. This vision or series of visions differs from earlier Jewish apocalyptic material by the way Jesus, his person and his work, affects and shapes the vision. This document is not purely world-denying in character because the author believes that the Lamb has already been slain in history and has triumphed beyond death. Thus we cannot appropriately call this an escapist document or even one that minimizes the importance of the temporal or history. History is seen as the place where the most crucial events affecting humans take place, even if those events are first planned and announced in heaven. The author is affirming what he does about the churches because he believes in divine intervention in those churches' situations.

This vision or revelation shows what must soon or suddenly take place. The phrase *en taxei* can in some cases mean suddenly speaking of how something will happen, but in view of the end of vs. 3 ("for the time is near") the author probably means soon here. The author anticipates that much of what he has seen is likely to be on a near historical horizon not one 2,000 years hence. The revelation, as noted, is mediated through an angel, which is typical of apocalyptic literature. This may provide the clue to the reference to the angels of the churches shortly after this introduction. Just as the Word is mediated to John through an angel so it is mediated to the churches through angels, for this is visionary material that requires special handling and care. The idea of angels being guardians of nations is familiar from Jewish literature, and so there may be the sense here of angels being on the scene and protecting these churches, including its worship services (see, e.g., 1 Cor. 11.10). What John conveys is meant to be taken as the word of God and also the testimony of Christ. The term *marturian* in this document, while not quite having its full later meaning of martyrological testimony, once studied in relationship to its semantic field shows that the term *martus* seems to imply death at Rev. 1.5, 3.14, and 17.6 (see the discussion in the next section). Notice the language used here – this testimony of Jesus was something signified to John through an angel. Thus we are meant to think of images being given to John, an indirect means of revelation. Clearly we are not to think of these images as snapshots of heaven since they draw on and modify OT images over and over again, with which our author was already familiar.

A CLOSER LOOK – FORENSIC LANGUAGE AND THE MEANING OF MARTYR

The root meaning of *martus* is one who bears witness, possibly in a legal setting, and so came to connote a guarantor of the truth about something. In Christian contexts it came in the second century to have the sense of one who bears witness to the truth of one's faith by laying down one's life. Though we have not yet arrived at the equation *martus* = martyr in Revelation, the usage is heading in that direction. There are five uses of *martus* in Revelation – 1.5 and 3.14 of Jesus, 2.13 of Antipas who also died for his faith, the reference to the two witnesses in 11.3, and the reference to the *martures 'Insou* (plural) who will be killed and lie in the streets (17.6–8). While it is not until the second-century document *The Martyrdom of Polycarp* that we find the term *martus* used in the sense of martyr, all the texts in Revelation imply martyrdom or death as the context. The term "faithful" along with the term "witness" means faithful unto death in Rev. 2.5, 10, 13. In both 1.5 and 3.14 the death of Jesus is involved in his attestation to God's word. The forensic use of the term in 2.13 and 11.3 refers to being a witness before a court, but the context suggests that the testifier goes on to die. The only place in Revelation where *martus* really does not carry overtones of death is at 15.5, where reference is to the OT institution of the tent of witness.[2]

There are important conclusions to be drawn. First, the use of legal language helps set the forensic rhetorical tone from the outset. It is going to be a document about faithful witnesses under pressure and prospect of death, and so a document about justice and vindication of those mistreated. Second, we are put on notice from the outset by the way that Jesus is described and then by the reference to Antipas that martyrdom is a live issue for John's audience and one with which they have already come to grips. This should not be trivialized by statements about "perceived crises" generating this document.[3] John's audience is being called to be faithful unto death, a prospect they did indeed face, not least because they could not participate in things like the emperor cult and would

---

[2] In all of this I am following some of the suggestions of A. A. Trites, "*Martus* and Martyrdom in the Apocalypse," *NovT* 15 (1973), pp. 72–80.

[3] See the critique of L. Thompson and A. Y. Collins in the Introduction.

not renounce their *superstitio*, something that Domitian had required even of some of the elite in his own circle in Rome.

❧

Vs. 3 tells us that prophecies are involved and that these words are given so that they may be kept. In short the function of these prophecies is hortatory. They are not given to satisfy idle curiosity about the future. They are imperatival, entailing a call to action. Unlike in some apocalyptic works, here the revelation is to be unsealed, not sealed up. It is to become known, not hidden for some remote future generation to discover. For John, since the eschatological time is at hand, the time for unsealing the revelation is now.

One of the most important tasks of a speaker in a rhetorically saturated environment was to establish credibility and authority with the audience at the outset. In his insightful doctoral thesis, W. G. Carey has shown at length that part of the way John establishes his authority is how he introduces this document and refers to it as a "revelation of Jesus Christ" and thereby coming from the highest authority. The speaker's character was also something that needed to be addressed as a concern at the outset of a discourse.[4] John is depicted at the beginning as (1) having had the great honor of having received a revelation from God in Christ that is about the future and especially the role Jesus plays in it, showing his intimate relationship with God, and (2) a person who could be "in the Spirit on the Lord's Day," which is to say he is a prophetic figure, in this case a seer. John is a person who can offer his audience divine insight that they would not otherwise have into their situation, and thus he becomes indispensable to them, an authority figure of the first magnitude, especially in a crisis.

Why did John choose to introduce his book in the fashion he does rather than simply to open with epistolary elements? R. Royalty suggests that John's rhetorical aims were involved.

But rather than presenting itself as a letter from John, the Apocalypse presents itself as the revelation . . . of Jesus Christ. This shift is a subtle rhetorical move designed to increase the authority of the visions in the text (the external proofs) by ascribing them to God and Christ while establishing the ethos or character of the narrator as trustworthy to deliver these visions to the audience (an internal, artistic proof).[5]

But what is the connection between the visions found in Rev. 4 up to the letters and what precedes them in Rev. 1–3? If, as Royalty suggests, the visions provide the external proofs supporting the arguments found in the letters, we have our

---

[4] See R. Royalty, *The Streets of Heaven: The Ideology of Wealth in the Apocalypse of John* (Macon, Ga.: Mercer University Press, 1998), pp. 132–35.
[5] Ibid., p. 134.

answer. In other words the visions enforce and reinforce the exhortations given to the churches particularly in Rev. 2–3. They provide the reasons why those exhortations should be obeyed: judgment and vindication are coming, and God's people must be awake, alert, prepared. Precisely because judgment will fall on the dominant culture, John is urging that his audience refuse to assimilate to the ungodly aspects of that culture, characterized as various forms of idolatry and immorality. Worshiping the true God and worshiping the Greco-Roman gods are mutually exclusive options in John's mind. John agrees that one of the primary tasks for Christians as they look forward to the return of Christ is worship. But of what sort, and who should be the object of that worship? John will indicate repeatedly that it ought to be God and Christ and that it ought not to be angels or human beings. John, by argument and letter and vision, is trying to convince his audience of what the world is really like and where their allegiances really ought to lie.

In a community that highly prized the word of God, there was a derived authority to be credited to anyone who could speak that word, especially in a fresh and new way. Furthermore it is the task of the rhetorically adept speaker to establish an attentive, receptive, and well-disposed audience, as Quintilian stresses (*Inst. Or.* 4.1.5). He does this by establishing his authority at the outset, making clear he has something important and indeed imperative for his audience to hear. But to establish ethos, emotions also come into play. John deals with the stress that exists in his audience by offering them conditional blessings at the end of his introductory remarks. The blessings are contingent on his audience heeding what he says following this introduction. In this way he instills both attentiveness and earnestness in his audience as his visions begin to unfold.

Apocalyptic rhetoric deals with ultimate and highly emotive issues such as good and evil, and justice and vindication. Consider, for instance, the quote from 4 Ezra 4.22–25 where the seer says,

I did not wish to inquire about the ways above, but about those things which we daily experience: why Israel has been given over to the gentiles as a reproach; why the people whom you loved has been given to godless tribes, and the Law of our fathers has been made of no effect and the written covenants no longer exist; and why we pass from the world like locusts, and our life is like a mist, and we are not worthy to obtain mercy. But what will he do for his name, by which we are called? It is about these things that I have asked.

Ezra had said just before this, "It would be better for us not to be here than to come here and live in ungodliness, and to suffer and not understand why" (4.12). Likewise in the case of John of Patmos, he is not really interested in writing about tours of heaven, unlike Dante, but rather about what will soon happen to remedy the injustices he and his audience experience. Heaven is brought into the picture to provide divine perspective on the earthly situation past, present, and future. John will help his audience understand why there is suffering and death within the Christian community. "Crisis rhetoric demonstrates the visionary's goodwill while affirming the audience's sense that its struggles are of cosmic significance. From a rhetorical perspective, apocalyptic discourse is especially effective for establishing authority."[6]

BRIDGING THE HORIZONS

Martin Marty, the great church historian, once said,

Notice that the Book of Revelation is at the end of the Bible. It barely made it into the scriptures. It's one of the two or three biblical books that calls itself a vision, a dream, yet it's a book that many people seem to take more literally than they do the non-dream books. Try interpreting your dreams and you'll see why people expound weird ideas based on this book.[7]

Marty has a point, but it is a mistake to treat John's revelation as if it were nothing more than a dream. His revelation is intended to be referential to things he believes to be true about human history and also the supernatural realm. This does not mean, however, that John would have been thrilled with the use of his work by sensationalist dispensationalist writers such as Hal Lindsey, John Walvoord, or Tim La Haye. John was writing for his own audiences in the first century A.D. not for late Western Christians in the twenty-first century. The text was a revelation to those Christians first. Any reading of these texts that suggests it could only have relevance for or make sense to Christians who lived many centuries after John does an injustice to this remarkable book. John is unveiling the secrets and unsealing the scrolls for his audience not sealing them back up for a much later audience to uncover.

The text's meaning must be understood in terms of the plausibility structure that existed between the original author and audience of this work. On the one hand, what the text meant back then is what it still means today, though of course with multivalent images it can have ever new applications and fresh significance. On the other hand, what the original author and audience could not possibly have understood the text to mean (e.g., the Beast is the European Common Market, or the anti-Christ is the Pope, etc.) cannot be the meaning of the text today either, if one believes meaning is not in the eye of the beholder but rather resides in the text, encoded by the original author.

It is true that an author can say more than he or she realizes, and this may well be the case with John. However, the trajectory of meaning must be grounded in what John did understand he was talking about and must be consistent with it. For example, John's message is about being prepared for suffering and death,

---

[6] W. G. Carey "Attention-Seeking Behavior: Rhetoric, Resistance, and Authority in the Book of Revelation" (Ph.D. diss., Vanderbilt University, Nashville, Tenn., 1996), p. 134.
[7] M. Marty, "M.E.M.O.: A Revelation," *The Christian Century* 114 (14 May 1997), p. 495.

even if one lives in the last generation of believers on the earth. His is not a rapture theology. He wishes to talk about the church enduring and in a sense about being protected from extinction through various sorts of tribulation (see, e.g., Rev. 12 and what happens to the woman). While John may or may not envision a millennium at the end of human history (and Rev. 20 suggests he does), he cannot possibly envision a church that is not required to suffer in this vale of tears, as the Lord did, until Christ returns.

The beatitudes at the close of this opening section of Revelation remind us that God's promises to his people are sometimes conditional on the people's obedience to God's demands. Blessing follows obedience. Hearing and heeding, comprehending and keeping the word leads to blessedness. This does not necessarily mean less suffering, but it means among other things that one gains the satisfaction of having done God's will and of having been faithful to the end. John is about to call the troops to a red alert. He promises that such vigilance will be worth it. Later in Revelation he will tell his audience what the blessing consists of, but here he simply announces its potential existence.

There are some seven beatitudes in Revelation, a number signifying completion or perfection – 1.3; 14.13; 16.15; 19.19; 20.6; 22.7, 22.14. The first and next to last are very much alike and seem to echo Luke 11.28 (see also John 12.47). Most of these beatitudes occur in the last third of the book. As the storm clouds grow darker and darker, so also the beatitudes begin to amass, until beatitude becomes reality in the closing vision in Rev. 22. About these beatitudes Bauckham observes,

Together they spell out the adequate response to John's prophecy (reading/hearing and keeping: 1.3; 22.7; faithfulness as far as death: 14.13; 22.14; readiness for the Lord's coming: 16.15) and the fulness of divine blessing that attends that response (rest from labours: 14.13; invitation to the Lamb's marriage supper: 19.9; participation in the first resurrection: 20.6; the tree of life and entry into the new Jerusalem: 22.14; but these are only *representative* of the complete blessing indicated by the number seven). The seven beatitudes comprise a kind of summary of Revelation's message.[8]

If this is true, then Revelation is primarily about two things – obedience unto death and preparation for the end with the reward being eschatological blessing. In other words the behavior of those who are already Christians is seen to affect their eternal status and standing. They are not eternally secure until they are securely in eternity, hence the form the exhortations of the seven churches take and the warnings about apostasy and the like. It is striking that the biblical book that maybe more than any other emphasizes God's sovereignty over human history also is emphatic about human responsibility and its connection with

---

[8] R. Bauckham, *The Climax of Prophecy* (Edinburgh: T + T Clark, 1993), p. 30.

final blessedness. Like the prophets of old, John dishes out one part moral instruction, one part promissory note, one part prediction.[9]

It was A. Einstein who once said, " 'the imagination is more important than intelligence,' meaning that there can be no meaningful use of intelligence unless there is imaginative perception."[10] Revelation is a book that must be grasped by the imagination not merely by intelligence. The idea is not just to inform us but to transform us by what we see and perceive through this work. "What is required is not that we read more but that we listen carefully; not study more but see believingly."[11] But Revelation is not a picture book, it is a book of words, and words that John does not want us to add to or subtract from. E. Peterson in his helpful study helps us to see one reason why:

Our capacity for language is the most distinctive thing about us as humans. Words are that by which we articulate who we are. Nothing about us is more significant than the way we use words. If words are used badly, our lives are debased. . . . The most distinctive feature of the Christian faith is its respect for the word: God's word first of all and secondarily our words of prayer, confession, and witness. The most-to-be-feared attacks on the Christian faith go for the jugular of the word: twisting the word, denying the word, doubting the word. It is impressive how frequently the Psalmists denounce and cry out for help against lying lips and flattering tongues. Far more than they feared murderers, adulterers, usurers, and Egyptians, they feared liars. God made himself known to them by word, and it was by words that they shaped their response to him. When words are ruined, we are damaged at the core of our being.[12]

Revelation's call to hear what is said is a call not merely to listen but to obey, for God's word is exacting in its demands and precision. The Scriptures, unlike some kinds of rhetoric, do not seek to please us but rather to persuade us to change. If we do not hear and heed them then they are mere words on a paper, and printer's ink can sometimes become embalming fluid when it comes to the living Word.[13] Revelation is not meant merely to enthrall us like a great work of fantasy, such as J. R. R. Tolkien's *Lord of the Rings*.

There is a fitness to Revelation being the last book in the canon, for in a sense it is the summing up of all that has come before, both in the Hebrew Scriptures and in the Christian tradition that John knew. That there are over 500 allusions to the OT in the 404 verses in this book makes evident that it should not be read in isolation from those earlier Scriptures. Peterson says, "no one has any business reading the last book who has not read the previous sixty-five. . . . Much mischief has been done by reading the Revelation in isolation from its canonical

---

9 See R. H. Mounce, *The Book of Revelation*, 2d ed. (Grand Rapids, Mich.: Eerdmans, 1998), pp. 43–44.

10 Quoted in R. E. Browne, *Ministry of the Word* (Philadelphia: Fortress, 1976), p. 115.

11 E. Peterson, *Reversed Thunder* (San Francisco: Harper and Row, 1988), p. 24.

12 Ibid., p. 14.

13 The phrase is E. Peterson's from *Reversed Thunder* (1998), p. 13.

context."[14] But the canonical reading of Revelation as an appropriate climax to the canon is a second-order reading, appropriate for and in the church, that must come after the historical reading of the work in its original context.

In particular, there was no NT canon for Revelation to be the climax of when John was writing. Nevertheless, there is a sense in which Revelation takes all that has come before and reimages it "in a compelling, persuading, evangelistic vision which has brought perseverance, stamina, joy and discipline to Christians for centuries, and continues to do so."[15]

REVELATION 1.4–1.20 – THE HEAVENLY SON OF MAN

NRSV Revelation 4 John to the seven churches that are in Asia: Grace to you and peace from him who is and who was and who is to come, and from the seven spirits who are before his throne,

5 and from Jesus Christ, the faithful witness, the firstborn of the dead, and the ruler of the kings of the earth. To him who loves us and freed us from our sins by his blood,

6 and made us to be a kingdom, priests serving his God and Father, to him be glory and dominion forever and ever. Amen.

7 Look! He is coming with the clouds; every eye will see him, even those who pierced him; and on his account all the tribes of the earth will wail. So it is to be. Amen.

8 "I am the Alpha and the Omega," says the Lord God, who is and who was and who is to come, the Almighty.

9 I, John, your brother who share with you in Jesus the persecution and the kingdom and the patient endurance, was on the island called Patmos because of the word of God and the testimony of Jesus.

10 I was in the spirit on the Lord's day, and I heard behind me a loud voice like a trumpet

11 saying, "Write in a book what you see and send it to the seven churches, to Ephesus, to Smyrna, to Pergamum, to Thyatira, to Sardis, to Philadelphia, and to Laodicea."

12 Then I turned to see whose voice it was that spoke to me, and on turning I saw seven golden lampstands,

13 and in the midst of the lampstands I saw one like the Son of Man, clothed with a long robe and with a golden sash across his chest.

14 His head and his hair were white as white wool, white as snow; his eyes were like a flame of fire,

---

[14] Ibid., p. 23.
[15] Ibid., p. 24.

15 his feet were like burnished bronze, refined as in a furnace, and his voice was like the sound of many waters.

16 In his right hand he held seven stars, and from his mouth came a sharp, two-edged sword, and his face was like the sun shining with full force.

17 When I saw him, I fell at his feet as though dead. But he placed his right hand on me, saying, "Do not be afraid; I am the first and the last,

18 and the living one. I was dead, and see, I am alive forever and ever; and I have the keys of Death and of Hades.

19 Now write what you have seen, what is, and what is to take place after this.

20 As for the mystery of the seven stars that you saw in my right hand, and the seven golden lampstands: the seven stars are the angels of the seven churches, and the seven lampstands are the seven churches."

*I*t was always crucial in a work seeking to persuade someone of something that there be an effective start that got the audience's attention and foreshadowed what was to come. Especially the tone of a rhetorical piece would be established at the outset (see Quintilian, *Inst. Or.* 6.1.5), and there would be some sort of preview of coming elements in the discourse. Rev. 1.5–6 suggest that Christology will indeed be a major theme.[16]

One of the major features by which ancients judged a discourse or speech to be rhetorically effective and persuasive was in regard to "invention." While John's Revelation is certainly one of the most creative pieces of NT literature, it is by no means very inventive, unless one counts the combining and reshaping of preexisting images and ideas as invention.[17] Narrative rhetoric, however, needs to be seen as a means to an end. In forensic rhetoric the *narratio* needed to be told in a fashion favorable to one's client – in this case to the churches facing persecution and, if they commit apostasy, possibly eternal as well as temporal judgment. Therefore, John must tell the story in a way that does not lead his audience to despair. He must encourage them at the same time he is exhorting them. They must be told about the favorable judgments their predecessor martyrs had received for being faithful to the end. Make no mistake: John sees his audience as on trial and under fire. He must prepare them for the worst, while reassuring them that, in the end, it will be for the best. He must also defend their honor, and that of the Christian cause in general, by presenting them as being in the good hands of Christ and protected from the Evil One. They are depicted as being on the right and winning side in the battle against evil.

Narratives persuade by catching the hearers up into the drama and making them feel a part of what is happening. The reassurance comes from the beginning

---

16 C. Keener, *Revelation: The NIV Application Bible Commentary* (Grand Rapids, Mich.: Zondervan, 2002), p. 69.

17 This fact was pointed out to me by D. de Silva.

of the book, for the judge who is sitting on the dazzling throne is none other than the divine Christ whom they love and serve, and by whom they will finally be vindicated.

According to **vs. 4** John is writing to seven churches in Asia, by which is meant churches in western Asia Minor not in all the province of Asia.[18] He is writing to the area that was once the ancient kingdom of Pergamum, which Rome eventually conquered. John then seems to be using provincial designations. John extends the Pauline greeting of grace and peace, but his audience may have heard more than that in this phrase. Domitian, according to Suetonius, would regularly preface his cruel sentences and punishments on the unfortunate with the phrase, "It has pleased the Lord our God in his grace . . . ," a signal that something horrible was about to come to pass.[19] John is suggesting that his audience lives by a very different sort and source of mercy and grace.

In vs. 4 we find both bad grammar and good theology. Probably Exod. 3.14–15 lies in the background here, but notice that God or Christ is called the one who is to come. The eschatological coming is thus stressed. God awaits the believer in the future. He is behind, among, and ahead of the church. The name Jesus Christ appears only here in this book; elsewhere the personal name Jesus is used. The author, as we noted in the Introduction, has a high Christology, predicating divine character and attributes of Jesus. One of the major themes of John's prophecy will be "the One who is to Come" and what that will entail for believers.

Who then are the seven spirits that stand before the throne of God? Probably this is not an allusion to the gifts of the Messiah in Isa. 11.2, for they are sixfold. According to Rev. 5.6 the seven spirits are something Jesus sent throughout the earth and are equated with the Lamb's seven eyes. At. 4.5 they are equated with the blazing lamps. At 3.1 they are associated with the seven stars, which we have already been told are the angels of the seven churches. It seems unlikely then that John is referring to a sevenfold division of the Holy Spirit. Rather the reference is to the angels who are the eyes of the great King, keeping watch over the church for the Lamb (cf. Heb. 1.14; Jub. 1.25, 2.2; 1 En. 61.12). Early Jewish texts clearly refer to seven archangels before the throne of God (Tob. 12.15; 1 En. 20.1–8; 4 Qserek). Lest this image suggest that Christ is distant, we are reminded in this first chapter of Revelation that Christ stands among the lampstands, which represent the seven congregations. A major point of this entire book is that

---

[18] It is interesting that John's seven cities are the same as the seven cities where the Asiarchs' council met, except John lists the centrally located Thyatira, which replaces Cyzicus. See C. Keener, *Revelation* (2002), p. 67. Christianity had basically imbedded itself in important cities in the region.

[19] See A. Boesak, *Comfort and Protest: The Apocalypse from a South African Perspective* (Philadelphia: Westminster, 1986), p. 47.

heaven and earth are very close indeed; in fact they are juxtaposed in such a way that heaven is already active in and for earth and will descend to it at the end in the form of the New Jerusalem.

At **vs. 5** Jesus is called the faithful witness, the firstborn from the dead (cf. Col. 1.18), and the ruler of the kings of the earth. These three images may echo Ps. 89.24–40.[20] The close association of his faithful witness and his resurrection implies that the witness entailed his death. All three of these traits are presented as models for John's audience – they should be faithful unto death, they will receive a good resurrection like Christ's, and they will rule with him over the earth (see Rev. 20). Put another way, John is reassuring his audience that the major factor that they might fear at this juncture, namely a shameful death at the hands of their own rulers, will be overcome, as it was for Christ. Neither death nor rulers are beyond the control of Jesus. He is already ruling over them, and so Christians should not fear such authorities. The wording in **vs. 5b** is significant. Christ is the one who loves (continual present tense) and loosed us (past tense) from our sins by his blood, and made us (past tense) into a kingdom.[21] This sentence has something of a liturgical flavor (cf. Gal. 2.20). Christ is said to save believers *from* sin, but *for* the task of being a saved zone on earth, and priests to the world and to God's people.[22] There is nothing here about a clerical class of Christians called to be priests. Rather the whole kingdom of believers are to be priests.

There is a large stress on Jesus as the Lamb in this work. It can be said to be the central Christological image in the book, and it reminds us that Christ's atoning death stands at the heart of this book as God's answer to the problem of sin, seen here as bondage or slavery. This is the only place in the NT where the phrase "freed us from our sin" occurs. But it is not just what he freed us from, but what he made us to be – a kingdom and priests to God. This is likely an allusion to Exod. 19.6, perhaps in the Greek versions other than the LXX. Whether referring to a kingdom of priests or kings and priests, it alludes to going from the status of a slave to the upper echelon of society, a message of hope for Christians being oppressed in their social situation. All believers are said to be kings and priests (cf. 1 Pet. 2.5). Contemplating the great work of Christ leads John to offer a doxology in vs. 6b. It is perhaps no accident that John mentions this everlasting kingdom at the very outset. In A.D. 90, shortly before this work was written, the Roman Empire received a new name – *Imperium Aeternum*, the eternal empire – and the Emperor was meant to be the eternal king, as the court poet Statius suggested to Domitian.[23] But John's theology is that Jesus

---

[20] See D. E. Aune, *Revelation 1–5*, 3 vols. (Dallas: Word, 1997; Nashville, Tenn.: Nelson, 1998), pp. 37–38.

[21] See M. Reddish, *Revelation* (Macon, Ga.: Smyth and Helwys, 2001), p. 35.

[22] C. Keener, *Revelation* (2002), p. 71.

[23] See A. Boesak, *Comfort and Protest* (1987), p. 43.

alone is King of Kings,[24] and his followers are not slaves but rather kings and priests.

Vs. 7 is perhaps a hymn fragment referring to the second coming, but it is certainly an allusion to Dan. 7.13. Everyone will see the pierced one coming (see Zech 12.10b), a way of putting things that stresses Christ's previous historical existence. When he is seen, the earth's tribes will mourn (Zech. 12.12).[25] Zech. 12.10–12 is echoed here, but as always the author feels free to mix his metaphors and mold the scriptural language to suit his purposes.[26] One could say he is using scriptural language homiletically to describe Jesus. He is not trying to stress Scripture fulfillment.

There is some question as to whether this mourning of the nations is contrition or grief over being lost now that the judge descends. It is probably the latter. The nations will regret what they did to Christ and his people in the end. At **vs. 8** we hear not only God's name predicated of the Lordly Christ, but he is called Alpha and Omega, letters that begin and end the Greek alphabet. Christ is the beginning and end of history, and by implication, he is in control of everything in between. It is plausible that this usage reflects Isa. 44.6, where God is called the first and the last.

A CLOSER LOOK – GOD AND CHRIST AS THE ALPHA AND OMEGA

The prophetic outlook of Revelation is exclusively monotheistic, but it is a Christologically redefined monotheism that John touts. If we compare Rev. 1.8, 1.17, 21.6, and 22.13, we discover that God and Christ are both associated with the beginning and the end of something, or the first and the last. R. Bauckham notes that "the one designation of God which appears in Revelation as a self-designation by God also appears as a self-designation by Christ."[27] God was before all things and brought them into being as the Creator, and God will bring everything to its proper eschatological conclusion. In addition God is the originator and the goal of human history. "He has the first word, in creation,

---

[24] See p. 244.
[25] L. Thompson, "Lamentation for Christ as a Hero: Revelation 1.7," *JBL* 119 (2000), pp. 700–1, suggests we see the text in light of the way deceased heroes were honored by mourning. He urges, "Jesus Christ has everything to do with death, the grave, and Hades, and it is his continued affiliation with death and funerary ritual that makes the Christology in John distinctive. . . . John emphasizes Christ's appearance as a slain victim, and for that he is honored and remembered: 'Worthy are you . . . for you were slaughtered.' As in Rev. 1.7, the appearance of the heavenly Christ is accompanied by reminders of death and mortality." This suggestion makes good sense because elsewhere John does seek to make his images words on target, drawing on familiar ideas and concepts from the Greco-Roman world in his narrative, in this case ideas about lamentations for a deceased hero.
[26] See D. E. Aune, *Revelation 1–5* (1997), pp. 55–56.
[27] R. Bauckham, *The Theology of the Book of Revelation* (Cambridge: Cambridge University Press, 1993), p. 19.

and the last word, in new creation. Therefore, within John's literary structure, he speaks twice, declaring himself Alpha and Omega first, before the outset of John's vision (1.8), and last, in declaring the eschatological accomplishment of his purpose for his whole creation: 'it is done' (21.6)."[28] The claim is being made that Christ shares in the eternal being of God, but not only so. Notice that in Isa. 44.6 it is Yahweh declaring, "I am the first and last, and besides me there is no god," making it all the more remarkable that Jesus uses this phrase to identify himself. He shares in the work of both creation and new creation that God brought about precisely because he shares in the divine being.[29] It is not a surprise then that Christ is the proper object of worship in Revelation.

We also learn something of how rhetorically effective and carefully crafted Revelation is by examining the occurrences of this title. Bauckham notes the chiastic pattern that frames the book, making clear to the audience the inclusion of Christ in the godhead.

A	B	B′	A′
1.8	1.17	21.6	22.13
End of prologue	Beginning of vision	End of vision	Beginning of epilogue
God	Christ	God	Christ
Alpha and Omega		Alpha and Omega	Alpha and Omega
	First and last		First and last
		Beginning and end	Beginning and end
Connection with	Connection with	Connection with	Connection with
Parousia (1.7)	New life (1.18)	New life (21.5–6)	Parousia (22.12)[30]

God is also called the *pantocrator* here – the almighty one. This is a favorite term in Revelation (cf. 1.8; 4.8; 11.17; 15.3; 16.7; 19.6; 21.22) and again is grounded in the divine name (cf. 2 Sam. 5.10; Jer. 5.14; Hos. 12.5; Amos 3.13; 4.13), but it is only found once elsewhere in the NT and there as part of an OT quote. The stress in this book is not on divine sovereignty in the abstract but on the exercise of that sovereignty on behalf of the church. The Lord is in control, the churches are being reassured, despite appearances to the contrary.

In **vs. 9** John calls himself a fellow sharer in three characteristics of the faith – suffering, kingdom, and endurance. The word *thlipsis* can also be translated tribulation rather than suffering. Either way, John believes he is already undergoing the eschatological tribulation just as his audience is. Such is the

---

[28] Ibid., p. 27.
[29] Ibid., p. 58. Christ is not a second god but one who participates in the eternal being of the one and only God of Israel.
[30] Ibid., p. 57.

paradox of Christian existence under pressure and persecution. John, of course, did not coin the phrase, "the blood of the martyrs is seed for the church" (Tertullian did), but he seems to believe that God's power is made perfect or evident in weakness. It was also Tertullian (*Baptism* 20) who tells us that Jesus said, "No one can obtain the kingdom of heaven without first passing through testing." John would have agreed.

John, we are told, was put on Patmos due to his witness to the Word. Patmos was one of the Sporades islands thirty-seven miles southwest of Miletus and some fifty miles from Ephesus. In short, by ancient standards it was well off-shore. The chains of islands most used in this region by the Romans for exile were indeed the Sporades and the Cyclades. Philostratus tells us that these small islands off the coast of Asia were full of exiles during the time of Domitian (*V.A.* 8.5). The trip could take some fourteen hours to reach the mainland. Patmos was not a deserted island for we have inscriptions dating to at least the second century B.C. (see SIG 1068.2) that speak of a torchbearer, games, and a gymnasium. This island had belonged to Miletus and had a fortress on it. It was precisely the sort of place the Romans would use to exile people using a minimum of troops to garrison the island.

The use of the aorist verb "was" here possibly indicates John was no longer on the island when he wrote this document. Could he have returned to the mainland to compile the document after the reign of Domitian ended? This is not impossible, for those banished by one emperor might get amnesty after his demise. This would answer the question how the document finally got to the churches from a remote island. Eusebius in fact tells us John returned to Ephesus (*Hist. Eccl.* 3.20.8–9). Furthermore we know that Nerva, who succeeded Domitian, recalled Domitian's exiles in A.D. 96 (see Pliny, *Epistles* 1.5.10; 9.13.5). The first real commentator on Revelation, Victorinus of Pettau (d. approx. A.D. 304), says that John was condemned to the mines on Patmos by Domitian and that he published the apocalypse he saw there after being released after Domitian's death (*Comm. In Apoc.* 10.3). This suggestion is probably unlikely for three reasons: (1) we do not know of any evidence of mines on Patmos; (2) being sentenced to an island was different from the punishment of being sent to the mines, and these punishments were used for differing kinds of offenses. But for John "Patmos, the infamous island, place of banishment, place of punishment, place of lonely wanderings, became a place of learning, of seeing, of understanding."[31] Probably John was seen as a ringleader of a particular group

---

[31] A. Boesak, *Comfort and Protest* (1987), p. 41. E. H. Peterson, *Reversed Thunder* (1988), p. 89, reminds us of the social and psychological effect of banishment on someone like John. "The worst punishment possible in ancient Israel was banishment. To be separated from family and country, from community worship and family faith – that was the cruelest decree. The severest judgment that the nation experienced was exile to Babylonia. A person created for personal relationships of love cannot live adequately without them. Exile dehumanizes. It sentences us to death by bread alone." John was exiled, however, by Babylon rather than to Babylonia.

of proselytizing Christians. C. Keener aptly sums up the evidence about John's probable situation:

> He may have been treated less harshly than others on account of his age or because the governor rather than the emperor sentenced him, but in any case banishment involved loss of honor. The severest form of banishment – probably not what John experienced – involved loss of one's civil rights, including the forfeiture of nearly all one's property to the state. Unless the government lifted the ban, those banished to an island remained there until they died. Those of higher social status could work on the island and earn some money; those of lower status were scourged . . . chained, given little food or clothing, left to sleep on the bare ground, and sentenced to hard labor.[32]

In other words, John probably experienced relegatio, in which case it was not the Emperor directly who punished him. This form of punishment was a common one for those found guilty of promulgating a superstition.[33] Under *relegatio* one could return home after a period of time.

Vs. 10 suggests that the revelation that follows came to John in a state of ecstasy.[34] This is what the Greek phrase here and in 4.2 suggests, as does 17.3 and 21.10. He was "in the Spirit" on the Lord's day. This use of the Spirit language is more like the references to the Spirit falling on prophetic figures (see Ezek. 3.12, 14) than like the NT discussions about being filled with the Spirit.[35] Probably we have the first clear reference to Sunday as the Christian day of worship, with "Lord's day" becoming something of a technical term (cf. *Did.* 14.1; *Ignatius Mag.* 9.1). We have confirmation of worship on Sunday in this vicinity from the early second century when Pliny writes to Trajan about Christians meeting in early morning on the first day of the week to sing and worship (see *Epistle* 10.96.8 ff.). This practice must be seen in the context of Emperor worship, which included a special day set aside in Asia once a month called "emperor's day" (Sebaste Augustus Day). Just as certain rulers claimed particular days as their own, so too did the Lord Christ.[36]

---

[32] C. Keener, *Revelation* (2002), p. 82.

[33] As Craig Koester has helpfully pointed out to me. I am grateful for his reading of the manuscript while it was being completed.

[34] M. R. Mulholland, *Revelation: Holy Living in an Unholy World* (Grand Rapids, Mich.: Francis Asbury Press, 1990), p. 18, makes a very good point when he says that language is sequential whereas a vision may be more holistic. "In other words one must relate a visionary experience a piece at a time, even though the experience may have been a single, unified, holistic encounter with reality." The language has to be used to describe a vision, for it could be described in many ways and at great length and still not exhaust what was seen.

[35] This is one of the mistakes made by R. L. Jeske, "Spirit and Community in the Apocalypse," *NTS* 31 (1985), pp. 452–66, who seeks to interpret this text on the basis of his understanding of the communal presence of the Spirit spoken of in Paul's letters. But John is not in community; he is isolated from his churches on the island of Patmos.

[36] See C. Keener, *Revelation* (2002), p. 83.

This revelation came to John rather like the sudden beginning of a loud rock concert. He heard coming from behind him a loud noise like a trumpet blast. Sometimes John also compares the voices he hears to the sound of roaring waters or of thunder. In addition the noun phrase "a loud sound" occurs some twenty times. This book speaks frequently of noisy revelations and startling sounds.[37] In Rev. 1 there was no warning, and John was not looking for this. He was commanded to write down this vision on a scroll or in a book and to send it. In other words it is meant to be a written revelation from the outset, though it is not clear whether John wrote while he was seeing the vision or, perhaps more likely, saw it, reflected on it, and finally wrote. If *Biblion* here actually means book, Revelation was possibly one of the first Christian documents to be produced in book form.

John turns and sees seven gold lampstands or candlesticks, suggesting a temple setting.[38] Already in Jewish circles there was the familiar seven-armed menorah, but here the seven are separated, perhaps suggesting a full representation of God's people in each church. There is a rather clear message that the church made up of Jew and Gentile united in Christ is the fulfillment or successor to Israel as the people of God. The menorah was widely recognized in the Mediterranean world as the symbol of Judaism (CIJ 1.8 #4; 1.16 #14). In **vs. 13** Jesus is described as one "like a son of man," using the exact language of Dan. 7.13. We find one other reference to the son of man in Rev. 14.14, again in its Danielic sense, betraying no indebtedness to the Gospel tradition. It is, of course, the language of analogy. Jesus is being identified with this human and yet more-than-human figure, who is seen in Daniel as a representative of God's people to God, and of God to God's people. While in Daniel the son of man is distinguished from the Ancient of Days, here the son of man is described as if he were the Ancient of Days.

The image of Jesus seems to combine some divine features with an attempt to depict him as the high priest in heaven wearing a full-length robe and the priestly breastplate. The snow-white head of hair comes from Dan. 7.9–10 and particularly associates Jesus with the God of the ages, the so-called Ancient of Days, while the reference to fiery eyes likely echoes Dan. 10.6, as does the reference to Christ's face shining like the sun at full strength. But there is perhaps more going on here with the Son of Man tradition than meets the eye. John Collins has shown that in the early Jewish literature of relevance the Son of Man is sometimes seen as a preexistent heavenly figure (whether an angel or something else), sometimes as a messianic figure, but never as just a corporate symbol of Israel. All of these texts, whether in the parables of Enoch or in 4 Ezra, are indebted to (but develop ideas further than in) Dan. 7 rather than to Ezekiel. It is not surprising to see a heavenly or even a divine Son of Man figure

---

[37] See D. E. Aune, *Revelation* 1–5 (1997), p. 85.
[38] Ibid., p. 90.

in Revelation.[39] For our purposes what is crucial is that the heavenly figure in question is identified with Jesus in Revelation, suggesting that he is more than a mere human being, even an exalted one who might have experienced apotheosis.

When you see God it is quite natural to fall as though dead, as John did (cf. Ezek. 1.28; Dan. 8.17, 10.9–11; Rev.19.10, 22.8). The sight is completely overwhelming. But John is told, "Stop being afraid." The bronze feet refined in the furnace likely are meant to indicate his stability or unmoveableness. He is no god with feet of clay. His voice sounded like the rushing of many waters. The two-edged sword that issues from his mouth may in fact be an allusion to the Roman short sword, which looked something like a tongue. His word is powerful and sharp and is an instrument of judgment, as a sword is. Yet the Lord who judges his own people also holds the church's guardian angels in the palm of his hand. **Vs. 17** makes clear that this cannot be taken literally for the hand that holds the stars also comforts John. Jesus is first and last and the living one who died and yet lives forever. That he is said to have the keys of Death and Hades means he now has power over death and the grave. Hades here is probably not a reference to hell but to the OT concept of the land of the dead – Sheol. This description may owe something to the Asia Minor myths about Hecate, who was said to be the key bearer to the gates of Hades. It may also owe something to typical descriptions of Hecate: "Beginning and end are you and you alone rule all. For all things are from you, and in you do all things, Eternal One, come to their end" (PGM IV .2836–37).[40] According to one Greek myth, Heracles had the power to bring up a few people from the dead (Diodorus Siculus 4.25.4; 4.26.1), and according to Jewish tradition only God could bring someone back up from Hades (Wisd. of Sol. 16.13), but here Christ as the divine Son of Man is given plenipotentiary power over all the dead. In one Egyptian papyrus, Anoubis is said to hold the keys to Hades (SIG 1717).

Vs. 19 is often taken as the hermeneutical key to interpreting the book. Rev. 1 is about what John had seen, Rev. 2–3 are about "what now is," and the remainder of the book is about what will be. Though Rev. 1–3 should be taken together as dealing mainly with "what is now," Rev. 11 makes evident that the whole book involves the past, present, and future. Thus vs. 19 should probably not be overly pressed as a way to divide up and understand Revelation. Reddish suggests it is simply a reference to the totality of the contents of John's vision.[41] All of the book ranges from the present to the end of the world, as Rev. 1.7 has already suggested. But we must keep in view that John is unveiling a mystery not something clear or obvious or straightforward. He is peeling back the veil of history to show the

---

[39] John Collins, "The Son of Man in First Century Judaism," *NTS* 38 (1992), pp. 448–66, should be compared to T. B. Slater, "One Like a Son of Man in First-Century CE Judaism," *NTS* 41 (1995), pp. 183–98, who also shows how prevalent it was to use this imagery to refer to a heavenly figure.

[40] See the discussion by D. E. Aune, *Revelation 1–5* (1997), p. 104.

[41] M. G. Reddish, *Revelation* (2001), p. 42.

supernatural forces at work behind the now and the not yet. The Pauline use of the term *musterion* to refer to something only God knows unless he unveils it to others seems close to John's conception of the content of his visions. Herein then lies an open secret, an unsealed one, which John lays before the eyes and ears of his audience. "John does not adopt a pseudonym probably because he is not interested either in communicating esoteric knowledge or in predicting schedules for the coming of the end of time. Instead he seeks to provide prophetic interpretation and eschatological exhortation for the Christian communities in Asia Minor to whom he writes."[42]

Upon analysis of the rhetoric of this section of Revelation, it becomes clear that it is the rhetoric of display, where the more hyperbolic and fantastic the image, the better. John cannot find words big enough to describe the awesome reality he saw, and so he is reduced to saying "it was like" over and over again. The visual images are intended to be stunning, with the audience reacting similarly to the way John reacted. If this work was performed, meaning read aloud in dramatic and rhetorical fashion, one can only imagine the impact when first heard – vivid descriptions followed by loud sayings from heaven. There is not a syllogistic logic to Revelation, but there is a narrative logic, and later in this study I will talk about the story that John seeks to tell. The audience is meant to locate themselves in the entire story and not merely in the parts addressing the churches. One of the major techniques of the rhetoric of display is the "making terrible" of the opponents by the use of vivid and dramatic language, the negative counterpart of the "making appealing" of the heroes of the story. This technique, called amplification, involves the substitution of stronger words for weaker ones (*Inst. Or.* 8.4.1–8).

John's heroes and paradigms are Christ, the martyrs, and the prophetic figures. The first two share in common suffering and death, and the message to the audience is that they must be prepared to go and do likewise. John does not offer up the false hope of exemption from suffering and death. Rather he suggests that if violent death happened to Jesus it may well happen to his followers. J. Christian Beker once said, "Cheap hope will not be able to speak a redemptive word either to the profound and new questions about the meaning of suffering today or to the projects of hope which our culture produces."[43] John's message, clothed in visual rhetoric, is the same as that of Jesus in the Gospel of John, "Be of good cheer, in this world you have trouble. But I have overcome the world." Though death may come, God in Christ's yes to life is louder than death's no. Quintilian reminds us that the form of amplification that relies on comparison seeks to rise from the lesser to the greater (*Inst. Or.* 8.4.9). John seeks to have his audience compare their behavior to that of Christ or someone like Antipas.

---

[42] E. Fiorenza, *Revelation* (1991), p. 47.
[43] J. Christian Beker, *Suffering and Hope: The Biblical Vision and the Human Predicament* (Grand Rapids, Mich.: Eerdmans, 1994), p. 30.

This is a shaming device to get them to pursue a higher standard of Christian living.

BRIDGING THE HORIZONS

Throughout the history of the church there have been various approaches to the book of Revelation, each relating to what has just been said about Rev. 1.19–20. The first, called the preterist approach, has had both ancient and modern exponents. Perhaps the most notable modern exponent was G. B. Caird in his influential commentary. This approach has sometimes been called the *zeitgeistliche* approach, which makes clear that the book is seen as being about the time contemporary with the author. Most scholars who see this book as referential adopt some form of this view. The second, known as the *endgeschichtliche* approach, suggests that at least Rev. 4–20 is speaking about final history, what will happen in the end, and thus not about what was already happening in John's day. The third, called the *kirkengeschichtliche* approach, argues that what is depicted is the history of the church through the ages. From this approach is derived a sort of Christian philosophy of history (see, e.g., Augustine's *The City of God*).

One problem with all these approaches to the text is that none adequately comes to grips with the nature of apocalyptic prophecy. They all tend to assume that a purely horizontal time line determines a proper approach to Revelation, and so all one needs to do is to determine where one is on the time line of recorded events. Yet most apocalyptic literature takes the perspective that these happenings occur not by historical causation but by divine intervention. In short no view that operates with a time line excluding God's periodic intervention now and at the end of history will be a satisfactory approach. This book is about the interface of time and eternity and more crucially about how time is controlled by the eternal God. The unsealing of the scrolls by the heavenly Christ is what precipitates the earthly events. God's intervention, not calculation of signs and events, determines the action. Revelation, unlike various other apocalyptic works, does not engage in the periodization of history to reckon the time until the end.

History is not to be seen as a self-contained homogeneous process where the normal laws of cause and effect apply. As Fiorenza points out, for John the most important events in human history have *already* transpired – the death and resurrection of the Lamb. All else after that has to be seen as the eschatological denouement.[44] The end has already broken into time and space through the Christ event. Here is a chronicling not of history as we know it, but rather of God's eschatological judgment on history. Since Christ has died and risen, there are no theologically significant events that need to happen before the end events

---

[44] See her *Revelation* (1991), pp. 15–19.

of the eschatological age. Thus the author can speak of the time as short or near. God could bring down the curtain on history at any moment. John interprets the present in light of both the realities above and the realities yet to come, which in some cases will come down from above. Christ already reigns in heaven and the victory song is already sung there, but Satan is currently loosed upon the earth and victory there has not yet been fully realized.

The focus in Revelation is on eschatology, not on salvation history. History receives its meaning and interpretation from the future, in particular from the future intervention of God in Christ. The focus on coming judgment shows that our author is not interested in esoteric discussions about the meaning of history; rather his focus is on the meaning of and divine response to suffering, in particular the suffering of God's people. The three sets of seven judgments all climax in judgment, and indeed the climax of the book in Rev. 17–20 is about final judgment and final salvation. The comfort for the suffering is not in the events leading up to the end, even when they go as God plans. Rather it is in the very final events when death and evil are eliminated and tears are wiped away as the vale of tears is transformed by the unveiled New Jerusalem. God's people are already a kingdom in this world, a locus where God's saving will is revealed and done, but they must still pray thy kingdom come, which refers to the point where Christ makes the kingdoms of this world his own. In short this book is about what is behind and at the end of history, but it does not seek to present a timetable about history. We will have occasion to say more about interpretive approaches when we discuss Rev. 20 and the millenium later in the text.

Because we live in an age where there are more and more visual learners, the book of Revelation becomes increasingly appealing to readers of the Bible. It is visual in content and triggers visual images more than any other book in the NT. It is not surprising that this work has always fired the imaginations of artists, Christian and otherwise. Already in the fifth century A.D., we have churches in Italy with mosaic images of the exalted Christ taken directly from the pages of Revelation on the churches' apses. Often they are images of worship in Revelation that are reproduced in stained glass (such as at Chartres) or in other media. "Moreover the Apocalypse's visions of heaven were reflected in the general impression conveyed by medieval churches and cathedrals. With their windows, paintings, sculptures, columns, and their soaring arches, spires and towers, they symbolized the new Jerusalem and provided a glimpse of the glory of eternity. A pledge of the heavenly city they rose above the meanness of the world around them."[45]

But it was not just in ancient Christianity that the appeal of the book has been strong to the aesthetically minded. Throughout Christian history the image of

---

[45] A. W. Wainwright, *Mysterious Apocalypse: Interpreting the Book of Revelation* (Nashville, Tenn.: Abingdon, 1993), p. 190.

the four horsemen of the apocalypse has inspired artists ranging from A. Dürer to W. Blake. There is the famous painting by Holman Hunt, a late nineteenth-century hanging in so many modern churches. Entitled *The Light of the World*, it depicts Christ standing at a door, which has no handle on its outside, and knocking. But there is yet more. Images and ideas from Revelation have inspired modern rap artists coming out of marginalized situations and identifying with the gestalt and cries for justice in this work. A paper given by A. Barsam and M. Bell of Oxford at the 2000 national meeting of the SBL was entitled "Millennial Rejections of Modernity: Rap and the Year 2000." While there is more going on in Revelation than meets the eye, its visual content nonetheless continues to provide material for artists of all kinds.

There is in modern worship some move toward making worship less of an entirely aural experience and more visual through video screens that project film clips, music videos, song and hymn lyrics, and the like. Oddly enough, this move toward the visual is happening largely in low church Protestant circles, not in high church settings where there have always been stained glass windows, for example. Perhaps popular culture has caused this sea change of attitude in low church conservative cultures, which were always wary of images in the past. It certainly did not come from the original Protestant reformers, who were very wary of the book of Revelation and its complex and confusing images.

One does need to be wary of using visual material in worship because if it is powerful it can so dominate the minds of the congregation that they fail to pay attention to the sermon or other aspects of the worship. There is, furthermore, a grave danger that indiscriminate use of visual material will only further the trend toward seeing worship as entertainment or a performance to be received rather than as a congregational event to be shared. Perhaps too it is time for the church to rediscover or further its role as a patron of the arts so that the images used come out of the theology and milieu of the church, even as they seek to speak to the casual observer.[46] The recovery of the arts in local churches can only enhance the degree of ministry that is effectively done, especially for those who learn primarily by seeing. I will speak about the use of the Apocalypse in music and drama at a later point in this study (pp. 123–26).

Rev. 1.10 raises the age-old debate about the relationship between the Jewish sabbath and the Lord's day. It seems that the earliest Jewish Christians continued to go to the synagogue, but they also held their own meetings in homes as well. For them it did not seem to be an either/or proposition. We do not find in the NT any arguments that Sunday should be seen as the Christians' sabbath. In fact, by the time we get to Ignatius (see *Magnes.* 9.1), a clear contrast is set between the Jewish sabbath and the Lord's day. The earliest canonical evidence

---

[46] F. Bond has provided us with an excellent tool, entitled *The Arts in Your Church: A Practical Guide* (Carlisle, Pa.: Piquant, 2001).

that something distinctively Christian was going on, and on Sunday, the first day of the week, is in 1 Cor. 16.1–2, which literally speaks of "the first of the sabbath," meaning the first day of the week. On that day Paul enjoins his converts to set aside funds for the collection. In light of his other comments in 2 Cor. 8–9, one may assume that Paul means that this money should be set aside for the day when the congregation gathers to meet, when it could be collected. Rev. 1.10 provides further evidence that there was a special day of worship for Christians, now called the Lord's day, because Jesus rose from the dead on Sunday morning. It is no accident that John says he is in the Spirit on that day, a day for worship and inspiration, and he was in a doxological mode when he received his visions.

Texts like Rom. 14.5–6 make evident that Paul recognized that some worshiped on a particular day, while others saw every day as the Lord's day and so appropriate for worship. His word is appropriate for today as well: "Let each be persuaded in their own mind." Worship is mandated, but a particular day is not, in the NT. Heb. 4.9 suggests that, in a sense, we can enjoy Jesus' sabbatical rest continually, on any and every day. As Keener says, "The connections between the 'Lord's Day' and the Sabbath on the one hand and between the Sabbath and church services on the other are postbiblical, and we should be charitable for differences of practice on this point."[47]

REVELATION 2–3 – POSTCARDS FROM THE EDGE

NRSV Revelation 2.1 "To the angel of the church in Ephesus write: These are the words of him who holds the seven stars in his right hand, who walks among the seven golden lampstands:

2 "I know your works, your toil and your patient endurance. I know that you cannot tolerate evildoers; you have tested those who claim to be apostles but are not, and have found them to be false.

3 I also know that you are enduring patiently and bearing up for the sake of my name, and that you have not grown weary.

4 But I have this against you, that you have abandoned the love you had at first.

5 Remember then from what you have fallen; repent, and do the works you did at first. If not, I will come to you and remove your lampstand from its place, unless you repent.

6 Yet this is to your credit: you hate the works of the Nicolaitans, which I also hate.

7 Let anyone who has an ear listen to what the Spirit is saying to the churches. To everyone who conquers, I will give permission to eat from the tree of life that is in the paradise of God.

8 "And to the angel of the church in Smyrna write: These are the words of the first and the last, who was dead and came to life:

47 C. Keener, *Revelation* (2002), p. 87.

9 "I know your affliction and your poverty, even though you are rich. I know the slander on the part of those who say that they are Jews and are not, but are a synagogue of Satan.

10 Do not fear what you are about to suffer. Beware, the devil is about to throw some of you into prison so that you may be tested, and for ten days you will have affliction. Be faithful until death, and I will give you the crown of life.

11 Let anyone who has an ear listen to what the Spirit is saying to the churches. Whoever conquers will not be harmed by the second death.

12 "And to the angel of the church in Pergamum write: These are the words of him who has the sharp two-edged sword:

13 "I know where you are living, where Satan's throne is. Yet you are holding fast to my name, and you did not deny your faith in me even in the days of Antipas my witness, my faithful one, who was killed among you, where Satan lives.

14 But I have a few things against you: you have some there who hold to the teaching of Balaam, who taught Balak to put a stumbling block before the people of Israel, so that they would eat food sacrificed to idols and practice fornication.

15 So you also have some who hold to the teaching of the Nicolaitans.

16 Repent then. If not, I will come to you soon and make war against them with the sword of my mouth.

17 Let anyone who has an ear listen to what the Spirit is saying to the churches. To everyone who conquers I will give some of the hidden manna, and I will give a white stone, and on the white stone is written a new name that no one knows except the one who receives it.

18 "And to the angel of the church in Thyatira write: These are the words of the Son of God, who has eyes like a flame of fire, and whose feet are like burnished bronze:

19 "I know your works – your love, faith, service, and patient endurance. I know that your last works are greater than the first.

20 But I have this against you: you tolerate that woman Jezebel, who calls herself a prophet and is teaching and beguiling my servants to practice fornication and to eat food sacrificed to idols.

21 I gave her time to repent, but she refuses to repent of her fornication.

22 Beware, I am throwing her on a bed, and those who commit adultery with her I am throwing into great distress, unless they repent of her doings;

23 and I will strike her children dead. And all the churches will know that I am the one who searches minds and hearts, and I will give to each of you as your works deserve.

24 But to the rest of you in Thyatira, who do not hold this teaching, who have not learned what some call 'the deep things of Satan,' to you I say, I do not lay on you any other burden;

25 only hold fast to what you have until I come.

26 To everyone who conquers and continues to do my works to the end, I will give authority over the nations;

27 to rule them with an iron rod, as when clay pots are shattered –

28 even as I also received authority from my Father. To the one who conquers I will also give the morning star.

29 Let anyone who has an ear listen to what the Spirit is saying to the churches."

NRSV Revelation 3.1 "And to the angel of the church in Sardis write: These are the words of him who has the seven spirits of God and the seven stars: "I know your works; you have a name of being alive, but you are dead.

2 Wake up, and strengthen what remains and is on the point of death, for I have not found your works perfect in the sight of my God.

3 Remember then what you received and heard; obey it, and repent. If you do not wake up, I will come like a thief, and you will not know at what hour I will come to you.

4 Yet you have still a few persons in Sardis who have not soiled their clothes; they will walk with me, dressed in white, for they are worthy.

5 If you conquer, you will be clothed like them in white robes, and I will not blot your name out of the book of life; I will confess your name before my Father and before his angels.

6 Let anyone who has an ear listen to what the Spirit is saying to the churches.

7 "And to the angel of the church in Philadelphia write: These are the words of the holy one, the true one, who has the key of David, who opens and no one will shut, who shuts and no one opens:

8 "I know your works. Look, I have set before you an open door, which no one is able to shut. I know that you have but little power, and yet you have kept my word and have not denied my name.

9 I will make those of the synagogue of Satan who say that they are Jews and are not, but are lying – I will make them come and bow down before your feet, and they will learn that I have loved you.

10 Because you have kept my word of patient endurance, I will keep you from the hour of trial that is coming on the whole world to test the inhabitants of the earth.

11 I am coming soon; hold fast to what you have, so that no one may seize your crown.

12 If you conquer, I will make you a pillar in the temple of my God; you will never go out of it. I will write on you the name of my God, and the name of the city of my God, the new Jerusalem that comes down from my God out of heaven, and my own new name.

13 Let anyone who has an ear listen to what the Spirit is saying to the churches.

14 "And to the angel of the church in Laodicea write: The words of the Amen, the faithful and true witness, the origin of God's creation:

15 "I know your works; you are neither cold nor hot. I wish that you were either cold or hot.

16 So, because you are lukewarm, and neither cold nor hot, I am about to spit you out of my mouth.

17 For you say, 'I am rich, I have prospered, and I need nothing.' You do not realize that you are wretched, pitiable, poor, blind, and naked.

18 Therefore I counsel you to buy from me gold refined by fire so that you may be rich; and white robes to clothe you and to keep the shame of your nakedness from being seen; and salve to anoint your eyes so that you may see.

19 I reprove and discipline those whom I love. Be earnest, therefore, and repent.

20 Listen! I am standing at the door, knocking; if you hear my voice and open the door, I will come in to you and eat with you, and you with me.

21 To the one who conquers I will give a place with me on my throne, just as I myself conquered and sat down with my Father on his throne.

22 Let anyone who has an ear listen to what the Spirit is saying to the churches."

*R*evelation 2–3 constitute a highly structured epistolary section that picks up some of the elements we saw in the vision in Rev. 1. It is most unlikely that these letters were independent and later incorporated into the document in view of their dependence on ideas in Rev. 1. "Since both the messages and the following visions aim at prophetic exhortation, the messages may not be divided from the so-called apocalyptic visions but must be understood as an integral part of the author's overall visionary rhetorical composition."[48] D. Aune has made a good case for seeing the form of these letters like edicts the Emperor would issue. In this case, however, the edicts come from the heavenly divine King Jesus and function as evidence that Christ knows and cares about the particular situations of these churches.[49] An even better case can be made for seeing these letters like prophetic letters in the OT (2 Chron. 21.12–15; Jer. 29 cf. 2 Bar. 77.17–19, 78–87; Ep. Jer. 1), and to some degree like OT oracles (Isa. 13–23; Jer. 46–51; Ezek. 25–32; Amos 1–2).[50]

The rhetoric involved in these letters is deliberative and also highly emotive. Quintilian has a good deal to say about speakers who seek to arouse the deeper emotions of the audience, namely the emotions of fear or pity or grief or love. "The prime essential for stirring the emotions of others is, in my opinion first to feel those emotions oneself . . . our eloquence must spring from the same feeling that we desire to produce in the mind of the judge" (*Inst. Or.* 2.26–27). Quintilian then asks how are emotions that move people to action excited. His answer is very instructive for our study – "There are certain experiences which the Greeks call *phantasiai*, and the Romans visions, *whereby things absent are presented to our imagination with such extreme vividness that they seem to actually be before*

---

[48] E. Fiorenza, *Revelation* (1991), p. 47.

[49] D. E. Aune, "The Form and Function of the Proclamations to the Seven Churches (Revelation 1–3)," *NTS* 36 (1990), pp. 182–204. G. H. R. Horsley et al., eds., *New Documents Illustrating Early Christianity*, vol. 2 (Grand Rapids, Mich.: Eerdmans, 1982), pp. 32–33, presents papyri examples to support this suggestion.

[50] See C. Keener, *Revelation* (2002), pp. 104–5.

our eyes. It is the man who is really sensitive to such impressions who will have the greatest power over the emotions" (italics added) (*Inst. Or.* 6.29–30). John, by recounting his visions, seeks to make a vivid impression on his audience so as to stir their emotions with the ultimate aim of them heeding his exhortations in these letters. In other words the visions in the main serve to amplify or make vivid or reinforce the exhortations. This must be kept in view when considering the function and purposes of Revelation.

The structure of these letters is as follows:

1) address to the angel of the particular church in question
2) the "thus sayeth" (*tade legei*) formula indicating prophetic communication ultimately from the Lord himself
3) a description of the one sending the message, drawing on descriptions found in Rev. 1
4) a word of commendation for a church's good qualities, if appropriate
5) the formula "but I have one thing against you" followed by a description of the fault and an exhortation to repent
6) indication of judgment or consequences of not following the exhortation
7) Gospel-like conclusion of "he who has ears, let him hear what the Spirit is saying to the churches"[51]
8) promise of what the conqueror or victor will receive from Christ for con-quering.

Among other things, this highly schematized form suggests that this material is a literary product carefully constructed after John received his visions, rather like an author writing the introduction after having written the rest of the work. With attention to the rhetorical shaping of this material, we find deliberative rhetoric letting the churches know what will benefit them in the future and what will make for peace and reconciliation with their Lord and among themselves. If this is indeed the last portion of Revelation to be written, it tells us that the work's primary function is exhortation to modify behavior and to comfort the afflicted and give them hope for the future.

Revelation is not a work of arcane or abstract speculation about the future, nor is it merely a chronicling of John's visions. The epistolary framework indicates that the visions are meant to be seen in a particular context or social location, namely the life of those first-century churches addressed by John. John is offering apocalyptic prophecy about the future in a way that is relevant to and reinforces the exhortations offered in Rev. 2–3. The rhetorical analysis of this material further highlights this point.

---

[51] On this hearing formula, see A.-M. Enroth, "The Hearing Formula in the Book of Revelation," *NTS* 36 (1990), pp. 598–608. She points out that the formula is directed to the churches, correctly surmising that this whole work is directed to Christians. John is not addressing the sort of general public Jesus was when he used the formula.

The authority and ethos of the speaker is established at the beginning of each of these brief letters – he is the one who holds the stars in his right hand, the one who is the first and the last, and so on. It is made clear that it is Jesus, not John, speaking and that his judgments are the judgments of God and cannot be gainsaid. There is then an exordium of sorts in which the speaker establishes rapport with his audience by commending them in some way, if he is able to do so. In fact this exordium blends together with the *narratio*, for the speaker will list something he knows to be already true about the audience. There is then the essential proposition or bone of contention that is listed in summary form normally following the "I have one thing against you" formula. There is no extended argument offered, as these are simply summaries of speeches that would have been made had John been present with these audiences at the time. Instead the speaker moves directly to the final exhortation or emotive *peroratio*, calling the churches to beware or be faithful or other similar exhortations. There is a final word of encouragement ("whoever conquers . . .") to once again establish good feeling among the audiences so they will be strengthened to do what needs to be done. The audiences are called to be moral athletes in a hostile environment.

The rhetorical analysis of J. T. Kirby of Rev. 2–3 deserves to be reviewed at this juncture.[52] First, Kirby is likely right that we should not simply see Revelation as an example of secondary rhetoric, rhetoric applied to literary vehicles that are not part of some oral proclamation. As Kirby says, Revelation takes the form of a text meant to be heard, not merely read. The author has been attentive to the aural potential of his material. Kirby suggests the material was meant to be read aloud in worship in the seven churches. Second, Kirby states that John is trying to establish the authority of the document in part by his claims to have received a revelation and so be a true prophet. Aristotle stressed that the trustworthiness of the character of the speaker is perhaps the most crucial element in making something persuasive (*Rhetoric* 1356a). John does not try to hide behind a pseudonym nor offer up *ex eventu* prophecy. He has a public face with these congregations, and he is counting on them to accept his prophecies in part on the basis of their knowledge of who he is as a reliable and authoritative figure.

An interesting feature of Revelation is that it partakes of the character of both deliberative and forensic rhetoric at the same time. Kirby discusses the basic future-oriented nature of most of the work. John is largely speaking about things that are yet to come and helping his converts make right decisions in preparation for the future.[53] However, and it is a big however, John believes that God already has a plan set down in writing for that future. God has already passed judgment on sin and wickedness, and Satan has already been cast out of heaven

[52] J. T. Kirby, "The Rhetorical Situation of Revelation 1–3," *NTS* 34 (1988), pp. 197–207.
[53] Ibid., p. 200.

before Revelation was written. Furthermore the essential history-changing act of redemption has already transpired in the coming, death, and exaltation of Jesus (see Rev. 12). The forensic character of the work is also undeniable. One could say that John encourages his converts about the future by reassuring them that God not only already has a plan to deal with evil but has already set it in motion and has already judged Satan by means of the Christ event. The unveiling of judgment in Rev. 4–19 is simply the revealing of the further progress of the redemptive-judgments God has already set in motion.[54]

Kirby proposes the following rhetorical structure to the letters in Rev. 2–3:

Proem	*Narration*	*Proposition*	*Epilogue*
2.1	2.2–3	2.4–6	2.7
2.8	2.9	2.10	2.11
2.12	2.13–15	2.16	2.17
2.18	2.19–21	2.22–25	2.26–29
3.1a	3.1b	3.2–4	3.5–6
3.7	3.8, 10	3.8–11	3.12–13
3.14	3.15–18	3.19–20	3.21–22[55]

This analysis comports with what I have suggested. The proem or exordium serves to establish the authority of the speaker, Jesus. Thus his credentials are established by indicating his names and character. Kirby could be right that these letters are judicial in character, indicating what Jesus has against this or that church. But judicial rhetoric does not really have a hortatory character, and furthermore there is at least one of these churches that is not criticized. It is better to see these letters as deliberative in function.[56]

A CLOSER LOOK — PROPHETS IN THE POSTAPOSTOLIC AGE

In the postapostolic era there was something of a power vacuum at the top of the leadership pyramid in early Christianity – a vacuum filled by prophets or teachers or elders, or, in due course in the second century, by monarchial bishops in some parts of Asia Minor. One of the clues in Revelation that John writes in such an era is precisely the sort of leadership structure the letters in

---

[54] R. G. Hall, "Arguing Like an Apocalypse," *NTS* 42 (1996), p. 436: "Apocalyptists assume a world that depends on God's decrees. In such a world arguments based on balanced probabilities and judicious distinctions of Greek philosophy and rhetoric are irrelevant. . . . Argumentative force depends not primarily on a chain of deductive or inductive reasoning but on the explanatory power of the world view disclosed when God reveals his judgments." Thus, John attempts to immerse his audience in his world view by immersing them in the narrative and symbolic world of his apocalyptic prophecy. Powerful images and ideas amount to a powerful form of persuasion.

[55] J. T. Kirby, "Rhetorical Situation of Revelation 1–3" (1988), p. 201. Cf. the similar conclusions in E. Fiorenza, *Revelation* (1991), p. 119.

[56] Ibid., p. 26.

Rev. 2–3 reflect. John's rivals and adversaries are false apostles and false prophets. Nothing is said about extant true apostles in this document. They are rather a part of the foundation of the New Jerusalem according to Rev. 21.14, and there the reference is to the original twelve apostles, a distant memory when John writes. It is useful to compare what John says about prophets with what is said in another document written probably about the same time as Revelation, the *Didache*.

The *Didache* paints a portrait of itinerant prophets whose actions as well as words are to be closely scrutinized. When we compare the portrait of prophets in the *Didache* with what we find in Revelation, we find a highly critical attitude toward such prophets, except in the author's evaluation of himself. The attitude in both these documents is quite different from what we find, for instance, in 1 Cor. 12–14 or in Acts, reflecting the earlier period of the Christian movement before A.D. 70. The *Didache*, like Revelation, reflects a time when the church seems to be less of a prophetic movement and more of a localized phenomenon. The advice in *Did.* 11–13 has to do with how to handle prophets or teachers who might show up. The primary concern is with those who might want to locate in a particular congregation and become an authority figure there. It does not appear, however, that John is dealing with itinerant prophets. The two false ones he mentions seem to be indigenous to the churches they are bothering.

As in Revelation, the phrase *en pneumati* crops up in the *Didache*. Prophets speaking "in the Spirit" are not tested or examined (*Did.* 11.7). But the *Didache* warns that not everyone who speaks in the Spirit is a prophet, and the ultimate test of true prophets is whether they model the behavior of the itinerant Lord (11.8). It would appear that speaking in the Spirit here refers to speaking in an ecstatic state, not necessarily speaking by means of the Holy Spirit. *Did.* 11.12 urges "whoever shall say in the Spirit 'Give me money or something else' you shall not listen to him. . . ." This verse must mean that not everything spoken in an ecstatic state is from the Lord. This may help explain why John must go out of his way to establish his ethos and authority with his audience. Prophets were critically evaluated in his day, and so he must connect himself not just with the Spirit but with Christ to establish his credentials. Prophets are seen as inspired but not infallible, and they are held responsible for what they say. The *Didache* seems to reflect a time or place or both when the number of prophets is dwindling and if true prophets are willing to locate, they are to be honored and provided for (13.1).[57] We learn two things from this brief comparison. John lives in an age when his authority is not automatically accepted as a prophetic figure. He also lives in an age when there is prophetic competition, and he has disadvantage of being at a distance from those he writes to, but his competition

---

[57] In addition to this "closer look," see my *Jesus the Seer: The Progress of Prophecy* (Peabody, Mass.: Hendrickson, 1999), pp. 343–48.

is within two of these churches. One can see why authority-building rhetoric is necessary in such a state of affairs.

The Message to Ephesus

Without question Ephesus was the most important city of those John addressed, and it is appropriate that it was addressed first. It was both a commercial and religious center, though its power in the commerical realm was beginning to decline due to the silting up of its harbor.[58] By the time John wrote his letter, the city had a population of 250,000 or more and was noted for its striking architecture, especially for the Temple of Artemis, one of the seven wonders of the ancient world. The Christian faith had existed in this city for over four decades by the time Revelation was penned, so we are not talking about a new congregation. Rather John is mostly addressing those who have been Christians for some time but whose initial enthusiasm has waned. Bear in mind that Ephesus was the most powerful city in the region and was indebted to the Emperor and his cult even more than Smyrna was. There were two temples built in Ephesus to Augustus, and, more important, Domitian had named Ephesus the guardian of the imperial cult.[59] Only a few years before Revelation was likely written, Ephesus had a new cult site for the emperors and celebrated the Olympic games in honor of Domitian.[60]

Notice at **vs. 2** an image of power – Christ is one who not only holds the angels of the churches in his hand but also walks in the midst of the lampstands that symbolize the churches. This is not simply an image of comfort for Christ is coming to inspect this church and exhort it. John is likely referring to a pre-Parousia judgment of Christ that is coming now, before all the events described in Rev. 4–22 transpire. It is the invisible Christ who already walks among the churches and inspects them and calls them into account in the present. His work always involves redemptive-judgment, or in this case beatitude follows correction of behavior.

The Ephesian church is praised for its works, which include endurance and lack of toleration for that which is evil or false. It has put to the test some false apostles and found them wanting. This seems to be in the past, while the trouble with the Nicolaitans seems to be a present matter.[61] Nothing is said about true apostles existing or doing the inspection and correction. John obviously agrees

---

[58] On this now, see my *New Testament History* (Grand Rapids, Mich.: Baker, 2001), p. 280.

[59] The most recent discussion suggests that the Imperial cult temple in Ephesus was dedicated to the Flavian emperors in general and contained a statue of Titus, rather than Domitian.

[60] See J. N. Kraybill, *Imperial Cult and Commerce in John's Apocalypse* (Sheffield, UK: Sheffield Academic Press, 1996), pp. 27–28; S. Friesen, "Ephesus: Key to a Vision in Revelation," *BAR* 19 (1993), pp. 24–37.

[61] See D. E. Aune, *Revelation 1–5* (1997), pp. 142–43.

that the Ephesian church's endurance, perseverance, and discernment about falsity are good things, but its concern for holiness and truth has apparently not been balanced with compassion and love. The Ephesians are said to have left their first love.

The word used for love here is "agape," referring to either the love of God or to the love of fellow believers or more broadly of fellow human beings. But the use of the term suggests priorities, and the context favors the suggestion that brotherly or sisterly love is mainly in view here.[62] This view is confirmed by what Christ tells them to go back and do – the works of love for each other. Perhaps, in their zeal for orthodoxy or orthopraxy, they have lost their ability to distinguish between hating the sin and loving the sinner. The alternative is that Christ will come and take away their lampstand, their source of spiritual light and life. Without love the church loses its status as the church.[63]

At **vs. 6** we are told of something Christ himself hates, namely the deeds of the Nicolaitans. We have no reference to this group outside the book of Revelation, and it is difficult to know what the nature of their error was. If their name gives any clue, they were the "Victory people" (combining *nike* and *laos*). We also do know that their error affected more than one of these churches. The Victory people may be contrasted with those who are said to conquer. It may be of significance that in **vs. 7** churches (plural) are mentioned. Though these words are addressed to the Ephesians, they are meant for all these churches to hear and heed. In other words we are dealing with circular letters.

The promise at the end of this first letter is drawn from Genesis. The one who conquers will be given to eat from the tree of life, which is in the paradise of God. In apocalyptic literature the tree of life is regularly the reward for the righteous following judgment (cf. 1 En. 24.4–25.6; Test. of Levi 18.11; 2 En. 8.3).[64] This paradise must be seen as otherwordly. There is a question as to whether the term *nikonti* refers to only martyrs or to all believers who are faithful to the end. If one compares 3.20 and 3.21, probably we should not see this as a technical term for martyr in Revelation, though it would include martyrs. As Reddish remarks, "the term 'conquerors' used for the faithful, reflects the apocalyptic worldview that sees the world engaged in a cosmic struggle between the forces of good and evil – God versus Satan."[65]

A CLOSER LOOK — JOHN AND SECTARIANISM

It has become almost a commonplace to argue that early Christianity was sectarian and world negating. There is a good deal of truth in this observation, and

62 See C. Hemer, *The Letters to the Seven Churches of Asia in Their Local Setting* (Sheffield, UK: JSOT Press, 1986), p. 41.
63 See C. Keener, *Revelation* (2002), p. 106.
64 See R. H. Mounce, *Book of Revelation* (1977), p. 72.
65 M. G. Reddish, *Revelation* (2001), p. 54.

the phrase "conversionist sect" does convey something about the early Christian movement, which was so focused on evangelism. One could also speak about John's attempt to create a millenarian sect, and his work has been used to further such an undertaking. But it is important to maintain a sense of historical balance when one uses such terminology. These letters that begin Revelation reflect that John thinks various of his converts or communities are not sectarian enough. They have, in his view, compromised too much with the world and the social milieu of Asia Minor, and they need to do a better job of disengaging from their pagan environment.

In fact, as P. A. Harland has argued, there was a range of responses by early Christians in Asia Minor to the dominant culture, including the religious aspects of that culture.[66] There is the entire spectrum of possible responses to something like the emperor cult from both early Jews and early Christians, ranging from full participation to absolute repudiation. John's sectarian attitude was not shared by all in his audience. We need to bear in mind that before there was ever a Roman presence in Asia Minor, this entire region was thoroughly Hellenized, and the values of Hellenistic culture were such that within the polis considerable diversity of religion and religious views were accommodated.[67] Before Christians were present in this region, there had been many Jews and Jewish communities that found ways to acclimate to their surroundings without giving up the distinctiveness of their Jewish identity. To the extent that the Christian communities John addresses had grown out of the Jewish communities, they had already had some practice in dealing with the issues of accommodation and deenculturation. For example, many Jews participated in guilds and associations in this region, and there was a religious dimension to such groups. Many also participated in activities at the gymnasiums.[68] Some early Christians in the region did so as well. The environment was inherently syncretistic, and John's appeals to stricter boundaries with other religions would have gone against the grain and nature of that society. Part of the problem John faced was that various of the guilds and associations that his converts likely were a part of had themselves taken up honoring the Emperor during their meetings. Depending on what form this honoring took, John's exhortations might mean dissociation from the guild itself, which would be costly in a place where one could not easily practice one's trade unless one "joined the union."[69] Thus Harland stresses that

---

[66] P. A. Harland, "Honouring the Emperor or Assailing the Beast: Participation in Civic Life among Associations (Jewish, Christian and Other) in Asia Minor and the Apocalypse of John," *JSNT* 77 (2000), pp. 99–121.

[67] See P. R. Trebilco, *Jewish Communities in Asia Minor* (Cambridge: Cambridge University Press, 1991).

[68] See A. Harland, "Honouring the Emperor" (2000), pp. 109–10.

[69] See ibid., p. 119: "if a person were to sever all such contacts with fellow-workers once affiliated with another group such as the Christians or the local synagogue removing oneself would sever the network connections necessary for business activity, thereby threatening one's means of livelihood."

John's sectarian stance was likely a minority opinion among Christians in the cities of Asia Minor.[70] It is important then, when using sociological models and concepts, that one takes into account archaeological and social historical data from the region about early Jews and Christians before one makes sweeping generalizations about the sectarian nature of Christianity in the region. John's perspective is John's perspective. If all or most of his audience shared it, there would be little need for some of his exhortations and many of his visionary accounts about the Beast and other things.

The Message to Smyrna

The phrase used to describe Christ in **vs. 8b** fits the content of the message that follows, for he is said not only to be the first and the last but also to be the one who died and came back to life. This is especially germane when we read of the suffering in Smyrna in **vs. 9**. Furthermore the congregation is said to be in poverty, and yet in another nonmaterial way, they are said to be rich. This is the opposite of what is later said of the Laodicean church. Smyrna, like Pergamum, Thyatira, and Philadephia, is one of the original seven cities still in existence. It was some thirty-five miles north of Ephesus, had an excellent harbor, and was a prosperous city. Smyrna had both strong ties to Rome and a large Jewish population, making it doubly difficult for Christians.[71] The poverty of the Christians here and elsewhere was possibly based in the guild system. To work at a particular trade one had to be a member of a guild, but the latter required participation in various pagan religious ceremonies.[72] It was the second city in the region in preeminence after Ephesus and the second allowed to have the imperial cult (Tacitus, *Ann.* 4.55–56).

A CLOSER LOOK — THE QUESTION OF JEWISH AND CHRISTIAN
RELATIONSHIPS IN REVELATION

One factor that may explain the polemic against Jews in Revelation is the possibility that Jews distinguished themselves from Christians, thus forcing the latter to honor the emperor cult. If Christians were said to be non-Jews, then there were implications. We also cannot rule out the sort of scenario depicted in Acts 18 in which Paul was taken to court in Corinth by Jews wanting him out of the picture. The Roman justice system depended on informants, and almost anyone

[70] Ibid., p. 116.
[71] According to one estimation of a total population in the Empire of 60 million, some 5 million were Jews and only 50,000 were Christians. See D. E. Aune, *Revelation 1–5* (1997), p. 164. The size of the Jewish population is in part indicated by the enormous synagogue, built in the third or fourth century A.D., that was about the length of a football field. See D. G. Mitten, "A New Look at Sardis," *BA* 24 (1966), p. 65.
[72] See E. Fiorenza, *Revelation* (1991), p. 56.

could be a snitch (or in Latin, a *delatores*). Normally it was only a higher-status person who would go to court and file a suit or claim against someone else, for the system was heavily weighted in favor of such people. If a Christian was found guilty of practicing an illegal religion, a *superstitio*, the penalties ranged from corporal punishment, to exile (as in John's case), to capital punishment. Torture could also be part of the fact-finding process before the sentence was handed down. All of these prospects led to the need for John to make sure that the faith of these converts was strong so they could face such things.

We know that many of the cities in Asia had a significant Jewish population, and many of those Jews were well-established citizens with connections, perhaps like Paul's family in Tarsus. "Archaeological and literary sources indicate that the Jewish community in each of the cities mentioned in Revelation was well integrated into both the colonial Roman and the indigenous Asian cultures. They did not live in a Jewish ghetto but had social intercourse with their neighbors and held local municipal, provincial, and imperial offices."[73] This and the webs of power being what they were, Christians could get in lots of trouble pretty quickly if they refused to worship the Emperor, especially if Christians had been witnessing within the synagogue, as Paul is depicted as having done repeatedly in Acts. The usual charge against those who refused to honor any of the traditional gods was "atheism," and if one couples that with evidence of practicing a *superstitio* as an alternative, it was twice as serious.

Jews of course had a right to practice their own religion (something Rome allowed most ethnic groups they conquered to do), but in the Jews' case abstaining from other gods was a component of their faith. If Christians could be shown to be Gentiles or no longer as Jews, they could not claim the benefits of an exemption from emperor worship, a precarious position in which to be.[74] This whole social scenario may help to explain the letter to Smyrna and the reference to a synagogue of Satan.[75] But there is a further factor, namely that the position of Jews in the Empire had become more tenuous after A.D. 70. It was the Flavians who waged the war against the Jews between A.D. 66 and 72. Thereafter it was the Flavians who imposed a major tax on the Jews. Since their own temple had been destroyed, they were now to give to the Temple of Jupiter in Rome. Domitian had stressed especially that the God-fearers and proselytes must pay this tax. It was the penalty for their seeking to become Jewish. It thus behooved Jews in Asia Minor and elsewhere to root out any messianic Jews or

---

[73] Ibid., p. 135.
[74] See G. Theissen, *The Religion of the Earliest Churches* (Minneapolis: Fortress, 1999), p. 244: "As long as the Christians were still part of Judaism, in principle they were free of any contact with the Emperor cult. Only after they had been perceived by those around them as an independent group alongside the Jews could they be perplexed by their confrontation with the Emperor cult."
[75] On the Jewish "exemption" from pagan worship, see my *The Acts of the Apostles* (Grand Rapids, Mich.: Eerdmans, 1998), pp. 539–44.

proselytes in their midst who might cause their own position in society to be further compromised.[76]

In regard to that potent polemical language about the synagogue of Satan, such language was characteristic of ancient rhetoric, and most ancients would have known there was a measure of hyperbole in such rhetoric.[77] Invective was a way of stigmatizing one's opponents and of putting them on the defensive. It was not to be used as a way of perpetrating injustices or justifying persecution, but rather as a way of winning an argument in court. Though there had apparently already been a parting of the ways by John's day of church and synagogue, they were apparently vying for some of the same clientele, and so the art of persuasion and dissuasion was used to win converts.

Fiorenza is right that we must beware of using John's rhetoric today, not least because Jews have often been the persecuted minority during Christian history, including in the twentieth century. "Revelation's defensive rhetoric of self-preservation of Jewish identity has been turned into a language of hate."[78] Instead of being seen as a cry of injustice, John's rhetoric has been used as a tool of injustice in the modern era! This shows how socio-historical and rhetorical contexts are everything in determining the meaning of a volatile work like John's. It also demonstrates that, in terms of hermeneutics, a simple transfer of John's ideas to a different cultural situation can be a very dangerous enterprise and can even lead to the opposite of what John fought to accomplish through his work, namely a reassuring that injustices will be remedied in due course by God.

⟨⟨⟨❦⟩⟩⟩

It is difficult to know whether or not we should take vs. 9 literally. John clearly blames at least some Jews connected with the synagogue for what has happened to the Christians in Smyrna. He calls them so-called Jews. Indeed they are quite the opposite. It seems likely that he means not that Satan was actually being worshipped in the synagogue but rather that their action in persecuting was "of the Devil."[79] Implied here as well is the sentiment found in Rom. 9.6, namely that not all of Abraham's seed are true Jews. John tells the Smyrneans not to fear what they are about to suffer. Apparently more persecutions or perhaps Roman trials and being cast into jail are in view. But imprisonment in the Roman world was only a temporary expedient until one's case was heard and the issue resolved legally. We have the independent testimonies of both Paul's letters and

---

[76] E. Schüssler Fiorenza, "The Followers of the Lamb: Visionary Rhetoric and Socio-Political Situation," *Semeia* 36 (1986), p. 137.

[77] See L. T. Johnson, "The New Testament's Anti-Jewish Slander and Conventions of Ancient Rhetoric," *JBL* 108 (1989), pp. 419–41.

[78] E. Fiorenza, *Revelation* (1991), p. 136.

[79] Cf. 1 QH 2.22 and 1 QM 4.9, which refer to a congregation of Belial.

Acts that Jews sometimes brought Christians before the Roman authorities (see Acts 18), as did pagans.[80] But whatever human agencies were involved, John clearly places the ultimate blame on Satan. He is the one who casts them into prison.

Vs. 10 is probably not a literal reference to ten days of suffering. More likely it means a definitive short period of time. In any case the Christians are told that if they will just be faithful unto death Christ will reward them with the crown of life (i.e., eternal life; cf. 1 Cor. 9.25; James. 1.12), which will prevent them from experiencing the second death.[81] Probably the crown is the laurel wreath won and worn by victors at Olympic and other Greek-style games.[82] Pausanias says that Smyrna was famous for such games, but it was also famous for being the home of Homer. More important, there may be local knowledge in this reference to a crown for Smyrna had as a symbol of its city a wreath emblem, which is often found on inscriptions there.[83]

The letter to Smyrna is the only letter that seems to address with any clarity the relationship of Christians to the world outside the Christian community. The references to Jewish harassment, suffering, potential imprisonment, and death all indicate a distressing situation for Christians.[84] The letter to Pergamum mentions the death of a Christian (2.13), and the letter to Philadelphia mentions Jewish harassment and perseverance despite pressure to recant Christian beliefs (3.8–10). This brings up a crucial point. It is a mistake to overlook that

the only references to the wider Roman Asian milieu are to the repression of Christians. Those who argue against persecution or oppression as a contributing social factor for Asian Christians based upon their absence in the letters have failed to note: 1) that the letters contain only one full comment (2.8–11) and two passing references (2.13; 3.8–10) to any external issues; and 2) that *all three passages refer to Christian suffering.*[85]

It is a large mistake to underestimate the context of persecution in which the book of Revelation was written.

---

[80] There is, in addition, evidence from the second-century document called *The Martyrdom of Polycarp* that Jews of Smyrna joined in with their pagan neighbors in cheering for the death of Polycarp, and indeed they even added fuel to the fire by gathering wood for the execution. Also, it was in Smyrna that Ignatius stopped on his way to being executed in Rome in A.D. 107. This evidence coupled with what one finds in Revelation reminds us that our author is hardly writing to a situation of only perceived danger or crisis.

[81] The phrase "the second death" occurs in rabbinic sources and refers to the death that the wicked will endure in the next world.

[82] But cf. Heb. 2.9 and *Mart. Poly.* 17.1 where the wreath is given to the one who is faithful even unto death (cf. 2 Tim. 2.5). Interestingly in 4 Macc. in various places the imagery of victorious athletes is used of Jewish martyrs (cf. 6.10; 11.20; 13.15; 15.29; 16.16; 17.11–16).

[83] See Horsley et al., eds., *New Docs.*, vol. 3, p. 52.

[84] Needless to say this polemical language should not be used by Christians to reverse the process, wherein a Christian majority persecutes a Jewish minority. See C. Keener, *Revelation* (2002), p. 118.

[85] T. B. Slater, "On the Social Setting of the Revelation," *NTS* 44 (1998), p. 241.

The Message to Pergamum

At **vs. 12** we find the image of Christ as judge, coming with his sharp two-edged sword.[86] This forewarns us that the message to Pergamum is likely to be strongly negative. Pergamum was the capital city of the region and, like Corinth and Athens, had a huge acropolis on which sat various temples, such as those to Athena and Zeus. There was also a famous temple on the plain below the acropolis for the god Asclepios, the god of healing (see Pausanias 2.26.9). The reference to the serpent in 12.9 may well have conjured up in the minds of the audience the symbol for the god Asclepios. R. H. Charles says that Pergamum had become the Lourdes of its day.[87] It also had a temple dedicated to Augustus and Rome, so we know emperor worship was prevalent here. Indeed it had had such a temple since 29 B.C., and the city had become the center of emperor worship for the entire region.[88] At the very top of the city's acropolis was an imposing altar to Zeus "the Savior." This sculpture also included images of snakes, so perhaps this is what John is alluding to when he refers to the throne of Satan. Both Christians and Jews saw this city as such a center of false religion that it was destined for destruction (Sib. Or. 5.119). Pergamum was also famous for its 200,000-volume library. Here above all the church was likely to clash with the dictates of Hellenistic culture and the imperial cult. While Satan's throne could refer to the altar to Zeus, which was visible for miles around, a more likely reference is to the worship of the Emperor, for worship of a mere mortal would be seen by a monotheistic person such as John as an abomination that could only be prompted by Satan. The antagonism toward Rome in Revelation makes this conjecture quite plausible and confirmed by what we find in 13.2 and 16.10.[89]

The Christians in this town are commended for holding on to the faith even in the days when Antipas, "my witness," is killed for his faith.[90] It is striking that Antipas is given the same title as Jesus, "the faithful witness," which suggests that the translation "the faithful martyr" is close to the mark. Against this group of Christians Jesus has more than one complaint. In particular some of the audience hold to the teaching of Balaam. This is not likely the person's real name, but it is given because of the character of his actions (see Num. 22–24). John sees him as a false prophet leading God's people astray to immorality and idolatry (Num. 31.16). Here we have the association of "idol food" with fornication, not fortuitous association. Many take the term "fornication" as a metaphor for idolatry.

---

[86] The term *roumphaia* normally refers to a large sword used for both cutting and piercing, in contrast to the *machaira*, which was the short sword or dagger.
[87] R. H. Charles, *The Revelation of Saint John*, vol. 1 (Edinburgh: T + T Clark, 1920), p. 60.
[88] M. G. Reddish, *Revelation* (2001), p. 59.
[89] See the discussion by D. E. Aune, *Revelation 1–5* (1997), pp. 182–83.
[90] See discussion on *martus*, pp. 67–68.

I have argued elsewhere at length that the term *eidolothuton* in early Christian literature refers to meat sacrificed and then eaten in the presence of an idol, which is to say within a pagan temple (cf. 1 Cor. 8–10 and Acts 15).[91] Whether John has in mind sex with sacred prostitutes (which would mean that *porneia* is used in its technical and root sense) or, more likely, the sexual dalliance that went on at dinner parties held in the temple precincts is uncertain. In either case John is warning against going to pagan temples and participating in events there.[92]

It is not clear whether **vs. 15** is telling us that there were Nicolaitans in Pergamum as well, or whether the Nicolaitan heresy involved dining and fraternizing in pagan temples. G. R. Beasley-Murray makes the appealing suggestion that the Nicolaitans may have been high-status Christians who believed a certain amount of compromise with the dominant culture was all right.[93] They could have argued, "Even the Romans don't really believe the Emperor is a god, so why not just go along, and have a good living as a member of a guild?" They might also have been dualists like some of the Corinthians (see 1 Cor. 8–10), arguing that what one did with the body did not affect one's spiritual condition and status. The complaint against Balaam is a complaint against syncretism, the luring of Christians into participation in pagan cults.[94] In the early second century, there is clear evidence that when Romans discovered that Christians refused to eat meat offered to idols, they reacted sternly because such a practice could affect not only Christians but others they proselytized (Pliny, *Epistle* 10.96).

The people of Pergamum are called to repent or Christ will come and attack them with the sword of his mouth (i.e., with his word of judgment). To those who conquer is offered not idol food but hidden manna (i.e., bread that is not currently visible and that comes from heaven). Here is the promise of a much more lasting and satisfying fellowship than one could get at a pagan feast, drawing on Jewish messianic traditions about the repetition of the manna miracle in the messianic kingdom (2 Bar. 29.4–8). Also offered is a white pebble with one's new name inscribed on it, which no one knows except the one taking it. Perhaps this is an allusion to the white pebble used in antiquity for admission to

---

[91] See my "Not So Idle Thoughts about *Eidolothuton*," *TynB* 44 (1993), pp. 237–54.

[92] G. Biguzzi, "Ephesus, Its Artemision, Its Temple to the Flavian Emperors, and Idolatry in Revelation," *NovT* 40 (1998), pp. 276–90, points out that John's main polemic is not against traditional pagan religion, though here it is critiqued, but against the newly ascendant form of idolatry in the imperial cult. As Biguzzi says, John devotes chapter after chapter to a critique of the Beast and the worship of the Beast but only briefly critiques the traditional gods. This is indeed a key clue to understanding the likely date of the work's composition. In the fifties and sixties the imperial cult in Asia Minor was not nearly the prominent religious factor that it became under the Flavians.

[93] G. R. Beasley-Murray, *The Book of Revelation* (London: Oliphants, 1974), pp. 92–94.

[94] C. Keener, *Revelation* (2002), pp. 124–25.

some feasts or to the one used to vote acquittal in a trial.[95] We should perhaps see these stones as an engraved invitation to the messianic banquet. The new name implies a new identity and being someone special in the kingdom. Christians did not have to compromise on earth by socializing with pagans in temples when they had a much better engraved invitation to a much better banquet.

The Message to Thyatira

At **vs. 18** we have the one and only reference in this book to Jesus as the Son of God. It is probably used here because of the quotation of Ps. 2.9 at vv. 26–27. The eyes of fire and the feet of bronze are mentioned, picking up on the vision in Rev. 1. The image is of one who sees all, penetrating right to the heart. The bronze feet suggest stability and firmness. Thyatira was a relatively unimportant city of merchants and artisans and so was full of trade guilds. In fact C. Hemer has called it "the least known, least important, and least remarkable" of the seven cities referred to in Rev. 2–3.[96] Here too there would be considerable economic pressure on Christians.

The Christians of Thyatira are highly commended in **vs. 19** for their love, faith, service, and endurance. They are the opposite of the Ephesians, for the Thyatirians are commended for their latter works being greater than their form ones. Yet this church, perhaps out of love, had tolerated aberration in the form of a prophetess, here called Jezebel. The suggestion is that this woman was leading them astray into idolatry and immorality, just like the ancient queen of Israel (see 1 Kings 18–19; 2 Kings 9.22). In **vs. 20** we hear mention of the same sin referred to in vs. 14. This woman was given time and opportunity to repent. She did not, and thus Christ has cast her into a sickbed. She has been plagued with some sort of illness that causes suffering. John certainly believes that, on occasion, there is a connection not merely between sickness and sin but between sickness and judgment, the former being a result of the latter. It is not clear from **vs. 22** whether literal adultery characterizes Jezebel's followers, but this is not impossible. Christ inflicted great suffering in hopes of repentance not because he wanted even Jezebel to undergo final judgment at the eschaton.

Vs. 23 uses the idiom "to kill unto death," which seems to mean to kill with a pestilence or with suffering (cf. Ezek. 33.27 with Rev. 6.8 where death equals pestilence). Jesus is called in vs. 23 the searcher of all hearts and minds. He knows all our motives. Strikingly, the first word, *nephos*, means literally kidneys, which

---

95   See ibid., p. 126: "the most significant allusion is a reference to some ancient courtrooms, where jurors voted for acquittal with a white stone and for conviction with a black one. Here a capital case is probably in view (2.13), and Jesus will overturn the verdict of the Pergamum Christians' persecutors at the final judgment. . . ."

96   See Hemer, *Letters*, p. 106. For a critique of the overreading of potential allusions to local factors, see C. H. H. Scobie, "Local References in the Letters to the Seven Churches," *NTS* 39 (1993), pp. 606–24.

were seen as the seat of affections, much as we would use the term "heart." Whereas heart in the text has a sense closer to what we mean by mind – the rational faculty or intellect. We are told that Christ gives to each according to a person's works. There is indeed a judgment of Christian works, with rewards and punishment depending on the evaluation. It appears that the heresy in question involved some sort of promise to know the deep things of God, which actually turned out to be the deep things of Satan. Real necromancy or Satan worship is unlikely to be meant.

The faithful Christians are to hold fast to their faith until Christ comes. To the victors goes the highest possible honor – power over the Gentile nations, with the ability to rule with absolute power. Thus a share in Christ's worldwide sovereignty is envisioned. But when would this transpire? John suggests in the millennium (see Rev. 20). In addition **vs. 28** promises the gift of the morning star, which probably should not be associated with Rev. 22.16. The morning star is Venus, which to the Romans was the symbol of victory and sovereignty. Christians will not obtain such things through pagan rituals or by following pagan teaching, but from Christ.

The Message to Sardis

"Jesus' oracle to Ephesus challenges a loveless church; his oracle to Smyrna encourages a persecuted church; his oracle to Pergamum addresses both persecution and compromise; but Jesus' word to Sardis summons a sleeping church to wake up."[97] This message is the most strongly negative of the seven. This church had the reputation of being alive but was really dead. The town was living basically on past historical prestige, having been the location where the famous King Croesus had lived. It was destroyed in the huge A.D. 17 earthquake that wracked the region and indebted to Rome for its rebuilding. According to Josephus this city had a good-sized Jewish population (*Ant.* 14.259–61; 16.166, 171). Its church had passed on from its better days. Rev. 3.2, however, suggests that there was a flicker that could be rekindled. None of the city's works were perfectly acceptable to God. The verb *pepleromena* could mean completed, suggesting that Sardis had never finished the work it was called to do in the first place. **Vs. 2a** should likely be translated "strengthen those who remain but are at the point of death."[98] This would seem to refer to the real possibility of martyrdom. **Vs. 3** is important for it speaks of Jesus' coming as a thief if the Sardisians did not become watchful about their behavior. This image likely goes back to the original parable of Jesus and image is reused where the subject is the Parousia (cf. Luke 12.39–40; 1 Thess. 5.2–8; 2 Pet. 3.10). The elaboration in **vs. 3b** suggests that the timing of Jesus' coming will be surprising. While the reference could be

---

[97] C. Keener, *Revelation* (2002), p. 142.
[98] D. E. Aune, *Revelation 1–5* (1997), p. 219.

to the Parousia, it is more likely to the invisible coming of Christ to judge this particular church in the present. Reddish suggests this image would have been especially striking to the Sardisians because twice in their history they had fallen prey to devastating sneak attacks because of their lack of diligence or alertness.

At **vs. 4** we hear of a few who have not defiled their garments. White garments are mentioned seven times in this book as a symbol of purity and holiness. In a city of garment workers, this promise was especially meaningful. The soiled garment in a city famous for its dyed garments and fancy clothing products would be antithetical to civic pride. In Asia Minor a soiled garment often prohibited a person from participating in an act of worship. The promise to those who are steadfast is a garment of absolute white and that their names will not be blotted out of the book of life. In the OT the phrase "book of life" refers to earthly life (cf. Exod. 32.32; Ps. 69.28; Isa. 4.3), but in the NT it refers to eternal life. The image suggests it is possible to be in such a book and then to be blotted out of it because of unacceptable beliefs and practices. The victor will be acknowledged in the highest throne room of all, namely before God and his angelic entourage.[99]

The call for the Christians in Sardis to wake up may have some basis in local knowledge. While Sardis had never been conquered through normal warfare, it had twice been taken because Sardisian forces had failed to be vigilant (see Herodotus 147.91). The same Greek word that can be translated "watch" could also be rendered "wake up."

The Message to Philadelphia

Philadephia was a city dedicated to Hellenistic culture and called "little Athens" for all its temples. It was in the midst of a vine-growing region, and so Bacchus was its favorite deity. In the message to Philadephia's church is the only description of Christ not drawn from the vision recorded in Rev. 1.[100] We are told that Christ has the key of David and the power to open so that no one can shut and vice versa. Isa. 22.22 is in the background here, and the verse means that Christ has the key to the royal household, referring to the New Jerusalem. In all likelihood the open door mentioned in **vs. 8** refers to the door into the heavenly city or royal and heavenly mansion. At least a few Christians here have kept Christ's word and not denied his name. As at Smyrna the problem relates to the synagogue, and, in an abrupt turn around from older Jewish expectations, these so-called Jews worship at the feet of the faithful Christians.

Vs. 10 sounds congenial to dispensationalism at first. Christ will keep the faithful from the hour of trial to come upon the whole earth. This is followed

---

[99] In some places in the Greco-Roman world the names of errant citizens could be blotted out of the city register immediately prior to execution. See Hemer, *Letters*, p. 148.

[100] See M. G. Reddish, *Revelation* (2001), p. 73.

by "I will come quickly." Notice, however, that the author says nothing about taking the Christians out of the world; rather he speaks of Christ coming and protecting Christians.[101] In this message it seems clear the author has begun to speak of the final eschatological events and not just what now is. Instead of being a pillar of pagan society, the victor will become a pillar in God's temple, with the most crucial of all things inscribed (i.e., impressed upon and so identified with the believer) – God's name, Jesus' name, and the name of the new city. The victor will belong to God and be a part of the heavenly city (see Rev. 6.9–11). As Reddish says, Christ is offering the Philadelphians a place of honor and security in the very presence of God. "Now those who kept 'the name' will be inscribed with the name."[102]

The Message to Laodicea

At **vs. 14** Christ is called both the Amen (as God is at Isa. 65.16)[103] and the beginning of God's creation, an explicit reference to Christ's preexistence. Our author possibly knew of the letter that went to Colossae and Laodicea and is reflecting his knowledge of Col. 1–2. The town of Laodicea was well known particularly for its banks and famous medical school (Strabo 12.8.20).[104] John clearly knows some of the social and religious particulars about each of these seven cities.[105] The weakness of the city, however, was its lack of a good water supply (Strabo 13.4.14). Six miles away Hierapolis had its hot medicinal springs, and there was also pure water in Colossae. Just across from Laodicea the hot springs went over limestone cliffs and became lukewarm and brackish.[106] Anyone drinking it would spit it out. The imagery seems pointedly directed toward the audience's life situation. There is no commendation at all for Laodicea. The Laodiceans are faulted for being neither hot nor cold. They claim to be rich and have no needs, but the result of complacency and status quo thinking is a loss of real self-knowledge. The Laodiceans have in fact become poor and naked spiritually speaking, and only Christ can apply the necessary ointment, the white garment,

---

[101] See ibid., p. 76: "To keep them from the coming trials does not mean the church will be exempt from the difficulties. Rather, this is a promise of Christ's abiding presence with the church that will strengthen and sustain it regardless of the trials ahead."

[102] Ibid., p. 78.

[103] On this text as a background for Rev. 3.14, see G. K. Beale, "The Old Testament Background of Rev 3.14," *NTS* 42 (1996), pp. 133–52.

[104] C. Koester has pointed out to me via email that it is not at all clear that Laodicea was famous for its eye salve, despite many commentators who think so.

[105] See Hemer, *Letters*, pp. 188–94. That this city was destroyed by earthquake in A.D. 60 and was able to rebuild itself with imperial assistance tells us something about how prosperous the city was.

[106] Lukewarm water for bathing was not seen as a bad thing, but for drinking it was another matter. In the ancient baths there was a caldarium (hot water in the form of steam), a tepidarium (warm water), and a fridgidarium (cold water).

the necessary spiritual currency to help them. He will reprove and discipline the ones he loves.[107] Even with such people as the Laodiceans, Christ does not give up.

Notice that he still calls to repentance this church that he cannot commend, and we hear the famous words about standing at the door and knocking. But each individual must respond. The victor gets to have ongoing fellowship with Christ and to sit with him on his throne. Finally, note the use of the rhetorical device of irony in this letter. Things are not as they appear in Laodicea, and John points out the incongruity through ironical words and images.[108]

If we consider the social situation described in these brief epistles, we discover several pertinent facts. First, the social makeup of the churches differed: some were predominantly poor, others had as members a number of high-status Christians. The variety in the exhortations reflects these social differences. Second, there are both internal and external problems plaguing these churches. The internal problems involve prophetic figures other than John who may have been the ones who filled the power vacuum when John was exiled. There was also the problem of the relationships with the synagogues. Third, there were the larger social issues of how to relate to pagan culture, and especially its religious culture, including the emperor cult. In pagan society Christians are being marginalized and persecuted for their faith. It appears that John believes that, in his absence, things have gone awry in these churches and that only the strongest exhortations may help right these ships. Some congregations are seen as being in better shape than others, but none are without difficulties.

BRIDGING THE HORIZONS

Probably Rev. 2–3 are the most frequently used sections of John's book when it comes to preaching and teaching. It is easy to find contemporary parallels of things to commend or condemn about Christian behavior. One can use the "if the shoe fits, wear it" kind of principle when preaching from this material.[109] What is missing in most Western contexts, however, is the atmosphere of menace and persecution underlying what we find in Rev. 2–3. Yet, it is not so in many places in the world. Having returned from teaching and preaching in Africa in 2001, it is clear to me there are some contexts where oppression, suffering, and death are Christians' regular companions. It is no accident that A. Boesak chose the book of Revelation to preach many sermons during the dark days of apartheid. Revelation is a book about justice and God's sovereignty even in the face of evidence of great evil on the loose in the world. And it is difficult to convince some parts of a church that it has been complicit with structural and governmental systems that have perpetrated great evils on many people. One of

---

[107] He even threatens to vomit (*emeo*) them out of his mouth.
[108] See C. Keener, *Revelation* (2002), p. 161.
[109] Ibid., pp. 108–9.

the things that one can do with the materials in Rev. 2–3 is to reflect on the sort of problems that arise when a church has been in existence for a good period of time. How does one deal with complacency, lack of zeal, self-centered behavior, and, most of all, too much accommodation to the secular culture outside the church?

The sociological literature has a good deal to say about millenarian sects and their attempts to build firm boundaries around their communities. This is difficult to do in a cosmopolitan urban setting, especially when one is a member of an evangelistic religion. One of John's problems is that he is dealing with churches that do not seem to have strong indigenous leadership structures. Indeed they seem far too susceptible to false apostles and false prophets. John would like to create a "high group" sense of identity[110] or community among his audiences, but there seems to be little leadership on the ground that he can appeal to, to assist in this group formation.

John attempts to instill certain accountability factors into their lives by making ethical demands in the context of eschatological warnings about Christ and coming judgment, both imminent and more remote. Bear in mind about millenarian sects such as those John is trying to nurture that they do not simply look for heavenly compensation for earthly deprivation. Rather they expect matters to be rectified on earth in the millennium when the Lord returns. It is no accident that the saints under the altar in heaven in Rev. 6 are crying out "How long?" and are given robes while they continue to wait. They too have not reached the eschaton. But rectification comes not by a call to arms but rather by prayer for divine intervention. John's vision of how justice is finally done is theocratic, not bureaucratic, which is not surprising when addressing a tiny minority that one does not set forth a major social program of societal reform, especially when one believes that God in Christ will intervene both imminently and on the more distant horizon.

Another important sociological issue raised by these letters is that of social networks. These churches are in effect being encouraged to read each other's mail, even if it's embarrassing! The issue, however, is one of accountability. In an honor-and-shame culture such as John is addressing, being shamed or embarrassed in public was a severe remedy. By airing churches' dirty laundry, John is applying pressure to these churches, and in the rhetorical realm, effectively. These letters imply that there was a rather strong social network between the churches, such that John could count on this document being passed from one to another and another, and so on. Then, too, John's assuming authority over them strongly suggests that there was some sort of already extant common leadership structure. But what kind? There is no evidence of apostles, but there is evidence of prophets. It would seem to be then more of a pneumatic type of

---

[110] In sociological terms "high group" refers to the great degree of cohesiveness and unity a particular collection of people have.

leadership structure. To use technical language John is trying to inculcate a high group sense of identity without a high grid authority structure.[111] This is a tall order and may explain why John uses such strong rhetoric to communicate his point. Only ultimate sanctions bring home the point in an environment where there is inadequate spiritual leadership.

In his fine commentary on Revelation, Keener points out that the only two churches unequivocally commended were those of Smyrna and Philadelphia, that is, the churches that had or were experiencing suffering. "Suffering has a way of reminding us which things in life really matter, forcing us to depend radically on God, and thus purifying our obedience to God's will."[112] I can personally testify to the truth of this statement. Two years ago, in addition to my seminary teaching, I had taken on the pastoring of a small church that had some difficulties. Shortly after I began this pastoral work, I had to go into the hospital and have two feet of my colon removed. The recovery proved to be slower than I had hoped, and in the process I was unable to continue in my church. My seminary gave me leave in the fall to recover. I found myself not teaching or preaching for the first time in twenty years. While the physical suffering was not insignificant, the sudden loss of my vocation, albeit temporary, led to a serious depression. The suffering became emotional and spiritual as well as physical. It became a time of going back to basics and of realizing that the most central truth in my life was not my ministerial tasks but my relationship with my God. Like Elijah in 1 Kings 19, I had to listen to the still small voice. Having been depressed enough to die, God recommissioned me to return to the tasks at hand. Suffering does indeed make one see what is most important in life.

One of the major functions that Revelation can serve for the Christian community today is as a warning against too much assimilation into the dominant non-Christian culture. In this sense Revelation is certainly sectarian literature.

It speaks harshly to those so-called Christian prophets who eagerly advocate assimilation to an alien ethos as something compatible with Christian faith. It also speaks a word of warning to the unthinking mass of Christians who simply want to share in the economic fruits of Babylon's wealth and luxury and are quite willing to assimilate in order to reap the temporal benefits. Revelation addresses not so much those alienated from the larger society because they belong to the "have-nots" as it does those with upward social mobility who want to be totally immersed in the larger society and are consciously or unconsciously willing to lose their souls in order to do so.[113]

---

[111] A high group, high grid congregation would have a very clearly demarcated hierarchial leadership structure, an equally clear degree of cohesiveness within the group, and a clear sense of who they are. The leadership structure seems lacking in various of these churches, but very few of their problems seem to involve internal conflict or inside troublemakers, with the exception of Jezebel and Nicolaitans.

[112] C. Keener, *Revelation* (2002), p. 120.

[113] C. H. Talbert, *The Apocalypse: A Reading of the Revelation of John* (Louisville, Ky.: Westminster/J. Knox, 1994), p. 112.

If Talbert is correct in this assessment, then John's apocalypse is not like those seeming to reflect a social ethos where the audience is simply poor and lives on the margins of society.[114] Rather John writes to those who are being oppressed, but some of them are certainly not on the margins of society. Indeed some are in grave danger of entering into a societal pattern that involves the worship of the Emperor, among other idolatries.

Finally we should reflect on some of the wisdom Peterson shares with us about this section of Revelation.

The gospel is never for individuals but always for a people. Sin fragments us, separates us, and sentences us to solitary confinement. Gospel restores us, unites us, and sets us in community. The life of faith revealed and nurtured in the biblical narratives is highly personal but never merely individual: always there is a family, a tribe, a nation – church.... A believing community is the context for the life of faith.... Love cannot exist in isolation: away from others, love bloats into pride. Grace cannot be received privately: cut off from others it is perverted into greed. Hope cannot develop in solitude: separated from the community, it goes to seed in the form of fantasies.[115]

There are very few documents in the NT written to individuals. It is primarily the church as a corporate entity that is addressed. The book of Revelation is especially not intended for private devotion and private readings. Especially with an esoteric book like this, private readings are more likely to be wrong than right since few if any modern Christians live in the world of Jewish apocalyptic prophecy. Isolation from the socio-historical context in which this material was written has led to misuse of this book. It is also true that this book was not intended to be read by those with mere idle curiosity about the future. It was meant to be read in the context of Christian faith, and it was meant to be obeyed, not merely studied.

REVELATION 4–5 – THE THRONE ROOM VISION

NRSV Revelation 4.1 After this I looked and there in heaven a door stood open! And the first voice which I had heard speaking to me like a trumpet said "Come up here, and I will show you what must take place after this."
2 At once I was in the spirit, and there in heaven stood a throne, with one seated on the throne!
3 And the one seated there looks like jasper and carnelian, and around the throne is a rainbow that looks like an emerald.

---

[114] Contrast, e.g., what N. Cohn discovered about some medieval forms of millenarianism in his *The Pursuit of the Millennium* (London: Granada, 1970).
[115] E. Peterson, *Reversed Thunder* (1988), pp. 42–43.

4 Around the throne are twenty-four thrones, and seated on the thrones are twenty-four elders, dressed in white robes, with golden crowns on their heads.

5 Coming from the throne are flashes of lightning, and rumblings and peals of thunder, and in front of the throne burn seven flaming torches, which are the seven spirits of God;

6 and in front of the throne there is something like a sea of glass, like crystal. Around the throne, and on each side of the throne, are four living creatures, full of eyes in front and behind:

7 the first living creature like a lion, the second living creature like an ox, the third living creature with a face like a human face, and the fourth living creature like a flying eagle.

8 And the four living creatures, each of them with six wings, are full of eyes all around and inside. Day and night without ceasing they sing, "Holy, holy, holy, the Lord God the Almighty, who was and is and is to come."

9 And whenever the living creatures give glory and honor and thanks to the one who is seated on the throne, who lives forever and ever,

10 the twenty-four elders fall before the one who is seated on the throne and worship the one who lives forever and ever; they cast their crowns before the throne, singing,

11 "You are worthy, our Lord and God, to receive glory and honor and power, for you created all things, and by your will they existed and were created."

NRSV Revelation 5.1 Then I saw in the right hand of the one seated on the throne a scroll written on the inside and on the back, sealed with seven seals;

2 and I saw a mighty angel proclaiming with a loud voice, "Who is worthy to open the scroll and break its seals?"

3 And no one in heaven or on earth or under the earth was able to open the scroll or to look into it.

4 And I began to weep bitterly because no one was found worthy to open the scroll or to look into it.

5 Then one of the elders said to me, "Do not weep. See, the Lion of the tribe of Judah, the Root of David, has conquered, so that he can open the scroll and its seven seals." He had been slaughtered, having seven horns and seven eyes, which are the seven spirits of God sent out into all the earth.

6 Then I saw between the throne and the four living creatures and among the elders a Lamb standing as if it had been slaughtered, having seven horns and seven eyes, which are the seven spirits of God sent out into all the earth.

7 He went and took the scroll from the right hand of the one who was seated on the throne.

8 When he had taken the scroll, the four living creatures and the twenty-four elders fell before the Lamb, each holding a harp and golden bowls full of incense, which are the prayers of the saints.

9 They sing a new song: "You are worthy to take the scroll and to open its seals, for you were slaughtered and by your blood you ransomed for God saints from every tribe and language and people and nation;

10 you have made them to be a kingdom and priests serving our God, and they will reign on earth."

11 Then I looked, and I heard the voice of many angels surrounding the throne and the living creatures and the elders; they numbered myriads of myriads and thousands of thousands,

12 singing with full voice, "Worthy is the Lamb that was slaughtered to receive power and wealth and wisdom and might and honor and glory and blessing!"

13 Then I heard every creature in heaven and on earth and under the earth and in the sea, and all that is in them, singing, "To the one seated on the throne and to the Lamb be blessing and honor and glory and might forever and ever!"

14 And the four living creatures said, "Amen!" And the elders fell down and worshiped.

*I*f we were to characterize the rhetorical problem that helped engender the production of the book of Revelation,[116] it would be this: "To whom does the earth belong? Who is the ruler of this world? The book's central theological symbol is therefore the *throne*, signifying either divine and liberating or demonic and death-dealing power."[117] The rhetorical exigence to be overcome in this book involves power and justice and, more particularly, the lack thereof for pressured Christians in John's and his audience's world.

It is no accident that, after the epistolary opening salvo, John turns immediately to the vision of God and the Lamb as the rulers of all that would transpire in human history and as rulers of the cosmic realm. Also John's portrayal of the throne room scene owes something to both ANE throne room scenes but more pertinently to Roman scenes of the enthroned Emperor surrounded by his council and holding an open scroll in his hand. The hymns that emanate from the throne room in heaven can be seen in the light of hymnic acclamations and acts of bowing down before the Emperor not only in the Roman court but also in the imperial cult in Asia, where a statue of the Emperor might have obeisance done before it.[118] The scenes in Rev. 4–5 then become John's rhetorical means of offering an alternative vision of who is really in charge of the world in which

---

[116] This may be something different from what engendered the visions encoded in this book.

[117] E. Fiorenza, *Revelation* (1991), p. 120.

[118] See Ibid., p. 123. C. Koester, *Revelation and the End of All Things* (Grand Rapids, Mich.: Eerdmans, 2001), p. 75, summarizes it this way: "Public appearances of the emperor often featured him sitting on a throne and accompanied by a crowd of friends, advisors, and attendants. When the emperor traveled, communities would send representatives, sometimes dressed in white, to greet him and present him with golden crowns to show their recognition of his sovereignty. Those who approached the throne would prostrate themselves, sometimes even bowing down before the throne when the emperor is absent." But the applause that admirers of the human emperor offered was flattery, as were the acclamations that the Emperor was lord and god (cf. Tacitus, *Ann.* 14.15; Martial, *Epigrams* 5.8; 7.34; 10.72).

John's audience lives. But there is an epideictic quality to the throne room scenes in heaven, especially those of heavenly worship.

Epideictic rhetoric is commonly called the rhetoric of display, and its proper function is to amplify or embellish the main themes or subject matter. It focuses on lavish praise or blame. The throne room scenes comport with this approach in the lavish descriptions and effusive praise of God or the Lamb found in these sections in Revelation. Quintilian reminds us that this sort of rhetoric is directed to the praise of the gods (*Inst. Or.* 3.7.6).

In praising the gods our first step will be to express our veneration of the majesty of their nature in general terms. Next we shall proceed to praise the special power of the individual god and the discoveries by which he has helped the human race (3.7.7). . . . Next we must record their exploits as handed down from antiquity. Even gods may derive honor from their descent (3.7.8). . . . Some again may be praised because they were born immortal, others because they won immortality by their valour, a theme which the piety of our sovereign has made the glory even of these present times" (3.7.9).

This passage is interesting in several respects. "Our sovereign" refers to Domitian and that he deified his father, Vespasian, and his brother Titus. Since John is writing at almost exactly the same time that Quintilian is, we now must compare what the latter says to the two parallel descriptions found in Rev. 4–5.

There is a clear attempt at parallelism between Rev. 4 and Rev. 5, as Talbert has shown.

Rev. 4 (about God)	Rev. 5 (about the Lamb)
God's glory (4.2b–8a)	The Lamb's glory (5.5–7)
Worship of God (8b–11)	Worship of the Lamb (8–12)
First hymn (8b)	First hymn (9–10)
Narrative (9–10)	Narrative (11–12a)
Second hymn (11)	Second hymn (12b)[119]

The rhetoric of display is fully evident in Rev. 4 and 5, and the beginning of both chapters focuses on the majesty of God and of Christ. In the hymn of praise in Rev. 5 there is praise of Christ because of his death, by which he provided incredible benefit to all, but also by which, and the reason why, he came to be raised from the dead and exalted on high. There are then at least four elements in John's descriptions that suggest he knows the conventions about epideictic praise of a divine being. Start with their majesty, speak of their benefits on behalf of humankind, speak of their immortality or the means by which they won such immortality, and in all of this amplify their merits using lavish words of praise of various sorts. One of the major virtues regularly praised in epideictic oratory is justice, something God and Christ are being praised for in Revelation as a whole. Quintilian also reminds us that, if there is a hero figure, such as Christ,

---

[119] C. H. Talbert, *Apocalypse* (1994), pp. 26–27.

"what most pleases an audience is the celebration of deeds which our hero was the first or only man ... to perform.... emphasizing what was done for the sake of others rather than what he performed on his own behalf" (*Inst. Or.* 3.7.16). In both of the hymns in Rev. 5, at vs. 9 and at vs. 12, Christ is praised for his unique atoning sacrifice for the salvation of humankind. John is sensitive to how his audience would hear his words, living as they did in a rhetoric-saturated environment, and he has shaped his presentation accordingly.

Clearly Rev. 4 begins a new section in this book, with a time indicator ("after this I looked. . . ." See also the subdivisions that begin this way at 7.1; 18.1; 19.1). What John sees is a door opened in heaven, and a voice speaks to him that is identified as the first voice he originally heard speaking to him. This vision is then from the same source as the first one, namely Christ. That John must look through an open door in heaven suggests that he will see something in heaven about which an ordinary mortal would not know. Koester sees the visions in Rev. 4–5 as the heart of the book and stresses that before the visions of the seals comes the vision of worship, and it is worship of God that concludes the book. This means that part of the essential message of Revelation is that the one true God must and will someday be universally recognized properly, which is to say that God will one day be properly worshipped.[120]

The word heaven (singular) is the usual usage in this document by contrast with heavens, which is found in so much apocalyptic literature.[121] As G. B. Caird says the word used here (*ouranos*) could in some instances be translated sky, so it is difficult to know whether what is envisioned is an unearthly and nonmaterial scene in heaven or a vision of the sky.[122] Texts such as Rev. 4.6, 12.7, and 13.1 suggest to Caird that this cannot be heaven since symbols of evil are present. This, however, is to forget that in apocalyptic literature there is an open heaven from which evil things are certainly within God's purview and control. The point of mentioning evil in God's throne room is in order to insist on his sovereignty over it.[123] There is no absolute dualism in this book. God and his Son reign, and the major message of the throne room vision is that God is in his heaven and ruling, no matter what the earthly appearances of things may suggest. Beasley-Murray and others rightly see this vision as crucial and pivotal for all that follows in this book because it introduces the judgment oracles and visions.[124]

John is commanded in **4.1** to come up here, and he will be shown what must happen after this. The theme of determinism ("what must happen ...")

[120] C. Koester, *Revelation and the End* (2001), pp. 71–72.
[121] Rev. 12.12 is an exception to this, and it appears to be influenced by the OT text it echoes.
[122] G. B. Caird, *The Revelation of St. John the Divine* (New York: Harper, 1966), pp. 62–63.
[123] A minority view held by some scholars is that the reference to the sea here is a reference to Solomon's bronze sea, which was in his temple (see 1 Kings 7.23–44; 1 Chron. 18.8; 2 Chron. 4.2, 6). This suggestion does not adequately come to grips with Rev. 13.1, where the Beast arises out of the sea, or with 21.1. But cf. C. Keener, *Revelation* (2002), p. 173.
[124] G. R. Beasley-Murray, *Book of Revelation* (1978), pp. 108–11.

is a regular feature of apocalyptic literature, not surprisingly since its major message is often that God controls human history. The time reference in vs. 1 though is very vague, and it cannot be deduced whether John has the near or more distant future in view.[125] John's visions range over the past, present, and future, and here one may ask if John has in mind something that transpired just after Jesus' death and resurrection, which of course would be in John's past. One must not press the time references and sequences. The crucial issue is *what* has happened and will happen, not *when*. The point is that it will happen according to God's plan. What may be of more significance is that the verb referring to the door standing open is in the perfect tense, suggesting that it is permanently open, perhaps as a result of Jesus' death and resurrection. The church has permanent and open access to heaven and to their God.[126]

It is quite unwarranted to make out of this chapter a proof text for the rapture of the church since this text can be paralleled in other apocalyptic literature (and cf. 1 Kings 22.19). What is in view is not bodily transportation into heaven but an ecstatic state in which John received a vision.[127] It may be possible to learn something from this vision about how John views the nature of revelation and about how God uses the human imagination and familiar images in the mind of his human author to relate his message. Much of the imagery is a new version of Ezekiel's throne–chariot vision (see Ezek. 1), but a careful comparison will show how flexible the images are. For example, in Rev. 4, we don't have multiple eyes within wheels but rather living creatures that surround or uphold the throne. This means we are to take this not as a picture of what heaven looks like but as a vivid description of God's character and influence. The images cannot and were not meant to be pressed to yield information on the inhabitants or nature of heaven. For example, it is possible to take the four living creatures as representative symbols indicating that God rules and is served by all sorts of living creatures.[128] We are dealing here with highly metaphorical speech meant to convey a heavenly message by vivid images. Notice that, unlike the case with Ezekiel, John does not try to describe God at all or what form he may have taken. This is not an exercise in satisfying overly curious piety. Notice too how often in this section John uses the term *homoious*. He keeps saying, "it was like." He is grasping for images that may approximate an experience that was so much greater than any combination of images he could assemble.

---

[125] It is perhaps apt to remember the famous aphorism of Niels Bohr: "Prediction is always difficult; especially of the future."

[126] See P. Barnett, *Apocalypse Now and Then: Reading Revelation Today* (Sydney: Aquila Press, 1989), p. 67.

[127] Another difference from other apocalyptic literature like 1 Enoch is that John is not really given a guided tour of heaven; he simply sees things in heaven from his own locale.

[128] Commentators have often puzzled over why it is said that the creatures are in the midst of the throne. R. G. Hall, "Living Creatures in the Midst of the Throne: Another Look at Rev. 4.6," *NTS* 36 (1990), pp. 609–13 has suggested they are part of the furniture so to speak; they are components of the throne.

A multicolored, stone-inlaid throne is envisioned around which are twenty-four thrones, belonging to the twenty-four elders. There is much debate as to what these represent and why the number is twenty-four. The elders could be any of the following: (1) angelic figures, possibly God's heavenly retinue or council; (2) the saints in heaven; (3) the twelve apostles and the twelve patriarchs (cf. 21.12 ff.); (4) angelic representatives/spirits of the church in heaven; (5) the people of God both Jew and Gentile (hence twice twelve); the image then represents the whole church;[129] (6) twenty-four represents the hours in the day, that is, God is offered round-the-clock praise.[130] Whatever the twenty-four are, their function in the drama is secondary, for all they do in this book is fall down and worship God or play a harp and so are contributors to heavenly worship (cf. 5.8, 14; 11.16; 19.4 cf. 5.5; 7.13 where an elder is an interpreter). One thing is certain: there is no known parallel to these twenty-four elders in other Jewish apocalyptic literature, so this is a new and perhaps important element in John's vision.

In an important article L. Hurtado points out that these elders are always distinguished from the angels, though they have similar privileges and functions to the angels in heaven (cf. 5.11; 7.11). They announce the appearance of the Lamb at 5.5, they identify the elect at 7.13–17, and they strike up the chorus when God's action for the elect is mentioned in 11.15–29. They cast their thrones before God at 4.10. All of this suggests that these elders represent human beings, whether we are to see them as saints in heaven or simply as representative symbols of the elect or people of God. If the number twenty-four does not come from the apostles plus the patriarchs, then 1 Chron. 24.4–6, which speaks of twenty-four courses of priests and Levites, is worth a mention. Notice the elders are wearing white and help lead worship. Hurtado calls them heavenly archetypes of what we are supposed to do and be on earth – priests and kings (noting the crowns) who lead God's people to worship the one on the throne. That these are symbols of the Christian elect is shown by their reaction when God acts on behalf of earthly Christians.[131]

Vs. 5 describes a theophany not unlike what Exodus says happened on Sinai. The burning lamps before the throne are said to be the seven spirits, again the angelic representatives of the churches keeping the churches' fires burning, in part by returning and being in the presence of God. Then, there is something that looks like a sea of glass or, better said, clear crystal. In view of 13.1, where the sea monster rises out of the glass sea, it is probably a reference to the reality of evil symbolized by the ancient image of the chaos waters. Even the source of evil is not outside the control of God.

---

[129] See H. B. Swete, *Commentary on Revelation* (Grand Rapids, Mich.: Kregel, 1977), p. 69.

[130] J. Roloff, *The Revelation of John: A Continental Commentary* (Minneapolis: Fortress, 1993), p. 69.

[131] L. Hurtado, "Revelation 4–5 in the Light of Jewish Apocalyptic Analogies," *JSNT* 25 (1985), pp. 105–24.

At **vs. 6b** we hear of four living creatures with eyes before and behind, and these creatures are said to be in the middle of and around the throne. The first is to be like (*homoin*) a lion, the second like a calf, the third having a face like a human being, and the fourth flying like an eagle, but all the creatures have six wings and eyes inside and out. The similarity of this vision to the throne–chariot vision in Ezek. 1 is obvious, but do the figures symbolize the same thing? Isa. 6 also provides John with some of this imagery. Some have conjectured that the four creatures represent the four signs of the zodiac, but if so it is impossible to say why the eagle has replaced the sign for Aquarius. Beasley-Murray quotes a late rabbinic saying, "The mightiest of birds is the eagle, the mightiest among the domestic animals the ox, the mightiest among wild animals is the lion, and the mightiest of all these is a human being. God has taken all these and secured them to his throne."[132] The point would be not only that God controls all these creatures but that they were all made for his ceaseless praise and support. They were, so to speak, meant to lift up the one who is on the throne. The throne is the central image in this vision because it symbolizes God's rule and control. Furthermore, "The praise of God as creator is not an incidental doctrine that John happens to include only in passing. God's creative activity is at the heart of God's sovereignty. God is sovereign over the world because this is *God's* world."[133]

We cannot equate these creatures with the four Gospels. They probably should rather be seen as heavenly archetypes of the whole of the animate creation. Their function is unceasing praise, day and night. The praise is the same as we hear in Isa. 6 except that we have the now-familiar line about who was, is, and is to come. To him they give glory, honor, and thanksgiving. Likewise, the elders fall down and worship. Especially pertinent to the audience is that the one sitting on the throne is called our Lord and God. Domitian not only accepted this title, he may have introduced it into the cult of emperor worship (cf. Suetonius, *Dom.* 13.2; Dio Cassius, *His. Rom.* 67.4.7).[134] But here believers are told those words should be applied only to the living one – the true God. He is worthy of all praise because he created all things. The phrase *dia to thelema* could mean "because of thy will" and could imply either the operating cause or the intention of creation. R. H. Charles may be right that here is being countered the idea that the world was created for human beings.[135] Rather it was created by and for God. It is a useful observation that the function of the heavenly hymns is to provide the divine commentary or perspective on the events in the book.[136] This chapter

---

[132] G. R. Beasley-Murray, *Book of Revelation* (1978), p. 117.

[133] M. G. Reddish, *Revelation* (Macon, Ga.: Smyth and Helwys, 2001), p. 101.

[134] See the discussion on pp. 5–8.

[135] C. H. Charles, *Revelation* (2000), vol. 1, p. 134.

[136] See C. Keener, *Revelation* (2002), p. 171, who suggests it functions rather like the chorus in a Greek play.

is a vision in praise of the Creator God. The next is a vision in praise of the Redeemer God.

Rev. 5 is about God's work not in creation but rather in redemption. It starts by talking about a book or a scroll, one written on both the front and the back.[137] The terminology may suggest *Biblion* should be translated scroll here. Possibly lying in the background is Ezek. 2.9. If so, we should see what is on the scroll as a group of sealed-up prophecies, a hidden revelation that no human being has the power to unveil. The inability of all parties, except the Lamb, to open it indicates a special revelation that only one can give and interpret. Nevertheless some have insisted that rather than prophecies what is in view is some sort of legal document or covenant treaty sealed with seven seals for protection.

A CLOSER LOOK — ON ANCIENT SCROLLS

It was the normal practice in antiquity to write only on one side of a papyrus roll, the front or recto side, which had the fibers aligned horizontally, which made for easier writing. The back or verso side would only be used if one ran out of space. The point in the case of John's scroll is that it is very full. Once the scroll was inscribed, it would be rolled up and usually tied with one or more pieces of thread.

If the document was a legal document, it would normally be sealed with hot wax on top of the threads, then seals, usually from signet rings of the official witnesses, would be used. The seals were not merely to indicate whom the document was from but to reserve the contents of the scroll for its proper recipient. It also made clear that the content was valid, important, and official. If the seals were broken, it would be evident that someone unauthorized tried to read the document. In some apocalyptic texts such tampering led to angels being sent forth to execute judgments (3 En. 32.1). There is precedent in Isa. 29.11 for a sealed book of judgments. The difficulty is that Rev. 6.1–17 has sometimes been read to associate the judgments with the witnesses rather than with the contents of the book. But the four living creatures are not per se witnesses, so it seems more likely that judgments are indeed the contents of this scroll.[138] The primary background for what John is going to say about the scroll is surely Ezek. 2.10, a scroll containing judgments.

❧

Against the idea that John has in mind a covenant document is the content of what follows, which reads not like a covenant document or treaty but like a series

---

[137] There are minor textual variants here: "on the inside and on the back" or the corrected "on the front and on the back."

[138] On all this, see C. Keener, *Revelation* (2002), pp. 184–85.

of judgment oracles. It is true that in Egypt a treaty might be sealed with seven seals and that it was written in part in more than one place. But here it is likely that the number seven is used because it suggests perfection or completion. Also intriguing is the suggestion that this is something of a testament, a last will and testament to be exact, that the reader is not only to read but to execute. In this case only the Lamb can read it because it is his will, for he died. In the OT and elsewhere there is also the notion of a book of oracles about the future course of history (Cf. Ps. 139.16; 1 En. 47.3, 81.1–2, 106.19, 107.1). That there are seven seals simply indicates the importance of this revelation and the need to keep it hidden until the appropriate time.

This is certainly a very strange scroll for each seal seals only a part of the revelation. A strong angel proclaims in a loud voice, "Who is worthy to open the scroll?" No creature on earth was worthy, and so John weeps. Some have suggested this is the angel Gabriel, but if it was important to know the name, John would likely have told us. Caird is right that in some cases the oracles are *descriptive* but in some cases they are *directive*.[139] It would be a mistake to see nothing here but future prophecies since, for instance, when the fifth seal is broken reference is made to a past as well as to a future martyrdom. In these oracles God's plan of redemptive-judgment spanning human history is revealed and involves not only the future but also the past and the present. Thus care must be taken when one reads each oracle, to bear in mind that it is what happens and not when it happens that is crucial. Timing is not what is most important to John.

John is consoled by one of the elders (a further clue that the elders are representatives of humankind) for there is one who is worthy to open the scroll and look inside – the Lion of the tribe of Judah who is also called the Root of David. Yet in **vs. 6** when John looks, he sees not a lion but a lamb, the slain Lamb of God. Caird is likely wrong to suggest that the lion image is replaced by the lamb image for both are appropriate in the text that follows, which speaks of both judgment and redemption, both justice and mercy, both punitive action and sacrifice by the one reading the scroll.[140] Caird is right, however, that God achieves his purpose of overthrowing the powers of evil through the slain lamb and his death on the cross. "Jesus conquered not by force but by death, not by violence but by marytrdom. The Lion is a Lamb!"[141]

Standing, not sitting, right in the middle of the throne and of the four creatures and twenty-four elders is a Lamb, seemingly slain. And it had seven horns, symbols of strength, and seven eyes, symbols of omniscience. This last feature has suggested to various commentators that the proper translation of *arnion* here should be ram (see, e.g., 1 En. 90.9, 38; Dan. 8.3). In fact *arnion* is a diminutive

[139] G. B. Caird, *Revelation* (1998), pp. 72–73.
[140] Ibid., pp. 73–75.
[141] C. Keener, *Revelation* (2002), p. 186.

of *arne* (sheep) and so literally means little sheep. Though rams were used in OT sacrifices, normally lambs were offered, and lambs were eaten as part of the Passover sacrifice. The term chosen, coupled with the emphasis on this being the *slain* lamb, favors the translation lamb rather than ram.[142] But this lamb had horns, and so we have a fusion of sacrificial lamb and ram features, conveying a deliberate paradox. The lamb is vulnerable and is slain, but the lamb is strong like a ram as well. A. Boesak makes the additional good point that the slain lamb is standing, whereas we might have expected it to be a limp corpse lying on an altar. The enemy may have thought they conquered it, but they did not. It overcame death though bears scars. This is at the heart of John's message of hope to his congregations facing and no doubt fearing persecution and even execution.

The angels/spirits of the churches are the eyes of the Lamb in the churches and in all the earth. Just as God was worshiped in the previous chapter, here the Lamb is worshiped for he is worthy to take the scroll and read it. The implication is clear that the Lamb is divine. The elders (and the creatures?) are each said to have harps and bowls full of incense. The former are used to sing the Lamb's praises, while the latter represent the prayers of the "holy ones." This is probably a reference not to angels but rather to human saints. If the elders are the heavenly representatives or archetypes of God's people, then it is appropriate that they convey the church militant's prayers to the Lamb. These elders are singing a new tune, for no one has been worthy or able to open the scroll and unseal its seals. There has been a pattern to the praise in Rev. 4–5. The first two hymns in Rev. 4 are to the Creator, the next two to the Redeemer, and the last one to both God and the Lamb.[143]

At **vs. 9b** we find a doctrine of the atonement reflected. The Lamb is worthy because he was slain and bought for God by his blood – some from every tribe and tongue and people and nation. Furthermore all of these are made and meant to be kings and priests and are told they will reign upon the earth. This repeats what was earlier said about priests and kings except the new motif about reigning on earth. But when is this reign to happen? One could argue it will transpire in the millennium, but only the martyrs are said in Rev. 20 to reign. It is equally unlikely to mean a present spiritual reign with Christ.[144] Nor can it be a future reign in heaven, since the venue is said to be *on earth*. It seems then that the believer will reign with Christ in the new heaven and the new earth. The Lamb has paid the price of redemption for believers by his death and has created a worldwide people of God, not just a people from one tribe or nation. One of the resulting benefits is that we too shall one day reign. It was good news to the oppressed and persecuted Christians to know the wrongs would one day

[142] But see the discussion by D. E. Aune, *Revelation 1–5* (1997), pp. 323, 368–69.
[143] See E. Peterson, *Reversed Thunder* (1988), pp. 66–67.
[144] See R. H. Mounce, *Book of Revelation* (1977), pp. 136–37.

be righted. Caird is right to stress that the events that are about to be recounted in fact hinge on past historical events – the death and resurrection of the one called the Lamb.[145]

Thus unlike some apocalyptic visions this one has an earthly foundation and in the end involves more than just judgment upon or elimination of the earth. There is a sense that believers are already kings and priests, but it is not said that they already reign or will immediately in this life. Beasley-Murray stresses the Exodus imagery here and that Christ is seen as the Passover Lamb.[146] We seem to have in this chapter a throne room vision that parallels the stages of a coronation ceremony in antiquity – there is the announcement, the exaltation, and the enthronement of the king. At the end of this chapter the Lamb is apparently seated on the throne. The elders and the living creatures lead the heavenly praise, and suddenly their number is said to be myriad. They recognize that because of what he has done on earth he is worthy to receive power and wealth, wisdom, strength, honor and glory, and praise. At vs. 13 ff. we have the earthly counterpart of these heavenly elders and creatures likewise echoing the acclamation. Indeed all of creation, not just believers, give praise and honor to the Lamb sitting upon the throne. At the conclusion of this scene the living creatures pronounce the Amen, the "so be it" to this act of worship, and the elders fall and worship again. "The song of praise to the Lamb shows that from John's perspective Christ's position does not reflect the deification of human power and practices."[147] To the contrary, the Lamb is a divine as well as human being. All is now in readiness for the reading of the contents of the scroll.

BRIDGING THE HORIZONS

In the wake of the enormously popular Left Behind series of Christian novels (with untold millions of copies sold worldwide), written by Timothy LaHaye and others, Rev. 4 has become an important text again. In some conservative circles a pretribulation rapture that exempts the church from going through the final suffering in human history is assumed to lead up to the return of Christ and the final judgment and redemption.

These issues are complex, but the following needs to be stressed. Rev. 4 is not about bodily transport into heaven. It is about a visionary or ecstatic experience in which John sees things in heaven, and the way it is described is characteristic of many such apocalyptic texts. Furthermore Rev. 4 is about an experience John the individual seer has, not the church collectively. Keener is quite right to point out that the language used in Rev. 4.1 is not different from what we find in

---

[145] G. B. Caird, *Revelation* (1998), pp. 72–73.
[146] G. R. Beasley-Murray, *Book of Revelation* (1978), pp. 127–28.
[147] C. Koester, *Revelation and the End* (2001), p. 79.

Rev. 17.1 or 21.9. Those texts are not seen in the same light by dispensationalists because of where they occur in Revelation and because they would mess up things if there were several raptures of the same person.[148] Keener points out that the phrase "after these things" cannot be pressed chronologically for it refers sometimes to events that follow the time the phrase is uttered (Rev. 9.12; 20.3) but sometimes to revelations that follow chronologically earlier revelations (7.9; 15.5; 18.1; 19.1).[149]

It is also a misinterpretation to read the reference to the seven lampstands before the throne as a reference to the raptured church (it refers to the churches' angels in the presence of God). The churches are all still on earth suffering through what is described in Rev. 4–20, and this is one reason John must write his audience to encourage them to go forward and be prepared for possible martyrdom. Furthermore we are not told that the saints in heaven got there by means of rapture. Indeed the suggestion is that they got there by death, in particular by martyrdom. "The pastoral purpose [of Rev. 4–5] is to assure suffering Christians that God and Jesus are sovereign and that the events that the Christians are facing are part of a sovereign plan that will culminate in their redemption and the vindication of their faith through the punishment of their persecutors."[150]

Unlike modern Americans, John's audience regularly had occasion to see the pageantry of royal events involving rulers, thrones, processions, festivals, and the like. But John's audience knew, because of the imperial cult in their area, that the Emperor was demanding divine worship while he was still living. It is quite possible, as Keener suggests, that one of the functions of Rev. 4–5 is to make the following clear: before John's portrait of the most majestic throne room of all, "... the emperor's claims fade into absurdity, and worshipping Christians find the strength to withstand the falsehood of the emperor's claims."[151] True Christian worship clarifies where our ultimate loyalties are and should be. Worship reminds us that we do not owe our ultimate loyalties to ourselves, our colleges, our sports teams, our nation, our human rulers or even to the human race in general, but rather to God in Christ.

These scenes of worship in Revelation, which are not interludes, remind us too that worship is to be God directed. A worship service should not be so taken up with humanly directed events that the focus on God is lost. Several of the problems encountered in contemporary worship could be remedied if one actually studied and patterned worship on the model in Revelation. For example, in Revelation John is rebuked when he falls down and does obeisance before the interpreting angel, yet in worship now we allow applause for those

---

[148] C. Keener, *Revelation* (2002), p. 177.
[149] Ibid., p. 178.
[150] G. K. Beale, *Revelation* (1999), p. 311.
[151] C. Keener, *Revelation* (2002), p. 180.

on the podium, as if the musicians were performing for the congregation's entertainment rather than for God. This is misdirected praise when we are in the midst of worshiping God and not ourselves and our own talents. We can also learn from Revelation that true worship inculcates a sense of awe and wonder in the worshiper, that is, a sense of both distance from and proximity to God. Worship should make clear we are not God in our own world. The Creator–creature distinction so vividly presented in Rev. 4 must be affirmed. But worship also makes clear that God has drawn near, that Christ is walking in the midst of the churches, but at his own gracious initiative, not because we feel we can relate to God as our chum or buddy in an overly familiar way. That tension between difference/distance and proximity without irreverence is inculcated in Revelation.

There is also the matter of the function of God's word in worship. There is far too much feelings- or needs-based preaching in the modern church that encourages people to focus more on themselves and their own problems rather than on God. But, in fact, God is the ultimate source of their help, though some self-help programs can be a means God uses. In the "preaching" in Rev. 2–3 to the churches, we see offered some stern critiques as well as some true solace and comfort. John is prepared both to comfort the afflicted and to afflict the comfortable and complacent. Good preaching should draw on the Word as its primary source (not on human need, experience, tradition, or rational considerations) and should be prepared to apply that Word vigorously to the congregation, even if it hurts. Perhaps the best compliment I ever got after preaching came from a small woman in one of my churches: "You really stepped on my toes today, Pastor. Thanks, I really needed that."

Some Christians, indeed some ministers, have a real difficulty with the concept of God's judgment. Perhaps they don't understand that God's love is a holy love, or their passion for justice does not match their compassion and desire for mercy. Whatever the cause of this attitude, it fails to do justice to what Revelation is teaching us. Keener suggests that "if we feel uncomfortable with the idea of judgment, perhaps it is because we have become more comfortable with the world than with suffering among Jesus' witnesses."[152] I am afraid this is all too true for most Western Christians.

For John the central event in human history is the death and resurrection of Jesus, and because Christ has gone through these events, he alone is worthy to unseal the seals on the document of judgment. In other words, he who endured grave injustice is alone the one who can unleash appropriately God's judgment on a sinful world. But several crucial aspects about these judgments need to be kept in mind as we explore Rev. 6–20. (1) These temporal judgments are not the final judgment, and part of their function is indeed to call people to

---

[152] Ibid., p. 193.

repent. (2) The focus here is on vindication of God's people, not vengeance on the wicked. (3) The concept of redemptive-judgment is important. Unless the oppressor is made to cease oppressing, the oppressed never get deliverance. Boesak understands and speaks profoundly of this in his work on Revelation, written while he was in the throes of combating apartheid.[153] We will have occasion to interact with what he says later in this study. Here I quote Bauckham as we prepare to consider Rev. 6 and following: "In the subsequent account of the fall of Babylon, the parousia and the battle of Armageddon (chapters 18–19) there is never any suggestion that those who suffer final judgment finally acklowledge God's rule in enforced worship. Revelation seems to offer only two possibilities for the nations: repentance, fear of God, genuine worship of God (11.13; 14.6; 15.4) or persistence in worshipping the Beast, refusal to repent, refusal to worship, cursing God, final opposition to God's rule, leading to final judgment (14.9–11; 16.9, 11, 21; 17.14; 19.17–21)."[154] Bauckham goes on to stress that the reaction to the judgments recorded in Rev. 6 ff. in some cases is repentance by nations (11.13; 15.4) and in some cases not (16.13–16; 17.14; 19.19). Temporal judgments soften the hearts of some and harden the hearts of others. It is also pertinent that before the seventh in each series of judgments is unleashed there is a pause in heaven to listen to prayers, and these may well be prayers of repentance by those now ready to acknowledge God. The book of Revelation gives us a picture not of a vengeful or vindictive God but of a God who through acts of redemptive-judgment calls all to repent, even though in the end some will refuse to do so and will face final judgment. It is the wisdom of John of Patmos that, for justice to be truly done, it must be seen to be done in or at the end of human history. Boesak thus correctly judges that Revelation is not an example of "comfort through escapism"[155] because it is precisely through and in history that God renders justice. Because Revelation's language is referential, it has much to tell us about the God of justice and how he operates in space and time. "[A]pocalyptic literature's primary concern is precisely the situation in which God's people find themselves in this world, a situation that is caused by political, social, and economic forces which are identified, challenged, and called to account in a unique way in this type of literature."[156]

How Christian is the book of Revelation? Is it basically a Jewish apocalypse only slightly modified in a Christological way? The answer to these questions must be no, not merely because this is not a pseudonymous work nor does it involve *ex eventu* prophecy. No, the Christology and soteriology of this book comports quite well with other portions of the NT, especially the Pauline

---

[153] See A. Boesak, *Comfort and Protest* (1986).
[154] R. Bauckham, *Climax of Prophecy* (1993), pp. 307–8.
[155] A. Boesak, *Comfort and Protest* (1986), p. 17.
[156] Ibid., p. 18.

portions. For example, P. Barnett has compared the following Christological motifs in Revelation and in Paul:

Rev. 2.18	the Son of God	cf. Rom. 1.3, 4
Rev. 5.5	the Root of David	cf. Rom. 1.3
Rev. 1.5	who loved us . . .	cf. Gal. 2.20
	And freed us from sin	
Rev. 1.5	first born from the dead	1 Cor. 15.4
Rev. 12.5	caught up to God	Acts 1.2
Rev. 1.5	the ruler of the kings of the earth	1 Cor. 15.25
Rev. 1.7	he is coming with the clouds	1 Thess. 3.17.[157]

Furthermore, like Paul, John believes that Christ's death is the fulcrum and turning point in human history and in particular in the battle between good and evil. Thus, for example, Barnett points to Rev. 5.5. The Lion of the tribe of Judah has already triumphed, has already conquered (the aorist tense of the verb *nikan*). Even more striking is that John insists that the basis of Jesus' Lordship over all things is not his divine status but rather his redemptive death and resurrection (cf. Rom. 1). "The crowning paradox of the gospel is that Jesus is the Lion of Judah, the Christ authorised to exercise his Father's dominion over history, precisely because he is the Lamb who is slain."[158]

When one couples this with the obvious connections with the Pauline epistolary form in Rev. 2–3, and that in both sources very little is said about the historical Jesus' ministry or life prior to his death, one begins to believe that John during his time in Ephesus and elsewhere in Asia had absorbed a good deal of the Pauline Gospel. No, the book of Revelation has as its main actor and central character Christ. John's Christological material is no mere appendage to a Jewish apocalypse. His Christological vision has transformed the whole way he approaches this genre of material as well as the way he views future history and its consummation.

REVELATION 6.1–8.5 – THE SEVEN SEALS

NRSV Revelation 6.1 Then I saw the Lamb open one of the seven seals, and I heard one of the four living creatures call out, as with a voice of thunder, "Come!"
2 I looked, and there was a white horse! Its rider had a bow; a crown was given to him, and he came out conquering and to conquer.
3 When he opened the second seal, I heard the second living creature call out, "Come!"

[157] P. Barnett, *Apocalypse Now and Then* (1989), p. 18.
[158] Ibid., p. 17.

4 And out came another horse, bright red; its rider was permitted to take peace from the earth, so that people would slaughter one another; and he was given a great sword.

5 When he opened the third seal, I heard the third living creature call out, "Come!" I looked, and there was a black horse! Its rider held a pair of scales in his hand,

6 and I heard what seemed to be a voice in the midst of the four living creatures saying, "A quart of wheat for a day's pay, and three quarts of barley for a day's pay, but do not damage the olive oil and the wine!"

7 When he opened the fourth seal, I heard the voice of the fourth living creature call out, "Come!"

8 I looked and there was a pale green horse! Its rider's name was Death, and Hades followed with him; they were given authority over a fourth of the earth, to kill with sword, famine, and pestilence, and by the wild animals of the earth.

9 When he opened the fifth seal, I saw under the altar the souls of those who had been slaughtered for the Word of God and for the testimony they had given;

10 they cried out with a loud voice, "Sovereign Lord, holy and true, how long will it be before you judge and avenge our blood on the inhabitants of the earth?"

11 They were each given a white robe and told to rest a little longer, until the number would be complete both of their fellow servants and of their brothers and sisters, who were soon to be killed as they themselves had been killed.

12 When he opened the sixth seal, I looked, and there came a great earthquake; the sun became black as sackcloth, the full moon became like blood,

13 and the stars of the sky fell to the earth as the fig tree drops its winter fruit when shaken by a gale.

14 The sky vanished like a scroll rolling itself up, and every mountain and island was removed from its place.

15 Then the kings of the earth and the magnates and the generals and the rich and the powerful, and everyone, slave and free, hid in the caves and among the rocks of the mountains,

16 calling to the mountains and rocks, "Fall on us and hide us from the face of the one seated on the throne and from the wrath of the Lamb";

NRSV Revelation 7.1 After this I saw four angels standing at the four corners of the earth, holding back the four winds of the earth so that no wind could blow on earth or sea or against any tree.

2 I saw another angel ascending from the rising of the sun, having the seal of the living God, and he called with a loud voice to the four angels who had been given power to damage earth and sea,

3 saying, "Do not damage the earth or the sea or the trees, until we have marked the servants of our God with a seal on their foreheads."

4 And I heard the number of those who were sealed, one hundred forty-four thousand, sealed out of every tribe of the people of Israel:

5 From the tribe of Judah twelve thousand sealed, from the tribe of Reuben twelve thousand, from the tribe of Gad twelve thousand,

6 from the tribe of Asher twelve thousand, from the tribe of Naphtali twelve thousand, from the tribe of Manasseh twelve thousand,

7 from the tribe of Simeon twelve thousand, from the tribe of Levi twelve thousand, from the tribe of Issachar twelve thousand,

8 from the tribe of Zebulun twelve thousand, from the tribe of Joseph twelve thousand, from the tribe of Benjamin twelve thousand sealed.

9 After this I looked, and there was a great multitude that no one could count, from every nation, from all tribes and peoples and languages, standing before the throne and before the Lamb, robed in white, with palm branches in their hands.

10 They cried out in a loud voice, saying, "Salvation belongs to our God who is seated on the throne, and to the Lamb!"

11 And all the angels stood around the throne and around the elders and the four living creatures, and they fell on their faces before the throne and worshiped God,

12 singing, "Amen! Blessing and glory and wisdom and thanksgiving and honor and power and might be to our God forever and ever! Amen."

13 Then one of the elders addressed me, saying, "Who are these, robed in white, and where have they come from?"

14 I said to him, "Sir, you are the one that knows." Then he said to me, "These are they who have come out of the great ordeal; they have washed their robes and made them white in the blood of the Lamb.

15 For this reason they are before the throne of God, and worship him day and night within his temple, and the one who is seated on the throne will shelter them.

16 They will hunger no more, and thirst no more; the sun will not strike them, nor any scorching heat;

17 for the Lamb at the center of the throne will be their shepherd, and he will guide them to springs of the water of life, and God will wipe away every tear from their eyes."

NRSV Revelation 8.1 When the Lamb opened the seventh seal, there was silence in heaven for about half an hour.

2 And I saw the seven angels who stand before God, and seven trumpets were given to them.

3 Another angel with a golden censer came and stood at the altar; he was given a great quantity of incense to offer with the prayers of all the saints on the golden altar that is before the throne.

4 And the smoke of the incense, with the prayers of the saints, rose before God from the hand of the angel.

5 Then the angel took the censer and filled it with fire from the altar and threw it on the earth; and there were peals of thunder, rumblings, flashes of lightning, and an earthquake.

*R*ev. 4–5 and the visions therein have prepared the way and set the stage for the Lamb to open the seven seals. Indeed Rev. 4–5 have prepared the way for the threefold set of seven judgments in Rev. 6–16. Following these sets of sevens, we also have several unnumbered judgments. Caird makes a helpful analogy between our material and a tour guide explaining a painting. The unnumbered judgments may be likened to close-up examinations of particular facets of what is to follow, while the three sets of sevens present the broad overall framework and picture.[159] Caird argues a version of the recapitulation theory, which suggests that we do not have three sets of seven judgments presented sequentially (for a total of twenty-one judgments presented in chronological order), but all three series present the entire process of judgment leading up to and culminating in the end of human history. However, each succeeding set of seven presents a more intensified or wide-angle version of these judgments. The seven trumpets present a more developed and intensifed version of the seven seals, and similarly the seven bowls present a more intensified version of the seven trumpets. It is as if the author first saw a fourth of the world affected and then looked again and saw a third of the world affected; the final look showed the full picture of how the whole world was affected. As with a camera with a wide and wider angle and higher powered lens, things come increasingly into focus.

As helpful as this analysis is, it is not entirely correct. One could say these sets of sevens overlap, with the second set beginning before the end of the first and then carrying things further, and the third picking up in the midst of the second set and carrying things even further. Bauckham has pointed out that all three sets of sevens conclude with the same final judgment reached in the seventh of each of the three series. This is demonstrated by the repeated use of the terms thunder, lightning, earthquake, and heavy hail in varying order at 4.5, 8.5, 11.19, and 16.18–21. This phrase is an echo of Exod. 19.16. "The seven seal-openings are linked to the seven trumpets by the technique of overlapping or interweaving."[160] But the whole sequence of bowls is a development of the seventh trumpet, and the three woes are identical with the judgments inaugurated by the last three trumpets. In other words there is recapitulation to a degree, but there is also interweaving and development in these sets of sevens as well. With the bowls being a development of the seventh trumpet, one wonders if the trumpets are

---

[159] See his influential series of articles "On Deciphering the Book of Revelation, *ExpT* 74 (1962–63), pp. 13–15, 51–53, 82–84, 103–5.

[160] R. Bauckham, *Climax of Prophecy* (1993), pp. 8–9.

not also a development of a closer look at the seventh seal. Whatever is the case, the three sets of sevens end at the same place – the culmination of history. One further structural observation of Bauckham needs to be reiterated: "all parts of Chapters 6–11 [are linked] into the vision of heaven in chapter 4–5. The two series of sevens – the seal-openings and the trumpets – develop sequentially out of the vision of the Lamb and the scroll in chapter 5.... [and] both series at their climactic conclusions (8.5; 11.19) are linked back to the vision of the divine throne in chapter 4 (4.5)."[161]

In terms of rhetoric, several things can be said. First, John is following the rhetorical conventions in regard to recapitulation or repetition. Rhetorica ad *Herrennium* 4.42.54 is quite specific: "We do not repeat the same thing precisely – for that to be sure, would weary the hearer and not elaborate the idea – but with changes." As Talbert points out, recapitulation is an especially popular rhetorical technique when one is arguing by means of narrative.[162] Second, the rhetoric of this section is that of justice, or forensic rhetoric. It is, therefore, all about judgments, witnesses, legal documents, and the like. It is about crime and punishment, or misbehavior and threats/warnings. There are a whole series of judgments that happen *prior* to what amounts to final judgment. This suggests that these preliminary temporal judgments should not be seen as purely puni-tive. Rather they are calls to repentance and opportunities for amendment of life. There is a clear use of the rhetorical interlocking structural technique.[163] So, for instance, the trumpet judgments are actually introduced at Rev. 8.2, but they are not recounted until 8.6 ff. after the conclusion of the first set of sevens. This is meant to suggest that the seven trumpets are somehow included in the judgments unleashed when the seventh seal is opened.[164]

The structure of these multiple sets of sevens material is, to say the least, intricate. It even involves what appear to be straightforward repetitions (e.g., the persecution in 13.7–8 does not appear to be different from that in 11.7–10). The unity of this book is literary and artistic, not arithmetic and chronological. Caird is likely right that the unnumbered visions/judgments are probably close-ups of

---

[161] Ibid., p. 14.
[162] C. H. Talbert, *Apocalypse* (1994), p. 7.
[163] On which see pp. 17–18 for the comments of B. Longenecker.
[164] One could argue that we are dealing with deliberative rhetoric here, but there are problems with that, not the least of which is that there is not usually any *narratio* in a deliberative piece, for as Aristotle says in *Rhetoric* 3.16.11, who can narrate the future? Actually the prophet can and does attempt to do that. But how then can this be forensic rhetoric if John is mainly speaking about the future, not the past? This overlooks John's belief in a divine plan for the future that God has already set in motion. The prophet in effect looks at history from the end of the process or from the heavenly perspective that sees the whole. It is as if his churches are already before the divine tribunal. Thus John speaks of the events that will "definitely soon take place" as if that were a certainty, as if they had already transpired. This is why he is able to use the conventions of forensic rhetoric in these portions of Revelation.

particular spots on the larger picture describing the time frame of the three sets of judgments. Almost all the imagery used in the three sets of sevens is traditional, though the way John has modified and used it is original. Nevertheless there is little here in this segment of the book that one could not find in other Jewish apocalypses. It is primarily in the unnumbered judgments where we see John's original Christian theology.

A CLOSER LOOK — ON HOW TO READ REVELATION 6–16

When one works through Rev. 6–16, one needs to be prepared for shifts in point of view. Sometimes the perspective is that of those on earth; sometimes it is the heavenly viewpoint through the so-called hymnic interludes. All at once in Rev. 12.1–6 we are talking about the past birth of the Messiah or about the seven-headed monster with heads of deceased emperors. This material is not *just* about the future, nor should we have expected it to be since it is narrative forensic rhetoric meant to prepare and exhort John's audience. A purely futurist reading of these sets of seven judgments will not do. It is hard to escape the impression that John believed he was living in the midst of the inauguration of these judgments or put another way in the age when the seals were being unsealed. It is then inadequate to suggest that these events are describing things in John's, much less our own, future. John believes the church is already in the period of the beginning of the eschatological judgments. We are not told how long this process of judgment will take, and it is inappropriate to say that just because John believed the beginning of the end had already transpired he also thought the end of the end was near. The point is that the world is living on borrowed time. Most of these judgments are so general they could represent events in many ages of human history. It may well be that John sees the events around him as types or archetypes. These visions can be seen as multivalent or, better said, generic or universal, and while the events of the author's age can in some measure be correlated with some of these symbols, so could they in other ages of church history. The symbols are deliberately universal or vague and thus universally relevant and available to the church. Precision would have limited reference to one particular small set of historical events, but I doubt this was John's thought. Certainly one thing he wants to accomplish in recounting the three sets of seven judgments is to make clear God is in control, even of all the bad things, some of which were already happening to John's churches. Some of these things happening should be seen as divine judgment on sin, according to John. The purpose of this material is also to say that however dark these dark times may be, in the end there will not only be the personal triumph of the martyrs in heaven but cosmic triumph for God on earth. The whole book is straining forward to reach the end that will bring in the new heaven and new earth. It is therefore inappropriate to read the somber and serious judgments in these chapters as anything other than the penultimate chapters in human history. They are the dark tunnel the church must go through, but as it does the light at the end of the tunnel becomes progressively brighter.

Koester has suggested that the "principle purpose of the visions in Revelation 6 is to awaken a sense of uneasiness in readers by vividly identifying threats to their well-being. The four horsemen are designed to shatter the illusion that people can find true security in the borders of a nation or empire, in a flourishing economy, or in their own health. Subsequent visions promise that God will not allow injustice to continue forever – which is assuring to the victims, but disturbing to the perpetrators – and warn that no place on earth and no position of power or wealth will protect people from the judgment of God and the Lamb."[165] He may be right about the effect of the vision in Rev. 6 on the complacent, but as Koester also says John had several audiences, and some of them needed reassurance about the justice of God and God's control of the historical process. This vision speaks to that need as well. The forensic character of this material must be taken seriously.[166]

❧

Rev. 6 begins with the Lamb opening the first seal. These judgments happen because of Christ's action of taking the scroll and unsealing the seals.[167] He is then in some sense sovereign over them and responsible for them. As R. Mounce says, we are not talking here either about personal vindictiveness on Christ's part nor about an inevitable impersonal process of "what goes around, comes around" in human history as if history were preprogrammed for ultimate justice. Rather, we are talking about divine judgment on sin, which unfortunately also involves judgment on sinners. Justice, not personal vengeance, is at issue, as is the vindication of those who have given their life for Christ. Though the Lamb is merciful, he must also be just. Ultimately justice must be served or God has reneged on his promises to the oppressed and has been untrue to his Word.

---

[165] C. Koester, *Revelation and the End* (2001), p. 82.

[166] Koester (ibid, p. 86) is also right that John has a healthy sense of secondary causes, knowing that Satan has power and humans have the ability to sin and so violate the will of God. It is therefore a matter of revelation to be able to tell whether a particular event or happening is attributed to God or some lesser being or to both. The ambiguity of life extends to the question – particular people suffering because they are sinners or because they are being faithful to God in a wicked world or perhaps neither? John does not do disteliology or theodicy in this work, but his prophecies suggest certain views on the subject. The higher one's view of God's power and sovereignty over the universe, the more problematic sin and evil become, if God is a good and loving and holy God.

[167] It appears we must envision a truly unique scroll that is cut horizontally into seven different strips with a seal sealing each segment. When each seal is broken, that particular part of the scroll is unrolled and sets in motion a particular judgment. See M. G. Reddish, *Revelation* (2001), pp. 124–25.

Christ acts here in a fashion that divine permission is given for these things to happen.

One of the living creatures says, "Come," but despite the textual variants this is not likely addressed to John but rather to each horseman. First comes a white horse, and the one riding on it has a bow. He is given a crown and sent forth conquering and to conquer. This figure is not likely Christ nor a image of the spreading of the Gospel, evident from Rev. 19.[168] Rather in this segment of the book we have four figures of judgment. In Rev. 19 the figure has a stack of diadems on his head, whereas the figure in Rev. 6 wears just the *stephanos*, a victor's wreath. When Christ rides forth on his white horse in Rev. 19, he carries only the sword of his mouth. Here then we have a very different figure of conquest, and probably the different colors represent the different aspects of judgment each horseman brings.

We may find a form of these symbols in Zech. 1.8–17 and 6.1–8, but our author modifies the symbols, for instance, in regard to the horses' colors, to make his own points. Some have seen here a reference to the Parthian archers, who in A.D. 62 (as well as in 53 and 35 B.C.)[169] came riding from the east and won against the Romans. Favoring the allusion to the Parthians are the following: (1) we seem to have allusions to these dreaded cavalrymen elsewhere in Revelation (9.14; 16.12); (2) Parthians were famous for their horses, and white was the Parthians' sacred color, and every one of their armies included some sacred white horses; (3) Parthians were known for being highly skillful mounted archers; (4) many Jewish writers expected Parthians to play a role in the eschatological war against Rome (1 En. 56.5–7; Sib. Or. 5.438); and (5) the Romans most often feared the Parthians as a threat to the Pax Romana.[170] While to some degree we have here a general symbol of military conquest,[171] John has chosen his general image so it would be familiar and thus on target for his audience.[172]

The second living creature calls forth the second horseman, who is riding on a fiery red stallion and carrying a massive sword with the commission to take the peace on earth away (the Pax Romana may be primarily in view) and to engage in slaughter. There is a logical order to the presentation of the four. "Conquest (6.2) would be followed by bloodshed (6.4) and in their wake would follow famine because of economic destabilization (6.5–6), and widespread death (6.8)."[173] It may be that this figure represents civil or internal strife, which was tearing the world apart during this and earlier periods. Each of these horsemen is said to

---

[168] But see the discussion in J. Herzer, "Der erste apokalyptische Reiter unter der König der Könige. Ein Beitrag zur Christologie der Johannesapokalypse," *NTS* 45 (2, 1999), pp. 230–49.

[169] See E. Fiorenza, *Revelation* (1991), p. 63.

[170] See the discussion in C. Keener, *Revelation* (2002), p. 202.

[171] R. H. Mounce, *Book of Revelation* (1977), pp. 139–45.

[172] A second possibility is that the allusion is to Apollo, who carried a bow. See A. Kerkeslager, "Apollo, Greco-Roman Prophecy, and the Rider on the White Horse in Rev. 6.2," *JBL* 112 (1993), pp. 116–21.

[173] C. Keener, *Revelation* (2002), p. 203.

be given permission to do something, making clear that a sovereign God is in charge of or has authorized these calamities.[174]

The third living creature summons a third horseman on a black horse carrying in his hands a pair of scales, as a symbol not of justice but of the necessary rationing of food at exorbitant prices. It will cost one a whole day's wages just to feed oneself, never mind the family. Famine and want is foreshadowed, and yet the effect is not allowed to be total for some of the main foodstuffs will not be wiped out – the oil and the wine. It is possible that the immediate audience would have remembered the act of Domitian in A.D. 92 whereby he destroyed half the vineyards throughout the provinces (Suetonius, *Dom.* 7.2; 14.2). But again the symbol is a general one. As Mounce points out, these preliminary judgments are not the last judgment and do not intend to wipe out everything before the unsealing of the seventh seal. We may take the exempting of the vineyards and the olive trees as a sign of how God was merciful in comparison to Domitian. The loss of a grain crop could be endured, for another one would come along the following year, but the destruction of vines and olive trees could cripple the region's economy for years, and there were indeed areas in Asia Minor where this judgment would be particularly devastating (e.g., Philadelphia with its vineyard culture).

The fourth living creature calls forth the fourth horse. The word used for his color is *chloros*, which normally and elsewhere in Revelation means yellow-green. Probably this should be seen as the color of a putrifying corpse, for the figure riding the horse is Death and he is followed (on foot apparently) by Hades, the term for the underworld or the land of the dead.[175] Power is given to Death to wipe out one-fourth of the earth by various means – sword, famine, death, wild beasts. This may suggest that the previous three horsemen were just agents of the fourth one. Ezek. 14.21 lies in the background here.[176]

Beasley-Murray proposes that in these seven seals the author is following a traditional order of judgment events, also found in Mark 13, which suggests he is drawing on an eschatological discourse or judgment oracle that had circulated previously. In Mark 13.7 ff. and 24 ff. and in Rev. 6 we hear of the following – basically in the same order – war, international strife, famine, earthquakes (though John leaves earthquakes until last to make it part of the final cataclysm). Famine is followed by persecutions and then cosmic signs (eclipses, falling stars). Beasley-Murray also suggests that the discussion about anti-Christ and the false prophets in Rev. 13 and 17 is a development of what we find in Mark 13.14 ff. If the author is presenting Jewish or early Jewish Christian traditional material, this may explain the lack of specific Christological or Christian elements.[177]

At **vs. 9** we hear of the lives of those who were slain because of the Word of God and their witness to it. They are said to be under the altar, a place of honor in a

---

[174] See E. Fiorenza, *Revelation* (1991), p. 63.
[175] The Greek word *thanatos*, translated 'death' here, can also mean pestilence, a frequent cause of death in antiquity. See M. G. Reddish, *Revelation* (2001), pp. 127–28.
[176] R. H. Mounce, *Book of Revelation* (1977), pp. 145–46.
[177] G. R. Beasley-Murray, *Book of Revelation* (1978), pp. 129–31.

Jewish tradition attributed to Rabbi Akiba, which says to be buried in the Holy Land is as if one is buried beneath the altar (B. T. Shabb. 152B). E. Boring offers a unique reading of this scene. "The chopping block of the Roman executioner has become a cosmic altar. Christians who refuse to sacrifice to the image of the Emperor are nonetheless Christian priests who sacrifice themselves on the true altar of God."[178] The word *psuche* should probably not be translated 'soul' here, for it means the living person or personality, without a body. The martyrs cry out, "How long O Master" [*despotes*], will you not judge and vindicate our blood from among those who dwell on earth?" Instead of an immediate positive response, they are each given long white robes, not likely to be equated with resurrection bodies which they do not receive until the millennium when the full number of martyrs is complete. Elsewhere in Revelation white robes are symbols of purity (see 3.5) and bliss, and there is no reason to doubt this meaning here. The martyrs are beneath the altar perhaps because the altar is a symbol of protection. The horns of the altar were seen as the place where one made contact with God's presence. Blood was applied to the horns, indicating the spot of atonement, where one could reestablish contact with God. But also blood was collected at the bottom of the altar (Lev. 17.11), so perhaps this is why the martyrs are beneath the altar. The Lamb does not respond but tells them to rest for a while until the full number of martyrs is complete. This idea of a preset number of the righteous who must die before the end is found elsewhere in apocalyptic literature, for example, in 1 En. 47.3–4 and 4 Ezek. 4.35–37. Of course, the "little while" is being reckoned on the clock in heaven where the martyrs are, so it should not be pressed (cf. 10.6; 12.12; 17.10; 20.3). "John is telling the prospective martyrs that their deaths are a necessary part of God's plan for conquering evil."[179]

At **vs. 12** at the opening of the sixth seal, we find the great earthquake with the sun turning black (eclipse) as sackcloth made of black goat hair, the moon appearing as blood (notice the *hos*), and the stars falling upon the earth, as late figs fall from the fig tree under a great wind. In the apocalypse in Mark 13 the cosmic signs are linked only to the very end of history when Christ will return. The preliminary eschatological judgments do not include such cosmic signs.[180] The opening of the sixth seal brings us to the end of the cosmos as we know it (cf. Isa. 13.9–11; 24.21–23; 1 En. 102.2–3). Here human beings finally recognize the unleashing of the final wrath of God. **Vs. 14** speaks of the splitting open of the sky and of each part rolling up like two great scrolls. Even the mountains and the islands are moved out of their places. Yet this is not quite a description of the end for all kinds of human beings – from kings to magnates to generals, and from the rich to the slaves and the freedmen and women hiding themselves in caves and in the rocks in mountains. They ask for their refuges to cover them

---

[178] M. E. Boring, *Revelation* (Louisville, Ky.: John Knox, 1989), p. 125.
[179] M. G. Reddish, *Revelation* (2001), p. 132.
[180] See my *The Gospel of Mark: A Socio-Rhetorical Commentary* (Grand Rapids, Mich.: Eerdmans, 2000).

and hide them from the one sitting on the throne and from the wrath of the
Lamb (see Hos. 10.8). It is clear that the wrath is coming from the Lamb. John's
audience, when hearing 6.12–17, may have thought of the eruption of Vesuvius
in A.D. 79 (see Pliny, the Elder Book 6, *Epistles* 16, 20), which indeed caused
the sky to turn black and fire to afflict the cities of Pompeii and Herculaneum.
Then, too, the cities to which John wrote were in a prime earthquake zone, and
Colossae had experienced an earthquake in living memory.

John takes us to the brink of the end but does not go on to describe the end
itself. We have here a sevenfold categorization of humanity, again a symbol of
completeness or totality. The point of this material may in part be that natural
disaster is not to be equated with the wrath of the Lamb but rather is preliminary
to it. But clearly the natural disaster is preferable to facing the Lamb's wrath. In
any event the text indicates that the wealthy and powerful will especially face
the judgment of God.

When **Rev. 7** begins, it is hard to know if the four winds are an alternate
form of the four horsemen. Four angels are restraining these winds so that they
won't blow away the earth, sea, or trees. Yet these angels are authorized to do
harm, but not until another angel comes down and seals the servants of God
upon the forehead, all 144,000 of them. There are many points here to note. Who
are the servants of God here? Is this Israel? Is this the last generation of Christians?
Is the reference to all Christians or just to the martyrs? Are Jewish Christians in
view? Should we contrast what is said here with what is said in the later material
about an innumerable multitude? Beasley-Murray thinks that once again the
author has incorporated some traditional Jewish material in his list of the twelve
tribes and that that accounts for some of the confusion. Christians have nothing
to fear from the coming wrath or even from the preliminary events so long as
they persevere in faith.

Mounce points out how frequently in apocalyptic literature angels are said
to be the ones in control of the natural forces (cf. Rev. 14.18; 16.5). He adds also
that in Zech. 6.5 a correct translation does not identify the horsemen and the
winds, though they are closely associated with one another. On the destructive
winds one may compare 1 En. 76.[181] What sort of sealing is in mind? Possibly
it is the sort mentioned in Ezek. 9.4, or possibly the Exodus painting of blood
on the doorpost is being echoed. If the former, the symbol painted was the
Hebrew letter tau, sometimes written in the form of a cross or X. This would
indeed be appropriate as a symbol for the people of the cross. The sealing likely
does not refer to baptism, though many medieval commentators thought so.
Those who are being sealed are *already* servants of God; we are not talking about
conversions here. Keener points out that the word *sphragizo* can imply a special
stamp of ownership or approval (see 4 Ezek. 6.5; cf. Isa. 44.5). He adds that this

[181] R. H. Mounce, *Book of Revelation* (1977), pp. 155–58.

seal should be contrasted with the mark of the Beast in Rev. 13.16–17.[182] There may also be some contrasting of the seals on the scrolls that once opened unleash wrath and of those on foreheads in protection from that wrath.

A clue about who these servants are is found in Rev. 9.4, where everyone but believers is called upon to repent, and they are said to be the ones without the sealing. This suggests that the 144,000 are coterminous with the total number of believers. Here as elsewhere the language about Israel is applied to Jew and Gentile united in Christ. Clearly enough, 144,000 is a symbolic number: 12 × 12 × 1,000. Just as the twelve tribes equaled all of Israel and the twelve disciples equaled all of the first apostles, here is a symbolic number for the whole people of God.[183] This is made abundantly clear when we are told of an innumerable multitude of the saved (and that may even refer to those saved at the end not to all the saved). There is no conflict between these two figures since 144,000 simply means the whole or complete number of the people of God who will be sealed.[184]

Some controversy continues as to why the tribes are listed as they are. It is impossible to maintain that John has the literal twelve tribes of Israel in mind, for even in his own day he knew there were no such tribes. The amphictyony had long since been dissolved in the wake of the Assyrian and Babylonian conquests, and the tribal unities were never fully reestablished after the exile. Judah is perhaps mentioned first because the Savior comes forth from that tribe. But why no mention of the tribe of Dan? It has been conjectured that the tribe was omitted due to its early connections with idolatry (cf. Judg. 18; 1 Kings 12.25–33) and later its association with the anti-Christ, and so Manasseh was substituted. This is a possibility, but the author does not explain and we shouldn't make too much of it. It is encouraging to hear that God's people will be completely

---

[182] C. Keener, *Revelation* (2002), p. 235. There is a slight chance that the branding of slaves is in the background here, though that was a rare practice in John's day. If it is echoed here, the point would be to stress ownership. The servants belong to their master, who will look after them.

[183] This conclusion is also supported in the following considerations: (1) these people are called "servants," which elsewhere in Revelation always refers to all believers or witnesses (1.1; 2.20; 6.11; 10.7; 11.18; 19.2, 5, 10; 22.3, 6, 9). To take "servant" here in a narrower sense leads to the untenable conclusion that God affords his special protection to only some in the church based on their ethnicity, gender, and marital status! This is hardly likely; (2) the sealing of the 144,000 connects them with believers mentioned in Rev. 3.12 and 22.4; (3) the 144,000 do not fit a literal description of Israel, and in any case a tribe is missing. See C. Keener, *Revelation* (2002), p. 232.

[184] M. G. Reddish, *Revelation* (2001), p. 147, wants to argue that the martyrs only are referred to by the 144,000, and so 7.1–8 could be seen as a response to the martyr's cry of "How long?" But, as mentioned in the previous note, this view requires that God give his protection to only one particular group of believers. C. Koester, *Revelation and the End* (2001), p. 90, makes the case for the 144,000 being the same as the multitude. He fruitfully compares these two images to describe one reality with the two images of Christ – Lion and Lamb – in Rev. 4–5.

international and interracial from every tribe and tongue and people and nation. It is perhaps likely that John is presenting us with two images – one Jewish, one Gentile – of God's end-time people or, more specifically, God's end-time army. "We vanquish our foes not by killing them but by martyrdom at their hands (11.7; 12.11; 13.7; 15.2; 21.7)."[185] If this is correct, then the "innumerable multitude" is a more literal interpretation of the image of the 144,000. Although at the end of the first century the total number of Christians cannot have been huge, the point would be that this vision encourages John about the eventual success of the Christian mission.[186]

At **vv. 9–10** we have a picture of the time of triumph when the saints celebrate in the kingdom, waving palm branches in their hands, when they will indeed be able to shout, "Salvation belongs to our God." It is possible that *soteria* has its nonsoteriological sense of 'rescue'; God is the rescuer of his persecuted people. We then are told of the falling down and worshiping of the four living creatures and the elders when God has completed his rescue operation.

Vs. 12 is another typical doxology from these heavenly archetypes. But who are these robed saints, and where are they from? These creatures do not partake of the omniscience and insight of God and have to be informed. The elder who raises the question is simply answered, "You know good sir" (cf. Ezekiel). The elder's is a sort of rhetorical question that does not expect a real answer from the hearer, not knowing enough to provide one (cf. Zech. 4.2, 5, 13; 5.2; Apoc. Paul 19). The multitude came through the great tribulation (see Dan. 12.1) or suffering (the grammar does not allow the reading "came *from* the great suffering"). By coming through it faithfully, they have washed and rolled their garments in the Lamb's blood. Christ has cleansed them, perhaps through death. We must bear in mind that the speaker is a heavenly one and so perhaps looking at things from the end of the historical process. These are aorist verbs because of the speaker's perspective. Because of what the designated multitude went through, they are given a special place right before the throne of God. They are given their own thrones, and God's presence dwells upon them and so they worship him day and night. They are finally beyond the deprivations of the world and in a place where hunger nor thirst nor heat can harm them for the Lamb stands in their midst, caring for them, leading them unto the springs of eternal life, and wiping away all their tears.

At the opening of the seventh seal, there is silence in heaven. Is this a dramatic pause before the end so that God can hear the prayers of the saints? The silence is during the time that the angels burn the incense on the altar to accompany the prayers of the saints (cf. 8.1 to vv. 3–4). "The incense in heaven accompanies the prayers of God's people and ensures they reach the throne of God. The early Jewish belief that the angels bring human beings prayers to God (Tob. 12.12, 15; 1 En. 47.1–2; 99.3 . . . 3 Bar. 11–16 . . .) is here dramatized in terms of the

---

[185] C. Keener, *Revelation* (2002), p. 243.
[186] See D. E. Aune, *Revelation 6–18* (1998), pp. 466–67.

liturgy in the heavenly temple."[187] The eschatological judgments that follow are in response to the prayers of the saints.[188]

The reference to half an hour of silence simply means a short period of time. P. Wick suggests that the silence was the normal procedure when one was offering a sacrifice.[189] In fact the connection between the offering of incense and praying is also found in Luke 1.9–10. Silence would seem to be the divine response, not the proper human protocol when offering a sacrifice. Thus, it apparently represents God's listening to the saints' prayers.

The seven angels standing before the throne are given seven trumpets.[190] This is an instrument to announce the presence of God, as well as the Parousia elsewhere in the Bible, but also an instrument used in battle, as at the city of Jericho. Does the adding of incense by the angel mean that the angels' prayers are being added to those of the saints, or does the incense simply facilitate the prayers of the saints reaching and being acceptable to God? **Rev. 8.3** reads literally that the angel stands before the altar so that the prayers of all the saints are given upon the altar. Bear in mind that daily the priest in the Temple in Jerusalem would take hot coals from the altar of sacrifice and carry them into the holy place to the golden incense altar (cf. Luke 1.9). It seems likely that the angel is seen as the saints presenting their prayers to God. Once the prayers are offered, they are just as quickly answered as the angel becomes an avenging angel, casting coals from the altar upon the earth, which produces immediate thunder, lightning, and earthquakes (cf. Ezek. 10.2–7).

BRIDGING THE HORIZONS

In one of the great ironies of my life, I was working on this particular segment of Revelation when the disasters of 11 September 2001 happened at the World Trade Towers, the Pentagon, and the field in Pennsylvania. It seemed that life was imitating art as I watched the pieces of the Trade Towers fall from the sky, all the while reading "and its rider in the sky was permitted to take peace from the earth." The next thing I knew, I was watching price gouging at the gas pump, while reading about the rider with the scales in his hands speaking of exorbitant prices. These multivalent symbols can speak to major disasters in any age. But there is also a pointedness to some of this material. As Boesak has noted, "During the siege of Jerusalem, Titus gave explicit orders not to destroy the oil and wine because he wanted those luxuries to be enjoyed by the rich, who can afford them

---

[187] R. Bauckham, *Climax of Prophecy* (1993), p. 81.

[188] R. H. Charles, *Revelation* (1920), 1:224, puts it this way: "The praise of the highest order of angels in heaven are hushed that the prayers of all the suffering saints on earth may be heard before the throne. Their needs are of more concern to God than all the psalmody of heaven."

[189] P. Wick, "There Was Silence in Heaven (Revelation 8.1): An Annotation to Israel Knohl's 'Between Voice and Silence,'" *SBL* 117 (1998), pp. 512–14.

[190] These angels may be seen as the angels of the presence as in Jub. 1.27–29; 2.1–2; Tob. 12.15.

even in times of want. The black horse states the hard facts of the matter, that the harsh inequalities in distribution of the necessities of life are exacerbated in situations of dire need. God's judgment on this injustice follows in subsequent chapters."[191] Injustice, war, and terror are our companions in any and every age of human history in this vale of tears.

Certainly there are several major messages that John wishes to convey by the vision of the seven seals. (1) God is a God of justice and will not forbear from judging human wickedness forever. But, at the same time, not all judgments are punitive in nature. Some are meant to call us to repentance. (2) God hears the prayers of the saints, whether they cry out for redemption or justice. (3) Sooner or later there are moral consequences to wicked human actions. (4) There are indeed urgencies on earth that can interrupt or silence the doxological activities in heaven. This reflects God's great concern and compassion for his people. (5) The Savior of the world is in charge of the judgments and has them under control. (6) God will protect his people's spiritual life even though they have to go through great suffering and perhaps even martyrdom. (7) There are agents of God in heaven interceding for the saints or aiding their prayers and responding to them.[192]

These passages give an opportunity for reflecting on the nature and meaning of prayer. The book of Revelation is quite clear about God's omniscience. There is nothing God needs to be informed about, as he knows all actualities as well as all future possibilities. The question then becomes, What is the function of prayer, if it is not a matter of informing God of something? Several answers are forthcoming. (1) Though God already knows what will be said, God still listens to prayer, like a parent listening to a child confess something that the parent already knows. That is, prayer helps the pray-er come into better conformity to God's will and recognize what that will is in the first place. (2) Prayer, by God's own choice, not by necessity, is used by God to shape human history. God chooses to respond positively to prayer when it is in accord with the divine will. (3) Prayer involves something other than just petitions or requests. There are prayers of thanksgiving and adoration, as we find in Revelation. (4) Prayer is cathartic for the pray-ers. It allows them to get something off their heart or mind. Therefore it becomes a means of healing. (5) Prayer makes those praying dialogue partners with God and so puts them into the right relationship with God. Through prayer one comes to know God, not just God's will. George Herbert wrote a wonderful poem defining prayer:

PRAYER (I)
Prayer the Churches banquet, Angels age,
God's breath in man returning to his birth,

---

[191] A. Boesak, *Comfort and Protest* (1986), p. 64.
[192] It is interesting to compare what we find here to what we find in Hebrews, where it is Christ in heaven who is said to intercede for the saints.

The soul in paraphrase, heart in pilgrimage,
The Christian plummet sounding heav'n and earth;
Engine against th' Almightie, sinners towre,
Reversed thunder, Christ's side piercing spear,
The six-daies world transposing in an houre,
A kind of tune, which all things heare and fear;
Softnesse, and peace, and joy, and love, and blisse,
Exalted Manna, gladnesse of the best,
Heaven in ordinarie, man well drest,
The milkie way, the bird of Paradise,
Church-bels beyond the starres heard, the souls bloud,
The land of spices; something understood.[193]

There are many daring images in this poem. Though most Christians today might think of prayer as essentially a matter of petitioning the Almighty, it is clear that Herbert sees it as far more than that. For one thing, he sees prayer as communion with God and therefore something of a feast in and of itself. Even if one does not get what one asks for, one always gets what is most needed through prayer, namely a drawing closer to God. For another thing, Herbert sees prayer as the natural spiritual response of a human being, who is after all created in God's image, to God. It is like breath returning to its ultimate source, and as such it helps resuscitate the breather. Herbert also sees real prayer as the distillation of what is truly on one's mind or in one's heart, as if the heart were setting out on a journey toward God (line 3), pouring out one's very life blood. Prayer then is seen as a sort of spiritual sacrifice offered up to God.

Perhaps the most daring portion of the poem comes in lines 4–6, where there may be an allusion to the story of the Tower of Babel, the human attempt to reach heaven on its own terms. If this is such an allusion then prayer is a chastened form of such an attempt that brings forth not God's judgment but rather God's succor. Prayer sounds out or takes the measure of the will of the Almighty (line 4); it is like a tower raised up with the intention to get the Almighty to capitulate on some subject. In line 6 it is suggested that prayer can pierce God like lightning and cause him to release a blessing, or that prayer is like the spear that pierced Christ. This last is an allusion to the medieval interpretation of John 19.34 that saw the reference to the blood and water coming from Christ's side as referring to the sacraments, the Lord's Supper and Baptism (see, e.g., Dürer's famous woodcut of this, in which a communion chalice is held up to catch the blood and a small font to catch the water). Thus Herbert suggests that, through prayer, one obtains the benefits of Christ's death.

Another of the many images in this poem is that prayer sums up the trials and tribulations of the week in a short span. It is also suggested that prayer, being

---

[193] Found in *The Poems of George Herbert* (London: Oxford University Press, 1961), p. 44.

powerful, is something that human beings instinctly do but also fear. "Beware of what you pray for, for you may receive it." Prayer is seen in line 11 as a garment that clothes a person and makes her or him properly presented before God, rather like spiritual fig leaves.

In the end Herbert suggests that prayer is not just importuning but also an opportunity for a person to come to understand God's will, be fed, and become content that things in God's hands will turn out for the best. It thus produces gladness, peace, joy, love, and a recognition that one has been constantly receiving exalted manna, albeit unaware much of the time. The good news is at the end of the poem, where we are reminded that when prayer, like a church bell, peals out to God, it is most certainly heard.

Peterson points out a further function of the seven seals material in relating how a friend of his who had suffered greatly had her life changed by studying Revelation, "None of the evil was abolished, but it was all in a defined perspective. The nameless evils had names. The numberless wrongs were numbered. She was hardly aware of the point at which the proportions shifted, but now it was the good that seemed endless, and the glories that were beyond counting. Nothing in her life had changed; everything in her life had changed."[194] There can be little doubt that one of the major intended rhetorical effects of Revelation is to change the perspective from which John's audience viewed their life situation. John seeks to give them the bird's-eye view rather than the worm's-eye view. In other words he looks to unveil the divine perspective and control of the situation. This in itself, even without material aid or comfort, can comfort and guide troubled souls.

The worship scenes in Revelation are drawn upon over and over again in the lectionaries, the liturgies, and the hymnals. P. Claudel once said that our primary concern should be not to understand the book of Revelation but rather to walk inside it like one would walk in a cathedral and be led to fall on one's knees in awe and wonder and worship God.[195] This is certainly one of the purposes of Revelation. The author's rhetoric seeks not merely to persuade but to enthrall and help the audience to be caught up in wonder, love, and praise. J. Wesley believed that the scenes of heaven and its worship were special means of conveying religious experience. "It is scarcely possible for any that either love or fear God not to feel their hearts extremely affected in seriously reading either the beginning or the latter part of the revelation."[196] This brings up an important point, namely that this book is written for the faithful, and it is to be best understood and responded to adequately by those who are prepared to do what John is trying to get his audience to do. The book of Revelation has, as part of its purpose, much the same intent as the famous hymn of R. Heber,

[194] E. Peterson, *Reversed Thunder* (1988), p. 86.
[195] P. Claude, *Oeuvres complètes*, vol. 26 (1965) (Paris: Editions Gallimard, 1955–65), pp. 11–12.
[196] J. Wesley, *Explanatory Notes on the New Testament* (London: Epworth, 1950), p. 932.

"Holy, Holy, Holy," which calls the hearer to bow down and worship and to "cast down their golden crowns around the glassy sea."

There is a connection between the history John speaks about and the hearts he seeks to move. John believes that God is Lord of time and history. But, insofar as human actors affect the course of affairs in history, John believes hearts create history. It is out of the human heart that sinful and sanctified behavior comes. He is busy exhorting people to change their ways and to have their hearts transformed by the grace of God. He believes the images he conveys will help in that transformative function. In other words, the work is soteriological in intent to some degree, and it intends to lead the audience to doxology.[197]

Selective listening is something we all tend to practice at times, especially when the message is not what we want to hear. There has been a tendency in the church, reflected in the lectionaries, liturgies, and hymnody, to avoid Rev. 6–19 precisely because this portion deals with judgment, an unpleasant topic. There is in human nature the tendency to want to whittle off the hard edges of life, and the same can be said about the hard edges of Scripture. But the portions of Scripture that make one most uncomfortable are those that one may most need to hear. M. McLuhan once said the Almighty did not make us with earlids but we compensate for that by selective listening. "We are conveniently deaf to sounds that challenge our pride, or command our obedience, or interrupt our fantasies, or call attention to our lapses."[198] The sections of Revelation dealing with judgment remind us that, whether we like it or not, a holy God will ultimately hold us all accountable for what we believe and how we behave. No amount of covering our ears will prevent God from pronouncing the final benediction or malediction on life. We can fail to listen, but we do so at great cost, for there is time for amendment of life. If nothing else Rev. 6–19 call us to "go and do otherwise" when we observe the negative examples that call forth the judgment of God.

REVELATION 8.5–11.19 – THE SEVEN TRUMPETS

NRSV Revelation 5 Then the angel took the censer and filled it with fire from the altar and threw it on the earth; and there were peals of thunder, rumblings, flashes of lightning, and an earthquake.
6 Now the seven angels who had the seven trumpets made ready to blow them.
7 The first angel blew his trumpet, and there came hail and fire, mixed with blood, and they were hurled to the earth; and a third of the earth was burned up, and a third of the trees were burned up, and all green grass was burned up.
8 The second angel blew his trumpet, and something like a great mountain, burning with fire, was thrown into the sea.

[197] On all this, see A. W. Wainwright, *Mysterious Apocalypse* (1993), pp. 203–22.
[198] Cited in E. Peterson, *Reversed Thunder* (1988), p. 49.

9 A third of the sea became blood, a third of the living creatures in the sea died, and a third of the ships were destroyed.

10 The third angel blew his trumpet, and a great star fell from heaven, blazing like a torch, and it fell on a third of the rivers and on the springs of water.

11 The name of the star is Wormwood. A third of the waters became wormwood, and many died from the water, because it was made bitter.

12 The fourth angel blew his trumpet, and a third of the sun was struck, and a third of the moon, and a third of the stars, so that a third of their light was darkened; a third of the day was kept from shining, and likewise the night.

13 Then I looked, and I heard an eagle crying with a loud voice as it flew in midheaven, "Woe, woe, woe to the inhabitants of the earth, at the blasts of the other trumpets that the three angels are about to blow!"

NRSV Revelation 9.1 And the fifth angel blew his trumpet, and I saw a star that had fallen from heaven to earth, and he was given the key to the shaft of the bottomless pit;

2 he opened the shaft of the bottomless pit, and from the shaft rose smoke like the smoke of a great furnace, and the sun and the air were darkened with the smoke from the shaft.

3 Then from the smoke came locusts on the earth, and they were given authority like the authority of scorpions of the earth.

4 They were told not to damage the grass of the earth or any green growth or any tree, but only those people who do not have the seal of God on their foreheads.

5 They were allowed to torture them for five months, but not to kill them, and their torture was like the torture of a scorpion when it stings someone.

6 And in those days people will seek death but will not find it; they will long to die, but death will flee from them.

7 In appearance the locusts were like horses equipped for battle. On their heads were what looked like crowns of gold; their faces were like human faces,

8 their hair like women's hair, and their teeth like lions' teeth;

9 they had scales like iron breastplates, and the noise of their wings was like the noise of many chariots with horses rushing into battle.

10 They have tails like scorpions, with stingers, and in their tails is their power to harm people for five months.

11 They have as king over them the angel of the bottomless pit; his name in Hebrew is Abaddon, and in Greek he is called Apollyon.

12 The first woe has passed. There are still two woes to come.

13 Then the sixth angel blew his trumpet, and I heard a voice from the four horns of the golden altar before God,

14 saying to the sixth angel who had the trumpet, "Release the four angels who are bound at the great river Euphrates."

15 So the four angels were released, who had been held ready for the hour, the day, the month, and the year, to kill a third of humankind.

16 The number of the troops of cavalry was two hundred million; I heard their number.

17 And this was how I saw the horses in my vision: the riders wore breastplates the color of fire and of sapphire and of sulfur; the heads of the horses were like lions' heads, and fire and smoke and sulfur came out of their mouths.

18 By these three plagues a third of humankind was killed, by the fire and smoke and sulfur coming out of their mouths.

19 For the power of the horses is in their mouths and in their tails; their tails are like serpents, having heads; and with them they inflict harm.

20 The rest of humankind, who were not killed by these plagues, did not repent of the works of their hands or give up worshiping demons and idols of gold and silver and bronze and stone and wood, which cannot see or hear or walk.

21 And they did not repent of their murders or their sorceries or their fornication or their thefts.

NRSV Revelation 10.1 And I saw another mighty angel coming down from heaven, wrapped in a cloud, with a rainbow over his head; his face was like the sun, and his legs like pillars of fire.

2 He held a little scroll open in his hand. Setting his right foot on the sea and his left foot on the land,

3 he gave a great shout, like a lion roaring. And when he shouted, the seven thunders sounded.

4 And when the seven thunders had sounded, I was about to write, but I heard a voice from heaven saying, "Seal up what the seven thunders have said, and do not write it down."

5 Then the angel whom I saw standing on the sea and the land raised his right hand to heaven

6 and swore by him who lives forever and ever, who created heaven and what is in it, the earth and what is in it, and the sea and what is in it: "There will be no more delay,

7 but in the days when the seventh angel is to blow his trumpet, the mystery of God will be fulfilled, as he announced to his servants the prophets."

8 Then the voice that I had heard from heaven spoke to me again, saying, "Go, take the scroll that is open in the hand of the angel who is standing on the sea and on the land."

9 So I went to the angel and told him to give me the little scroll; and he said to me, "Take it, and eat; it will be bitter to your stomach, but sweet as honey in your mouth."

10 So I took the little scroll from the hand of the angel and ate it; it was sweet as honey in my mouth, but when I had eaten it, my stomach was made bitter.

11 Then they said to me, "You must prophesy again about many peoples and nations and languages and kings."

NRSV Revelation 11.1 Then I was given a measuring rod like a staff, and I was told, "Come and measure the temple of God and the altar and those who worship there, **2** but do not measure the court outside the temple; leave that out, for it is given over to the nations, and they will trample over the holy city for forty-two months.

3 And I will grant my two witnesses authority to prophesy for one thousand two hundred sixty days, wearing sackcloth."

4 These are the two olive trees and the two lampstands that stand before the Lord of the earth.

5 And if anyone wants to harm them, fire pours from their mouth and consumes their foes; anyone who wants to harm them must be killed in this manner.

6 They have authority to shut the sky, so that no rain may fall during the days of their prophesying, and they have authority over the waters to turn them into blood, and to strike the earth with every kind of plague, as often as they desire.

7 When they have finished their testimony, the Beast that comes up from the bottomless pit will make war on them and conquer them and kill them,

8 and their dead bodies will lie in the street of the great city that is prophetically called Sodom and Egypt, where also their Lord was crucified.

9 For three and a half days members of the peoples and tribes and languages and nations will gaze at their dead bodies and refuse to let them be placed in a tomb;

10 and the inhabitants of the earth will gloat over them and celebrate and exchange presents, because these two prophets had been a torment to the inhabitants of the earth.

11 But after the three and a half days, the breath of life from God entered them, and they stood on their feet, and those who saw them were terrified.

12 Then they heard a loud voice from heaven saying to them, "Come up here!" And they went up to heaven in a cloud while their enemies watched them.

13 At that moment there was a great earthquake, and a tenth of the city fell; seven thousand people were killed in the earthquake, and the rest were terrified and gave glory to the God of heaven.

14 The second woe has passed. The third woe is coming very soon.

15 Then the seventh angel blew his trumpet, and there were loud voices in heaven, saying, "The kingdom of the world has become the kingdom of our Lord and of his Messiah, and he will reign forever and ever."

16 Then the twenty-four elders who sit on their thrones before God fell on their faces and worshiped God,

17 singing, "We give you thanks, Lord God Almighty, who are and who were, for you have taken your great power and begun to reign.

18 The nations raged, but your wrath has come, and the time for judging the dead, for rewarding your servants, the prophets and saints and all who fear your name, both small and great, and for destroying those who destroy the earth."

19 Then God's temple in heaven was opened, and the ark of his covenant was seen within his temple; and there were flashes of lightning, rumblings, peals of thunder, an earthquake, and heavy hail.

$\mathcal{T}$he second series of sevens centers around the blowing of trumpets. Trumpets are especially associated as warning instruments in a war situation, whether calling for attack or retreat or just alerting (cf. Judg. 3.27 ff., 7.8 ff.; Neh. 4.18; and especially Joel 2.1). From this association, it became natural to understand a trumpet blast as announcing a coming judgment, rather like an air raid siren. Beasley-Murray, in addition, points out that on Tishri 1, the beginning of the new year was proclaimed with trumpets as a day of holy convocation and seen as an anticipation of the Day of Judgment.[199] The judgments announced by these trumpets are more specifically directed; the first four are attacks on nature and the cosmos, the last three are directed against wicked humanity – the destroyers of the earth (11.19).

Though these judgments are much more fearsome than the seven seals, they are balanced in a way the seals are not; namely, there is an announcement of coming salvation as well. The trumpet scenes end in joy with a virtual coronation scene, like in Rev. 5. These judgments, however gruesome, are not (at least in the case of the preliminary ones) punitive or final but rather are chastisements meant to lead humans to repentance. John's ultimate aim is to proclaim the calm and victory after the storm, though he gives us the storm in graphic detail as well.

Images like the demonic grasshoppers, or little things like in 8.7 where all the grass is burned up, or in 9.4 where the locusts are told not to harm the grass, make evident that there is no way to take this material literally.[200] These horrific images don't even have one-to-one correspondences with something in reality. The point simply is that God's judgments are horrific and that their effects will be devastating to humans.[201] Likewise his redemption will be greater than the wildest imaginations or dreams. Thus we should not be concerned about little inconsistencies here and there. The aim is the overall effect of the material not a detailed map of the end times.

Though there is general correspondence between the seven seals and the seven trumpets, we cannot match up the four horsemen with the four angels in

[199] G. R. Beasley-Murray, *Revelation* (1978), p. 153.
[200] See C. Koester, *Revelation and the End* (2001), p. 97. This also shows that it is difficult to take this material as chronologically linear in some respects.
[201] C. Koester (ibid., p. 100), however, argues that the "judgment depicted here is not direct divine punishment, but a revelation of what it would mean for God to hand over the world to other powers." But God's permissive will is still within the scope of God's will in the broad sense.

this vision. John might be saying, "Here are two different ways of looking at the coming storm, using differing not corresponding images." The author obviously draws on the Exodus/Sinai traditions for his plagues but freely modifies them as he chooses. Again there is no exact paralleling; rather the OT is used as a font for images and ideas. The general idea of a new exodus for God's people that will usher them into the promised land is no doubt a theme here, only in this case the promised land is the New Jerusalem at the end of time and space. The judgment like the salvation involves all of humanity. Thus it is Exodus/Sinai on a grander scale not mere repetition of a previous pattern of deliverance. The use of OT images to describe the fate of the church proves once more that the author sees in the church the new Israel. God's true people are Jew and Gentile united in Christ.

Rev. 8.5 begins with a statement that there are seven angels with seven trumpets all prepared to blow them upon order. Following the blowing of the seven trumpets are judgments that though they will affect the church on earth they are not directed against the church. Notice that while the first four judgments affect the church, the last three do not. The last three are demonic attacks from which the church is protected. These judgments are not final any more than those involved with the seals. We are told they are meant to lead people to repentance.[202] The division of four and then three judgments with a pause before the seventh one is also like the seals. Mounce suggests that what is happening to the church during the plagues is described in Rev. 11–13.[203] There are several keys to understanding this segment of the book. (1) The three woes should be seen as identical to the last three trumpet blasts, describing the same reality. (2) The third woe and seventh trumpet are important for John's purposes in this segment (see 10.6–7). (3) While the delay in the seven seals sequence before the last seal is opened has to do with protecting God's people from judgments, the delay in the second sequence of seven before the seventh trumpet is for the sake of the witness of the people of God to the world. (4) There is an intricate structure to the judgments sequence. In 4.5; 8.5; 11.19; and 16.18–21, we have a formulaic listing of calamities basically in the same order used to link this material together. The "seventh seal-opening, the climax of the first series, described by this formula in 8.5 encompasses the whole course of the judgments of the seven trumpets, and similarly the judgment of the seventh trumpet described by this formula in 11.19b, encompasses the whole series of bowl judgments, climaxing in the fullest elaboration of the formula in 16.18–21."[204]

The first trumpet blast corresponds to some degree with the seventh plague in Exod. 9.23 ff. except that this hail is mixed with blood – a gruesome rain indeed.

---

[202] See E. Fiorenza, *Revelation* (1991), p. 73: "Revelation's mythological rhetoric represents the repulsive and grotesque powers of Satan and the abyss in order to shock the audience to repent of idolatry and to reject completely destructive powers."

[203] R. H. Mounce, *Book of Revelation* (1977), p. 177.

[204] See R. Bauckham, *Climax of Prophecy* (1993), pp. 11–13.

The effect on the earth is that a third of it is burned up, including all the grass and a third of the trees. There is no specific significance to the one-third except it indicates a larger fraction than the effect of the seven seals. It also indicates that this judgment is not total or final. Unlike the Egyptian plagues listed in Exodus, it is impossible to provide any sort of naturalistic explanation of all these plagues. They are to be seen as divine and supernatural judgments.

The second trumpet blast produces a great mountain on fire that falls into the sea, turning a third of the sea into blood and destroying a third of the sea life and a third of the boats in the vicinity. Possibly the audience would visualize this by remembering the great eruption of Vesuvius in A.D. 79. Jews had seen the eruption of Vesuvius as a judgment on Rome, and Rome may soon come into the picture in our material here as well. It is not clear whether John envisions a sea full of blood, or just a boiling blood-red sea.

The third trumpet is blown, and a great star falls from heaven, on fire like a lighted lamp. Possibly we are to think of a meteorite that falls on and affects a third of the rivers and springs, polluting the water and making it taste like wormwood. Wormwood was not poisonous but very bitter.[205] The star itself is called Wormwood because of its effect on the water. Many died because when they drank the water they got sick. So poor was the state of medicine in that era that people died of even minor ailments. Jer. 9.15 and 23.15 speak of drinking wormwood as God's punishment on his people.

The fourth trumpet blows, and a third of the earth's sources of light and thus life is cut off. The result, however, is somewhat different than one might think. It is not that the earth gets light a third less intense but rather that a third more of the day ends up in total darkness. Caird points out in all of this that for those for whom death is seen as the ultimate tragedy, these events are horrible indeed. But that is not John's point of view.[206] He will go on to make clear that for many death is going to be preferred to a living hell or nightmare. The saints who face death then are not to see it as the worst possible thing that could happen to them. After the fourth trumpet blast John sees a bird flying high overhead crying, "Woe, woe, woe" on those dwelling upon the earth and those remaining to hear the last three trumpet blasts. Those who remain to hear the last three blasts will have to undergo what they herald. The Greek noun ***aetos*** can certainly refer to an eagle, but at Luke 17.37 it appears to mean vulture, as is the case in the LXX. One may compare Hos. 8.1: "Set the trumpet to your lips, for a vulture is over the house of the Lord." It would be much more appropriate for this bird to be a bird of prey, a carrion bird, in light of the human slaughter that follows

---

[205] See Prov. 5.4; Lam. 3.15, 19, cf. Deut. 29.18; Jer. 9.15; 23.15). The plant seems to be *Artemisia herbalba Asso*, a small bush with gray leaves. It seems to have gotten its name because its leaves were used as a folk remedy for intestinal worms. See M. G. Reddish, *Revelation* (2001), p. 167.

[206] G. B. Caird, *Revelation* (1998), pp. 111–17.

(cf. Matt. 24.28; Luke 17.37; Rev. 19.17–18).[207] Here and in the rest of these plagues John has taken some of his audience's worst fears and experiences of wars and natural disasters and "blown them to apocalyptic proportions, and cast them in biblically allusive terms. The point is not to predict a series of events. The point is to evoke the meaning of divine judgment which is impending on the sinful world."[208]

The fifth trumpet is blown, and a star falls from heaven at **Rev. 9.1**, but this star is obviously a being of some sort for it is given the key to unlock the well of the abyss. There is significant debate as to whether we should see this figure as the same as the angel in 20.1 who comes down from heaven with the key to the abyss. Caird, however, points out that the former figure releases the destroyers upon the earth, while the latter shuts them up, but also he sees the former purpose as evil and the latter as good.[209] This latter distinction can probably not be made, since the former creature was given the key by someone in heaven, suggesting it is part of the divine purpose. Thus Mounce is perhaps right in identifying the two figures at one point acting for God in judgment, at another in mercy. The term abyss originally denoted the chaos waters at the beginning of creation that covered the earth and that God then confined (cf. Ps. 33.7). It was thus the location of the great sea monster Leviathan. In a natural development of ideas, the abyss came to be thought of as being the place where evil creatures (demons and fallen angels) were kept (see 1 En. 18–21).

From this great abyss or well arose smoke like that coming from a great furnace, and the sky and the sun were covered over in blackness. With this effective smoke screen set up, a swarm of locusts comes forth with the power of scorpions – that is, with stingers in their tails. Unlike normal locusts, these are told not to consume the vegetation but rather to attack the human beings without the essential mark on their foreheads. The stings did not kill but rather produced a situation of torture. These locusts were given five months to do their worst. Of course, a locust plague could indeed darken the sky for they have been known to swarm one hundred feet deep and four miles long. It is also true that the life cycle of a grasshopper is five months long, so this could explain the five-month figure.

There is some confusion about how we should relate the sealing of the saints as in 7.1–8 to this event where the foreheads are marked. One would think this fifth trumpet event must be subsequent to the sixth seal, but these matters must not be pressed. The torment these creatures produce is so great that people will seek to die, but death will flee from them. The author describes the locusts as like warhorses ready for battle. On their heads they wore what looked like gold crowns, but hideously their faces were human-looking though they had teeth

---

[207] But since the eagle was the symbol on Roman military insignia, there may be an allusion to this here. See Josephus, *Ant.* 17.151. Rome is depicted as an eagle in 4 Ezra 11.1–12.39.

[208] R. Bauckham, *Theology of the Book of Revelation* (1993), p. 20.

[209] G. B. Caird, *Revelation* (1998), pp. 117–18.

like a lion (on their head or legs?). In addition they have a breastplate like iron, and the sound of their wings is like the sound of many chariots riding into battle. Their general or, in this case, their ruler or king (*basilea* is like a king) is the angel of the abyss, presumably the one who let them out of jail. His name is Abaddon in Hebrew and Apollyon in Greek. The intended impact is of awesome hideousness and cruelty. It may be that John wants us to think of these creatures as the size of horses.[210]

A CLOSER LOOK — FALLEN ANGELS IN EARLY JUDAISM AND CHRISTIANITY

There was much fascination with the notion of fallen angels or spirits, especially those referred to in Gen. 6.1–4 in both Jewish and Christian literature, not only the canonical literature but also the extracanonical literature. One of the most consistent elements in this tradition is the notion of their imprisonment in some pit or abyss.

Within the canon, our earliest text of relevance is found in Isa. 24.21–22, where we read, "On that day the Lord will punish the host of heaven and on earth the kings of earth. They will be gathered together like prisoners in a pit, they will be shut up in a prison, and after many days they will be punished."[211] While the identity of the host of heaven is not absolutely clear, the contrast of them with the kings of the earth makes it likely that rebellious powers in heaven are in view (cf. Deut. 32.8; Dan. 10.13). There is also the suggestion that these powers in heaven are the ones controlling or directing the rebellious kings and their nations, which are also mentioned. Crucial about this passage is the stress that these powers are put in something like an extraterrestrial prison or holding cell until the time comes for them to be punished.

The second passage from closer to the time of if not during the early stages of the NT era is in 1 En. 10:4–6. Here the picture of the two-stage defeat of these powers (or at least one of them) is clarified and particularized: "the Lord said to Raphael, 'Bind Azaz'el[212] hand and foot, throw him into the darkness!' And he made a hole in the desert which was in Duda'el and cast him there; he threw on top of him rugged sharp rocks. And he covered his face in order that he might not see the light; and in order that he might be sent into the great fire on the day of judgment."[213] The fallen angels are imprisoned in a place full of fire that

---

[210] G. R. Beasley-Murray, *Revelation* (1978), p. 162, suggests that the description owes something to an Arabian proverb that compared "the head of the locust with the head of a horse, its breast with the breast of a lion, its feet with the feet of a camel, its body with the body of a snake, its tail with the tail of a scorpion, its antennae with the hair of a maiden."

[211] The following paragraphs in this excursus are in a somewhat different form in my *Jesus the Seer*, pp. vii–xii.

[212] Clearly a demonic figure; see, e.g., D. P. Wright, "Azazel," in *ABD*, vol. 1, pp. 536–37.

[213] One should compare this text to 1 En. 10.12, 18.14–19, 21.6–10, 90.23–27 and Jub. 5.6–10, 10.5–9.

had a cleft reaching to the abyss, according to 1 En. 21.7. Jub. 5.6 says these angels have been placed and confined in the depths of the earth.

Our next port of call is found in several NT texts, the earliest of which is Jude. For convenience I present these three texts in columns to facilitate the comparison.

Jude	*2 Peter*	*1 Peter*
(vs. 6)	(2.4)	(3.19–20)
"and the angels who didn't keep their own position, but left their proper dwelling, he has kept in eternal chains in deepest darkness for the judgment of the Great Day"	"For if God did not spare the angels when they sinned, but cast them into Tartaros and commited them to chains of deepest darkness to be kept until the judgment"	[Christ] "went and made a proclamation to the spirits in prison, who in former times did not obey when God waited patiently in the days of Noah."

Obviously, the first two are more similar to each other than the third is to either of them. Bauckham has shown at considerable length that there is likely a literary link between Jude and 2 Peter, as this and other material from the same parts of these documents show.[214] The first two of these texts are not obviously of Christological import, though if the reference to Christ as Lord in Jude vs. 4 prepares for vs. 5, where the Lord is the one who saved the people from Egypt and then kept the angels in chains, then we have a comment on Christ's preexistence and roles in Israel's history, drawing on Wisdom ideas not unlike what we find in 1 Cor. 10.4 (cf. Wisd. of Sol. 11.4). The author of 2 Peter would seem to see God and not Christ as the one who chained the disobedient angels, and this comports with the font of this tradition found in Isaiah.

In all these NT texts, the reference is to the story in Gen. 6.1–4, where God was so outraged by what the angels (sons of God) did with the daughters of humanity that God brought a flood upon the earth. This context is more obvious in the 1 Pet. 3 use of this material, and it is in 1 Pet. 3 that we find something of clear Christological importance. Christ (vs. 18 makes clear this is who it is) goes and preaches to these angels in prison. Though the 1 Pet. 3 text has been the basis of the credal statement "he descended into hell" and also the basis of various "second chance" theologies it is doubtful this text has anything to do with such notions. Nothing is said about Christ's "descent" anywhere. We are simply told that after Christ died and was "made alive in the Spirit" he went and preached or made a proclamation to these spirits or angels. There may be a trace of this whole theological development in the hymn fragment in 1 Tim. 3.16, where we hear that Christ was "vindicated in spirit," a remark immediately followed by "seen by angels." Commentators have always thought this remark was out of place. If it referred to Christ's entry into heaven, it would be better placed just before or after the last line of the hymn, which reads "taken up in glory." This

---

[214] See R. Bauckham, *Jude and 2 Peter* (Waco, Texas: Word, 1983).

reference to being seen by angels may not be out of place, however, if it is about Christ's visit to Tartaros. Eph. 4.8 may be of relevance here as well for there it is said of Christ quoting Ps. 68.18, with alterations, "When he ascended on high, he led or made captivity itself captive."

To understand this material, a certain knowledge of Jewish angeology and demonology is necessary. For our purposes, it is only necessary to say that the powers and principalities and indeed Satan himself were believed to inhabit the realm between heaven and earth. This is one reason why the planets were sometimes assumed to be heavenly beings or angels ("the heavenly host") and is also why Satan is called in the NT "the Ruler of the Power of the Air" (Eph. 2.2). It would appear then that 1 Pet. 3, far from being about a descent to humans, is about Christ's ascent to the angels on his way to heaven, at which point he proclaimed his victory over such powers and thereby made their captivity all the more permanent and their doom sure. This material would provide us with another strand of evidence of the development of cosmic Christology or Christus Victor (over the powers) and would show this is not simply a Pauline development. It would also provide another piece of evidence for the phenomenon whereby actions predicated of God in earlier Jewish traditions are now predicated of Christ in the NT.[215]

There is actually a remarkable coherence between these five texts with signs of development in Enoch in the naming of the demon, in the NT in the naming of the prison itself, and finally in the focus in 1 Pet. 3 on the role of Christ in relationship to these beings. Yet, without hearing the echoes of or allusions to the earlier prophetic texts, it is understandable how especially the text in 1 Pet. 3 has so often been misread. Longitudinal studies in the trajectory of the prophetic tradition offer many such revelations.[216]

In light of the above, both Rev. 9 and Rev. 20.1–2 should be reconsidered. Both texts speak about the binding of the demonic in some pit and then of their later release. This stands clearly in the same line of tradition as the material just discussed. This shows that John is conversant with such Jewish and Christian traditions both in their apocalyptic and nonapocalyptic forms and that he makes good use of them.

⌘

Abaddon in Hebrew is just another name for Hades, the land of the dead (Job 31.12; Ps. 88.11; Prov. 15.11 cf. Rev. 6.8). The Greek word **Apollyon** is unique,

---

[215] For a compelling study of the material in the Petrine texts that leaves little doubt that they are angelic not human beings who are in this dark prison and that the land of the dead or hell is not meant, see W. J. Dalton, *Christ's Proclamation to the Spirits: A Study of 1 Peter 3.18–4.6* (Rome: Pontifical Biblical Institute Press, 1965).

[216] Another example of this sort of approach on a larger scale but dealing with one particular tradition is found in J. T. Greene, *Balaam and His Interpreters: A Hermeneutical History of the Balaam Traditions* (Atlanta: Scholars Press, 1992).

but obviously it ultimately comes from the word for "to destroy." One must ask whether there is also any connection with the god Apollo. When one pursues this, one discovers that the symbol for Apollo is the locust,[217] and Domitian gave himself out to be the incarnation of Apollo. This may mean that John is suggesting that the Emperor is the leader of the pack in hell. This would fit well with the descriptions of Rome that follow. As frightening as this sight is, there are yet two more woes to come. It becomes clear that woes one and two are to be identified with the fifth and sixth trumpet blasts and what follows from them. This leads to the correspondence between the seventh trumpet and the third woe.

The sixth angel blows his trumpet, and a voice from the horns of the altar commands the angel, "Loose the four angels who are bound at the great river Euphrates." These are probably not to be identified with the four angels who stand on the earth's corners. There are many many angels in Revelation, and we need not assume associations purely on the basis of numbers. The location of these angels is significant, for not only were the Romans frightened of the Parthian hordes that might charge out of the east, but Jews were as well, for their captors – both Babylonians and Assyrians – had come from beyond the Euphrates. That the voice comes from the four horns of the altar, where the sacrificial blood was applied, suggests that it is the voice of the martyrs.

These angels are in charge of a demonic horde of horsemen numbering 200 million, probably a larger number than the entire population of those who lived in the Mediterranean crescent![218] Their task is to kill a third of humanity. John would no doubt have laughed at attempts to identify this horde with a group of human beings for he is talking about powers and principalities. Though, as Caird says, evil has a human face like the locusts; even human evil may be guided and goaded by supernatural evil.[219] The angels had been readied for these actions and hour – a precise act at a precise time. The horses have fiery red, violet, and yellow breastplates, and it may be more than coincidence that Parthians did ride horses with breastplates, indeed brightly colored breastplates.[220] But the heads of these horses were like the heads of lions with fire and sulphur and smoke coming out from their months. The power of these creatures was both in their mouths and in their tails, which were like harmful snake heads.

Again the author is not describing what will happen but using images to create a sense of the horrible nature of undergoing God's wrath. In 12.9 Satan is called the old serpent, which is probably an indication of the demonic nature of these creatures. The point is that God allows evil but uses it for his just purposes – he makes the wrath of even Satan to serve Him. That the horses are harmful

---

[217] See Aeschylus, *Agamemnon* 1080–86.
[218] See C. Keener, *Revelation* (2002), p. 273.
[219] G. B. Caird, *Revelation* (1998), pp. 121–23.
[220] On the Parthians, see Horace, *Epistles* 2.1.112; *Ode* 1.19.12; 4.15.24; Martial, *Epigrams* 2.53.10.

before and behind may also be reminiscent of the Parthians, who shot both going forward and turning around facing backward. Yet, despite the horrific nature of these woes, the nonsaved humanity left did not repent and indeed, continued to worship their demonic deities. Why should they run away from the demonic or repent when they worshiped the demonic? As in Deut. 32.17 and elsewhere in the OT, as in Rom. 1, bad theology leads to bad ethics, and bad religion leads to immorality. Not only were idols and demons continually worshiped, but murder, fornication, theft, and other vices were continuing to be commited. *Pharmakon* probably refers to the use of magical charms to achieve some end. The word could be translated sorceries. The use of witchcraft and potions was part and parcel of pagan religion. It was used to gain control of supernatural forces or of events controlled by those forces. In any event, wicked humanity became even more hardened in their wickedness in the wake of these woes.

Some of the most debated material in the whole book of Revelation is to be found in **Rev. 10–11**. Mounce and various others have seen in the so-called interludes literary devices by which the church is instructed about its future and its role in the interim before the end.[221] It is argued that there is no interval between the sixth and seventh bowl because, by then, all warnings and preliminary judgment are over. We will draw conclusions about such matters as we proceed through these two chapters, but for now it is important to see the heavenly worship scenes not as interruptions to the action but as divine commentary on the action and to some degree divine precipitation of the action. Worship and adoration of God and the Lamb is one of the main goals of the rhetoric of this work, and so the worship scenes should not be seen as heavenly commercials or interruptions on that account either. This is made clear by the doxological conclusion in Rev. 22 when God comes to dwell with his people.

We are told at the outset of **Rev. 10.1** that another strong or mighty angel descends from above.[222] This obviously links with what precedes in this book, and we probably should see this as the angel or messenger of Christ who partakes of some of the features of Christ mentioned in Rev. 1.[223] The angel is wearing a cloud and a rainbow upon his head. The former emphasizes the mysterious nature of this revelation, and the latter is probably a reflection of the covenant made with Noah that involved the rainbow as a covenant sign. This angel should be then a harbinger of good news and mercy for a world judged by God in incredible fashion, as seen with the seals and trumpets. This angel has a face seeming to reflect the divine glory, and his legs are like fiery pillars, reminiscent of the Exodus events.

---

[221] See R. H. Mounce, *Book of Revelation* (1977), pp. 200–5.

[222] M. G. Reddish, *Revelation* (2001), p. 191, notes that the phrase "I saw" occurs over forty times in Revelation, indicating its very visual nature.

[223] It is interesting that this angel has even been identified with the emperors Justin or Justinian and with monks such as Benedict or St. Francis of Assisi. See A. W. Wainwright, *Mysterious Apocalypse* (1993), pp. 54–57.

In this angel's hand is a little scroll already open, unlike the previous sealed scroll. Yet is doubtful that the noun indicates a scroll any shorter than the previous one, for in Rev. 5 the word there is little book (Biblion). Beasley-Murray sees in Rev. 5 a document and in Rev. 10 a book roll.[224] The openness of the book roll suggests that what it reveals is no secret. It may also be significant that this revelation is on earth, and apparently John is on earth to receive it. This may explain the difference in perspective and in time references in this section.

The angel is a colossal figure bestriding both land and sea, possibly indicating the scope of the relevance of his message. He opens his mouth and roars like a lion, and when he did so seven thunders spoke in response. John tells us he was about to write down what the thunders said, but he is prohibited from doing so. This revelation is to be sealed up rather than written down. This may be because John is called upon not to reveal all he experienced or heard but only that which he is directed to communicate. In this case he may be called upon to communicate what is in the open little scroll the angel brings with him. The angel assumes the posture of one who is swearing to the truth of what he reveals, with a most solemn oath on God. He swears that there will be no more delay. As Mounce says, this phrase with *chronos* should not be interpreted to mean that there will be no more time, as if time was to be dissolved into eternity. Rather here we have the response to the cry of the saints under the altar who asked, "How long?" When the seventh angel blows his trumpet, the mystery of God is complete, as it has been made known to God's servants, the prophets. As 11.15 ff. makes clear, when the seventh trumpet is sounded, all is complete except the final eschatological celebration. The mystery of God would seem to refer to all that has been previously revealed in this book about the events leading up to the end. They are called mystery because apart from God's revelation, it is hard to see God's saving hand in them because of all the evil and suffering involved, especially during the tribulation. "The completion of the 'mystery' (10.7) probably indicates that the seven thunders will no longer remain secret (10.4); all will be revealed at the consummation (cf. 1 Cor. 13.8–12)."[225]

As **Rev. 11** shows, it is impossible to arrange all penultimate events, prior to the kingdom's coming, in any sort of clear chronological order. If Rev. 11 is about the destruction of the temple in Jerusalem in A.D. 70, then no sooner do we hear there will be no more delay before the final event when we backpedal to some earlier events. The mystery is made known to the prophets. This may or may not be a reference to Christian prophets contemporary with John. More likely John sees himself as in the line of OT prophets, for it is said of them in Amos 3.7 that God does nothing without telling his servants, the prophets. It seems unnecessary to identify these prophets with martyrs.

---

[224] G. R. Beasley-Murray, *Book of Revelation* (1978), pp. 168–69.
[225] C. Keener, *Revelation* (2002), p. 282.

John is exhorted to take the little scroll from the hand of the angel. John very politely goes and asks for the little scroll. He is exhorted to eat it up, and though it will be bitter in the stomach, it will be sweet on the lips and in the mouth. This is a variant of what we find Ezekiel is told in Ezek. 2.8–3.3. Jer. 15.16 ff. may also be in view. These OT precedents suggest that the message involves cause both for joy and for lamentation. If the message of this scroll is, "There is no more delay," we can see why there would be a mixed reaction.[226] No more delay means the kingdom is fully coming, but it also means no more chance for amendment of lives. Mounce and others hold that the contents of the scroll are found in Rev. 11 and following. If this is correct, this chapter involves both proclamation and martyrdom for the witnesses. To take the message of the little scroll to be Rev. 11 involves seeing in it a message for the church primarily, not for the world. Others, such as Beasley-Murray, stress that here we have the recommissioning of John and that vs. 11 indicates the real meaning of the scroll, namely that he must prophesy again about many peoples. If this is correct, the scroll is about what we find in Rev. 12 ff. Beasley-Murray sees in Rev. 11 a sort of intrusion of a Jewish apocalypse, which could be left out. But the truth is we are not told what the content is of the scroll. It seems that eating the scroll is a prerequisite to accomplishing the task set before him in vs. 11. Koester suggests that in Rev. 11 we have an overture to the last half of the book, introducing us in summary form to the conflict between God's people and the Beast that is recounted in Rev. 12–19.[227]

At the beginning of Rev. 11 John is given a cane and a staff and told to rise up and measure the temple of God and its surroundings.[228] This task also goes back to Ezek. 40–48, and there are at least a dozen suggestions as to the significance of the measuring. We may break them down to four basic ideas. (1) Measuring is preliminary to rebuilding and restoring. This is the case in Ezekiel, and it is understandable how a Jewish Christian prophet after A.D. 70 might see himself in the same position as Ezekiel. But how would this square with John seeming to see the church as the new temple of God? Would not any restoration of the old temple seem superfluous to someone with that theology? (2) The temple is being sized up for destruction. This would seem to be a possibility only if this book was written prior to A.D. 70, which is unlikely.[229] (3) The measurements are taken to indicate the parts to be protected from physical harm. This would not seem to fit with the theme of partial judgments before this point in the narrative, a theme that includes the notion that even Christians will suffer from the partial judgments to some degree. (4) The measuring signifies preservation

---

[226] It seems improbable that the content of the scroll is about a prophetic commission, since that was already depicted at the outset of Revelation. But see M. G. Reddish, *Revelation* (2001), p. 198.

[227] C. Koester, *Revelation and the End* (2001), p. 104.

[228] On which temple John had in mind, see M. Bachmann, "Himmelisch: Der 'Tempel Gottes' von Apk. 11.1," *NTS* 40 (1994), pp. 474–80.

[229] See the Introduction.

from spiritual harm. If the reference is to Christians, or some portion of the Christian community, this might be suitable. Against any sort of Jewish reference to the temple, the text refers not just to the building but to those worshiping in it. Furthermore, elsewhere in Revelation, the temple is symbolic (3.12; 13.6).[230] The structure of the Herodian temple involved three major inner courts – one for the priests, one for the Jewish men, and one for the Jewish women. There was a wall around these courts complete with a warning sign for Gentiles not to enter on pain of death, and outside that wall was the court of the Gentiles. In our text John uses the word *naos*, which normally refers to the inner sanctum of the temple not to the whole of the temple precincts. This comports with the view that spiritual protection, not necessarily protection of their physical temples, is what is being promised here.

The reference to forty-two months comes from Daniel and is just another way of rendering the period of three and a half years, that final penultimate period before the end of history. What is recorded as happening at **11.14** to the temple and in Jerusalem (the locale must be Jerusalem since it is identified as the city where the Lord was crucified) is the second woe, not the last one. Thus we must now broach the question of who the two witnesses are.

Whoever these witnesses are, it is clear that they are presented as being like Elijah and Moses. The background of these symbols is far clearer than the foreground. Not only do they bring the fire-breathing Word of God to earth, including plagues, but also they are taken back up into heaven. If this is a prophecy about the fall of Jerusalem, why is it put here and simply called the second woe? Or again, if, as G. Ladd maintains, this is a prophecy about the final preservation of the Jewish people, why are the witnesses identified with the figure used in the seven letters to identify the church?[231] Much more probable is the suggestion that we have a prophecy either about the whole church and its task in the world as witnesses and as the temple of God, or it is a specific reference to two churches that are undergoing persecution and even martyrdoms – for instance, Smyrna and Philadelphia.[232] This would explain why the number two is used here of the witnesses rather than the earlier seven for the churches in question. Some scholars see in the number two a reference to Deut. 19.15, where two validating witnesses are required to testify to the truth of anything. If John believed this still to be true, it might imply he needed someone outside himself to authenticate his revelation, which he obviously doesn't seem to think he needs. He is not really claiming this is his revelation but that of Christ through him and thus having its own inherent authority.[233] It is much easier to see here a

---

[230] See C. Koester, *Revelation and the End* (2001), pp. 106–7.

[231] G. Ladd, *A Commentary on Revelation of John* (Grand Rapids, Mich.: Eerdmans, 1972), pp. 160–61.

[232] Another conjecture is that Peter and Paul are alluded to but they were not raised as 11.11 suggests of these witnesses. See C. Keener, *Revelation* (2002), p. 291.

[233] On the issue of authority and ethos, see pp. 65–67.

reference either to the whole of the church and its prophetic role as witness or to two of John's churches undergoing persecution. This fits with the reference to the lampstands. Also if John could cast his own experience in the light of the prophet Ezekiel, there is no reason he could not cast the experience of two of his churches in the light of Moses' and Elijah's lives. After all the churches are to bear prophetic witness to the revelation of God as John does. "Their period of witnessing coincides with the time when persecution and suffering of the faithful will be at its worst."[234] Notice that the garb of the witnesses is sackcloth, that of those in mourning. This suggests that their message may deal with repentance from the state of moral apostasy.[235]

Furthermore the idea of only outward harm to the temple would imply that persecution and even physical death can do no spiritual harm to the witnesses in these and other churches. Here there is a relevant word of encouragement to John's audience or at least a part of it. This text would imply that the church will be on the earth during the great tribulation, during the penultimate three and a half years of human history.[236] The witnesses are called olive trees for they carry in them the fuel by which the candlestick could be lit.

In **vs. 8** we must see the reference to Sodom and Egypt as a statement about the spiritual status of Jerusalem. It was a city occupied and, in fact, trampled underfoot in A.D. 95 by Gentiles. " 'Sodom' was a prophetic title for Jerusalem that implied its judgment (Is. 1.9–10; Jer. 23.14; Lam. 4.6)."[237] In other words it is a place of oppression, slavery, and gross immorality.[238] That the bodies of the witnesses were not allowed to be buried was considered in the ancient near east the ultimate way to disgrace or shame someone (see Isa. 5.25; Ps. Sol. 2.30 ff.). There has already been clear indication of antagonistic relationships with Jews in this document,[239] and it appears to continue here. Possibly John has in mind that he is describing what happened to some of his fellow believers when on pilgrimage up to Jerusalem, but the flexibility of the symbolism is such that we can't be sure. Again Ezekiel is drawn on in **vs. 11** to speak of the resurrection of the two witnesses. This may refer to the first resurrection of the martyrs, which is treated further in Rev. 20.2.

In **vs. 12** we hear of the witnesses being caught up to heaven. This echoes what is said of Elijah in 2 Kings 2.11 (cf. Rev. 11.6). There were also ascent traditions about Enoch and Moses as well.[240] This is a sign of the vindication of these witnesses

---

[234] M. G. Reddish, *Revelation* (2001), p. 210.
[235] Ibid.
[236] Being half of seven, three and a half is a symbol of incompletion and so of imperfection.
[237] C. Keener, *Revelation* (2002), p. 295.
[238] Sodom was said to be destroyed by sulphur and fire in Gen. 19.24, 28. Cf. Deut. 29.23; Job 18.15; Ps. 11.6; Isa. 30.33, 34.9; Ezek. 38.22; Luke 17.29. On using symbolic names like Sodom or Babylon to refer to the character of other cities, see *P. Oxy.* 3314, cited in Horsley et al., eds., *New Docs.*, vol. 3, p. 141.
[239] See pp. 98–100 on the "synagogue of Satan."
[240] See 1 En. 39.3; Josephus, *Ant.* 4.326.

and occurs immediately preceding the end of the age, not as in dispensational theology several years before (see 11.15).[241] According to **vs. 13**, a tenth part of the city fell during supernaturally induced upheavals, and the number of dead is 7,000 (which is very close to a tenth of the population of Jerusalem in the early part of the first century A.D.). There is also the heartening reference to the repentance of the city in 11.11–13. Fiorenza argues that 11.13 "seems to anticipate the pronouncement of 15.3–4 that all the nations will come and worship God. It is crucial to recognize that Revelation's rhetoric of judgment expresses hope for the conversion of nine-tenths of the nations in response to Christian witness and preaching. Otherwise, one will not understand that the author advocates a theology of justice rather than a theology of hate and resentment."[242] Koester points out the reversal that John suggests when one compares 1 Kings 19.18 to Rev. 11.13. In the former, all but 7,000 embrace idolatry, in the latter all but 7,000 glorify God. "The conversion of the nations, rather than their destruction is God's will for the world (14.7)."[243]

The seventh angel sounds his trumpet, but instead of the third woe happening, we hear a song of praise in heaven that Christ's reign in heaven has now become his reign on earth (the word ***basileia*** could be translated either reign or kingdom/realm).[244] Notice in **vs. 17** the change of address to God. He no longer "was, is, and is to come." The end has arrived, and the coming has become a reality. Thus it can be said only that God was and is. In **vs. 18** we hear that the wrathful ones will receive wrath, and the destroyers will be destroyed in the end. Also God's faithful ones – prophet, martyr, and saint – will get their eternal reward for perseverance in the faith. **Vs. 19** closes this section with the vision of God's ark, not on earth but in heaven. The ark was the locus of God's Word and his presence, and in apocalyptic vision, it is quite proper to stress the heavenly nature and origin of these things. It is accompanied by the usual signs of theophany and of God coming down, which is the ultimate event. This vision promises God will be faithful to his Word and maintain fellowship with his covenant people.

BRIDGING THE HORIZONS

Apocalyptic literature is, by its very nature, resistance literature. Borne out of the traumatic experiences of exile and then repeatedly being conquered or oppressed by one Western power or another (e.g., Alexander and his successors),

---

[241] C. Keener, *Revelation* (2002), p. 296.

[242] E. Fiorenza, *Revelation* (1991), p. 79.

[243] C. Koester, *Revelation and the End* (2001), p. 111.

[244] Reigning in heaven is something predicated of Zeus in the papyri; see Horsley et al., eds., *New Docs*, vol. 3, p. 48. See P. Barnett, *Apocalypse Now and Then* (1989), p. 97. This announcement is not about the result of Christ's death and resurrection but about what will be the case when the seventh trumpet is blown, which John clearly sees as future.

this literature was always "insider" literature with a political edge. B. K. Blount, in his analysis of Revelation, remarks,

It is not simply the language of the oppressed and marginalized; it is also the language they used to survive and defy the colonized existence imposed upon them. Jewish apocalyptic writing had already staked out an identity as oppositional literature in works like Daniel and the Maccabees. Indeed Adela Yarbro Collins observes that the hellenizing crisis brought on by the aggressive efforts of the Seleucid empire and leaders like Antiochus IV Epiphanes stirred the fires of apocalyptic feeling and directly contributed to the Maccabean revolt.[245]

Blount suggests that, since this is resistance literature, it needs to be read as such. Would a nonoppressed, nonminority person in any culture be able even to hear this text as it was originally intended to be heard? And, in any case, what was a hearing of this text originally intended to do to or in John's hearers if they actually submitted to John's visionary world?

Blount's essential proposition is that John's call to bear witness, being faithful to the Gospel and to the witnessing task even to the point of death if need be, is indeed a call to active but nonviolent resistance to the oppressive powers that be. But how to do that? According to John it involves hearing but also sharing the testimony/witness of Jesus Christ. This could refer to what Christ says in Revelation or to the testimony about Christ; in either case the issue is Christological. In what way does "testimony of Christ" become nonviolent resistance? The answer must in part be that it calls one to honor only Jesus, not Caesar, as King of kings and Lord of lords. There were apparently various early Christians at the end of the first century A.D. who saw any sort of participation in the growing and increasingly popular imperial cult as a betrayal of one's recognition of only Jesus as Lord. Mutually exclusive social options and religious positions come into play.

Blount, following A. Callahan, suggests that John deliberately chooses to write in a Semitized Greek as a symbol of his resistance to the dominant culture, for most of the time when we find a grammatical flaw in one passage we find the same phenomenon rendered flawlessly elsewhere in Revelation.[246] John is not making a mistake; he is making a point. There may be some truth to this suggestion, but one wonders if it would have been lost on his largely Gentile audience. The apocalyptic images were off-putting enough for them.

But there is something to Blount's claims that being a faithful witness, even to the point of death, helps to bring in Christ's Lordship upon the earth.[247]

---

[245] B. K. Blount, "Reading Revelation Today: Witness as Active Resistance," *Interp.* 54 (Oct. 2000), p. 399.

[246] See A. D. Callahan, "The Language of the Apocalypse," *HTR* 88 (1995), p. 457.

[247] B. K. Blount, "Reading Revelation Today," p. 410: "The more who witness, the more intolerable will become the word as witnessed, and the more belligerently Rome will be forced to act. The witnessing, the provocative activity John has been commending all

For one thing it leads to converts. For another thing it leads to persecution and martyrdom, which in turn sets God's justice into motion as a response to the persecution of his people. Witnessing in a setting where exclusive monotheism is not acceptable and where pluralism and polytheism are the norm leads to persecution and often to prosecution. The proclamation of Jesus as Lord then is a profoundly political act. The issue was not merely the proclamation of king Jesus. There were kings and lords aplenty, and this was not a problem in the Greco-Roman world so long as the Emperor was honored as the ultimate king and lord and as divine. It was the rejection not merely of polytheism but also of emperor worship rather than the affirmation of Jesus as a king that was most offensive. The judgment tales we find in this segment of Revelation must be read as the divine response in part to what had been done and was being done to the church by the Empire and its Emperor.

Something more needs to be said about prayer at this juncture and in particular about prayer in extremis. The prayer that goes up to the throne of grace in this section of Revelation and is depicted as causing silence in heaven refers to prayers of great urgency for justice. Prayer is seen, as Peterson has realized, not as mystical escape but as historical engagement. Prayer actually prompts or is allowed to facilitate or participate in God's action. "God gathers our cries and our praises, our petitions and intercessions, and uses them."[248] B. Pascal once aptly said, "Prayer is God's way of providing [humankind] with the dignity of causality."[249]

But Rev. 8–11 does not give us lessons about just any kind of prayer. It depicts prayers for justice and judgment. It is the sort that a persecuted and suffering person would find most urgent. If we do not find them so, it is probably because we do not share the author's social location. Sometimes there has been an overreaction to this particular section of Revelation, and in some quarters judgment has been banished as a topic for Christian discourse or belief. In protest against the latter H. Richard Neibuhr once wrote that the essential message of liberal Protestantism was, "A God without wrath brought me without sin into a kingdom without judgment through the ministrations of a Christ without the cross."[250] This is a Gospel that John might have typified as one the Laodiceans or other complacent Christians might have preached or received.

But it needs to be recognized that a God without judgment is also a God who does not care about justice, which is to say a God who is neither holy nor

---

along, will set up the circumstances of Rome's response. It is the witnessing, then, that leads to the coming of God's justice and vengeance, God's kingdom. Dying is a result; witnessing is the cause. For it is witnessing that plays a synergistic role with God's own efforts to accomplish the universal and abiding lordship of Jesus Christ. *This* is the revelation of Jesus Christ."

[248] E. Peterson, *Reversed Thunder* (1988), p. 95.

[249] B. Pascal, *Pensées* (New York: Modern Library, 1941), p. 166.

[250] See the quote in C. Keener, *Revelation* (2002), p. 262, and his treatment of it.

righteous nor fair. According to John and other NT writers, God's love is a holy love, and therefore it could not neglect the issues of justice and fairness. If one is a persecuted believer, one could easily say that for God to neglect justice or judgment would not be a loving thing to do. God must in the end vindicate not only his own people but the divine nature itself, or people will never recognize the full character of God, nor will God's plan for rectification of a lost world come to fruition. Justice must be done, and it must be seen to be done in space and time. This is why John writes as he does in Rev. 8–11.

One aspect of the justice of course has to do with the fall and judgment of Satan. As R. Mulholland suggests, the death and exaltation of Christ provide the turning point in the story of Satan. Not only does he no longer have a role to play in the heavenly court, his fate is sealed. Mulholland describes the process this way:

At a certain point in many chess games, the one who ultimately wins makes a move that sets the mating net. That is, from that point on the outcome of the game is a foregone conclusion. There may be as many as ten or fifteen or even more moves left before the final checkmate move that seals the victory. During these endgame moves the loser is still playing the game, still capturing pieces from the winner. But inexorably, unavoidably, finally the winner makes the checkmate move and the loser is defeated. . . . Often the move that sets the mating net is costly, a sacrificial move that lures the loser into a trap. The winner may sacrifice the most valuable piece in the game, appearing to insure defeat."[251]

This is part of what John explains in his description of the judgments. Justice extends to the cosmic realm and involves the supernatural creatures as well as the human ones.

REVELATION 12 – THE WOMAN AND THE DRAGON

NRSV Revelation 12.1 A great portent appeared in heaven: a woman clothed with the sun, with the moon under her feet, and on her head a crown of twelve stars.
2 She was pregnant and was crying out in birth pangs, in the agony of giving birth.
3 Then another portent appeared in heaven: a great red dragon, with seven heads and ten horns, and seven diadems on his heads.
4 His tail swept down a third of the stars of heaven and threw them to the earth. Then the dragon stood before the woman who was about to bear a child, so that he might devour her child as soon as it was born.
5 And she gave birth to a son, a male child, who is to rule all the nations with a rod of iron. But her child was snatched away and taken to God and to his throne;

---

[251] M. R. Mulholland, *Revelation* (1990), p. 43.

6 and the woman fled into the wilderness, where she has a place prepared by God, so that there she can be nourished for one thousand two hundred sixty days.

7 And war broke out in heaven; Michael and his angels fought against the dragon. The dragon and his angels fought back,

8 but they were defeated, and there was no longer any place for them in heaven.

9 The great dragon was thrown down, that ancient serpent, who is called the Devil and Satan, the deceiver of the whole world – he was thrown down to the earth, and his angels were thrown down with him.

10 Then I heard a loud voice in heaven, proclaiming, "Now have come the salvation and the power and the kingdom of our God and the authority of his Messiah, for the accuser of our comrades has been thrown down, who accuses them day and night before our God.

11 But they have conquered him by the blood of the Lamb and by the word of their testimony, for they did not cling to life even in the face of death.

12 Rejoice then, you heavens and those who dwell in them! But woe to the earth and the sea, for the devil has come down to you with great wrath, because he knows that his time is short!"

13 So when the dragon saw that he had been thrown down to the earth, he pursued the woman who had given birth to the male child.

14 But the woman was given the two wings of the great eagle, so that she could fly from the serpent into the wilderness, to her place where she is nourished for a time, and times, and half a time.

15 Then from his mouth the serpent poured water like a river after the woman, to sweep her away with the flood.

16 But the earth came to the help of the woman; it opened its mouth and swallowed the river that the dragon had poured from his mouth.

17 Then the dragon was angry with the woman, and went off to make war on the rest of her children, those who keep the commandments of God and hold the testimony of Jesus.

18 Then the dragon took his stand on the sand of the seashore.

*R*ev. 12 is a classic example of how an author has drawn on various sources, including pagan myths, to make a Christian point. One gets the feeling that in apocalyptic prophecy all sources are fair game so long as they can be appropriately modified. Here, then, we have an example of "plundering the Egyptians," so to speak.

A CLOSER LOOK – THE MYTHOLOGICAL BACKGROUND
OF REVELATION 12

In her book *The Combat Myth in the Book of Revelation*, A. Y. Collins has spent considerable time demonstrating that this chapter is based in part on an ancient combat myth, probably in its Babylonian form. The myth in its basic form goes like this: a dragon usually led by another Beast threatens the reigning gods or the supreme god. Sometimes in these myths the supreme god is defeated or even killed, which results in the dragon ruling in chaos for a while. Finally the dragon is defeated by the god who had ruled before or by one of his allies. This plot is certainly in evidence in Rev. 12. In some ways the closest form of this myth to our material is the Greek one, which involves the birth of Apollo from the goddess Leto. This myth has various forms, but one tells of the great dragon Python who pursued Leto because he learned that she would bear a child who would kill him. Leto was carried off to Poseidon, the god of the sea, who placed her on a remote island and then sank the island beneath the sea for good measure! After a vain search, Python retired to Mt. Parnassus, and Leto's island was brought up from the sea. When her infant was born, he immediately gained full strength, and thus Apollo within four days went and slew Python on Mt. Parnassus. Another form of the myth tells how the earth helped hide Leto by raising up the remote island.

There is, however, another and more primitive Babylonian myth also being drawn on in our text. In it we find the war taking place between Tiamat, the seven-headed sea monster, and the gods of heaven. Tiamat's flaunting of these gods was ended by Marduk, a young god of light, who hewed the sea monster in pieces. Marduk's mother is portrayed similarly to the way the woman in Rev. 12 is portrayed. In addition we are told that in the war between Tiamat and the gods a third of the stars were thrown from the sky.

Egyptian mythology may also be in the background here. Isis, wife of Osiris, gave birth to Horus, the sun god. She is portrayed with the sun on her head. The dragon Typhon was pictured as red in color but also as a crocodile or serpent (further allusion to the old serpent). In the Egyptian form of the myth the dragon slays Osiris and pursues Isis, who is about to give birth. In a miraculous manner Isis gives birth to her child and escapes to an island in a papyrus boat. The son, Horus, eventually overcomes the dragon, and it is destroyed in due course through the fire (cf. Rev. 20.1 ff.). The parallels to these various myths are too striking to be accidental and too early to argue that they were derived from Revelation. Rather John has freely drawn on elements of these myths, adding certain elements to conform the story to the Christian narrative about their Savior.

It seems probable that at least some, if not many, of John's audience would have recognized what he was doing. One of the implications of such recognition would be that, in Christ, all the primal myths and the truths they enshrine come to fulfillment. He is the incarnation of these universal truths. He proves to be the archetype of which all these others are mere types or fictional copies. Or as J. R. R. Tolkien once put it – in Christ myths become reality in human history. Various Roman emperors used these and other pagan myths to refer to themselves and their pedigree. For instance, Domitian implied he was the incarnation of divine Apollo or another deity. It is probable that the woman in our text is being portrayed as the queen of heaven. On coins we see the Emperor and his wife portrayed as sun and moon. Roma, the goddess and patroness of Rome, was represented as the queen of the gods and mother of the savior. In Rev. 12 is a counterclaim to such notions. Jesus, the male child, not Domitian or another emperor, is the real conqueror of evil, and the woman from whom he comes (either Mary or the community of God's people; cf. below) is the real queen of heaven, the real mother of the Savior. Here is an antiestablishment mythology if there ever was one. Yet our author also draws on sources such as Dan. 7 and adapts his sources to biblical contours. It could be said that this story is an allegory of sorts, though not every element in it refers to something outside the story. Reddish warns us against the danger of "getting so involved in trying to uncover the sources of John's images and the historical and political referents underneath the symbolism that one fails to see the overarching vision that John is presenting."[252] "John produces a distinctively Christian perspective both from biblical and from pagan mythological language. Christianity reworks its biblical heritage and transforms pagan material in line with its own aim of communicating truth in its cultural context. Its tendency to inculturate the Gospel without adulterating it is as old as the NT itself."[253]

Commentators have often remarked on the abrupt transition from Rev. 11.19 to 12.1.[254] This is in part due to the different sources of the material in Rev. 11 and Rev. 12, but it is also because the author is providing something of a flashback, or a return to an earlier part of the story. One should not read Rev. 12–14 as simply the chronological sequel to what has come before it. Many scholars would see Rev.12.1–14.5 as a sort of parenthesis, but that is not a very helpful designation. While Rev. 12.1–14.5 (or 14.20) does seem to be a rhetorical unit, seeing it as a parenthesis is not appropriate. For one thing, some of our most explicitly Christian material is found in this section of Revelation, and for another, John makes clear in this material that the battle is with the powers and principalities, not just human forces. Here more than elsewhere John peels back the canvas and shows us the underlying and overarching supernatural forces at work.

I would choose to differ with Caird, who thinks we simply have heavenly symbols of a purely earthly struggle here.[255] I would suggest John believes he is describing supernatural realities, though he is freely using metaphorical language to do so (e.g., Satan is not really thought by the author to be a snake or a

---

[252] M. G. Reddish, *Revelation* (2001), p. 230.
[253] C. H. Giblin, *The Book of Revelation: The Open Book of Prophecy* (Collegeville, Minn.: Liturgical Press, 1991), p. 125.
[254] See, e.g., J. Roloff, *Revelation of John* (1993), p. 139.
[255] See G. B. Caird, *Revelation* (1998), pp. 147–56.

dragon). John believes that these realities exist and that they dramatically affect the course of human history. Nor is it just a matter of him thinking that heaven and earth are parallel universes so that war in heaven mirrors war on earth. Rather, in John's view, there is but one struggle, and it involves both heaven and earth. Furthermore John believes there is an open heaven with beings coming and going to earth and back again with great regularity. I would, however, agree that in Rev.12.1–14.5 we have a close-up of the whole tapestry of vision, or if we choose the portrait analogy, a looking behind the canvas at points.[256] Far from this material being a mere parenthesis, it is a close-up of some of the most crucial elements that are shaping and directing the drama that will unfold.[257] Here we have clues to unlocking various of the symbols elsewhere in the book.[258]

Rev. 12.1 begins by telling us that the author saw a great sign[259] or portent appearing in the *ouranos*. Mounce says that here and at 15.1 this language connotes a spectacle pointing us toward the consummation of the story.[260] Elsewhere the word sign or spectacle can refer to Satan's deceptive miracles. The question arises as to whether we should translate *ouranos* as sky or heaven. Either rendering is possible, but as the story unfolds heaven seems the more likely translation. We hear of a woman clothed with the sun, with the moon under her feet and a crown (*stephanos*) with twelve stars. Much conjecture has been offered as to whether this crown might represent the constellations or, more specifically, the twelve signs of the zodiac. The point is that in this woman the destiny of the whole race lies, drawing on the notion that stars control one's future or fate. But the question is, Who is this woman?

The conjecture still favored by most Roman Catholic scholars is that it is Mary. This is not impossible, but two factors are usually thought to counter this conclusion. (1) At vs. 17 we hear about "the rest of her offspring" (*semeia* – seed here). This is surely unlikely to be a reference to Jesus' other physical kin. It is more likely to refer to believers, perhaps in particular persecuted believers or those about to be persecuted. (2) The parallels to our text in Isa. 66.6–9 strongly suggest mother Zion is in view or, as Paul would put it, the New Jerusalem, which is our mother (Gal. 4.26). In short here is the community of God's people, and

---

256 D. E. Aune, *Revelation 6–22* (1998), pp. 400 ff., suggests that the three visions in Rev. 12–14 represent the past (Rev. 12), the present (the Beasts – Rev. 13), and the future (Rev. 14).

257 Though there are a few grammatical problems in this segment, there are not any significant textual problems except in regard to the last verse of this section, where it is either John standing on the sand by the sea or, more probably, the Beast standing near to the source from which it came – the chaos waters.

258 See C. Keener, *Revelation* (2002), p. 312.

259 This word can sometimes be translated constellation (e.g., virgo and draco), but the action that follows makes it clear that we are talking about earthly activities involving beings, including human beings. Where John sees these entities does not dictate their nature. See C. Keener, *Revelation* (2002), p. 312, against the suggestions of B. J. Malina and J. J. Pilch (on which see pp. 22–25 in the Introduction).

260 R. H. Mounce, *Book of Revelation* (1977), pp. 231–32.

there is a certain continuity between the OT and NT people of God. Jesus was born a Jew into the Jewish believing community. Gentiles are the community of God's other children. Jesus is in a sense a special child of God, as we shall see.

The woman is depicted as being in anguish to give birth. The red or fiery (or bloody) dragon is said to be a second portent in the sky or in heaven. That he has ten horns suggests awesome strength and draws on the apocalyptic imagery in Dan. 7–8, where it refers to nations. Notice the deliberate contrast between the dragon and the woman. The dragon has seven crowns (***diademata***), perhaps indicating his attempt to usurp all power; mother Zion's crown is the **stephanos**, the laurel wreath for victors. It is possible that the reference to twelve refers to the twelve tribes of Israel rather than to the zodiac and so would be a symbol for the whole people of God. This dragon's tail is said to have dragged a third of the stars from the sky. The stars are cast to earth, not into hell or the abyss or some other destination. Stars were seen as gods by pagans and as angels by Jews.[261]

One may ask when we are meant to think of these events as happening. There does not appear to be anything here about a primordial fall of Satan and his angels from heaven. Rather it is a depiction of either what happened as a result of the triumphant death, resurrection, ascension, and assumption of power by the male child (in which case the whole church age is seen as a time of being in extremis) or alternately what happened at the end of human history. This then would refer to a final tribulation before the end, since the Devil knows his time is exceedingly short. Some would say that this is a false dilemma. John never pictured a long church age, and thus he could depict the final tribulation as potentially near at hand.[262]

Perhaps it is helpful to look forward for a moment by offering a summary of the plot as it involves the powers of darkness in Rev. 12–20.

1) Satan thrown from heaven to earth (Rev. 12)
2) Beast and false prophet conquer (Rev. 13)
3) Harlot rides on the Beast (Rev. 17)
4) Harlot destroyed by the Beast (Rev. 17)
5) Beast and false prophet conquered (Rev. 19)
6) Satan thrown from earth into the abyss (Rev. 20).[263]

This outline shows not only how John systematically introduces the powers of darkness into his story but how he describes their defeat in reverse order – first the harlot, then the Beast and false prophet, then finally Satan himself. Satan

---

[261] For pagan beliefs, see Cicero, *De Nat. Deor.* 2.15.39–40; Seneca, *Benef.* 4.23.4; 1 En. 80.7–8. For Jewish equating of stars with angels, see 1QM 10.11–12; 2 En. 4.1; 2 Bar. 51.10; Philo, *Plant.* 12–14; Test. of Sol. 2.2; 4.6; 5.4; 6.7; 7.6. See Keener, *Revelation*, p. 317 and notes there.

[262] M. G. Reddish, *Revelation* (2001), p. 235, is right that John is interested not in describing the origin of evil but in chronicling its demise. His eschatological focus is clear.

[263] C. Koester, *Revelation and the End* (2001), p. 116.

breaks loose again briefly at Rev. 20.7–10 which reminds the hearer of the resiliency of evil. It must not be underestimated.

Vs. 4b depicts the dragon almost hovering in front of the woman who is about
to give birth so that it can devour the child as soon as it is born. This child was
a male child destined to shepherd all the nations with an iron rod. Ps. 2 is in
the background, and the imagery conveys the child's absolute power over the
nations and possibly even his power to judge. John is drawing on the traditions
in regard to the birth of Apollo, which were also appropriated by Domitian to
suggest that he was a divine being and the conqueror of evil. "John's reuse of
this ancient myth challenges the divine claims and arrogant presumptions of
the imperial cult. Christ, not the emperor, is the real victor over the malevolent
forces of chaos, darkness, and wickedness. John unmasks the Roman power for
what it truly is – a tool of Satan, and a god worthy of worship."[264] It was not
Roma but mother Zion who was the real mother of the divine Son of God.[265]

The text says that the male child was seized and carried off to God and to
his throne. Some commentators think that Jesus' birth, death, resurrection,
and ascension are in view here. Others think that the focus is the death and
resurrection and ascension, for it is at this point that Jesus becomes Son of God
in power, properly speaking. This last view requires that we interpret this text
by a text it likely has no relationship with (Rom. 1.3–4), and also we are told
explicitly that the woman bore a son. The only reference to sonship is connected
with birth, not the being seized or carried off. I thus conclude that the birth
and the death/resurrection/ascension is in view here, which is a sort of merism
circumscribing the whole earthly career of Jesus. The passive voice verbs "was
seized and carried off" implies that God did this. This means John sees God's
hand in Jesus' death. What the forces of darkness thought would mean the end
of the male child God used to give him a promotion and further power and
authority even over the dark powers.

In **vs. 6** the woman fled into the desert. Since she represents the people of
God, it is probable that this is an allusion to God's people fleeing into the desert,
that is, an allusion to the Exodus/Sinai events. The imagery will be developed
in vs. 13 ff. Perhaps John is especially drawing on the prophetic recasting of the
Exodus/Sinai events such as found in Isa. 40.3 or Hos. 2.14. There the reference
is to a new exodus into the desert when Israel's future redemption arrives. John
indicates in his vision that the people of God will be nourished (by God) just as

---

[264] M. G. Reddish, *Revelation* (2001), p. 233.
[265] See E. Fiorenza, *Revelation* (1991), p. 80: "A coin of Pergamum, for instance, shows the
goddess Roma with the divine emperor. In the cities of Asia Minor Roma, the queen of
heaven was worshiped as the mother of the gods. Her oldest temple stood in Smyrna. Her
imperial child was celebrated as the world's savior, incarnation of the sun-god, Apollo.
John probably intends such an allusion to the imperial cult and the goddess Roma insofar
as he pictures the woman clothed with the sun as the anti-image of Babylon, the symbol
of world power of his day and its allies (chaps. 17–18)."

the Israelites had been in the wilderness by manna and quail. This text does not say the people of God are raptured into heaven or any celestial place. The image is of protection on earth from the wrath of the dragon, something one does not need protection from if one is in heaven. The people of God are put in a place prepared by God and will stay there for a definite period of time – 1,260 days or Daniel's three and a half years. Beasley-Murray suggests that in view of 11.1–13 and 13.5 the period when Satan will rage upon the earth and try and crush the church out of existence is likely intended. This presupposes, as Mark. 13 suggests, that the church will be on earth and must endure the tribulation. Though the church collectively will be protected from final destruction, individuals need to be vigilant to persevere through such a severe trial, as Mark. 13 also indicates.[266]

At **vs. 7** the scene shifts to war in heaven. We might expect this to be war waged by Christ against the dragon, but instead Michael, the archangel, leads the fighting for the "good guys." This can only be explained by realizing that the author is adapting traditional material.[267] In Test. of Dan. 6.2 Michael is the mediator between God and humanity, and the angel of the nation Israel fighting against the angelic leaders of the Gentile nations (cf. Dan. 10.13 ff.; 12.1). In 1 En. 54.6 he is one of four archangels who casts the fallen angels into the fiery furnace on judgment day. In the Qumran literature, Michael is the Prince of Light who leads the children of light into battle against Belial (War Scroll 13.10–12; 17.6–8; Community Rule 3.20–4.1). Here his task is to take on the adversary of the people of God in general. Michael prevails, and the Devil and his minions are cast down to earth. A threefold fall of Satan can be noted in Revelation: (1) from heaven to earth (12.9); (2) from earth to the abyss (20.2); and (3) from the abyss into the lake of fire (20.10). The first casting down of Satan, the text seems to imply, transpires as a result of the death/ascension of the Messiah.[268] This is why tribulation comes on the earth after Jesus' ascension. Until that time Satan had had a role in the heavenly court as the prosecuting attorney (see Job 1–2). But in Rev. 12 Satan, having lost his legitimate place and role in that court, no longer plays a positive role of any kind. Before, he could accuse the people of God as well as the world of sin. Here in our text he is out for blood, out to destroy. Koester puts it well:

From a heavenly perspective . . . evil rages on earth not because it is so powerful, but because it is so vulnerable. Revelation likens Satan to a rogue animal that the forces of God have corralled, driving it off the expansive plains of heaven into the fenced-in area of earth. The Beast rampages within its newly limited circumstances seeking to do as much damage as possible during the short time that remains until the company of heaven slips the noose around its head, binds its legs and chains it up so that it can do no further

---

[266] G. R. Beasley-Murray, *Book of Revelation* (1978), pp. 191–206.

[267] It also presumes that some in the audience will be familiar with Jewish angelology, for John does not stop to explain. See C. Koester, *Revelation and the End* (2001), p. 120.

[268] Here we must distinguish between the event that causes the expulsion of Satan from heaven (namely the Christ event) and the agent of expulsion in heaven (namely Michael).

damage (12.11; 20.2). . . . those who recognize that Satan rages on earth because he has already lost heaven and is now desperate have reason to resist him, confident that God will prevail.[269]

In **vs. 9** Satan is called the deceiver of the whole ***oikomene***, the Hellenistic term for the civilized and Hellenized world. Less likely is the suggestion that this refers to the whole people of God. At **vs. 10** we hear a hymn sung in heaven. Salvation, power, and kingship/kingdom come when Satan is finally cast down. Who then are "our brothers" referred to in this verse? They may be the martyrs who are already dead. The accuser is no longer allowed to accuse because of the atoning death of the Lamb and because of the word of his testimony. This suggests that the casting down of Satan took place at the point of Christ's death when the benefits of that death began to apply and sins were covered. Satan was beaten from that point on and saw his days as numbered. Satan is also defeated by the testimony about the Lamb's death, and the martyrs' witness through the pouring out of their life blood. This is a word of encouragement to John's audience that, even if they must give their lives, it is not in vain. To the contrary, it is a powerful testimony about Christ and suffering love.

Vs. 12 makes clear that Satan knows his time is short. Unable to eliminate the Son, he vents his wrath on the people of God. Some have pointed out what a suitable commentary John 12.31 ff. is on this material. It seems also to relate to Christ's saying, "I saw Satan fall like lightning from the sky" (Luke 10.18).[270] Satan is not prevented from pursuing the woman (after the 1,260 days?), but she is aided in her flight with the wings of eagles. Exod. 19.4 is called to mind: "You have seen what I did to the Egyptians and how I bore you on wings of eagles. . . ." But we are told that this flight is into the desert. Thus we have backtracked to the same period of time referred to in vs. 6.

Vs. 15 indicates that Satan throws up a river to flush the woman out of the wilderness. This may again be an allusion to the Exodus/Sinai events. But since in the primal myth it is the sea monster who is the evil one, it is not surprising that water is his modus vivendi to do in the woman. This last great attack on the church will be described more in Rev. 13–14. It is difficult to say if any specific event is referred to by this flood. Mounce rehearses the various options, but none are entirely persuasive.[271] Unable to destroy the church collectively, Satan contents himself with attacking individual Christians, the ones keeping God's commandments and bearing the testimony of Christ.[272] The reference to the "seed" of the woman in **vs. 17** is a bit strange since that term is usually used of

[269] C. Koester, *Revelation and the End* (2001), p. 123.
[270] One can see this saying as Jesus' vision of what would soon or inevitably happen to Satan as a result of the Christ event.
[271] R. H. Mounce, *Book of Revelation* (1977), pp. 231–42.
[272] C. H. Giblin, *Book of Revelation* (1991), p. 129: "The major message of this final confrontation is that the people of God, represented by the woman and the rest of her children, remain at one and the same time immune to destruction, being providentially preserved during the whole period of tribulation, and yet vulnerable to diabolical attack."

a father's rather than a mother's offspring. But, perhaps as Michaels suggests, there is an echo of the story in Gen. 3.15, where it refers to the enmity between Eve's seed and the seed of the serpent. The only other allusion to that story in Gen. 3 treats the serpent as Satan, as in Revelation (Rom. 16.20).

John's vision expands a single text (Gen. 3.15) into an extraordinary two-stage account of an apocalyptic struggle between good and evil. Chapter 12 details the enmity between the serpent (the Dragon) and the woman; chapter 13, the enmity between the serpent's seed (the Beast from the sea) and the "seed" of the woman (Christian believers). It is no accident, therefore, that one of the Beast's heads is "as slain . . . to death, and his mortal wound was healed. . . ." Words spoken long ago to the serpent in Genesis, "he will strike your head," come true in John's vision."[273]

With all the Exodus/Sinai allusions and other OT events John gives his audience a larger perspective on things. "In the story of the woman, readers can see their story within the story of God's people generally."[274]

The image in **vs. 18** concludes this section with the sea monster/dragon standing next to his native element. Caird may be right that the dragon is returning to his native home for reinforcements, and it may also be true that the river is the river of lies, the reverse of the river of life flowing out of the stomach of the believer.[275] John seems to know this Gospel material and to draw on it here and elsewhere.

BRIDGING THE HORIZONS

One of the major controversies surrounding this text has always been who the woman in question was. Is it Mary, as Catholic tradition has long held, and called her as a result "The Queen of Heaven"? Is it the people of God in female persona? If the latter, John seems to see clear continuity between Israel and its Messiah and the other offspring. And there may be more going on here as well, for a coin from Pergamum shows the goddess Roma as the queen of heaven and the mother of the gods, depicted with the divine emperor. But it appears that John's main inspiration comes from the vision of the woman (Israel/Zion) in labor found in Isa. 26.16–27; 54.1; and 66.7–9. It seems that the woman must be seen as the messianic community that, like the 144,000 in Rev. 7, is protected on the earth and eschatologically saved, even though the war waged against it will harm and perhaps kill various members.[276] This woman is a survivor and an exemplar of durability and paradoxically of vulnerability, but the durability comes from the protection God affords, not from any inherent

---

273 J. R. Michaels, *Interpreting the Book of Revelation* (Grand Rapids, Mich.: Baker Books, 1992), p. 122.
274 C. Koester, *Revelation and the End* (2001), p. 125.
275 G. B. Caird, *Revelation* (1998), pp. 159–60.
276 See the discussion in E. Fiorenza, *Revelation* (1991), pp. 80–81.

strength. There is a lesson here for all believers. In this fallen and evil world, even believers, perhaps especially believers, will have trouble. But God is greater than the scope of our troubles, and God will see his people through the wilderness time.

Feminists have understandably been concerned about the extreme contrast of female images (between the woman in Rev. 12 and the harlot in Rev. 17). In part the concern has been that this sort of depiction encourages stereotyping of women as either saints or sirens. Fiorenza, however, encourages us to remember the following:

such female imagery for cities utilizes conventional language because then, as today, cities and countries were grammatically construed as feminine. In addition, centuries before Revelation, the Hebrew prophets had employed the image of the bride, the wife, or the harlot either for characterizing Jerusalem and Israel or for depicting other nations and their capitals. The female imagery of Revelation, therefore, would be completely misconstrued if it were understood as referring to actual behavior of individual women.... Just as, for example, the Lamb, refers to an actual historical person and not to animals, so the image of the heavenly woman, the bride, or the harlot symbolizes cities as places of human culture and political institutions and does not tell us anything about the author's understanding of actual women."[277]

To this may be added that one of the challenges for those who work with Revelation in English is to keep in view that Greek is a gender-inflected language while English is basically not. One must be wary of what conclusions are drawn about the use of female imagery in Greek. The rationale for using such imagery in Greek does not apply in English.

An odd version of the Christmas story is found in Rev. 12.

It is St. John's Spirit-appointed task to supplement the work of St. Matthew and St. Luke so that the nativity can not be sentimentalized into coziness, nor domesticated into drabness, nor commercialized into worldliness.... The splendors of creation and the agony of redemption combine in this event, this center where God in Christ invades existence with redeeming life and decisively defeats evil. It is St. John's genius to take Jesus in a manger attended by shepherds and wisemen and put him in a cosmos attacked by a dragon.... Our response to the Nativity cannot be reduced to shutting the door against a wintry world, drinking hot chocolate, and singing carols. Rather we are ready to walk out the door with ... high praises of God in our throats and two-edged swords in our hands."[278]

There is nothing maudlin about John's portrayal of the birth of the Messiah. He makes clear that Jesus did not just come to heal the sick or save the soul. He came to eradicate the evil that had so long bewitched, bothered, and bewildered humankind. He came to set up a worldwide kingdom. But what sort of kingdom

[277] Ibid., pp. 95–96.
[278] E. Peterson, *Reversed Thunder* (1998), pp. 121–22.

was it to be? Would it involve politics as usual? John's understanding of this matter comports with such diverse texts as the Sermon on the Mount and the discourse between Pilate and Jesus in the Johannine Passion narrative. Peterson sums up the matter ably:

[Jesus] clearly intended that everyone know that the rule of God was comprehensive, established over body as well as soul, over society as well as individual, in our external behavior as well as our internal disposition, over cities and nations as well as in homes and churches. He just as clearly repudiated the accustomed means by which that rule was exercised: he rejected the devil's offer of a position in government, rebuked the brothers Boanerges for wanting to call down fire from heaven to incinerate their enemies, ordered Peter to put up his sword, reassured Pilate that the governor's job was in no danger, and finally to make sure no one missed the point, arranged that his coronation take place on a cross."[279]

This sort of theological and ethical stance undergirds what John urges of his converts, namely a martyrological approach to violence and suffering. He urges them to be prepared to give their lives but not to take lives. Conquering takes place through dying not killing. The kingdom of Jesus, while definitely in this world, does not take up the values of this world or engage in politics as usual. A stance of passive resistance or even of nonresistance is nonetheless a profoundly political posture and act. It is not quietism or a retreat into mysticism; it is a way of saying no to the demands of the powers and principalities, no to idolatry and immorality, without resorting to the tactics of one's opponents. Part of this has to do with a profound commitment to forgiveness, which breaks the cycle of reciprocating violence, and part has to do with the commitment to witness. Let there be no mistake: in a violent world it takes far greater strength of character to take Jesus' approach to these matters than to take up arms. The meek are not the weak. It takes far more grace not to retaliate than to respond in kind. When one has been harmed or had evil done to oneself, retaliation is the natural response, but John points out it was not the response of the slaughtered Lamb, and it should not be the response of his sheep.

REVELATION 13.1–14.5 – 666 AND HIS SPOKESMAN

NRSV Revelation 13.1 And I saw a Beast rising out of the sea, having ten horns and seven heads; and on its horns were ten diadems, and on its heads were blasphemous names.

2 And the Beast that I saw was like a leopard, its feet were like a bear's, and its mouth was like a lion's mouth. And the dragon gave it his power and his throne and great authority.

[279] Ibid., p. 118.

3 One of its heads seemed to have received a death-blow, but its mortal wound had been healed. In amazement the whole earth followed the Beast.

4 They worshiped the dragon, for he had given his authority to the Beast, and they worshiped the Beast, saying, "Who is like the Beast, and who can fight against it?"

5 The Beast was given a mouth uttering haughty and blasphemous words, and it was allowed to exercise authority for forty-two months.

6 It opened its mouth to utter blasphemies against God, blaspheming his name and his dwelling, that is, those who dwell in heaven.

7 Also it was allowed to make war on the saints and to conquer them. It was given authority over every tribe and people and language and nation,

8 and all the inhabitants of the earth will worship it, everyone whose name has not been written from the foundation of the world in the book of life of the Lamb that was slaughtered.

9 Let anyone who has an ear listen:

10 If you are to be taken captive, into captivity you go; if you kill with the sword, with the sword you must be killed. Here is a call for the endurance and faith of the saints.

11 Then I saw another Beast that rose out of the earth; it had two horns like a lamb and it spoke like a dragon.

12 It exercises all the authority of the first Beast on its behalf, and it makes the earth and its inhabitants worship the first Beast, whose mortal wound had been healed.

13 It performs great signs, even making fire come down from heaven to earth in the sight of all;

14 and by the signs that it is allowed to perform on behalf of the Beast, it deceives the inhabitants of earth, telling them to make an image for the Beast that had been wounded by the sword and yet lived;

15 and it was allowed to give breath to the image of the Beast so that the image of the Beast could even speak and cause those who would not worship the image of the Beast to be killed.

16 Also it causes all, both small and great, both rich and poor, both free and slave, to be marked on the right hand or the forehead,

17 so that no one can buy or sell who does not have the mark, that is, the name of the Beast or the number of its name.

18 This calls for wisdom: let anyone with understanding calculate the number of the Beast, for it is the number of a person. Its number is six hundred sixty-six.

NRSV Revelation 14.1 Then I looked, and there was the Lamb, standing on Mount Zion! And with him were one hundred forty-four thousand who had his name and his Father's name written on their foreheads.

2 And I heard a voice from heaven like the sound of many waters and like the sound of loud thunder; the voice I heard was like the sound of harpists playing on their harps,

3 and they sing a new song before the throne and before the four living creatures and before the elders. No one could learn that song except the one hundred forty-four thousand who have been redeemed from the earth.

4 It is these who have not defiled themselves with women, for they are virgins; these follow the Lamb wherever he goes. They have been redeemed from humankind as first fruits for God and the Lamb,

5 and in their mouth no lie was found; they are blameless.

_J_ohn's rhetoric takes fresh turns in this section of his work. He uses the strategy of appealing to symbolic numbers to concretize some of what he wishes to say. This segment is part of the larger project of persuasion by constructing a symbolic universe that captures the imagination of the audience and carries them along to the point where they are in agreement with John's vision.[280] The more impressive the images, the more persuasive the rhetoric. John was urging a difficult course of action, namely exclusive loyalty to Christ and a disengagement from the gods of this world. Thus the image of the anti-Christ had to also be set over against its antidote, namely the Christ. John could not afford simply to criticize the powers-that-be. To be persuasive, he had to offer a positive alternative. Koester has recognized that John is quite deliberately setting Christ against the Beast, and the worship of the former against the worship of the latter as mutually exclusive options in Rev. 13. Just as the Lamb shares the throne and authority of God (5.6, 12, 13), so the Beast shares the throne, power, and authority of Satan (13.2). It is no accident that the same word used to describe the head wound of the Beast, namely slaughter (_sphazein_) is also used of the Lamb (cf. 13.3 to 5.6, 9, 12). "The outcome of the Lamb's work is that the world worships God the Creator (5.10, 13), but the outcome of the Beast's work is that the world worships Satan the destroyer (13.4)."[281]

Of all the verses of Revelation, 13.18 has received the most speculation and attention by commentators. Since there are several symbolic numbers in this central section of Revelation, here is the best place to say something about the ancient art of gematria.

A CLOSER LOOK — 666, NERO, AND THE ANCIENT ART OF GEMATRIA

Gematria is the practice of assigning numerical values to letters of the alphabet, a favorite practice not only of Jews but also of people in the Greco-Roman world.[282] In the first century none of the cultures of the Mediterranean crescent used an Arabic numbering system. The Romans of course used Roman numerals.

---

[280] See E. Fiorenza, "Followers of the Lamb" _Semeia_ 36 (1986), p. 130.

[281] C. Koester, _Revelation and the End_ (2001), p. 127.

[282] See, e.g., the graffito found at Pompeii that reads, "I love the girl whose number is 545." Reported in A. Deissmann, _Light from the Ancient East_ (London: Hodder, 1910), p. 276.

Gematria is different from merely using numbers in a symbolic way, as we have already seen done in Revelation (e.g., seven = completion or perfection). The number 666 is significant because not only is it symbolic (the number just short of perfection and completion, and so the number of incompletion and chaos), but it has gematric value, as Rev. 13.18 clearly implies. It is the enumeration of a name, but which name is much debated. Gematria works such that it is easy to get from a name to a number if one knows the numerical value of the alphabetic letters. But to get from a number to a name is much more difficult and usually results in a wide number of conjectures, as the centuries-long speculation about Rev. 13.18 shows. John is using a literary or rhetorical device that he shared in common with his audience. The human name represented by the number 666 must have been known to at least some of his audience. It was not the purpose of this material to create a conundrum that the church would puzzle over for 2,000 years. Adding to our difficulties is that we have a textual issue at Rev. 13.18. Some manuscripts read 616 instead of 666, though they are decidedly in the minority.

The most common explanation of the number 666 is that the sum of the letters in the name Nero Caesar written in Hebrew characters is 666. It has been argued that this can explain the variant reading 616 at 13.18 as well because, if the Latin of Nero rather than the Greek form (***Neron***) is transliterated into Hebrew, the numerical value of the name becomes 616. But there is a remarkable further fact that is often overlooked by commentators, namely that the numerical value of the Greek word for Beast (***therion***) when transliterated into Hebrew is also 666.[283] "Thus John is saying that the number of the word Beast ... is also the number of a man. The gematria does not merely assert that Nero is the Beast: it demonstrates that he is."[284]

But there is more to the number 666 than meets the eye in another respect. It is a triangular number, which is the sum of successive numbers. Indeed it is a doubly triangular number. It is the triangle of 36 (i.e., $1 + 2 + 3 \ldots + 36 = 666$), which is itself the triangle of the number 8 ($1 + 2 + 3 \ldots + 8 = 36$). In fact 666 is the eighth doubly triangular number in the sequence (1, 6, 21, 55, 120, 231, 406, 666). "Thus Nero's number 666 not only reveals by isopsephism that he is the Beast; it also, as the eighth 'doubly triangular' number, reveals that he is 'the eighth' and thus related to the seven heads of the Beast as an eighth ... the main point of the numerological connection between 666 and 8 must be to demonstrate Nero's relationship to the seven heads as an eighth."[285]

The legend that Nero would return from the dead and wreak havoc on the Empire took various forms and was part of Roman, Jewish, and Christian folklore. Nero was indeed worshiped as a god in the imperial cult in the eastern

---

[283] See S. R. Llewelyn, *New Documents Illustrating Early Christianity*, vol. 8 (Grand Rapids, Mich.: Eerdmans, 1998), pp. 165–66.

[284] See R. Bauckham, *Climax of Prophecy* (1993), p. 389.

[285] Ibid., p. 396.

provinces of the Empire even during his lifetime. Furthermore Nero was respected by the dreaded Parthians, with whom he had concluded a peace treaty. "Nero crowned the Parthian prince Tiridates king of Armenia and Tiridates worshipped Nero as the god Mithras."[286] We learn from Suetonius that, when Nero realized his number was up, he thought of fleeing to the Parthians (*Nero* 47), but he got no further than the villa of his freedman in a Roman suburb. However, his funeral was not a public event, and he was buried privately in the family tomb of the Domitii rather than in the mausoleum of Augustus (*Nero* 50). This private end to Nero's life fueled speculation that he had not died at all (see Tacitus, *Hist.* 2.8). There were a series of imposters posing as Nero after his death, first in A.D. 69, then in A.D. 80. Terentius Maximus, who was the imposter in A.D. 80, actually managed to win the support of a pretender to the Parthian throne. But, for our purposes, the most important of these imposters is the one who arose during the reign of Domitian in about A.D. 88–89 (Suetonius, *Nero* 57.2) and appears to have won the support of the Parthian king Pacorus II. This fact may have been fresh in the memory of John's audiences when he wrote Revelation. Important for our purposes is the fact that Domitian was himself considered a second Nero (Juvenal 4.38).

The Jewish forms of the return-of-Nero legend usually include the notion that Nero will return and wreak havoc on Rome itself. (See Sib. Or. 3.63; 4.363–80). In the Fifth Sibylline Oracle, Nero takes on apocalyptic features, becoming the eschatological adversary of the people of God (see Sib. Or. 5.107). It is not appropriate to call these various versions a Nero redivivus legend because the Roman and Jewish versions seem to imply that Nero had not died but rather had escaped to the east and was biding his time for return from the Parthian realm. But the Christian forms of this legend in Rev. 13 and 17 take on somewhat differing forms while preserving the general outline of the familiar legend about Nero's return.

John was not alone among early Christian writers in associating the anti-Christ figure with Nero. Another early Christian document of about the same period, the Ascension of Isaiah 4.2–14, appears to do so as well. Though the number 666 is not explicitly mentioned in Ascension of Isaiah, it seems to stand behind what the author says about the 1,332 days for the adversary's reign. The context of the discussion in Ascension of Isaiah suggests that the author knows that a reference to Nero was understood.[287] John is counting on his audience being aware of the returning Nero legends that were extant at the end of the first century A.D. But characteristically, he gives the legend his own unique presentation. Bauckham helpfully sums up the evidence that shows that John uses one form of the Nero legend in Rev. 13 and another in Rev. 17.

Bauckham notes that John in Rev. 13 makes a unique contribution to the legend by associating the return of Nero with a visionary interpretation of the

[286] Ibid., p. 409.
[287] Ibid., p. 427.

fourth Beast mentioned in Dan. 7. 4 Ezra 11–12 and 2 Bar. 36–40 interpret the fourth Beast as the Roman Empire of their own era, but there is no association of it with Nero in particular. Now John's vision of the Beast in Rev. 13.1–2 draws on features of all four of Daniel's Beasts (see Dan. 7.3–6) and on Dan. 7 right through 13.7.[288] Bauckham sums up some of the differences between John's use of the legend and that found in other sources:

> In the pagan legend Nero is a threat to the Empire, returning to wreak venegeance on the city of Rome that had brought about his downfall. He embodies the hopes of the east for reversing the supremacy of west over east. In the Jewish forms of the legend, this picture is continued and Nero is seen as an instrument of divine vengeance on Rome, destroying the city of Rome and conquering the empire. In Revelation 13 it is quite the contrary: the Beast's recovery from its mortal wound is not the overturning of the Beast's power but the restoration and enhancement of the Beast's power. The implication of the identification of the eschatological adversary with Nero is not here to identify the eschatological adversary with the threat to Rome but to identify the eschatological adversary with the imperical power of Rome. The chapter is not concerned with the downfall of the Roman Empire but with its apparent ability to oppose God and to persecute his people with impunity. In this respect, chapter 17 is quite different. Here John is primarily concerned with the fall of Babylon (the city of Rome). . . . The form of the Nero legend which is echoed in 17.7–18 is therefore, appropriately, one which portrays the returning Nero and his allies from the east as hating and destroying the city of Rome.[289]

The upshot of this discussion is as follows: (1) There is good reason to think that John saw Nero as an anti-Christ figure, indeed the paradigm of such tyrants. (2) Prophesying during the reign of Domitian, who persecuted Christians and demanded divine worship, it would be easy for John's audience to see that the author was suggesting that Domitian was Nero revisited, or at least another incarnation of such an anti-Christ figure. (3) John is capable of using various forms of a Nero legend to his own ends and of adding his own twists to the story. In Rev. 17 we have a variation of the Jewish version of the story found in the Fifth Sibylline Oracle, but in Rev. 13 John makes his own contribution to the legend. (4) The number 666 is a unique number, especially suited to identify Nero and identify him as "the Beast." (5) Nevertheless, the veiled nature of such gematric games allows John's text to have a certain multivalency.[290] Whether Nero, Domitian, or Adolph Hitler, this material portrays the nature of evil when it takes root in the leader of a large and powerful domain.

❧

The structure of **Rev. 13** is clear. This is a tale of two Beasts, neither of which is to be identified with the dragon, but both of which serve his cause and

---

[288] Ibid., pp. 423–34.
[289] Ibid., p. 429.
[290] Sib. Or. 1.324–29 indicates that the name Jesus in Greek letters adds up to 888.

purposes. The first of the two Beasts comes forth from the sea and, like Tiamat, is a seven-headed Beast with ten horns. As we shall see, a clear understanding of Dan. 7 ff. is required to understand some of the material in this chapter. The second of the two Beasts comes forth from the earth and appears like a lamb with two horns. While the former creature has its parallels with the OT water monster Leviathan, the latter parallels Behemoth. Jewish apocalyptic literature has a good deal to say about these two creatures (cf. 1 En. 60.7 ff.; 2 Esd. 6.49 ff.; 2 Bar. 29.4).

Tradition had it that these two Beasts were created on the fifth day, and humans were created on the sixth to rule over such Beasts. The most reasonable guess as to what these symbols refer to is that the former is a figure of the Roman Empire itself and its emperors, alluded to by the ten heads, while the latter stands either for the priests who propagated and maintained the emperor cult or, since this was written to an audience in Asia Minor, for the provincial council in charge of enforcing emperor worship throughout Asia Minor. Though the former Beast is not called "anti-Christ," this is not an inappropriate designation for him. Fiorenza suggests that "the Beast's arrival might have appeared to represent the proconsul emerging from the sea at the arrival for his annual visit in Ephesus. Similarly, according to the Jewish apocalypse of Ezra, the eagle symbolizing Rome comes from the sea (4 Ezra 11.1). However, the sea itself has both a geographical meaning and a mythological significance. For, according to ancient beliefs, the sea symbolizes chaos and evil and demonic powers (cf. Rev. 9.2; 11.17)."[291]

Thus, in this and subsequent chapters, we have the introduction of the unholy trinity – the dragon, the water monster, and the land Beast (the devil, the anti-Christ, and the false prophet – see 16.13). These three are striving for the religious allegiance of the world. The water monster can be seen as an anti-Christ figure for it has ten diadems just as Christ has many (cf. 13.1; 19.12). He has a blasphemous name (13.1) just as Christ has a holy name (19.11 ff.). He causes people to worship Satan (13.4) while Christ causes people to worship God (1.6). He has a mortal wound and possibly even dies but then revives or lives again (13.3, 12–14) just as Christ died and lived again. He has the power, throne, and authority of the Devil (13.2), and Christ shares the power, throne, and authority of God (12.5–10). In addition Beasley-Murray points out that the land Beast seems to function rather like an unholy spirit. It performs prophetic activity and is the instrument of revelation of the Satanic authority, just as the Holy Spirit mediates God's revelation. One must also recognize that the Beast combines features of the four Beasts in Daniel and features of Nero as well to create a composite portrait of evil incarnate. It is also a sort of universal image

---

[291] E. Fiorenza, Revelation (1991), p. 83. See A. Boesak, Comfort and Protest (1986), p. 94: "The sea is the nether resource of evil, the abode of Leviathan. Its eternal restlessness is the restlessness of a monster on the prowl, forever moving, forever threatening."

indicating the kinds of threats God's people have endured in many different generations.[292]

The echoes of Daniel 7 in this segment of text need to be noted:

Revelation	Daniel
13.1	7.2–3, 7
13.2	7.3–6
13.4	7.6, 12
13.5a	7.8, 25
13.5b	7.25 (cf. 12.7, 11–12)
13.6	7.25 (cf. 8.10–11; 11.36)
13.7a	7.21
13.7b	cf. 7.14[293]

With this background, it is possible to examine our text in some detail.

When we turn to the exegesis of Rev. 13, we come immediately to an interesting revelation. Though it is commonplace among scholars to interpret Daniel's empire with ten horns (i.e., the fourth Beast/empire) as referring to the Seleucid Empire, in Revelation we have another point of view. John sees Daniel's fourth empire as referring to the Roman Empire. There are other Jewish sources that made this correlation (cf. 2 Esd. 12.10; B. T. Shebu. 6b). The degree of freedom with which John handles Daniel is clear in **vs. 2** where he paints this sea monster as all four beastly empires rolled into one, or at least having some of the features of each. The more one studies Revelation, the more one realizes that the author must have expected some significant understanding of the OT as a prerequisite to understanding his revelation. Perhaps he expected those who were biblically literate to explain things to other parts of the audience.[294]

Each head of the Beast is said to have a blasphemous name, just as we have already heard of believers bearing the seal of God. We will shortly hear of followers of the Beast bearing the mark of the Beast on their foreheads. This Beast is an underling of the dragon and so bears his mark. Just as God bestowed on Christ his power, authority, and throne, so it is with this Beast, and the parallels are deliberate. **Vs. 3** reads literally, "and one from his heads like a wound unto death (or slaughtered to death) and the wound of his death was healed." It is not clear how we are to understand the crucial verb *esphagmene*. Is it referring to a nearly mortal wound, and so the head is dying, or is it suggesting that the wound was indeed mortal but that the head was revived? Elsewhere in this book (see 6.4, 9; 18.24), this verb means to slay or to murder and more strikingly the exact phrase of "like it had been slaughtered to death" is found

---

[292] C. Koester, *Revelation and the End* (2001), p. 128.

[293] C. Keener, *Revelation* (2002), p. 336.

[294] On the sea Beast Leviathan and the land Beast Behemoth in the Jewish tradition, see 2 Esd. 6.49–52; 1 En. 60.7–9; 2 Bar. 29.3–4.

in Rev. 5.6, referring to the death of the Lamb, which then rose. We are meant to see a demonic imitation of Christ. **Vs. 14** suggests that the mortal wound was inflicted by the sword. We are told the head was revived, although in this same verse the wound is predicated of the Beast and not just its head. This is not unrealistic since the Empire suffers when it loses its head.

We must focus, however, on what John mentions first – the wounded head. To whom could this possibly refer? The most probable candidate is Nero, who committed suicide in A.D. 68.[295] But the joy over his demise was soon replaced by fear that Nero had not in fact died.[296] Dio Chrysostom suggests that in his day most people thought Nero was still alive, despite the imposters who had arisen in his name (*Or.* 21; *On Beauty* 9–10). The Neronian imposter of most recent memory to John's audience actually persuaded the Parthians to march on Rome in A.D. 88–89. The return of Nero was actually the nightmare of stable Romans' dreams, but it was also alluded to in Jewish prophetic sources (Sib. Or. 5.33–34, 137–54, 361–85), including a prediction that Nero would return at the head of a Parthian army (Sib. Or. 4.119–20, 124, 137–39).[297] This figure that came back from the dead astonished everyone in the world in a way that Christ's death and resurrection didn't. The fallen world fell at the feet of this Beast and was led to worship the dragon as a result.[298]

Vs. 4b says, "Who is like this Beast?" This language imitates the language of the Psalms (see Ps. 89.6 ff.; Exod. 15.11–12; Isa. 40.25 ff.; Mic. 7.18 ff.). Emperor worship is being discussed, and the hymns of the Bible are being parodied. John is speaking of a phenomenon of his day when the government became so totalitarian that it arrogated to itself all the attributes of deity and demanded absolute allegiance. **Vs. 5** says this Beast is notable for its grandiose talk and the blasphemy that comes out of its mouth. The same verse also says it was given power to do this damage for forty-two months. Who gave him this power? Implied is that even wicked governments are given their power and are allowed to operate by the passive will of God.[299] The forty-two months = three and a half years = 1,260 days is again the prescribed duration for the tribulation. As Beasley-Murray says, it is hardly likely that Satan would limit his lieutenant's time

[295] Suetonius, *Nero* 49.
[296] See the excursus pp. 176–79.
[297] In the Armenian language, the word for anti-Christ was Nero, so prevalent was the myth of his return. See G. R. Beasley-Murray, *Book of Revelation* (1978), p. 211.
[298] The deification of the Emperor is especially clear in the case of Domitian as he was regarded in the cities to which John is writing. Ephesus, e.g., issued a coin of Domitian, but his image conformed to the image of Zeus. See F. N. Kraybill, *Imperial Cult and Commerce* (1996), p. 28.
[299] A. Boesak, *Comfort and Protest* (1986), p. 96, argues, "a government has power and authority *because and only as long as*, it reflects the power and authority of God." But this is not quite true. A government may have power illegitimately, e.g., when a coup happens. Presumably what a text like Rom. 13 is suggesting is that all legitimate power and authority is derived from God, but there are other sources of power.

to wreak havoc in any way.[300] That the rule of this Beast would be for a prescribed period of time would be good news to Christians under persecution. Deification of the ruler is savagely critiqued in this chapter. This Beast blasphemed not only God but his name and tent (i.e., his tabernacle in heaven). Perhaps the tabernacle referred to is in fact God's saints, depending on whether we take the last clause as appositional.

Vs. 7 says the Beast is allowed to make war on believers and to defeat them. The Beast is given power over every tribe, tongue, people, and nation. Such was the nature of the Roman Empire, which swallowed up most of the known Mediterranean world. But the worshipers of the Beast are only those whose names are not written in the Lamb's book of life. This must be compared to 17.8, where it says that the elect's names were written in the Lamb's book of life from before the foundation of the earth. However, at Rev. 3.5, we hear of someone's name being removed from this book of life. John is suggesting that whatever destining and purposing of God is involved, it does not rule out the human ability to opt out of God's best plan for a person's life. It is said at 20.12 that there will be a book of deeds in addition to the book of life. John is assuring his audience that God's salvation is something that God planned for human beings before they were ever created. Salvation is pure, unmerited grace. Human beings must simply receive it. The function of this language is comfort and assurance. It is not rhetoric attempting to instill some sense of fatalism or of irreversible predestination.

The last clause of **vs. 8** speaks of Christ mortally wounded from before the foundation of the cosmos, so Christ's coming and dying was also part of God's eternal plan. God knew humans would fall and planned for the remedy. This shows the incredible love of God for his creatures. At **vs. 9** we hear the by now familiar exhortation that closed each of the seven letters in Rev. 2–3 – "listen up." At **vs. 10** we come upon a partial quote of Jer. 15.2 (cf. 43.11). But what is its force? Is it an affirmation of the *lex talionis*? There is also a reminiscence of Matt. 26.52, and probably what is in view is a call for Christians to endure whatever persecution comes and to remain faithful. They are not to take the sword against their oppressors but, rather like their master, simply suffer the wrath of evil and so stop the vicious cycle of killing and revenge. The church then is called to follow the *Via Dolorosa*. In such endurance lies the faithfulness and witness of the saints, who when mistreated did not retaliate.

At **vs. 11** we hear of the second Beast arising from the earth. This Beast is in a sense also a parody of Christ in that it is said to have horns *like* a lamb. It is clearly no lamb for it speaks like the dragon. It is possible that John is echoing the description of the ram with horns in Dan. 8 (the Medo-Persian Empire), and so there may be no allusion to Christ. This Beast derives his power, authority, etc. from the first Beast. His task is to make the whole earth worship the first

---

[300] G. R. Beasley-Murray, *Book of Revelation* (1978), pp. 212–13. Luther once remarked that the Devil is God's Devil and ultimately still under God's control.

Beast. This second Beast is capable of Satanic miracles to deceive the people, even bringing down fire from heaven.[301] He imitates the true prophet or priest. This second Beast endeavors to get the earth dwellers to make a statue or image of the first Beast. There were legends about Simon Magus bringing statues to life or at least making them talk,[302] but more to the point are the attempts to deceive worshipers into believing a god was speaking to them through the artifice of having them addressed by a statue (see Lucian's *Alexander the False Prophet* 12, 26).[303] In addition Roman emperors were notorious for bringing magicians to court to practice various forms of astrology. We also know that Caligula tried to erect his statue in the Temple in Jerusalem. The Ascension of Isaiah 4.11 says the image of anti-Christ was set up in every city. Statues of the Emperor were indeed erected all over Asia Minor, for the goddess Roma and her imperial offspring were worshiped together throughout the region. It is possible that John has in mind here someone specific, namely the asiarch, the high priest of the imperial cult. "The council of priests responsible for the imperial cult was a body with civil authority."[304]

Vs. 15 says that the second Beast is given the power to give life or breath to the image. This second Beast has the function of the Holy Spirit. Worship of the Emperor in Domitian's day was a test of loyalty to the Empire for everyone. Those willing to worship in this way received the ***charagma*** of the Beast on their right hand and on their foreheads. What is this ***charagma***? This was a term used for the imperial stamp on commerical documents and for the impression of the Emperor's head on a coin.[305] If this practice is in view here, the implication

---

301 E. Fiorenza, *Revelation* (1991), p. 86, points out that Martial in his *Epigrams* refers a number of times to Domitian as the thunderer. She thinks that 13.13–15 alludes to actual worship practices in the imperial cult in Asia. The asiarches were those from whom the high priest of the imperial cult would be chosen. These priests wore unusually ostentatious crowns that had miniature busts of the Emperor on them. See Fiorenza, "Followers of the Lamb" (1986), p. 136.

302 See Justin, *Apol.* 1.26; Irenaeus, *Haer.* 1.23; G. B. Caird, *Revelation* (1998), p. 172.

303 This is carefully documented by S. J. Scherrer, "Signs and Wonders in the Imperial Cult," *JBL* 103 (1984), pp. 599–610. He also shows that Dio Cassius, *Rom. Hist.* 59.28.6, knows of emperors like Caligula who had thunder and lightning machines or mechanisms so they could be like Jupiter. John may be alluding to such practices. Plutarch even complained about emperors who imitated the gods in this way. See his *Moralia* 780E. On the attempts to give life breath to a statue of a god by strangling a bird and trying to transfer its breath into the statue, see my "Not So Idle Thoughts" *TynB* 44 (1993), pp. 237–54.

304 A. Boesak, *Comfort and Protest* (1986), p. 103.

305 There is now plenty of literature and evidence showing that the imperial cult was a pervasive and growing influence in the Empire, especially in Asia. For example, all seven cities that John addresses had imperial temples, and for all but Laodicea and Philadelphia there is evidence that they had imperial altars and imperial priests. This meant various festivals in honor of the Emperor and civic responsibilities linked to the worship of Emperor. Besides the work of Kraybill, one should consult D. Magie, *Roman Rule in Asia Minor* (Princeton: Princeton University Press, 1950); F. Millar, *The Emperor in the Roman World* (Ithaca, N.Y.: Cornell University Press, 1977); and S. R. Price, *Rituals and Power: The Roman Imperial Cult in Asia Minor* (Cambridge: Cambridge University Press, 1984).

would be that individuals with this sign on them belong to the Emperor, being his slaves or devotees. Slaves and defeated soldiers were branded if they joined the Roman army. 3 Macc. 2.28–30 says that Ptolemy IV required Jews to offer sacrifice to pagan gods. If they refused, they were killed. If they simply refrained from doing so, they were branded with the emblem of the god Dionysius. We cannot be sure whether we are meant to think of the mark of the Beast as visible or invisible, possibly the latter in view of the analogy with 3.12 and 7.1 ff. However, when one considers 13.17, which suggests that it was a trade requirement to see the mark, a visible mark is likely. The mark is said to be the name of the Beast or rather the number of his name. As we have observed, 666 likely refers to Nero.[306] Beasley-Murray is probably right that John is drawing on earlier Jewish and/or Jewish Christian traditions about Nero, for both groups had reason to despise Nero. Those who invented the numerical name 666 probably did not want outsiders to understand it, and gematria was a good way to convey the message. Like the number 888, which is the numerical value of Jesus found in the Sibylline Oracles, this number conveyed the notion that the Emperor was in thrall to, or in league with, the forces of chaos and darkness.

Rev. 14.1–5 involve a complete contrast to what we have just heard. Here the real Lamb is standing on Mt. Zion and with him the 144,000 who bear his name and that of the Father upon their foreheads. As I have argued, 144,000 is probably a symbol for the whole people of God, both Jew and Gentile in Christ. Caird's explanation of this text is as follows: (1) John is alluding to Ps. 2; and (2) what is being envisioned is the preparation of the army of the Lord for the final battle.[307] This would be a military role call such as in 1 Chron. 4–7.[308] Thus **vs. 4** is not an exaltation of celibacy. John is certainly not expecting the listeners to believe that all the victims of persecution would be male. Rather he is drawing on the provisions in the Pentateuch for preparing for a holy war (Deut. 20, 23.9–10; 1 Sam. 21.5; 2 Sam. 11.11).[309] Those going into battle were expected to abstain from sexual intercourse.[310] But in Revelation the issue is probably not physical but

---

[306] The objection of R. H. Mounce, *Book of Revelation* (1977), pp. 261–62, that this requires a defective spelling of Caesar cannot stand because this same defective spelling has been found at Qumran.

[307] Notice they are enumerated by tribes in 7.4–8.

[308] See G. B. Caird, *Revelation* (1998), pp. 178–79.

[309] With C. Keener, *Revelation* (2002), p. 371; against E. Fiorenza, *Revelation* (1991), p. 88, who oddly thinks that John is referring to the idolatry and immorality involved with the Emperor. John, however, is talking about the army of believers preparing to do battle.

[310] D. C. Olson, "'Those Who Have Not Defiled Themselves with Women': Revelation 14.4 and the Book of Enoch," *CBQ* 59 (1997), pp. 492–510, suggests that in 14.4a we have an allusion to the story of the Watchers in 1 Enoch. He points out that the Pentateuchal regulations for holy war require the soldiers not to be virgins, but only celibate for a period of time. Olson is thinking particularly of the material in 1 En. 7–15. He assumes, however, that John has an angelomorphic anthropology, believing humans become angels. But the evidence in Revelation makes clear that to keep company with angels is not the same as

spiritual. Believers are not to give in to the great whore Babylon (i.e., Rome) and to the adultery (i.e., idolatry) that she requires. The soldiers of the cross are expected to follow Christ unto death. The ones in Revelation are said to be the redeemed of God, the first fruits of the harvest of souls by God and the Lamb. In contrast to the followers of the Beast, there were no lies in the mouths of these believers, nor any blemishes, suggesting that, like their Lord, they will make a perfect sacrifice. John seems to be saying that the martyrs' sacrifice will be the first fruits of the great harvesting of souls, the opening act of bringing in the sheaves, a view confirmed by the allusion to Isa. 53.9. This loyalty calls forth a new song from heaven involving the sound of many harps but also of thunder and of rushing waters. The only ones able to learn this new song are those bought from the earth by the blood of the Lamb. We see proleptic celebration in heaven for the triumph of faith, and in particular the martyrs, who would be first fruits of the 144,000. They are soldiers of the cross, but if these martyrs are only the first fruits, John had vision beyond his own immediate situation of the rest of the harvest to follow. What is to come after that will increasingly preoccupy the author as the book progresses.

BRIDGING THE HORIZONS

The governing authority in Revelation is described as a brutal subhuman creature, a Beast. There can be little doubt that John speaks differently about governing authorities than what we find in Rom. 13 or in 1 Pet. But Rom. 13 is not a call to blind obedience to the governing authorities. It is a document written during the good years of Nero's reign, when he had helpful advisors, and well before the persecutions, whereas Revelation was written after the Neronian persecutions and during the troubles under Domitian. Paul assumes that government is operating in a normal mode and that justice is still possible through those authorities. John makes no such assumptions.

The reference to heads bearing blasphemous names reminds the hearer of the coins that have both the head and the names of the Emperor on them. Jewish belief, of course, forbade not only the worship of anyone but the one true God but also graven images. Both were seen as examples of blasphemy. What happens when one's ruler becomes a Beast? What happens when that ruler/Beast calls for worship and devotion in various forms? What happens when a ruler has no human feeling? On such occasions one must obey God rather than the idolatrous demands of human beings. John's book is written during and for such a time when one must choose between God and the existing political rulers. Boesak sees that a government has legitimate power and authority only insofar

being or becoming one of their number. The elders are not the angels, and the angels are not the elders, even in heaven. Later Christian speculation on such matters should not guide our interpretation of John's work.

as and as long as it reflects the power and authority and will of God. I tend to agree.

Boesak points out that Rom. 13 counsels submission, not absolute obedience, to the governing authorities, adding that Paul says not that government comes from God, but that the *exousia*, or power and authority by which they exist, is established by God.[311] Remember the story in Genesis where God gives the first couple authority to rule over the rest of creation, to fill the earth and subdue it. This does not mean that God endorsed any and all forms by which that governance was exercised by human beings. Paul says in Rom. 13 that government is supposed to be an agent or servant of God that knows the difference between justice and injustice, good and evil. But the actions of the Beast, far from upholding justice, perpetrate injustice and evil, and can only garner divine condemnation. "When government no longer distinguishes between good and evil, between what is humanizing and what is not, it is no longer the servant of God but the Beast from the sea."[312]

John's image of the anti-Christ is one part Nero, one part Antiochus Epiphanes. He refers to an oppressor who will come after the current one (see 17.8) who will embody evil as Nero did. As Keener says, the issue here is more the character and pattern of the oppressor than the particular person in view. "The ultimate incarnation of evil simply epitomizes and carries forward the character of his predecessors, so we may find many evil rulers whose behavior provides analogies."[313] John is using symbols that, on the one hand, have enough particularity to be a word on target for his audience, but, on the other hand, are universal enough that they could apply to various tyrannical rulers. The question has always been, How should Christians respond to tyranny in government?

Let us consider for a moment the case of Adolf Hitler. He, as much as anyone in the twentieth century, could be called an anti-Christ figure. Anyone who initiates the persecution of Jews and Christians, which leads to the extermination of some 6 million Jews and untold numbers of Christians, certainly can be seen as a diabolical ruler. Yet the German church responded in various ways to Hitler, some endorsing him, some trying to ignore him, and some denouncing him. There was no unanimity in the church about Hitler. One of the few German pastors to stand against Hitler was Martin Niemöller. He denounced Hitler from the pulpit, was imprisoned, and was visited by a chaplain who was shocked to find someone he knew in jail. When the dumbfounded chaplain asked Niemöller what he was doing in prison, Niemöller retorted "Why are you *not* in prison?"[314] The text that Niemöller and others often used to justify resisting Hitler was

---

[311] A. Boesak, *Comfort and Protest* (1986), p. 96.
[312] Ibid., p. 99.
[313] C. Keener, *Revelation* (2002), p. 342.
[314] See C. Colson, *Kingdoms in Conflict* (Grand Rapids, Mich.: Zondervan, 1987), p. 152.

Rev. 13, and one can say that the analogy is sufficiently close and strong between Nero or Domitian and Hitler that the use seems warranted. It is noteworthy, though, that Niemöller believed that protest and martyrdom were the extent to which he as a Christian could go in opposing Hitler. Dietrich Bonhoeffer and others, however, believed that Hitler had to be stopped by means of assassination. Revelation does not endorse bomb plots against the ruler, not least because it does expect divine intervention to solve the problem, but it does raise the question of the proper ethical response to tyranny.

On occasion some Christians think it futile to give up one's life in martyrdom rather than to oppose tyranny with force. This overlooks many powerful historical examples. For instance, there is the story of Boris Kornfield, a Jewish doctor who had become a Christian. When he refused to cooperate in the deaths of prisoners in the Soviet Gulag, he was brutally murdered. So short was his tenure in the Gulag, he had time only to witness to one prisoner before being killed. That prisoner was Alexander Solzhenitsyn, the great Christian witness against Soviet evil. He, of course, spread the message to millions, but he would not have been able to do so had God not used Kornfield to touch his life.[315]

REVELATION 14.6–14.20 – THREE ANGELIC MESSENGERS

NRSV Revelation 6 Then I saw another angel flying in midheaven, with an eternal gospel to proclaim to those who live on the earth – to every nation and tribe and language and people.

7 He said in a loud voice, "Fear God and give him glory, for the hour of his judgment has come; and worship him who made heaven and earth, the sea and the springs of water."

8 Then another angel, a second, followed, saying, "Fallen, fallen is Babylon the great! She has made all nations drink of the wine of the wrath of her fornication."

9 Then another angel, a third, followed them, crying with a loud voice, "Those who worship the Beast and its image, and receive a mark on their foreheads or on their hands,

10 they will also drink the wine of God's wrath, poured unmixed into the cup of his anger, and they will be tormented with fire and sulphur in the presence of the holy angels and in the presence of the Lamb.

11 And the smoke of their torment goes up forever and ever. There is no rest day or night for those who worship the Beast and its image and for anyone who receives the mark of its name."

12 Here is a call for the endurance of the saints, those who keep the commandments of God and hold fast to the faith of Jesus.

---

[315] See C. Colson, *Loving God* (Grand Rapids, Mich.: Zondervan, 1987), pp. 27–34.

13 And I heard a voice from heaven saying, "Write this: Blessed are the dead who from now on die in the Lord." "Yes," says the Spirit, "they will rest from their labors, for their deeds follow them."

14 Then I looked, and there was a white cloud, and seated on the cloud was one like the Son of Man, with a golden crown on his head, and a sharp sickle in his hand!

15 Another angel came out of the temple, calling with a loud voice to the one who sat on the cloud, "Use your sickle and reap, for the hour to reap has come, because the harvest of the earth is fully ripe."

16 So the one who sat on the cloud swung his sickle over the earth, and the earth was reaped.

17 Then another angel came out of the temple in heaven, and he too had a sharp sickle.

18 Then another angel came out from the altar, the angel who has authority over fire, and he called with a loud voice to him who had the sharp sickle, "Use your sharp sickle and gather the clusters of the vine of the earth, for its grapes are ripe."

19 So the angel swung his sickle over the earth and gathered the vintage of the earth, and he threw it into the great wine press of the wrath of God.

20 And the wine press was trodden outside the city, and blood flowed from the winepress, as high as a horse's bridle, for a distance of about two hundred miles.

*M*ounce sees this section of the book as progressive in nature.[316] There is a summons to worship God, which is followed by the consequences of not doing so, namely the fall of the unheavenly city, the bastion of paganism. This is followed by a portrayal of judgment. Caird notes that Rev. 13 ends with a death threat to those who refused to worship the statue of the monster, while Rev. 15 begins with a vision of the victorious martyrs who have won their freedom from the monster and its statue. What then would naturally intervene between these two events? Caird thinks that it would be a description of the battle in which the freedom was won.[317] But it is also perfectly possible that this chapter describes the ultimate consequences of what happens when one gives allegiance to the monster and his statue, as well as what happens when one does not. In fact this material has been interpreted in three different ways: (1) that it refers to the judgment of the wicked under two different images; (2) that it refers to the final judgment, which involves both the righteous and the unrighteous, at least under the first image; (3) that both segments of the chapter tell of the fate of the righteous and their eventual triumph. The last is a distinctly minority opinion defended by Caird in a tour de force argument. We will explore these options.[318]

---

[316] R. H. Mounce, *Book of Revelation* (1977), pp. 269–70.

[317] G. B. Caird, *Revelation* (1998), pp. 176–82.

[318] There are no textual problems in this section that have any real theological or ethical significance.

There is a certain literary or rhetorical structure to these oracles. Notice that vs. 6 mentions another angel, vs. 8 mentions a second angel, and vs. 9 refers to a third angel. It is not clear whom John is distinguishing the first angel from – the one in 8.13 or possibly the one at 10.1? All three of these angels proclaim the truth of God and come from heaven to do so. Their words are indeed Gospel. In his analysis of Rev. 14.6–13, D. De Silva suggests we have an admixture of deliberative and epideictic rhetoric.[319] The goal of all this material is stated plainly at Rev. 18.4: "come out of her, my people, so that you do not share in her sins and receive her plagues." It needs to be seen that the particular concern here has to do with the same matter in 2 Cor. 6.14–7.1, disengagment from the dominant culture's core values. The basic issue is worship – there should be no combining the worship of the true God with the worship or placating of false ones. There can be no fellowship between light and darkness, no syncretism of heart, mind, or practice between the temple of God and idols, and John, as well as Paul, believes that the Christian is the temple of God. One can't take the presence of Christ in one's own life into the presence of the dark forces by participating in idol worship. For John this is a nonnegotiable matter. Hence we hear the angel in our present text urge, "fear God and give God glory" (14.7). This is deliberative rhetoric at this juncture, making clear that "engagement with the cult of the Beast would be the most disadvantageous path for any believer to take. Participation there would mean exposure to everlasting torment at God's judgment. . . . [But John] is acknowledging that exclusive worship of the one God brings danger and dishonor (the potential for loss of status and property, and exposure to shameful execution)."[320] He had already indicated as much in Rev. 13.15–17. Therefore John must speak of eternal advantage and benefit outweighing temporal and temporary disadvantages. It is not until Rev. 21–22 that the full scope of the believer's advantages for following John's exhortations are made clear.

John says he saw the first of the three angels flying in midheaven literally (i.e., the highest point in the sky) to speak to the widest possible range of people. The message is for all those dwelling upon the earth – all nations, tribes, tongues, and peoples. What the angel proclaims is called an eternal *euangellion*. Is this the "good news" of salvation, or is it rather the last-ditch call to fear and honor and obey God? It appears to be the latter, one final call to repentance.[321] In the OT the announcement of judgment on enemies could be called good news

[319] D. A. de Silva, "A Socio-rhetorical Interpretation of Revelation 14.6–13," *Bulletin for Biblical Research* 9 (1999), pp. 65–117.
[320] Ibid., p. 83.
[321] See C. Koester, *Revelation and the End* (2001), p. 139: "The vision of divine wrath is properly read as a warning. Warnings are not given in order to make people despair of grace, but to bring about change and avert disaster." But would it not be better to say that this is a conditional prophecy, which if not taken as a warning leads to judgment of those to whom it is directed?

(Nah. 1.15). Mounce notes that there is no definite article before *euangellion*, so this is not some technical term for the good news.[322] Why the urgency of this proclamation, spoken in a loud voice? As the text says, "the hour of his judgment has come." At this juncture it seems quite improbable to follow Caird, who sees an allusion to the Fourth Gospel motif about Jesus' hour (i.e., the hour of his death).[323] Here the reference is to God's, not Christ's hour, though the Son of Man is one of the implementers of this judgment. All of creation is called one last time to worship God or face the consequences. As soon as the hour of judgment is announced, we hear that great Babylon (i.e., Rome) has fallen. John is thinking of the future fall of the eternal city and its Empire. He was right that this Empire would one day face its demise, though he may have been surprised how long it lasted after his own day.

The second half of **vs. 8** is problematic and has spawned numerous translations. Literally it reads, "who has made all the nations to drink from the wine of the wrath of her fornication." Since *thumos* can be translated as passion rather than wrath, some have thought the passion of her fornication is the better translation here. Against this, however, is the statement in vs. 10 that refers to the wrath of God using the same phrase. Probably we have here a combination of ideas – the wine that leads to fornication and the wine that symbolizes God's wrath. Clearly the author is drawing on Jer. 51.7 – Babylon is a cup in the Lord's hand making all the world drunk. God's wrath is also frequently portrayed in the OT as a drink of wine that causes one to stagger (cf. Job 21.20; Ps. 75.8; Isa. 51.17; Jer. 25.15 ff.). The sequence of thought is logical. The evil things that Rome has led the nations to do will result in the wrath of God falling upon them. It is clear from this verse that the subject of this chapter is the judgment on the nations, not the martyrdom of the saints.

The third angel (**vs. 9**) makes evident that whoever does what was described in Rev. 13, assuming the mark of the Beast and worshiping the Emperor, will face the wrath of God. And drinking from that cup will be like drinking undiluted wine mixed with spices. Such a brew will have dire effects. Recall that this material began with a call to repentance. These horrific effects are not inevitable unless one refuses to repent and to cease following the dragon. The latter half of this verse says they will be tormented in fire and sulphur before the holy angels and the Lamb. It does not say before the saints. The intertestamental notion that the saints would watch with glee the torment of the damned is not found in Revelation (contrast 1 En. 27.3 ff.; 48.9). Probably the idea of judgment by fire and sulphur draws from the story of the destruction of Sodom and Gomorrah. Jesus himself used this image, drawing on another biblical location, Gehenna, the burning sacrifice place (and possibly the garbage dump) in the Hinnom valley just outside Jerusalem. These images cannot be taken literally, but what

---

[322] R. H. Mounce, *Book of Revelation* (1977), pp. 270–71.
[323] G. B. Caird, *Revelation* (1998), pp. 183–84.

they imply is horrific. We are told that enduring the wrath of God will amount to real torment and, worse still, torment in the sight of those one has despised during life (i.e., the angels), an ultimate form of shaming. **Vs. 10** does not say anything about this torment being eternal. **Vs. 11**, however, suggests this, for the smoke goes up forever and ever (cf. 20.10). The punishment of the damned is not portrayed as a temporary matter.[324]

A CLOSER LOOK – THE EMPEROR'S NEW CLOTHES

The rise of the emperor cult parallels in time the rise of early Christianity. The emperor cult began at the turn of the era with Augustus. It was a new and exciting phenomenon spreading throughout the Empire and was especially enthusiastically received and practiced in the East, particularly in the province of Asia. The difference between the emperor cult and the worship of other Greco-Roman deities was exactly what was said about Demetrius Polikretes, the liberator of Athens, who was viewed as a god because of his deeds. About him it was said,[325] "The other gods must be far distant, or have no ears, or even do not exist, or if they do, care nothing for us but you we see as living and present among us, not of wood or of stone, but truly present. Thus we pray: above all, make peace, Most Beloved, for you are Lord [*kyrios*]." Both early Christians and Romans were identifying a historical person of the first century A.D. as a god upon the earth, and since Christians were monotheists, this was severely problematic.

A little historical background will help us view the imperial cult in Asia with a little more understanding. Asia was a resource-rich province and, unfortunately, before Julius Caesar and his successors came along, international trade and commerce were very difficult due to piracy on the high seas and a lack of good roads. Many merchants in Asia and elsewhere were grateful indeed for the Pax Romana, which put an end to numerous local wars and rebellions and established tranquility for sea trade as well. "When Augustus ushered in the era of the *Pax Romana*, it was the greatest benefit many of his subjects could imagine."[326] Indeed so grateful were many provincials in Asia that already in 29 B.C., a cult to Roma and Augustus had been established at Pergamum. There is a stele that was set up at that temple in about 9 B.C. that speaks of Augustus as the savior who brought peace to the world, having exceeded all expectations in regard to the "good news" provincials had expected. So grateful were these Asians that they redid their calendar so it would begin on the birthday of Caesar!

---

[324] For a dramatic development of this image, see Dante's *Divine Comedy*, the first segment on the *Inferno*.

[325] This quote is found in M. E. Boring, *Hellenistic Commentary to the New Testament* (Nashville, Tenn.: Abingdon, 1995), p. 548.

[326] J. N. Kraybill, *Imperial Cult and Commerce* (1996), p. 59.

In this environment the imperial cult emerged spontaneously in Asia and on the whole was not imposed from above. The money for building the temples and shrines was provided by local well-to-do citizens who saw it as a part of the "liturgy" they would provide for their city, in exchange for honor and sometimes office in the cult. So eager were the cities in Asia to recognize the Emperor as divine that they vied for the right to have the cult in their cities. It was a matter of enormous civic pride when in A.D. 23 Smyrna became the second city in the region, after Pegamum, to be a provincial center of the imperial cult. Pergamum had even organized a choral association whose sole function was to sing hymns to Augustus as a god in the temple precincts. In this setting, the hymns in Revelation to Christ as God become a good deal more than just positive, effusive praise of Christ. By implication they provide negative commentary on such practices in the imperial cult. While several emperors sought and expected divine honors after their death, Domitian sought such elevation to divine status while he was alive (see Suetonius, *Dom.* 13). In addition, his wife and deceased son, who died in infancy, are represented in divine terms on coins.[327] On one the infant Flavian is depicted as Jupiter sitting on a globe surrounded with seven stars.[328] A province so enamored with and enmeshed in the web of the emperor's cult and patronage could hardly have reacted indifferently to defections of citizens to a Jewish sect that called for the worship of another historical figure instead of the Emperor, a manual worker from Nazareth named Jesus.

A. Y. Collins stresses, "For some Christians of the first and second centuries, just as for some Jews, the imperial ruler cult must have been deeply offensive. The polytheism which was joined to it was equally distasteful. The imperial cult was enthusiastically supported in Asia Minor. . . . The trauma was compounded by the fact that their Gentile neighbors resented Christians' rejections of polytheism and ruler cult. The more enthusiastic their neighbors were about the ruler cult, the more precarious the Christians' public status became."[329] Christians increasingly became *personae non grata* the more it became evident that they were (1) not Jews and (2) still unwilling to participate in the emperor cult. While it is not clear that the emperor cult issue was a constant subject of concern during the Pauline era and in his churches, near the end of the century in Asia Minor it was a significant issue for John and his churches.

The late first century A.D. was a time of increasing urbanization, and early Christianity had an urban strategy in regard to its mission work. At a time when

---

[327] See the details in ibid., p. 63 and n. 26.

[328] E. P. Janzen, "The Jesus of the Apocalypse Wears the Emperor's Clothes," in *SBL Seminar Papers 1994*, ed. E. H. Lovering (Atlanta: Scholars Press, 1994), pp. 637–61. This is plausibly suggested as a background to John's depiction of Christ in Rev. 1.16, where Christ holds the seven stars in his hand. This connection may also provide another small confirmation of the nineties dating of John's work.

[329] A. Y. Collins, *Crisis and Catharsis: The Power of the Apocalypse* (Philadelphia: Westminster, 1984), p. 101.

the Empire's cities were more and more dependent on outside resources, being largely consuming rather than producing units (i.e., at a time when cities were increasingly dependent on merchants, commerce, and the patronage of the Emperor and his provincial representatives), John and other early Christians were challenging the very fabric of this tightly woven network of socioeconomic, religious, and political factors by challenging participation in the emperor cult. But it was primarily through the imperial cult that cities like those John addressed felt themselves linked to Rome and its ruler and his patronage. Participation in the cult was the grateful response of those who felt the Emperor had brought them peace and prosperity. Civic pride and civic competition among John's cities as they each sought to build statues and temples and altars to the Emperor were at stake.[330] Furthermore the "temples played a role in the economy of the cities of Asia operating both as banks and marketplaces. Large-scale financial transactions were impossible without recourse to the banking facilities in the larger temples.... The temple of Artemis in Ephesus was the financial headquarters of the province of Asia,"[331] a temple also connected to the Emperor in various ways.

What was at stake if Christians, especially higher-status ones, did not participate in the public ceremonies of the emperor cult? De Silva puts matters this way:

Emperor worship was no "sham religion" enforced from above. Rather, participation in this institution, as in the cults of the traditional pantheon, showed one's *pietas*..., one's reliability, in effect to fulfill one's obligations to family, patron, city, province, and empire. Participation showed one's support of the social body, one's desire for doing what was necessary to secure the welfare of the city, and one's commitment to the stability and ongoing life of the city. Moreover, participation was an important expression of gratitude toward those who were the city's benefactors. The imperial cult in all parts of the empire focused attention on the emperor as the patron of the world.... [It was believed that as] long as the emperor was strong and his clients faithful, peace and prosperity would remain and the horrors of civil war and foreign invasion would be prevented.[332]

In other words, if one didn't recognize the emperor's new divine clothes one was being ungrateful, antisocial, atheistic, unkind, and unpatriotic, to mention but a few traits bound to irritate and anger loyal citizens of cities such as Ephesus. Modern distinctions between religion and politics do not fit John's world at all well. A rejection of Greco-Roman religion, particularly of the emperor cult, was a political act as much as a religious act. Thus we must see John's strong words against worshiping the Beast as not merely an example of religious rhetoric. It is also a political manifesto of sorts. We are some distance from Rom. 13

---

[330] See S. R. Price, *Rituals and Power* (1984), in general.

[331] W. Howard-Brook and A. Gwyther, *Unveiling Empire: Reading Revelation Then and Now* (Maryknoll, N.Y.: Orbis, 1999), p. 103.

[332] D. A. de Silva, "A Socio-rhetorical Interpretation" (1999), pp. 100–1.

in this book in regard to the attitude about government, but this is in part because the government was behaving very differently in the A.D. midfifties toward Christians than Domitian and his emissaries were in the nineties, and the emperor cult had developed to be a major factor in religious life in Asia in John's day.

Many have seen **vs. 12** as an intrusion, which Charles, among others, excises and transplants to another place in the text. But this is unnecessary. We have **hode** followed by a positive message for the saints: "herein is the endorsement of the saints keeping of the commandments of God and the faith of Jesus." The implication is that this is the way to avoid the previously mentioned fate. Eternal issues are at stake when it comes to how one lives one's life and in whom one places one's ultimate faith.

At **vs. 13** we have the second beatitude of seven and probably the most quoted one: "Blessed are the dead who die in the Lord *ap arti*.[333] It is possible that these last two Greek words are one word – *aparti*. If the latter is the case, as Beasley-Murray argues, then what is meant is assuredly rather than henceforth.[334] Thus the saying would simply be emphatic and without time reference. It is equally plausible that here as in Rev. 13, where the first fruits were mentioned, John is expressing his belief that he lives on the eve of a significant number of martyrdoms. He would be thinking of what their faithful witness unto death would accomplish from now on. As Tertullian once said, "the blood of the martyrs is seed for the church." This beatitude is followed by "Yes, says the Spirit in order to give them rest from their toil, for their work follows with them." In Mishnah *Aboth* 6.9 we read, "In the hour of a man's decease neither silver or gold ... accompany him, but his knowledge of Torah and good works." Sometimes too we hear that a person's good works reach heaven before him or her and plead the case. This reflects at least covenantal nomism but perhaps not a works religion. John would be pointing out, by contrast, that the martyr's good deeds will not go unrewarded in heaven. Heaven itself is not the reward, but there are rewards in heaven.[335]

The second major section of this chapter begins at **vs. 14** and continues to the end of the chapter. Again we find a use of OT images with great freedom and imagination. John sees someone coming down from heaven on a white cloud.[336]

---

[333] For the seven beatitudes, cf. 1.3; 14.13; 16.15; 19.9; 20.6; 22.7, 14.

[334] G. R. Beasley-Murray, *Book of Revelation* (1978), p. 227.

[335] E. Fiorenza, *Revelation* (1991), p. 90, suggests that the grain passage contains a positive message while the grape image conveys a message of judgment.

[336] The reference to the white cloud is a unique feature, perhaps suggesting the purity of the Son or his coming in light and glory.

John says the one coming is *like* a son of man, which means he appeared to be a human being. He is wearing the crown of gold, indicating his royal status and his power to rule and conquer. He has in his hand a sharp sickle. In the OT both harvest and vintage are regularly used as symbols of judgment either on God's people or on their foes (cf. Hos. 6.11; Lam. 1.15; Jer. 51.33). Possibly the closest parallel is Joel 3.9–14, which refers to a double harvest of grain and grapes. Isa. 63.1–6 speaks of God returning from the winepress with garments dyed with the blood of the heathen. These images are here combined with Dan. 7.13, the familiar son of man image.

The angel comes from the heavenly temple and cries out in a loud voice to the Son of Man, "put in the sickle and reap, because the hour for reaping has come, for the harvest of the earth has dried up (i.e., is ripe)." Here the Son is said to cast his sickle down upon the earth and reap it. But is this a harvest only of the wheat or of the wheat and the tares or only of the tares? What is the relationship of this material to what follows in vv. 17 ff.? The grain harvest could be an image of the harvest of wheat, but there are passages in the Gospels that speak of the Son of Man coming for judgment (e.g., Mark 14.62; cf. 2 Thess. 2). Thus it is more probable that we have either a mixed harvest of wheat and tares or a harvest of those ripe for judgment. As Reddish says, the echoes of the text in Joel 3 suggest that judgment is in view.[337] Some have wanted to make a neat division between Christ's harvesting the righteous and the destroying angel in vv. 17 ff. harvesting the wicked. Against this it would seem that we simply have an alternate image of the same judgment in the grain and grapes segments of the narrative, only the process is taken a bit further, for we are told what happens after the harvest.

Vs. 17 says another angel comes from the heavenly temple with a sharp sickle. Yet another comes from the altar of God – a symbol that God requires rectitude, atonement for sin, justice. **Vs. 18** indicates that this angel has power over fire, a symbol of judgment (cf. 8.1 ff.). The fire expresses the holiness of God in action. The call goes up to harvest the grape clusters of the earth because they are ripe. **Vs. 19** portrays the fulfillment of this command but goes on to indicate that the grapes are cast into the winepress of the wrath of the great God. This surely is an image of judgment, given that in Rev. 19.15 ff. it is Christ himself who treads the winepress. This suggests that we should not distinguish the two images of grain and grape. They are just two differing ways of speaking of one judgment.[338] We hear in the Gospel tradition that the Son of Man will come with his angels for judgment.

Vs. 20 says that the winepress is trodden outside the city. This would be the normal location where the wicked were executed, and the author does not seem to have any particular city in mind (Rome or Jerusalem), nor does he hint at

---

[337] M. G. Reddish, *Revelation* (2001), p. 281. See also C. Koester, *Revelation and the End* (2001), p. 140.
[338] See the discussion in C. Keener, *Revelation* (2002), pp. 374–76.

comparisons with Christ's death outside Jerusalem. The chapter concludes with a gruesome image of blood coming forth from the winepress and going for miles around as high as the bridle on a horse.[339] The distance is said to be 1,600 stadia or about 184 miles. It has been suggested that this is about the length of the Holy Land. The point here is simply the great quantity of blood, suggesting a huge number judged by the Son of Man. Judgment is never a pretty sight, but this is the stuff of which nightmares are made. The consequences of human actions and faith, or lack of it, are seen to be awesome and eternal.

BRIDGING THE HORIZONS

It is often forgotten that God's love is a holy love, for God is a righteous as well as a compassionate God. Sometimes the tendency is to assume that God's love wins out over his holiness or righteousness. M. Reddish offers a helpful perspective on these matters:

God's wrath is a part of God's love. It is God's wrath, God's justice, that responds to the cries of the martyrs under the altar in 6.9–11. It is God's wrath that hears and responds to the prayers of God's people in 8.3–5. God's love for creation and the people of God created means that God can not ignore the cries of the people of the earth nor the whole creation that has been groaning for redemption (Rom. 8:18–25). For John, the wrath of God is the wrath of the Lamb – the Lamb, John never lets us forget, who was slain; the Lamb who conquered by his own death. That self-sacrificial death is a part of God's response to a world that cries for justice. So when we look for the justice of God, we should not be surprised if that justice is tempered by – even comes in the form of – mercy.[340]

It has been said that hell is the place where God reluctantly says to those determined to go there, "OK, your will be done." It is the perspective of the Johannine community that it is not God's will that any should perish. But C. S. Lewis, in his helpful small study *The Great Divorce*, suggested that those commited to sin all their lives might not choose life even after they had been banished to outer darkness.[341] While the quote from Reddish gets at a part of the message of John of Patmos, it does not get at the whole truth. It forgets that even mercy offered is not the same as mercy received, and for those who will not receive it, there is only the experience of what is fair and just. If one will not receive the mercy of God, then one cannot avoid experiencing God as the just judge of the world. The author of Revelation does not operate on the basis of the modern dictum of transactional analysis, namely "I'm OK, and you're OK." He operates with the belief that all have sinned and fallen short of the glory of God, and, if God were to be merely fair, then none would be

---

[339] Cf. 1 En. 100.1–3, which speaks of blood flowing in streams and horses walking up to their chests in human blood, with the chariots they pulled being covered in blood.

[340] M. G. Reddish, *Revelation* (2001), p. 318.

[341] C. S. Lewis, *The Great Divorce* (New York: Macmillan, 1946), pp. 6–9.

saved. Thus it is right to talk about God's justice tempered with mercy – this is precisely what the death of the Lamb demonstrates. But the benefit of that holy and compassionate love goes to those who will receive it by grace and through faith. It is not automatically received.

Though Christians have sometimes been accused of having a martyr complex, and no doubt some like Ignatius of Antioch have been guilty of such, many Christians have been persecuted and/or killed for their faith in every year since the beginning of the Christian movement. For example, in 1996 over 150,000 Christians worldwide lost their lives for their faith.[342] Just because we see very little of this in Europe or the United States does not mean it is not happening elsewhere in the world. R. Q. Tuttle tells the poignant tale of a man named Ranjit who lived in a small Asian country. This man was basically a paid assassin who had killed many police officers in his day. But he was converted through the witness of a minister. Ranjit became a well-known preacher through whom many others were converted. But the terrorist group he had been a part of demanded he continue to work for them. When he refused, they came after him, and he hid in his pastor's house. The pastor volunteered to die in his place, but at this juncture Ranjit came out and, rather than allow his pastor to die, accepted being beaten to death. His final words were, "Tell my pastor I died a believer."[343]

Just as it will not do to minimize the suffering and martyrdom of Christians in John's era, so it will not do to minimize its reality and impact today. While one can be a sincere believer and die for one's faith, and that faith still not be grounded in truth, when one thinks of the millions of Christians who have died for their faith in just over 2,000 years of church history, it demands respect. It also requires explanation. In some ways living the faith is more difficult than dying for it. Living the faith takes more than a momentary act of trust and bravery. It takes a day-by-day commitment. John understood and addresses this in the epistles in Rev. 2–3. He wants his converts prepared to go but also prepared to stay the course. In a sense all Christians should live like the warriors who, while stooping down to drink from the water right before them and so attend to their daily needs, nonetheless never stop keeping one eye on the horizon. The example of Noble Alexander demonstrates clearly that ongoing persecution may be far more difficult to face than martyrdom.

Noble Alexander had been a youth pastor of a Seventh Day Adventist church in Cuba. Because he refused to renounce Christ, he was imprisoned, forced to eat maggot-laden gruel that led to food poisoning, dunked in an icy lake while bound hand and foot, and he passed out three times from being whipped with

---

[342] See D. Barrett, "Annual Statistical Table on Global Mission: 1997," *International Bulletin of Missionary Research* (Jan. 1997), p. 25. See also P. A. Marshall, *Their Blood Cries Out* (Dallas: Word, 1997).

[343] R. Q. Tuttle, "Tell My Pastor I Died a Believer," *Mountain Movers* (Feb. 1992), p. 4.

electrical cables, sustained gunshot wounds to various parts of his body, and was dunked into a septic tank for three hours; but there was something worse than all this. His Christian wife divorced him while he was in prison, and this brought him so much despair that he did not remarry for twenty-eight years. Alexander says after this long ordeal, "No one can be truly certain of his faith and endurance until he is forced to test them."[344] John would say the same to us. Suffering and persecution may be far more difficult to bear than dying for Christ. John prepares his audience for either eventuality, and even for what to do if one becomes all too comfortable in the world.

The book of Revelation is full of references to angels, and there has been much discussion about them in the postmodern West, both on television and in the print media. John's angels are creatures that appear to him in visions and, as Peterson says, they are "apocalyptic angels – vast, fiery, sea-striding creatures with hell in their nostrils and heaven in their eyes." They are not "the plump darlings of the Rubens' oils, or the giggling, tinsel-fringed girls in Christmas plays, but real angels."[345] Angels are messengers for witness and encouragement; they are not for entertainment. It is strange how the existence of angels seems to be quickly dismissed in the corridors of education and academic research, even when the discussion has to do with the Bible. Peterson suggests that this is "not so much because of an atrophy of the ability to believe as of an anemia of the capacity to imagine."[346] There is a connection between faithful witness and angels. The latter, in John's view, deliver the messages from God, providing humans with a vision of God's hand in human affairs. Without such vision, such perspective, witness falters or fails. John does not, however, see angels, any more than human beings, as the unsealers of the scroll. That role is played by Christ. No, angels and humans both play the subordinate role of delivering the message, not creating or revealing it in the first instance.

There is a danger in focusing too much on the truth about and for the future, namely, procrastination. One does not have to deal with such truth today if one knows it will not come to pass for some time. Now is the day of reckoning according to John's word; very soon a witness of one's faith will be required of his audience. The attitude of a witness who has received the divine word is different than that of a scientist or a so-called objective inquirer into truth. "Witness is wary of discussions. It opposes an aloof objectivity that claims to preserve scientific truth by discouraging personal participation.... Witness demands an alert mind ... and an immediate response."[347] In Rev. 10.9, John is not asked to pass on information about God; he is commanded, as Ezekiel was, to consume the scroll, meaning to assimilate the Word of God into his very being. It should

344 J. W. Kennedy, "Bittersweet Cuban Memories," *CT* (Jan. 1998), p. 24.
345 E. Peterson, *Reversed Thunder* (1988), p. 104.
346 Ibid., p. 105.
347 Ibid., p. 107.

be clear from John's use of Biblese, with nearly every verse of his work echoing some previous Scripture, that he has taken heed of the command to take God's Word into his very being. John Wesley was much the same way. His mind was so saturated with Scripture that he would frequently use little catchphrases in relation to himself and others that, if one didn't know the scriptural context, would make little sense. For example, he called himself "a brand plucked from the burning" because he was rescued from a fire as a boy, and he believed God did this so that he might be called to witness. There are many who own Bibles, but in an age of biblical illiteracy only a minority really read them, and of that minority only a small portion really take the Word into the fiber of their being and become shaped deeply and profoundly by that Word, as John was. And of those who have been deeply and profoundly shaped by that Word, in our modern Western world that sees religion as a private matter, only some of them have heeded the call to witness.

One gets the sense that John peels back the tapestry of time and shows us the underlying forces at work partly because those who would be brave witnesses unto death need to have a glimpse of the great cloud of witnesses, both angelic and human, surrounding them, aiding them, and passing along the message to them. John himself needed to know this. But he was encouraged to be brave enough not to "unpack the contents of our own emotional suitcases for the titillation of voyeurs [but rather to] point to what *God* has revealed. . . . Prophecy is the call to *live* the revealed truth, not merely acknowledge it, and to discover new ways to live it in every aspect of life – while brushing my teeth, dialing the telephone, pulling a lever in a voting booth, signing a check."[348] John is not merely conveying information but persuading his audience to be changed and healed. It is about transformation, so they can be living witnesses, not mere repositories of knowledge.

REVELATION 15.1–16.21 – THE SEVEN ESCHATOLOGICAL PLAGUES

NRSV Revelation 15.1 Then I saw another portent in heaven, great and amazing: seven angels with seven plagues, which are the last, for with them the wrath of God is ended.
2 And I saw what appeared to be a sea of glass mixed with fire, and those who had conquered the Beast and its image and the number of its name, standing beside the sea of glass with harps of God in their hands.
3 And they sing the song of Moses, the servant of God, and the song of the Lamb: "Great and amazing are your deeds, Lord God the Almighty! Just and true are your ways, King of the nations!

---

[348] Ibid., p. 113.

4 Lord, who will not fear and glorify your name? For you alone are holy. All nations will come and worship before you, for your judgments have been revealed."

5 After this I looked, and the temple of the tent of witness in heaven was opened,

6 and out of the temple came the seven angels with the seven plagues, robed in pure bright linen, with golden sashes across their chests.

7 Then one of the four living creatures gave the seven angels seven golden bowls full of the wrath of God, who lives forever and ever;

8 and the temple was filled with smoke from the glory of God and from his power, and no one could enter the temple until the seven plagues of the seven angels were ended.

NRSV Revelation 16.1 Then I heard a loud voice from the temple telling the seven angels, "Go and pour out on the earth the seven bowls of the wrath of God."

2 So the first angel went and poured his bowl on the earth, and a foul and painful sore came on those who had the mark of the Beast and who worshiped its image.

3 The second angel poured his bowl into the sea, and it became like the blood of a corpse, and every living thing in the sea died.

4 The third angel poured his bowl into the rivers and the springs of water, and they became blood.

5 And I heard the angel of the waters say, "You are just, O Holy One, who are and were, for you have judged these things;

6 because they shed the blood of saints and prophets, you have given them blood to drink. It is what they deserve!"

7 And I heard the altar respond, "Yes, O Lord God, the Almighty, your judgments are true and just!"

8 The fourth angel poured his bowl on the sun, and it was allowed to scorch them with fire;

9 they were scorched by the fierce heat, but they cursed the name of God, who had authority over these plagues, and they did not repent and give him glory.

10 The fifth angel poured his bowl on the throne of the Beast, and its kingdom was plunged into darkness; people gnawed their tongues in agony,

11 and cursed the God of heaven because of their pains and sores, and they did not repent of their deeds.

12 The sixth angel poured his bowl on the great river Euphrates, and its water was dried up in order to prepare the way for the kings from the east.

13 And I saw three foul spirits like frogs coming from the mouth of the dragon, from the mouth of the Beast, and from the mouth of the false prophet.

14 These are demonic spirits, performing signs, who go abroad to the kings of the whole world, to assemble them for battle on the great day of God the Almighty.

15 ("See, I am coming like a thief! Blessed is the one who stays awake and is clothed, not going about naked and exposed to shame.")

16 And they assembled them at the place that in Hebrew is called Harmagedon.

17 The seventh angel poured his bowl into the air, and a loud voice came out of the temple, from the throne, saying, "It is done!"
18 And there came flashes of lightning, rumblings, peals of thunder, and a violent earthquake, such as had not occurred since people were upon the earth, so violent was that earthquake.
19 The great city was split into three parts, and the cities of the nations fell. God remembered great Babylon and gave her the wine-cup of the fury of his wrath.
20 And every island fled away, and no mountains were to be found;
21 and huge hailstones, each weighing about a hundred pounds, dropped from heaven on people, until they cursed God for the plague of the hail, so fearful was that plague.

*R*ev. 15 is the shortest chapter in the entire book and introduces the section 15.1–16.21, in which the judgment of the seven bowls/cups is explicated. 15.1 is a sort of introduction to the entire section that follows, for here the seven angels are introduced who will later pour out the seven bowls/cups of God's judgment on the heathen. Mounce suggests that, finally in Rev. 16, the divine retribution revealed by the seals and announced by the seven trumpets is implemented by the pouring out of the cups.[349] This suggests a certain progressiveness in the three sets of seven judgments. In Mounce's view, however, it appeared that judgment was implemented to some degree in the prior two sets of judgments. While Mounce is right that here we go further than in the two previous sets of judgments, it is better to speak of overlap rather than of either simple threefold parallelism or progression. The third set of seven judgments seems to be a fuller exposition or development of the seventh trumpet, just as the seven trumpets seem to have been a further exposition or explication of the seventh seal. Mounce goes on to suggest that the seven cups are to be identified with the third woe of 11.14, which is correct, but the third woe corresponds to the seventh trumpet.[350]

In view of the typology of this section, these seven plagues are but the beginning of the end, for the devil is yet to be thrown into the lake of fire and God's people have yet to experience the final redemption. The key to understanding this entire segment is found in the Exodus typology, for as Caird notes we not only have the seven plagues in Revelation, we also have a sea that the faithful seem to cross, a song of Moses that is also said to be the song of the Lamb, the

---

[349] R. H. Mounce, *Book of Revelation* (1977), pp. 282–83.
[350] D. De Silva, in "Final Topics: The Rhetorical Functions of Intertexture in Revelation 14.14–16.21," an unpublished paper, provides a study using the modern rhetorical approach of V. Robbins, which is not the orientation of this commentary. Nevertheless, De Silva sees this material as deliberative rhetoric if one analyzes according to Greco-Roman conventions. This is possibly correct, but on the whole it appears conform more to the conventions of forensic rhetoric.

smoke of the theophany at Sinai, and the tent of testimony.[351] John is trying to say that God's final deliverance will be like, though much greater than, that paradigmatic deliverance of the OT – the Exodus Sinai events. Once again he presumes a clear understanding of the OT among at least part of his audience.

A CLOSER LOOK – JOHN'S NARRATIVE AND NARRATIVE LOGIC

There is indeed a story behind the story we find in Revelation, and one must know that story of redemption in its proper order, for John takes the liberty of not telling it in strict chronological order. This is one of the things that has befuddled many a commentator. The story begins with the preexistent God, who as Father and Son as well as Spirit was, is, and will always be. The Alpha and Omega motif applied to both Father and Son in this work reminds the hearer of the pretemporal existence of God, the generator of the story, and that one day the Author plans to step on the stage and end the story with a new heaven, a new earth, and a true union between God and his people. But what is to happen in between these times?

John believes he is writing in the age of the beginning of the fulfillment and fleshing out of all the promises and prophecies of the OT era. He does not retell the old, old story, but at every turn he alludes to and echoes it, sometimes in the form of typology in Rev. 15–16 and sometimes in the form of prophecy fulfillment. One cannot really understand John's story without knowing the prequel. The nature of typology is to reassure an audience that, as God has rescued his people before, so he can and will do it again. It will be "déjà vu, all over again," as one famous American once wryly said. But it is a matter not simply of recapitulation but rather, as with the three sets of sevens in our text, of taking things a step further. This brings us to Rev. 12.

For John the change agent in the story is the male child born of the woman referred to in Rev. 12. John believes that redemption, though it may be planned in heaven, must be wrought on earth, and Jesus is the one who must bring it. John is first and foremost a theologian, and so for him it is enough to focus on the three moments of prime soteriological weight in the life of Jesus – that he came from above, that he died for our sins, and that God highly exalted him by resurrection/ascension/exaltation to the right hand. For John the fulcrum of history is at the death/exaltation of Jesus, when evil is dealt a decisive blow and Satan is cast out of heaven for good. John has a cosmic view of the soteriological story much as we find in Colossians. But what comes after the casting of Satan to earth? It can only mean trouble for the inhabitants of earth.

John believes that he lives in the eschatological age, the age of messianic woes when Satan bewitches, bothers, and bewilders even the people of God.

---

[351] G. B. Caird, *Revelation* (1998), pp. 196–97.

He believes and has seen that persecution and martyrdom and various other sorts of suffering are possible and likely. As a pastoral person, he is concerned to comfort the afflicted but also to alert them to spiritual danger. He does so by giving them not only an analysis of their current spiritual state of affairs (Rev. 2–3) but a symbolic preview of coming attractions. His message is both grim and grand. There is more suffering and judgment coming. The church will not be immune to suffering, but it will be spiritually protected while remaining on earth and will survive the onslaughts of the powers of darkness. But more than this, John also foresees the demise of the evil Empire, the final judgment on the wicked, and the final redemption of the believers. Contrary to what several have thought, John foresees many in the nations repenting during the preliminary judgments, turning the saved community into a great multitude. John even foresees a great spiritual battle at the end of this phase of human history, which will be won by Christ himself.

Is this the end of the end of the story? What then is to happen when the Son of Man finally returns to rectify all wrongs and reestablish all rights? For John the answer seems to be no. Satan is to be put in a holding tank once Christ returns (or just before), so that Christ may establish progressively and once and for all his kingdom upon the earth. In this part of the story, Christ will enlist the risen saints to aid him. The number 1,000 simply indicates a very long time for John, and thus he envisions a sort of golden age of human history after Christ's return. Yet, it is still history; the new heaven and new earth have not yet come to pass. At the end of this long period, which apparently involves the spread of the Gospel, we have the resurrection and judgment of the lost, a final unleashing of Satan and a placing of him and his great weapon, death, in its place. Then and only then have we reached the climax of the story with the new heaven and the new earth. The story ends not in heaven but rather with a merger of heaven and earth, the former coming down and transforming the latter into its likeness, with no more disease, decay, dying, and death, no more suffering and sorrow.

John's vision does not offer "heaven" or "dying and going to heaven" as the final solution to the problem of evil or as the final resolution of the story. Like many early Jews and Jewish Christians, he believed justice must be done on earth and must be seen to be done, and likewise so must redemption if God's word and sovereignty is to be vindicated. For John this included the expedient of a messianic age at the close of human history proper.[352] The eschatological age ushered in with the coming of the male child would climax when he returned and brought down the curtain on human history, having finally dealt with all things dark and dangerous.

---

[352] On which see pp. 245–52. John's historical focus becomes especially clear in Rev. 20–22, where he feels compelled to say that all things will eventually be resolved and solved in space and time, not in heaven.

This story has drama and tension precisely because although there is promise that the gates of Hades will not prevail against the church, there is still spiritual and physical danger to individual Christians between the first and second advents of Christ. There is no promise of a quick fix when the tribulation gets really bad toward the end of human history. John does not advocate a rapture theology. His word is that believers shall be conformed to the image of the Lamb, who bled and died, was crucified, and rose again. *Imitatio Christi* is a definite pattern in John's story. More will be said about this as we further explore the contours of John's tale. At the end of the day, John is saying, "God's yes to life and light and salvation is louder than Satan's and death's and evil's no."

The author looks and sees another sign. The language in Rev. 15.1–16.21 reminds us of that in Rev. 12, for once again we are hearing about a sign in heaven or in the sky – a portent of things to come. John is envisioning the future, not what was currently happening in heaven or on earth in his day. The sign is said to be great and marvelous, that is, awesome and awe-inspiring. We are told that these are the seven last, or eschatological, plagues by which the wrath of God is brought to consummation upon the earth and upon unbelievers.[353] The consummation of God's wrath on supernatural evil must wait until later in the story.

John looks and perceives a sea of glass as before, but this time it is mixed with fire. As in 8.5, fire is a symbol of God's holiness and wrath, which is hovering and about to be cast down, like fire on Sodom and Gomorrah.[354] By the sea John sees standing the conquerors with their harps, those who triumphed over the Beast, and the number of his name. These were singing the song of Moses and the song

---

[353] The term "last" here is problematic if one does not see the seven cups as a development toward the seals or trumpets. Yet there is a progressiveness involved when a previous set of judgments affects only a third of the earth, and a subsequent series affects the entire earth, or when a previous set of judgments involves a pause before the seven judgments. This is not the case with the seven cups judgments. It is far better to speak of development with some overlapping. M. G. Reddish, *Commentary on Revelation* (2001), p. 290, is forced to resort to the suggestion that the seven cups describe a judgment taking place in a different part of the battlefield where, at the same time, the seals or trumpets judgments are transpiring. This does not make the best sense of the text. He should have taken a clue from what he observes about Rev. 17–18 and the interlocking nature of things. He notes that those two chapters give the details of what is referred to in the seventh cup plague. This is also true about the trumpets developing the seventh seal and the cups fleshing out the seventh trumpet.

[354] Had John meant blood, as in the blood of the martyrs, he could easily have said so, but it is not impossible that the image has to do with the refiner's fire the martyrs had to pass through to enter heaven. See H. B. Swete, *Commentary on Revelation* (1977), p. 194. If this is so, it is an interesting oxymoronic image – they passed through the Red Sea and the fire at the same time.

of the Lamb, which presumably is one song, though two are a grammatical possibility.[355] The question is, What is in view here? The swan song of Moses in Deut. 32 or more likely Exod. 15 (cf. Rev. 15.4 and Exod. 15.11) is meant. The song is a patchwork quilt of OT phrases, and its content owes more to Deut. 32 than to Exod. 15.[356] This worship scene is perhaps to remind us of the one in Rev. 4–5.[357]

God's works are great and wondrous; his way is just and true. Exod. 15.11 speaks of God's wonders after God judged the Egyptians by means of the Red Sea miracle.[358] He is the King of all the nations.[359] This is a song of praise and probably includes some dramatic hyperbole. We must nonetheless ask how we are to understand **vs. 4**. We hear that all nations will come and worship before the Lamb, because the Lamb's just deeds will be revealed. Is this a statement of universalism? Bauckham has dealt with this whole motif more than adequately, and his conclusions deserve to be followed. The Lamb's death and the prophetic and martyrological witness of believers are God's strategy for winning the nations. John envisions a great harvest of souls as the end of the ages come. But, as Bauckham says, "this does not of course mean that Revelation expects the salvation of each and every human being. From 21.8, 27; 22.15 it is quite clear that unrepentant sinners have no place in the new Jerusalem."[360] The material in Rev. 15 means that John believes that God's chastisements are intended to lead the lost to salvation and that God takes no satisfaction that some of the lost will remain lost. Revelation is a book not about vindictiveness but about vindication, not about the glee of the few over the damnation of the many but about the great cloud of witnesses there will be one day from every tribe, tongue, and nation. But when will this transpire? Probably these things are envisioned as happening during the time enunciated in Rev. 20.4–6, presumably after the plagues were implemented, while Satan is bound, and when the nations are not under his spell. The alternative is to suggest that John believes that the nations will be forced to recognize the Christ, even if unwillingly, due to the overwhelming nature of his second Advent. If so, that would be a response of

---

[355] See E. Fiorenza, *Revelation* (1991), p. 92. It is not impossible that the lamb referred to here is the Passover Lamb whose blood saved the Israelites in Egypt, but since elsewhere in this book it is a reference to Jesus, the latter is likely meant. On it being one song and not two, see C. Koester, *Revelation and the End* (2001), p. 141.

[356] R. H. Mounce, *Book of Revelation* (1977), p. 286. For example, the first stanza of the song draws on Ps. 111.3; Amos 4.13; Deut. 32.4; Jer. 10.7. He points out how in the Nestle-Aland Greek text, 80 percent of the words are italicized as coming from an OT source. See M. G. Reddish, *Revelation* (2001), p. 292.

[357] See M. G. Reddish, *Revelation* (2001), p. 289.

[358] Thus as C. Keener, *Revelation* (2002), p. 384, implies, the translation of marvelous is misleading unless we take the word in its root sense of a marvel or a miracle, rather than something that everyone thought was wonderful and heartwarming.

[359] Here there is a textual problem. Some manuscripts read, "King of the ages/eternity," and a few even read, "King of the saints." In view of what follows in the text, "King of the nations" seems to be the original reading.

[360] R. Bauckham, *Climax of Prophecy* (1993), p. 313.

awe and fear not of love and adoration. But, as Caird properly insists, there is nothing to suggest the nations' response here is coerced or given out of necessity or even given begrudgingly. Both in the OT (Ps. 86.9; Mal. 1.11) and in the NT (Phil. 2.9–11), we hear that the world will eventually worship the one true God.[361]

At **vs. 5** we hear of the temple of the Tent of meeting, the heavenly counterpart to the tent of Moses' age. The temple opens and the seven angels come forth bearing seven plagues. The Mosaic plagues were but foreshadowings of these greater plagues. The angels are clothed in gleaming white, clean linen, the symbol of purity and holiness,[362] for they are to execute God's holy wrath. They are clad with breastplates and golden girdles. This is similar to the appearance of Jesus in Rev. 1.13, but Dan. 10.5 may also be echoed, as it describes an angelic figure clothed in linen with a belt of gold.[363] That the angels wear such clothes makes clear that what they are about to do they do as agents of a holy God who sent them. At **vs. 7** we hear that the four living creatures themselves, those supporting the divine throne, give seven **phials**. This word does not mean vials or test tubes; rather it can refer to anything from a bowl used as a saucepan for cooking to a bowl-shaped cup used for drinking. The Targum on Isa. 51.17 uses the equivalent Aramaic word to refer to the cup of God's wrath. Thus it seems we are referring to a drinking cup shaped like a bowl, for surely Isa. 51.17, 22 stands in the background here.[364] These cups are said to be full of the eternal wrath of God. At **vs. 8** we have a description of a theophany – the coming of God's presence into his temple. Like the vision in Isa. 6, smoke fills the temple. This is the signal not merely that God is coming but that God is about to act. No one can stand in the way or even in his presence when his wrath is executed or, in this case, until the seven plagues have been fulfilled.

Rev. 16 continues what has been introduced in Rev. 15. Notice the parallels between the judgments of the seven trumpets and those of the seven cups. Both sets of visions are based on Exod. 7 and 9. In both sets of judgments, the following things are affected in the same order: (1) the earth; (2) the sea; (3) the rivers and fountains; (4) the sun; (5) darkness comes and torments humankind; (6) judgment comes from beyond the Euphrates; and (7) loud voices in heaven, lightning, thunder, earthquake, and hail climax the series of disasters. The new

---

[361] G. B. Caird, *Revelation* (1998), pp. 198–200.

[362] According to Lev. 16.4 worshipers in the temple normally wore linen or white.

[363] The Greek word is **linon**, but a few manuscripts have **lithon** instead, which means stone. This involved a one-letter slip of the pen by some scribe, but some scholars have actually thought that this is the correct reading based on Ezek. 28.13. This is unlikely, as M. G. Reddish, *Revelation* (2001), p. 295, says, but it demonstrates how establishing the original Greek text of a manuscript is the first task, but when there are interesting or viable alternate readings, the task is never quite finished.

[364] The same word is used at Rev. 5.8 where it refers to the incense bowls, but here the context is different, especially the inter-textual echo.

judgments are directed at the followers of the anti-Christ. They are specific, like the plagues in Egypt were. Also, the cup judgments affect the whole earth, not just a third of it. There is no mention of an intermission between the sixth and seventh judgments, or, better put, of a pause to allow for repentance. This should demonstrate that the three sets of sevens are not simply parallel ways of describing exactly the same events. Caird points out that we should not interpret Rev. 16 as suggesting the dissolution of the universe and its elements.[365] What is being described is judgment on fallen humanity, not the dissolution of the universe. Thus we should concentrate on that focus of the story and less on the means by which the judgment is accomplished. As Caird notes, the final three plagues are directed so as to accomplish the dethronement of the monster, the invasion of his realm by the demonic hordes, and the destruction of his capital city, Babylon.[366] Beasley-Murray suggests that John explains more fully the implications of the sixth cup in Rev. 17–19.[367]

The command to go and pour out the cups upon the whole earth comes from the great voice within the heavenly temple. Though this refers to another angel, in view of 15.8, it probably means the voice of God himself. It is God who is behind all this. The first evil that falls upon those who bear the mark of the Beast is "evil ulcers" – presumably boils, if the analogy with the Exodus Sinai events is in view. Obviously the theme of this section is that God's final redemptive-judgment will be like the Exodus Sinai events although on a much grander scale. The turning of the seas and springs into blood divides a single Egyptian plague into two parts, thus showing the author is not attempting to follow slavishly the literary pattern. Notice that **vs. 3** says that every living thing in the sea dies. The term **psuche** here means a physical being or creature, not a soul, especially since we are talking about nonhumans here. At **vs. 5** we hear of an angel of the water. There is little doubt that the author is following apocalyptic ideas here, as he does at 7.1 ff. where he speaks of angels that control the wind and, at 14.18, control the fire (cf. 1 En. 60.11 ff.).

In what follows, John seems to be drawing on some other intertestamental Jewish ideas such as those found in Wisd. of Sol. 5.7 – God makes the whole creation a weapon to repel his enemies. "The very means by which their enemies was punished was used to benefit God's people in their need" (Wisd. of Sol. 11.5), and "the medium of humanity's sin is the medium of their punishment" (Wisd. of Sol. 11.5). There is a sense throughout this material that the punishment fits the crime but also that what means judgment for the oppressors means redemption for the oppressed. This is truly a redemptive-judgment. For example, the invasion of the demonic hordes means destruction for Babylon but liberation for the saints. Blood is the punishment for the shedding of the saints' blood.

---

[365] G. B. Caird, *Revelation* (1998), pp. 209–210.
[366] Ibid., pp. 204–5.
[367] G. R. Beasley-Murray, *Book of Revelation* (1978), pp. 243–45.

The angel of the water sings another hymn of praise, and like all of them it praises God's redemptive-judgments. God is always the Holy One and righteous, as is shown by God's decreeing these judgments because the blood of his prophets and saints has been shed. The character of God, as revealed in acts of judgment and redemption, is the great theme of worship in heaven. This is hardly surprising since one of the functions of this book is to comfort the afflicted.

The fourth cup is poured out on the sun, not to extinguish its blaze but to make it scorch with great heat those who serve the anti-Christ. In this case there is no repentance. Indeed, there is none anywhere in this chapter. While some of the previous judgments seem not to have been punitive but were rather chastisements meant to produce repentance, these judgments appear to be a matter of pure justice falling on the obdurate. The result is merely that they curse God and God's ways. "Their response makes clear that they have not simply been bullied into worshipping the Beast in order to avoid affliction (cf. 13.16–17), because here they suffer affliction, yet still refuse to worship God. Moreover they do not remain silently obstinate, but reveal their true loyalties by blaspheming God as the Beast did (13.5–6)."[368] This vision makes evident the author is no universalist, but it does not justify the conclusion that he thought only a few would be saved. In **vs. 9**, it is said that repentance involves giving God glory.

The fifth cup falls quite specifically on the throne of the Beast so that his kingdom suddenly dwells in darkness. Those who aligned themselves with the Beast in the kingdom did not repent of their evil works but rather bit their tongues and blasphemed God. "Their blasphemy of God means that in their agony they clearly recognize the source of their punishments yet refuse to give up their idolatrous and rebellious ways."[369] In **vv. 12 ff.** we have reference to a subject covered in 9.14 ff., namely Rome's paranoia about the Parthians.

Here we learn of the Euphrates actually drying up and so paving the way for such an invasion. The Euphrates was an enormous river, and it never dried up under normal circumstances. Thus the divine source of this drying up as a judgment is emphasized (cf. Isa. 50.2; Hos. 13.15; Nah. 1.4).[370] This invasion was frequently connected with Nero. At 17.16 we will learn that these kings from the rising sun have as their goal the destruction of Babylon. At **vs. 13 ff.** we hear of the response of the evil ones to all this judgment, and in this regard we may distinguish our text from the frog plague in Egypt. Here literal frogs are not in view, but three unclean spirits that are like frogs come forth from the mouth of the unholy trinity. Frogs that came out of other creatures' mouths were seen as an evil omen (Apuleius, *Metam.* 9.34). Plutarch even says that Nero was reincarnated as a frog so he could continue his singing (*Divine Vengeance* 32)! "[A]ncients usually viewed frogs as unclean, ugly, and vicious."[371]

---

[368] C. Koester, *Revelation and the End* (2001), p. 150.

[369] M. G. Reddish, *Revelation* (2001), p. 306.

[370] See D. E. Aune, *Revelation 6–22* (1998), pp. 890–91; and C. Keener, *Revelation* (2002), p. 394.

[371] C. Keener, *Revelation* (2002), p. 395.

We are told at **vs. 14** that these are demonic spirits who make evil signs and go out into the kingdoms of the whole civilized world to summon the nations to war, which would amount to the great day of God. **Vs. 15** fits naturally in this context. Having just mentioned the great Day of God, we hear of the coming of the Son like a thief for judgment. We also hear the third beatitude – "Blessed are those who are alert and keep their shirts on lest they walk around naked and reveal their private parts."

These nations were mustered together at a place called in Hebrew "Armaggedon." Various aspects of vv. 14–16 call for our attention. First, though the evil trinity sends these spirits out, they serve God's purpose of bringing the nations together for God's final judgment. It is quite clear from Ezek. 38–39; Zech. 14; and 1 En. 56, 90 that various early Jews believed that, in the last days, their enemies would gather to war against them but that God would intervene and save them. Here this tradition has been blended with the idea of hordes invading the Roman Empire. Second, in the OT and especially in Joel 2.11 and 3.2, we hear of the great and terrible Day of the Lord when God will gather the nations into the valley of Jehoshaphat and execute judgment upon them. To this we must also add the idea that the plains of Megiddo were where various important OT battles transpired, including the defeat of Sisera by Barak and Deborah in Judg. 4–5 and the sad defeat of Josiah in 2 Kings 23.29. This then was a natural place to envision the final battle.

We heard of the coming of the thief in the night previously at Rev. 3.3, and again it is likely that John knew some such traditions as we find in Matt. 24.43–44; 1 Thess. 5.2–5; or 2 Pet. 3.10. The image of the person being found naked is a symbol of lack of preparation for the last day (cf. Ezek. 23.24–29; 2 Cor. 5.3). Captives in war were led away naked as part of their shaming, and so this image is especially appropriate here. Also, in the Mishnah, we hear that a guard caught napping on his watch had his clothes taken and burned and he was sent away naked, in disgrace. The word shame (*aschemosune*) is a euphemism for the genitals in Jewish contexts.

It appears from **vs. 16** that John expects some of the audience to know a bit of Hebrew. The word Armaggedon is almost as frequently debated as the number 666. One may debate whether the word should begin with a rough or smooth breathing mark. Is it Har-Magedon? If so, what could be called the mountain of Megiddo, which is in the midst of the great Plain of Esdraelon? But perhaps the word Har-Magedon means mountain of marauding or attack, in which case Jer. 51.25 could be compared, for Jeremiah speaks of a destroying mountain.[372]

---

[372] It might also be worth considering whether the phrase means the Mound of Megiddo, since there were more than twenty destruction layers underneath the city by NT times, and because of this it was a city set on a small hill. C. Koester, *Revelation and the End* (2001), p. 152, reminds us that John elsewhere uses such names as Babylon and Sodom in symbolic ways, and there is no reason to doubt he is doing so here as well. But note

This has led Caird to speculate that the battle transpires at Rome's seven hills.[373] If we take the opposite view and assume that the word is Ar-Magedon (**ap** in Greek being the equivalent of **ar** in Hebrew, which means city), we should interpret the text to mean that the last battle will transpire near the city of Megiddo. Or, perhaps John is just suggesting it will be as crucial as those battles at Megiddo, using the term Megiddo to conjure up the image of a climactic battle not to specify its location. Beasley-Murray urges we should see the text as specifying an event not a place.[374] Fiorenza puts it best: "The multivalence of the author's mythological-symbolic language cannot be reduced to a single one-dimensional definition! Such multivalence expresses the author's interest in giving prophetic interpretation rather than geographic-eschatological information. Rhetorically 16.13–16 announces the great eschatological battle, a motif that will be more fully developed in Revelation 19.11–20.10."[375] The one major demur I have about this is that John seems to believe there really will be an eschatological battle and climax at the end of human history, though he does use symbolic and metaphorical language to describe it. While John's interest may not be geography, it is certainly history and how history will turn out.

After the seventh cup is poured out on the air, we hear from heaven that "it is finished." Rev. 15.1 should be compared. It is doubtful John has the similar phrase in John 19 in view. Then at **vs. 18** we hear of the usual things that accompany a theophany – thunder, lightning, hail, earthquakes. Only now we are told that it was heavy weather unlike that which had ever been seen before. At **vs. 19** we hear of Babylon being split in three parts (perhaps because it is ruled by the unholy trinity, so that the punishment fits the crime). But it is also said that the cities of the Gentiles fell. Babylon is given to drink from the cup of the wine of fury of God's wrath. On that day there will be no place to hide. Even the mountains and islands such as John was on are said to flee away. This is, of course, metaphorical, but it draws on the OT notion that all of creation quakes when God comes down to visit, especially when he comes in judgment. The chapter concludes with a hailstorm without parallel. Even this leads to no repentance, only a blasphemous scream complaining about the severe weather.

BRIDGING THE HORIZONS

Boesak in his landmark study on Revelation makes the following observation: "But the visions of John are more than just a 'Christian' record of contemporary

that in the case the symbolic names were still referential, referring to real cities, and this may be the case here. However, it is possible to use a historical name and refer to a real battle but not necessarily to a specific location (e.g., John would be speaking of a Megiddo-like battle scenario).

[373] G. B. Caird, *Revelation* (1998), p. 207.
[374] G. R. Beasley-Murray, *Book of Revelation* (1978), p. 245.
[375] E. Fiorenza, *Revelation* (1991), p. 94.

history. His book is prophecy, and therefore it reflects depth and understanding that go beyond the mere recording of events. His visions are visions of prophetic insight; he knows that Nero and Caligula and Domitian are only *manifestations* of this condition of human history."[376] This approach to Revelation assumes that John sees what he is doing as a matter of using universal or multivalent symbols, which, while grounded to some degree in the rulers and institutions of the day, have a wider perspective. Perhaps the clearest proof that this is so is that John can take the prophecies and visions of the OT and use them in a flexible fashion, combining, for example, the four Beasts in Daniel into one in his work. This suggests, especially since John is offering us apocalyptic prophecy, that he would have us view his revelation in the way that Boesak suggests.

There is one further factor – the eschatological one. John is not into date setting, but he believes the return of Christ could come in his day and age, and he prays for that. While using universal symbols, myths, and types, he nonetheless conjures with the possibility that his generation may be the last. There is a sense of finality in what he writes. And yet John knows that many of the prophecies are conditional in nature. If, indeed, people heed the warnings of the preliminary judgments and repent, then the final judgment will at the least be postponed. It will be a matter of judgment deferred as God listens again to the prayers of those who need more time to evangelize or work for amendment of life. These things need to be kept in mind when reading Revelation, especially its judgment sequences.

Justice is sometimes, in our era, a cipher for vengeance or payback. Fiorenza helps us to see beyond such a notion of justice when she says,

Justice is not an alien imposition by some external authority. Rather, justice is understood as the conviction that each act brings about consequences which must be faced responsibly. It is God who has the power to make sure that all people have to bear the consequences of their actions. All receive what is their due. The Greek text does not speak of punishments, but about judgment and justice. Not the desire to inflict punitive torments but the values of equity and vindication motivate and direct God's wrath and judgment.[377]

It is a salutary reminder that only the judge of all the earth knows everything, including human hearts, and so only God's acts of judgment can be fully just. Human attempts at justice are often inadequate or even a travesty of true justice. The outcome of trials is often more a matter of legal wizardry, the quality of lawyer one can afford, or the degree of empathy a jury feels than of what is truly just. It is to John's credit that he does not call on some other human government or power (e.g., Parthians) to render judgment on the Roman Empire. Rather, he calls on God. God is the vindicator of the oppressed and persecution. John has little faith in human governments. It is an old saying, but true, that when

---

[376] A. Boesak, *Comfort and Protest* (1986), p. 94.
[377] E. Fiorenza, *Revelation* (1991), p. 95.

human beings respond in kind to vicious and injust actions, they simply become as bad as their tormentors. Even the *lex talionis* in the OT (a hand for a hand, a life for a life, etc.) probably was meant to limit revenge taking, not to license it, because at the end of the day only God knows what is truly a just response. Revelation suggests that a theocratic vision of the rendering of justice is the only adequate one, for only God is all-seeing, all-knowing, completely holy, and all-loving. This does not mean that governments should not try to approximate God's justice, but we must be ever mindful that that is all we can ever hope to do short of divine intervention.

Some may find it incredible that people facing utter destruction and death would not turn to God and implore him for rescue. Yet this is not the way many people react to a disaster happening to them. Keener tells the story of a man who miraculously survived an air crash. He "always expected people who were dying to cry out to God for mercy in their final moments, but noted that he heard many respond with cursing, following the habits they had spent their life developing. Whether God acts with justice or mercy, some refuse to believe (16.9)."[378]

As I have had occasion to say before, John's focus is on divine activity within human history, and even the heavenly scenes are providing commentary on that divine activity within history. John does not see the ultimate solution to the problem of evil as Christians face it as a matter of dying and going to heaven. As we saw in Rev. 6, even the martyrs under the heavenly altar are not satisfied but rather are crying out, "How long?" The comfort John offers is not merely heavenly compensation for earthly travail. Rather, he wants us to know that God is intimately involved in our history even in the darkest times. M. L. King Jr. puts the matter this way:

We must be reminded anew that God is at work in his universe. He is not outside the world looking on with a sort of cold indifference. Here on all the roads of life, he is striving in our striving. Like an ever-loving Father, he is working through history for the salvation of his children. As we struggle to defeat the forces of evil, the God of the universe struggles with us. Evil dies on the seashore, not merely because of man's endless struggle against it, but because of God's power to defeat it.[379]

REVELATION 17.1–19.10 – BABYLON THE HARLOT

NRSV Revelation 17.1 Then one of the seven angels who had the seven bowls came and said to me, "Come, I will show you the judgment of the great whore who is seated on many waters,

[378] C. Keener, *Revelation* (2002), p. 400.
[379] M. L. King Jr., "The Death of Evil upon the Seashore," in *Strength to Love* (New York: Harper and Row, 1963), p. 64.

2 with whom the kings of the earth have committed fornication, and with the wine of whose fornication the inhabitants of the earth have become drunk."

3 So he carried me away in the spirit into a wilderness, and I saw a woman sitting on a scarlet Beast that was full of blasphemous names, and it had seven heads and ten horns.

4 The woman was clothed in purple and scarlet, and adorned with gold and jewels and pearls, holding in her hand a golden cup full of abominations and the impurities of her fornication;

5 and on her forehead was written a name, a mystery: "Babylon the great, mother of whores and of earth's abominations."

6 And I saw that the woman was drunk with the blood of the saints and the blood of the witnesses to Jesus. When I saw her, I was greatly amazed.

7 But the angel said to me, "Why are you so amazed? I will tell you the mystery of the woman, and of the Beast with seven heads and ten horns that carries her.

8 The Beast that you saw was, and is not, and is about to ascend from the bottomless pit and go to destruction. And the inhabitants of the earth, whose names have not been written in the book of life from the foundation of the world, will be amazed when they see the Beast, because it was and is not and is to come.

9 This calls for a mind that has wisdom: the seven heads are seven mountains on which the woman is seated; also, they are seven kings,

10 of whom five have fallen, one is living, and the other has not yet come; and when he comes, he must remain only a little while.

11 As for the Beast that was and is not, it is an eighth but it belongs to the seven, and it goes to destruction.

12 And the ten horns that you saw are ten kings who have not yet received a kingdom, but they are to receive authority as kings for one hour, together with the Beast.

13 These are united in yielding their power and authority to the Beast;

14 they will make war on the Lamb, and the Lamb will conquer them, for he is Lord of lords and King of kings, and those with him are called and chosen and faithful."

15 And he said to me, "The waters that you saw, where the whore is seated, are peoples and multitudes and nations and languages.

16 And the ten horns that you saw, they and the Beast will hate the whore; they will make her desolate and naked; they will devour her flesh and burn her up with fire.

17 For God has put it into their hearts to carry out his purpose by agreeing to give their kingdom to the Beast, until the words of God will be fulfilled.

18 The woman you saw is the great city that rules over the kings of the earth."

NRSV Revelation 18.1 After this I saw another angel coming down from heaven, having great authority; and the earth was made bright with his splendor.

2 He called out with a mighty voice, "Fallen, fallen is Babylon the great! It has become a dwelling place of demons, a haunt of every foul spirit, a haunt of every foul bird, a haunt of every foul and hateful Beast.

3 For all the nations have drunk of the wine of the wrath of her fornication, and the kings of the earth have committed fornication with her, and the merchants of the earth have grown rich from the power of her luxury."

4 Then I heard another voice from heaven saying, "Come out of her, my people, so that you do not take part in her sins, and so that you do not share in her plagues;

5 for her sins are heaped high as heaven, and God has remembered her iniquities.

6 Render to her as she herself has rendered, and repay her double for her deeds; mix a double draught for her in the cup she mixed.

7 As she glorified herself and lived luxuriously, so give her a like measure of torment and grief. Since in her heart she says, 'I rule as a queen; I am no widow, and I will never see grief,'

8 therefore her plagues will come in a single day – pestilence and mourning and famine – and she will be burned with fire; for mighty is the Lord God who judges her."

9 And the kings of the earth, who committed fornication and lived in luxury with her, will weep and wail over her when they see the smoke of her burning;

10 they will stand far off, in fear of her torment, and say, "Alas, alas, the great city, Babylon, the mighty city! For in one hour your judgment has come."

11 And the merchants of the earth weep and mourn for her, since no one buys their cargo anymore,

12 cargo of gold, silver, jewels and pearls, fine linen, purple, silk and scarlet, all kinds of scented wood, all articles of ivory, all articles of costly wood, bronze, iron, and marble,

13 cinnamon, spice, incense, myrrh, frankincense, wine, olive oil, choice flour and wheat, cattle and sheep, horses and chariots, slaves – and human lives.

14 "The fruit for which your soul longed has gone from you, and all your dainties and your splendor are lost to you, never to be found again!"

15 The merchants of these wares, who gained wealth from her, will stand far off, in fear of her torment, weeping and mourning aloud,

16 "Alas, alas, the great city, clothed in fine linen, in purple and scarlet, adorned with gold, with jewels, and with pearls!

17 For in one hour all this wealth has been laid waste!" And all shipmasters and seafarers, sailors and all whose trade is on the sea, stood far off

18 and cried out as they saw the smoke of her burning, "What city was like the great city?"

19 And they threw dust on their heads, as they wept and mourned, crying out, "Alas, alas, the great city, where all who had ships at sea grew rich by her wealth! For in one hour she has been laid waste."

20 Rejoice over her, O heaven, you saints and apostles and prophets! For God has given judgment for you against her.

21 Then a mighty angel took up a stone like a great millstone and threw it into the sea, saying, "With such violence Babylon the great city will be thrown down, and will be found no more;

22 and the sound of harpists and minstrels and of flutists and trumpeters will be heard in you no more; and an artisan of any trade will be found in you no more; and the sound of the millstone will be heard in you no more;

23 and the light of a lamp will shine in you no more; and the voice of bridegroom and bride will be heard in you no more; for your merchants were the magnates of the earth, and all nations were deceived by your sorcery.

24 And in you was found the blood of prophets and of saints, and of all who have been slaughtered on earth."

NRSV Revelation 19.1 After this I heard what seemed to be the loud voice of a great multitude in heaven, saying, "Hallelujah! Salvation and glory and power to our God,

2 for his judgments are true and just; he has judged the great whore who corrupted the earth with her fornication, and he has avenged on her the blood of his servants."

3 Once more they said, "Hallelujah! The smoke goes up from her forever and ever."

4 And the twenty-four elders and the four living creatures fell down and worshiped God who is seated on the throne, saying, "Amen. Hallelujah!"

5 And from the throne came a voice saying, "Praise our God, all you his servants, and all who fear him, small and great."

6 Then I heard what seemed to be the voice of a great multitude, like the sound of many waters and like the sound of mighty thunderpeals, crying out, "Hallelujah! For the Lord our God the Almighty reigns.

7 Let us rejoice and exult and give him the glory, for the marriage of the Lamb has come, and his bride has made herself ready;

8 to her it has been granted to be clothed with fine linen, bright and pure"– for the fine linen is the righteous deeds of the saints.

9 And the angel said to me, "Write this: Blessed are those who are invited to the marriage supper of the Lamb." And he said to me, "These are true words of God."

10 Then I fell down at his feet to worship him, but he said to me, "You must not do that! I am a fellow servant with you and your comrades who hold the testimony of Jesus. Worship God! For the testimony of Jesus is the spirit of prophecy."

*R*ev. 17.1–19.10 is the first of two parallel sections that include a comparison and contrast between two cities – Babylon and the New Jerusalem. The second part of this parallel is at Rev. 21.9–22.9. From a rhetorical point of view, we are dealing with an epideictic ***sunkrisis***, or comparison and contrast, in which one city will be blamed and the other praised. There is also another feature of epideictic rhetoric found here, namely ***ekphrasis***, or vivid description. In her insightful study B. R. Rossing speaks of "a visual picture or ***ekphrasis***, of two feminine figures ... at the cross-roads, each described in vivid detail. The personified figures are physically contrasted (***sunkrisis***) in such a way that the audience is persuaded to resist Vice and follow Virtue."[380] John's rhetorical strategy has been to try and use the two women *topos* to paint Rome as undesirable, untrustworthy, and dangerous, so that his audience will focus on the community of faith and its values.[381]

It is necessary to speak briefly on "vituperations," as Quintilian calls the use of invective to blame or condemn someone or something using epideictic rhetoric. He notes that fame and distinction often will just highlight the vices that a person or a city may have (*Inst. Or.* 3.7.19). He tells us that vices may be condemned in two different ways. One can wait until the person has died and evaluate the whole of his or her career, or one can make an interim judgment if he or she is still living. It will be seen that, in Rev. 17, John is condemning the city as if from after its demise, telling his audience in advance what that end will be and why. He warns, however, that, if the generally received opinion of a city is favorable rather than unfavorable, then it will require better rhetoric and efforts at persuasion to convince the audience (3.7.23). He urges that the goodness or evilness of a city will be revealed through its deeds (3.7.26), something John highlights in his comparison.

Rev. 17 should not be seen as the sequel to Rev. 16. It is an expansion or close-up of the seventh cup or perhaps of the sixth and seventh cups.[382] The procedure of recounting a vision and then following it with an interpretation is common in apocalyptic literature, not least because such highly symbolic visions required interpretation, even to those who received them, hence the angelic interpreters (cf. Dan. 7–12). In Revelation the interpreting angel does not show up until Rev. 17, though this angel is mentioned in passing in Rev. 1 and 22.6. This larger section of 17.1–19.10 is followed in 19.11 ff. by a description of the Parousia of Christ. Rev. 17.1–19.10 demonstrates how Babylon is made to drain the cup of God's wrath. The lamentation in Rev. 18 and the worship in Rev. 19.1–10 underscore that the fall is final. A good deal of the description of Babylon draws on Jer. 51.

There are several difficulties of interpretation in this section, not the least of which is that we see the Beast become the agent of the city's destruction, when previously they seem to have been allies. Is it possible that two different Beasts are in mind (the sea Beast and the land Beast)? Some have thought that in this section the Beast is both the Roman Empire and the enemies of that Empire. There is then the further problem of the eighth ruler being identified

---

[380] B. R. Rossing, *The Choice between Two Cities: Whore, Bride and the Empire in the Apocalypse* (Harrisburg, Pa.: Trinity Press, 1999), p. 25.

[381] See also R. Royalty, *Streets of Heaven* (1998), pp. 125–30.

[382] J. Roloff, *Revelation of John* (1993), p. 193, calls it an enlarged photograph of the seventh cup or bowl. M. G. Reddish, *Revelation* (2001), p. 321, calls it a hypertext or window that provides more information on what was referred to in Rev. 16.17–21.

with the Beast. Beasley-Murray reminds us that a similar flexibility of imagery is found in Daniel when kings and kingdoms are spoken of interchangeably. In Dan. 7.17–18, the four Beasts are four kings, but, in 7.23 ff., the fourth one is called a kingdom.[383]

Several other background elements in this section should be noted. First, in the myth about Tiamat and the destruction of the chaos monster, the monster is seen as female. This concept may lie in the background of the portrayal in Rev. 17, only bifurcated into two parts. Second, the worship of Magna Mater was nearly universal throughout the ancient world. It has been suggested that she is parodied here. This is entirely possible, and that Cybele, the Roman form of this goddess, was worshiped in the area to which John writes might support this conclusion, not least because we have here the title "mother of harlots" for this city. The orgiastic rituals of this cult would provide further support for this deduction. In any case both spiritual degradation and immorality characterize Rome.

The connection between what precedes and what is in Rev. 17.1 ff. is made clear in **vv. 1–2**, which announce the theme of the entire section. The initial image revealed to John is of the great harlot who dwells upon many waters. This would seem to draw on the OT image of Babylon, the many waters alluding to that city's essential and extensive irrigation system bringing water to the city through various canals (cf. Jer. 51.23). The term harlot is used in the OT of foreign cities like Tyre but also of Jerusalem when she was unfaithful (cf. Isa. 1.21, 23.17; Nah. 3; Jer. 3; Ezek. 16, 23). We hear in **vs. 2** that the kings of the earth have committed fornication with this woman, getting drunk on the wine of her fornications. Thus John indicates the deleterious effect on the nations of their accepting Rome's patronage and, so to speak, getting in bed with Rome as a sycophantic client. But M. E. Boring has rightly noted that fornication here refers not only to participation in idolatrous worship of the Emperor but likely also worship of the city of Rome in the form of the goddess Roma. This in effect involves "accepting Rome as the point of orientation for life in this world, that is, making Rome herself a god."[384] There is then a sense in which John's caricature of Rome and its ruler is meant to demythologize both the myth of the divine Emperor and the myth of the eternal city. John hopes to help his audience resist being seduced by these religious and political forces in their culture.

There was a bronze coin minted during the time of the reign of Vespasian, Domitian's father, a coin that was still in circulation in John's day depicting Roma sitting on seven hills.[385] It was in any case typical to depict a city as a wealthy goddess enthroned next to a river.[386] John's depiction may owe something to this coin, but one must bear in mind he is doing a deliberate parody of such

---

[383]   G. R. Beasley-Murray, *Book of Revelation* (1978), pp. 248–50.

[384]   M. E. Boring, *Revelation* (1989), p. 158.

[385]   R. Beauvery, "L'Apocalypse au eisque de la numismatique: Babylone, la grande Prostituée et le sixième roi Vespasien et la déesse Rome," *RevBib* 90 (April 1983), pp. 243–60.

[386]   See C. Keener, *Revelation* (2002), p. 405.

images that involves comic exaggeration of features, such as we see today in political cartoons.

With **vs. 3** the introduction has been left behind and the actual discussion begins. Once more the prophet is being carried away in the Spirit into the desert. This does not mean either that the Spirit physically lifted him up and put him in the desert, though in light of Elijah one might think this. Nor are we to think of the author going into a literal desert by some other means. Rather, this is a stereotypical way of saying that John was having an ecstastic experience and, as we might say, really got carried away (i.e., in a vision he saw what follows in the text; cf. 1.10; 4.2; 21.10). Why the desert or the wilderness? Presumably, it is because of its associations with the presence of God and, one might add, of his judgment, though in other contexts it is mentioned as the locale where one encounters the Devil or his minions.

John sees a woman sitting on a scarlet Beast covered with blasphemous names, and once again we hear of the seven heads and the ten horns (cf. 12.3; 13.1). The color of the Beast is probably intended to recall the color of the dragon in 12.3. But Beasley-Murray may be correct that the color is meant to suggest royalty.[387] Scarlet and purple were colors much beloved by the wealthy and royalty of Rome. But it is also true that all purple outfits were worn by high-class prostitutes.[388] It is natural to interpret the woman as the anti-Christian city, while the Beast represents the Empire, and its heads are the leaders of the Empire. The woman herself has royal purple draped around her. In addition she is adorned with gold, precious stones, and pearls (i.e., she has all the trappings of royalty). But in her hand is a golden cup full of abominations and the uncleanness of her fornications (cf. Jer. 51.7 and Dan. 9.27). In view of Mark 13 and other texts, the reference to the abominations should probably be taken to mean idolatrous practices, since abomination was a common Jewish euphemism for "idol."

Upon the forehead of the woman was written the word ***musterion***, which here may mean secret. Also there was written, "Babylon the Great, the mother of fornication and abomination upon the earth." John was probably also drawing on the practice of Roman harlots of wearing a headband with their name on it. The word ***musterion*** combined with the idea of a name means a secret or, better said, a symbolic name, the symbolic name being Babylon. **Vs. 6** says she is drunk with the blood of the saints and the witnesses of Jesus. We have here two phrases following the preposition of *ek*, which most naturally suggests two different groups. Before we have had the tandem of the prophets and martyrs/witnesses.[389] The reference actually could be to the OT saints and the Christians (cf. Heb. 12.1 ff.).

John says he is astounded at the harlot he sees. I tend to agree with Boesak when he says that John is not marveling at the beauty or opulence of the city

[387] G. R. Beasley-Murray, *Book of Revelation* (1978), p. 252.
[388] See C. Keener, *Revelation* (2002), p. 406 and n. 14, and D. E. Aune, *Revelation 17–22* (1998), p. 935.
[389] On *martus*, see pp. 67–68.

but is dumbstruck by the mystery of inquity as encapsulated in and by Rome.[390] Here again the vision is meant to reveal the real character of various players in human history. Beginning at **vs. 7**, we have the interpretive section where the angel explains to John what he has seen, since he is so amazed by the sight. Probably *thauma* here connotes flabbergasted or even astounded and confused. At **vs. 8** there is a remarkable parody of the theophanic name (cf. 1.4, 8, and 4.8). The Beast is said to be the one who "was, and is not" and who must arise from the abyss, only to depart into destruction, an event that will astound those who do not yet have their names in the book of life. At the end of vs. 8, we hear again, "He was, he is not, and he *parestai.*" This last word is the verbal form of Parousia. The author is suggesting two things: (1) the figure in question obviously had made some sort of claims to divinity, but the joke is that at present "he is not." What kind of deity ceases to exist?; and (2) his second coming, like the real second coming, will mean bad news for many. But the figure in question is but a shadow or parody of the real Savior. Caird points out that at 11.7 we hear of a Beast that rises from the abyss. Rev. 13.1 ff. must be compared at this juncture.[391] There the monster in question was the Roman Empire, and it seems likely that that is true here as well. But the idea of the second coming refers to the epitome of evil (i.e., Nero back from the dead). This figure apparently does not exist while the author is writing but is expected again, having lived once in the past. Did John really believe Nero would return? Probably not, but he is drawing on common notions to convey the idea of an anti-Christ figure. Evil takes many shapes, though ultimately it all goes back to the same source – the abyss and the Devil.

A CLOSER LOOK – HOLY AND UNHOLY CITIES

The study of the religious meaning of urban space has been going on for some time, and moderns often underestimate the degree to which religion was literally and figuratively at the heart of ancient city life. A holy city is one in which there is an *axis mundi*, by which is meant a profound vertical connection between the city and the divine. The city, in addition, is seen as the epicenter of religious life and thus where pilgrimage should be made. This concept of holy city was already in place in the ANE before NT times, and in the Jewish tradition, Jerusalem was believed to be that city. It is no small thing for a Jewish Christian like John to have divested himself of that sort of belief by (1) calling Jerusalem Sodom and Gomorrah (in part because of the judgment that fell upon it in A.D. 70), and (2) substituting for such a city a heavenly city that descends from above and is called the New Jerusalem.[392]

---

[390] A. Boesak, *Comfort and Protest* (1986), p. 117.
[391] G. B. Caird, *Revelation* (1998), pp. 215–17.
[392] F. Winter, "Aspekte der Beschreibung des himmelischen Jerusalem auf dem Hintergrund der antiken Architektur- und Vefassungs-theories," *ProtoBib* 8 (1999), pp. 85–102, attempts

Holy cities were seen to be places where the cosmic order was mirrored in the design and architecture of things. The city indeed becomes the place where the deity takes up residence on earth, and so pilgrimage to such a city is not merely an attempt to enter a sacred area but an attempt to come into the very presence of God. In such a city, urban space is seen as one form of sacred space.[393] In some cases it was believed that a city was actually founded by some particular god. This sort of belief existed for Rome and was one of the reasons it was called the eternal city. It thus must have come as a total shock to some of John's audience that he portrays Rome as a very unholy city. This is important because the "images of cities are expressions of the religious system; they transmit a vision of the urban dimensions as a structured, transparent and functioning world."[394] What John is actually doing is undercutting the religious foundations of the Empire by stigmatizing Rome as an unholy city. This would suggest, at least to the pro-Roman part of his audience, that the gods had abandoned the city.

We will have occasion to deal with the argument that ancient urban spaces should be seen as servicing the rural surroundings of the basically peasant society of the day (see pp. 226–28), but here it is important to note that the propaganda of Rome and other large cities would not agree with this assessment. It was believed, for example, that the Empire and all its resources existed to serve the city and citizens of Rome. Rome was depicted as the stomach of the Empire, that is, as the consuming center of the Empire. The essence of the propaganda can be seen in Virgil's Fourth Ecologue and the sixth book of his *Aeneid*. "Rome was the city selected by the gods to rule forever, to usher in a new Golden Age of peace and prosperity, to extend law and order to the far reaches of the known world."[395] The rhetorical parody of the Roman boast in Rev. 18.7 needs to be taken seriously – "I rule as a queen; I am no widow, and I will never see grief."

"Most of the images are produced within cities; therefore, they support an 'urbanocentric' point of view. The city and all its aspects of urban space are seen as the ideal dimension where human life can be developed according to divine plans; they are valued in an absolutely positive way."[396] John would not have agreed with the modern cliché "it takes a village." In his view "it takes a city" to represent adequately human society, both at its worst and best as a spiritual entity. The holy city is at the center of divine order, and outside the city

to argue that John has modeled the New Jerusalem on the plan of an ideal Hellenistic city, but this judgment cannot stand. For one thing, no ideal Hellenistic city would omit temples altogether.

[393] See D. Pezzoli-Oligati, "Image of Cities in Ancient Religions: Some Methodological Considerations," in *SBL 2000 Seminar Papers* (Atlanta: SBL, 2000), pp. 80–102.

[394] Ibid., p. 83.

[395] D. A. de Silva, "Honor Discourse" *JSNT* 71 (1998), p. 99.

[396] Ibid., p. 84.

is seen as the place of evil and chaos. The city is the center of divinely sanctioned culture, whereas the countryside around is at best a place of agriculture. It is telling that John even includes food within the walls of the New Jerusalem. He wishes to portray the abolition of all, or almost all, nonsacred space upon earth. Cosmos triumphs over chaos once and for all, when the "sea is no more." "Interestingly, Babylon's condemnation does not lead to the abandonment of the very idea of city. Although Jerusalem comes from a divine dimension and is situated in a transcendent cosmos, it is still conceived as an urban space."[397] This is in part because John believes the final locale of all the saved will be on the eschatologically redeemed earth, not in heaven.

It has not always been well noted, but John had precursors, not only in but outside the Jewish Scriptures, in the portrayal of holy cities. For example, already in the third millennium B.C. in a document called *The Curse of Agade*, we have a portrayal of a city with a wall that touched heaven, like a mountain, full of all the most beautiful things and all the necessities of life, including wisdom as well as material resources. It is a city founded by a god named Inanna.[398] There can be little doubt that John, like Ezekiel before him, envisions a holy city of New Jerusalem on the ANE model and not on the Greco-Roman model of urban space. In this same document, it is chronicled what happens when a holy city is abandoned by its deity, namely, it degenerates into chaos and becomes a desolate and cursed place, where its people fall into poverty, starvation, and self-destruction. This was the fear of every great city in antiquity and explains why in Rome the cessation of the rituals of the Vestal Virgins or even the temporary extinguishing of the eternal flame were taken very seriously.

These things need to be kept in view as we evaluate what John says about both Babylon/Rome and the New Jerusalem. He understood quite well that such cities were profoundly religious in character, in design, in practice, and in belief structure. John does not oppose a secular to a sacred city in his visions. He opposes two categorically opposed visions of a holy city, one involving the deification of the human in the person of the Emperor and of the city, and of nature/creation in the form of a multitude of other gods and goddesses, and the other involving the deity of an only God who always maintains the creator/creature distinction and so makes relationships between the human and divine eternally possible.

⚜

At **vs. 9** the author says, "herein is a mystery that requires some human wisdom to decipher it." Many exegetes have scratched their heads over this one. We see in this verse just how flexible all this symbolism is for here the seven heads

---

[397] Ibid., p. 98.
[398] See ibid., pp. 88–92.

represent the seven hills of Rome where the woman is seated. Rome had for centuries been known as the city of seven hills, and there was even a yearly festival celebrating the enclosure of the seven hills within the city (Suetonius, *Dom.* 4). Yet they also represent the leaders of the Empire – five have fallen, one has not yet but he will last for only a while, and he will be followed by an eighth who is in fact one of the seven. In ancient Roman tradition there were seven kings from the founding of the city of Rome in 753 B.C. until the time of the last Etruscan king in 508 B.C[399] This eighth one too is destined to go onto destruction. The explanation that the seven heads represent seven hills helps in several ways: (1) it makes clear John sees these symbols as referential; (2) John is not really using the symbols to conceal all of his message for the reference to seven hills would have been apparent to most any ancient reader who knew about Rome. In other words, it is at best a half-truth to say John is writing in a sort of code language; but (3) that he has to offer *some* explanations from time to time also makes clear that he realizes various parts of the audience will not understand some of what he says without help.

If one draws up a list of rulers of Rome beginning with Julius Caesar, one comes to the point where Claudius has died, and Nero is now reigning as the sixth in the series. Some have taken this to indicate that Revelation was written during the time of Nero, which is not impossible. But there was no return of Nero myth while Nero was still reigning. Other scholars have suggested we must start counting with Augustus, but this still doesn't allow one to get up to Domitian's time. This is why some have argued the book was written during the time of Vespasian or Titus. Still others have suggested starting with Nero, the first persecutor of Christians, in which case Domitian is the seventh ruler. Probably it is best to see the number seven as symbolic, indicating a complete set of rulers of Rome, however many there actually were.[400] The only question would be, not who were the first five, but rather who is the eighth? None fits the notion of a second incarnation of Nero so well as Domitian, though it is just possible that Trajan could fill this role, in view of the letters we have between Pliny and Trajan.

Many, if not most, conservative commentators have insisted that the eighth ruler was not Domitian but an eschatological anti-Christ figure, in part, because it is feared that John will have mistakenly predicted the end of the Empire during Domitian's reign.[401] This overlooks that John himself speaks of a pause between the sixth and seventh judgments in the first two series of judgments, a pause for repentance and hearing of prayers. John could well have conceived of a scenario where God issued a stay of execution for a while out of mercy, so that more from the nations could be saved.[402] Thus, even on a very conservative approach

---

[399] D. E. Aune, *Revelation 17–22* (1998), p. 948.
[400] See C. Koester, *Revelation and the End* (2001), p. 161.
[401] See R. H. Mounce, *Book of Revelation* (1977), pp. 314–15.
[402] On mercy on and salvation for the nations, see pp. 205–8.

to this material, it is not necessary to insist that the final, or eighth, figure must be an eschatological figure. It could still be a type of the anti-Christ. Certainly Domitian could have been seen in that light by Christians of John's era.

At **vs. 12** we learn of the identity of the ten horns. We hear that they are rulers who have not yet come to the throne but whom the Beast will give power to for a short time. This makes it unlikely we should identify them with the kings mentioned at Rev. 16.14. All of these ten will be of one mind with the Beast to give him their power and authority. We may be talking about provincial governors or local officials who ran the imperial cult in Asia. S. Friesen has argued that

John's critique was, therefore, directed more at local enemies than at the distant emperor. . . . In the late first century in Asia, a denunciation of imperial cults constituted a denunciation of cities' efforts to define themselves, a rejection of proper legal decisions of the *koinon*, and a sarcastic commentary on the public religious activities of the wealthy and of many others. John not only prophesied against imperial power; he also declared illegitimate the presuppositions of the local elite claim to authority and condemned the general population for their compliance. If the author's trip to Patmos was punishment, it occurred because John was a nuisance to the province rather than to the empire. The book of Revelation must be understood in its local setting as part of a clash of religious ideologies, for it represents an assault on fundamental issues of social organization in late first-century Asia.[403]

Yet it is important to recognize that this was only one factor that troubled early Christians in John's region.[404]

These officials or rulers will go to war with the Lamb but will lose to him because he is the King of Kings and the Lord of Lords. G. Beale argues that this title is probably indebted to Dan. 4.37 (LXX), not least because the context of Dan. 4 refers to Babylon the Great and discusses the judgment on the Babylonian king.[405] The title indicates the divinity of the Lamb. Presumably, the end of **vs. 14** indicates that these ten rulers will lose not only to the Lamb but to those with the Lamb – the called, the elect, the faithful (three different ways to refer to the same group). The image may refer to the anger of the nations against God's people at the end of human history.

At **vs. 15** we hear that the waters themselves represent nations and groups of people. The harlot sits on them, which suggests heavy-handed ruling or squashing of local autonomy. Perhaps it is precisely because of the way she rules

---

[403] S. Friesen, "The Cult of Roman Emperors in Ephesos: Temple Wardens, City Titles, and the Interpretation of the Revelation of John," in *Ephesos: Metropolis of Asia*, ed. H. Koester (Valley Forge, Pa.: Trinity Press, 1995), p. 250.

[404] See T. B. Slater, "Social Setting" *NTS* 44 (1998), pp. 252–54.

[405] See G. Beale, "The Origin of the Title 'King of Kings and Lord of Lords' in Revelation 7.14," *NTS* 31 (1985), pp. 618–20. It may be significant that the conqueror of Tiamat, namely Marduk, was also called King of kings and Lord of lords. For further support for Beale's argument, see T. B. Slater, "King of Kings and Lord of Lords Revisited," *NTS* 39 (1993), pp. 159–60.

that the Empire and the ten horns (rulers connected with the Empire) come to hate the harlot and make her desolate, naked, and consume her flesh. Do the ten horns represent the Parthian satraps invading Rome and led by the returned Nero? This certainly makes sense of what follows in Rev. 19.16–18. Others have seen in them the governors of the senatorial provinces in the Empire. But, if that were the case, why is it said they have not yet come to power or have not given power to the Beast? Client states or Parthians are more likely to be in review. It is God who gives the ten the ability to be of one mind. He puts this idea into their hearts, and the idea to give their power to the Empire until God's purposes are fulfilled against the harlot, an idea expressed by saying until the Word of God will be accomplished. **Vs. 18** simply reiterates what we already know – the woman is the great city that holds sway over the world, Rome.

Rev. 18 is a perfect example of John's great indebtedness to the OT and his successful blending together of a variety of sources to serve his own purposes. But it is wrong to see this chapter as simply a pastiche of OT allusions. It is a maze of past, present, and future tense verbs. Notice how, for instance, the fall of the city is viewed as past in vv. 1–3 but as future in vv. 4–8. The text is divided into sections depending on who laments the fall of the city. In vv. 9–10, the kings of the earth do so; in vv. 11–16, it is the merchants; and, in vv. 17 ff., it is the sailors and sea captains. At the end of each of these sections, we hear the identical cry of astonishment, "It all happened in a single hour!" The suddenness and speed of the fall is a major theme of the lament. While Rev. 17 is more like an apocalyptic cartoon, Rev. 18 is far more according to prophetic style.[406] This shows that John thinks that the two sorts of material can be used in tandem to describe the same reality. The OT texts being drawn on in this section are chiefly Isa. 13, 34.8 ff.; Jer. 51; Ezek. 26–28; and Nah. 3, though there are small echoes from elsewhere in the OT. Rev. 17.16–18 have warned of Rome's destruction. Rev. 18 will lament its fall and the aftermath. So sure is John of the outcome that he offers a funeral dirge before the city is even attacked.

As Kraybill has shown, Rev. 18 is not merely a lament. John knows that some first-century Christians in Asia had close connections with merchants and the enterprises of commerce that were linked to Rome and the Emperor's dealings. John is not against commerce itself, but his call for Christians to "come out from them" in 18.4 shows that "John warned Christians to sever or avoid economic and political ties with Rome because institutions and structures of the Roman Empire were saturated with unholy allegiance to an Emperor who claimed to be divine (or was treated as such)."[407]

Rev. 18 begins with a strong angel descending from heaven, who is illuminated by his own radiance. The description alludes to the glory of the Lord described in

---

[406] This section gives clear indication why it is inadequate either simply to call this work a prophecy or to call it an apocalypse. It is both and set within an epistolary framework.

[407] J. N. Kraybill, *Imperial Cult and Commerce* (1996), p. 17.

Ezek. 43.2 in a context where judgment is the concern, as it is here. In Revelation the greater the angel, the greater and more significant the proclamation. Thus one must be clear that this lament is no mere musical interlude. Because the text has so many allusions to the OT, it raises the question of literary artifice. In my view John certainly had visions, but he reflected on them and described them in terms that reflect his own mind, which is thoroughly saturated with OT ideas, images, and texts. The mode of expression is his own. God uses the prophet where he is and as he is. The lament for a destroyed city was a well-recognized literary form in antiquity.[408]

Rome has fallen and has become desolate, so desolate it is like the proverbial wilderness, where it was believed demons dwelled.[409] Rome was to go from being a city of perhaps 1 million in John's day to only about 30,000 when the city fell several centuries later.[410] *Phulake* in vs. 2 can mean prison, though some think it should be translated watchtower. The image is meant to convey the city's desolation, which is perhaps why the New Revised Standard Version (NRSV) translates the word "haunt" here. It is a place where every unclean and hateful bird now dwells – the home of vultures.[411] This description comes from Jer. 51.37 speaking of Babylon and Isa. 34.11–15 of Edom. The punishment fell on the city because she made all other nations drink from the cup of her fornication, and so they committed fornication with her. The subject here though is not mere immorality. As we shall see, the subject in large part is materialism and greed – the wrongful orientation toward the good things of this world. Notice the immediate complaint in vs. 3. The merchants of the world became rich from the power of Rome's luxury and from Rome's desire for luxury. The seduction was in large part material and financial. The cry is immediately followed by the exclamation, "come out from them." This cry is common in the OT (Jer. 50.8, 51.6; Isa. 48.10, 52.11).[412]

Vs. 4 involves a call by a voice from heaven to God's people in Rome. While there might be a geographical reference in this call, since John apparently believed that Rome would one day fall, in terms of John's own immediate audience, Boring is right to say, "The call to 'come out' is not a matter of geographical relocation but of inner reorientation."[413] In our text it is a call for divorcing oneself from the materialistic orientation that characterized Rome. That orientation,

---

[408] See Lam. 1.1–5.22; 1 Macc. 2.6–13; Greek Anthology 9.151; Sib. Or. 5.98–99 (lament for a city's future demise).

[409] This would be seen as poetic justice in light of Rev. 16.9.20 and 16.14. The city once motivated and directed by demons would in the end be inhabited almost solely by demons.

[410] See C. Keener, *Revelation* (2002), p. 423.

[411] As M. G. Reddish, *Revelation* (2001), p. 340, says. The birds are considered unclean because they prey on corpses.

[412] In these texts, it is used to speak of a literal leaving of Babylon before it is destroyed. But, this clearly is not what it has come to mean in 2 Cor. 6.17.

[413] M. E. Boring, *Revelation* (1989), p. 189.

and the greed, gluttony, and immorality that go along with it, are being warned against by John. Mounce relates the exorbitant extravagances that characterized Roman nobility and royal families as well as the merchants who supplied them.[414] Vitellius, who was Emperor less than a year, somehow managed to spend more than $20 million, mostly on food. B. T. Kidd. 49a has a saying about Rome's legendary wealth: "Ten measures of wealth came down into the world; Rome received nine." Thus it is no exaggeration when John says that the sins of Rome are like a great pile of possessions stacked up as high as heaven.

In **vs. 5** we hear that God remembered (i.e., not merely noticed but judged) this sin.[415] Indeed, **vs. 6** says they were paid back double for her deeds. John believes in some form of divine *lex talionis* and, in particular, in the idea that the punishment should fit the crime. "Double unto her the double" is a conventional saying meaning full requital (cf. Jer. 16.18, 17.18 cf. Jer. 50.29). Rome will have to drink a double portion of the evil brew she mixed. The sin of Rome was both self-glorification and voluptuous living. Self-glorification also involves self-delusion. Rome had said to herself, "I sit as Queen and I am not a widow." Because of this arrogance and sin, she will experience death, mourning, and famine in the space of one short day (cf. Isa. 47.9). In **vs. 9** we have the first instance of the refrain, "it all happened in an hour." Caird suggests we compare the one hour in 17.12–14 in which the kings wage war against the Lamb.[416] One hour of persecution is balanced by one hour of judgment. **Vs. 8b** says the great city will be burned up, and perhaps we are meant to think of the experience under Nero, or more likely Pompey will still have been fresh in the memories of many during the reign of Domitian.

These things happen to Rome not merely because she has sinned, as if it were some historical process of what goes around comes around, but because the strong Lord who judges intervenes, and no matter what Rome's resources she will fall suddenly. Those client kings or rulers who had depended on Rome break out into weeping and mourning, watching the smoke rise from the city at a distance.[417] In short they are weeping over their own demise, for they do not rush to help. They think only of the implications for themselves, such is the fallen, selfish human nature. There is more involved though, for these rulers or officials also fear sharing in the same torment. This is why they stand at a distance and watch.

Beginning at **vs. 11 ff.** we hear the lament of the merchants, including a long list of imports that came to Rome from all over the Empire and beyond.

---

[414] R. H. Mounce, *Book of Revelation* (1977), pp. 326–29.
[415] There are texts, such as Gen. 15.16; Matt. 23.36; Luke 11.50, suggesting that God sometimes delays judgment until the sins have piled up so high that he is forced to act.
[416] G. B. Caird, *Revelation* (1998), pp. 225–26.
[417] This may be usefully contrasted with the other parallel city prophecy in Rev. 21, where righteous kings will bring glory into the New Jerusalem. See C. Keener, *Revelation* (2002), p. 426.

The merchants mourn for there will no longer be anyone to buy jewels and pearls from India, silk and cinnamon from China, gold and ivory and costly wood from Africa, spices and incense from Arabia, horses from Armenia, and slaves from everywhere. All of these items are luxury goods that only the wealthy could afford. The list here should be compared to the one in Ezek. 27.2–24, where there is a list of forty products traded in Tyre. Women of Rome in this period had a great passion for silver bathtubs, and Julius Caesar is said to have given a pearl worth $18,000 to Servilia.[418]

There are two words used here for slaves. The first is simply bodies, as in English we might talk about hired hands. There were perhaps 60 million slaves in the Roman Empire at this time. The second term, lives/souls of humans, basically refer to human livestock. Slaves did the work for the wealthy, filled the brothels, and performed in the arena. Rome could not have existed without slavery.

A CLOSER LOOK – SLAVERY AND THE ROMAN ECONOMY

Slavery in the Roman Empire was in many respects of a very different ilk than modern forms of slavery, including antebellum slavery in the southern parts of the United States in the eighteenth and nineteenth centuries. The whole of the Roman economy, not just the agrarian part, depended on slave labor. To a certain extent this was a result of the attitudes of the Greco-Roman elite about manual or menial labor, but that was only one factor. Slave trade was a burgeoning enterprise in the late first century A.D. Most of the slaves in this era had come from the eastern part of the Empire, though perhaps only about half had been obtained through capture during a war. Others were sold into slavery by their parents (indigent families who could not afford to keep all, or in some cases any, of their children) or even sold themselves into slavery to survive or advance economically.

Since the time of Aristotle, slaves had been defined as a piece of living property (see Rev. 18.13c). As a material good, slaves basically had no rights and were wholly subject to the will or whims of their owners. But there were masters who were kind, and often enough slaves were allowed to have families, pass down a part of an inheritance, own property (through the legal device called the *peculium*), start their own businesses, and a variety of other activities. Seneca satirizes the time of Claudius as an extended Saturnalia when slaves could not only become freedmen and freedwomen but could rise high in society and even intermarry with patricians (cf. *Apocolocyntosis* 3, 12; *On Benefits* 28.5–6).[419]

---

[418] Notice in **vs. 14** the aural play on words between **lipara** (riches) and **lampra** (splendor). This reminds us once more that this was to be a document that was in the first instance heard, not simply read. This is why the rhetorical dimensions of the document need to be taken seriously.

[419] See D. B. Martin, *Slavery as Salvation: The Metaphor of Slavery in Pauline Christianity* (New Haven, Conn.: Yale University Press, 1990), pp. 43–45.

It was not just that there were slaves doing all sorts of menial tasks in the Empire, such as working in the mines, they could also be teachers, pedagogues, artists, artisans, business agents, and a host of other things. Even the civil service of the Roman government was run to a large extent by slaves. The imperial slaves also had considerable clout and were widely respected.

Though many slaves were able to save up enough money so that, if given permission by their masters, they could buy themselves out of slavery, many chose not to do so, because there was often greater economic security being a slave than becoming a poor freed person. Thus we can understand the inscription of the freed slave who said, "Slavery was never unkind to me" (*CIL* 13.7119). The networks of reciprocity were such that there were enough benefits and opportunities for most slaves that revolutionary behavior was not seriously contemplated by any significant number of slaves. The patron–client system tended to mitigate the harsher realities of a highly stratified society.

What were ancient attitudes toward slavery? No ancient government ever sought to abolish slavery, not even a Jewish one. No former slaves who became writers ever attacked the institution of slavery. Even when there was a slave revolt, it was almost never intended to end slavery but rather to free a certain group of slaves from abuses. This may even be true of the famous Spartacus revolt.[420]

Estimates vary, but most scholars believe that one-third to one-half of the population of the Empire were slaves. The Empire ran on slave labor, and hence the bigger the Empire, the greater the need for slaves. Indeed, one could say that the Roman Empire as it was would have been impossible without slavery. Also it was far more likely that freedmen and freedwomen would be abused by their employers than slaves, since an owner stood to lose much if he damaged or killed his own slave. Good-quality, healthy slaves did not come cheap.

Once manumitted, a slave attained a restricted citizenship status, which even included the right to inherit the patron's estate. It indeed became the case that domestic servitude was a means of integrating talented foreigners into society, with the regular expectation that they would be freed and given certain civic rights in due course. It was a regular practice to leave one's estate to a trusted slave rather than to a dissolute heir. But it is largely domestic slaves that had opportunities for advancement in life and in their social standing. Agricultural slaves or mining slaves really did not often have such opportunities to obtain freedom.[421]

To a very high degree, slavery as an institution and the Roman economy were primarily set up to benefit the city of Rome itself, whether we think of

---

[420] See S. Scott Bartchy, *First-Century Slavery and the Interpretation of 1 Cor. 7.21* (Missoula, Mont.: Scholars, 1973), p. 63.

[421] See T. Wiedemann, *Greek and Roman Slavery* (Baltimore: Johns Hopkins University Press, 1981), pp. 3–5.

slaves harvesting the crops in Egypt that were then put on merchant vessels bound for Rome to be used for the dole, or imperial slaves, or temple slaves serving in the cults, including the imperial cult. Slavery helped create the 1–2 percent leisure class of rulers, patricians, and others in Rome exempt from having to do any manual labor. Thus when Rome itself falls or is destroyed, this meant the end of a whole way of life for merchants and ship owners and others who depended on the wealthy on the one hand to buy their goods and slaves on the other hand to provide, transport, and deliver their goods. Since Asia was the richest of provinces, and in some ways the one most dependent on Rome, John's audience would know at once what the impact was on them if Rome fell.

It is worthwhile to quote Aelius Aristides (*To Rome* 11–13), a second-century A.D. writer who saw Rome at its height, as did John. He knew very well the truth of the saying "all roads (and sea channels) lead to Rome."

Around lie the continents far and wide, pouring an endless flow of goods to Roma. There is brought from every land and sea whatever is brought forth by the seasons and is produced by all countries, rivers, lakes, and the skills of Greeks and foreigners.... Anyone who wants to behold all these products must either journey through the whole world to see them or else come to this city. For whatever is raised or manufactured by each people is assuredly always here to overflowing. So many merchants arrive here with cargoes from all over, at every season, and with each return of the harvest, that the city seems like a common warehouse of the world. One can see so many cargoes from India or if you wish from Arabia ... that one may surmise that the trees there have been left permanently bare, and that those people must come here to beg for their own goods whenever they need anything! ... The arrival and departure of ships never ceases, so that it is astounding that the sea, never mind the harbor, suffices for the merchants, and all things converge here – trade, seafaring, agriculture, metallurgy, all the skills which exist and have existed, anything that is begotten and grows, all the skills which exist and have existed, anything that is begotten and grows. Whatever cannot be seen here belongs completely to the category of nonexistent things.

All the pleasures that derived from all these products and people have now been taken away, never to be given back. Fallen is the great city. She was laid waste in but a single hour. At **vs. 18** we hear the cry of the seamen – "What city was like this great one?" **Vs. 19** says the merchants cast dust upon their heads in mourning for Rome. While there is mourning in Rome, **vs. 20** says that heaven and the saints, apostles, and prophets are called upon to rejoice. The bad news for the oppressors is good news for the oppressed. Who here are the saints? Are these prophets OT prophets or Christian prophets, or both? It is possible that all these terms simply refer to Christians, which might explain why prophets follow apostles, as in the Pauline list in 1 Cor. 12. Caird sees here a cross-reference to the other courtroom scene in Rev. 12.12.[422] He suggests, I think rightly, that the word **krima** here, as elsewhere in the NT, means the sentence passed by a judge. Thus **vs. 20b** must refer to the judgment Rome passed on the martyrs that is now being passed on her. The threat of the city burning, of course, was a real one, and many still living in John's day would remember the huge fire in A.D. 64 during the reign of Nero.

At **vs. 21** we hear of a strong angel who takes a millstone and casts it into the sea. This is comprehensible on the basis of the parallel in Jer. 51.63–64, where Jeremiah tied his prophecies about the fall of Babylon to a stone and threw them in the Euphrates, symbolizing the fall and sinking of the great city (cf. Luke 17.2). The fall is cause for striking up the heavenly band according to **vs. 22**. Vv. 22–23 draw on Jer. 25.10 and Ezek. 26.13 and refer to harpists, flautists, and trumpeters. There will be no more sounds of grinding grain, no more lights shining in the city, no more sound of the bride and the bridegroom, because Rome was the one who misled the nations with her sorcery. Her idolatry, immorality, and materialism wove a spell over the nations. **Vs. 23** refers to **pharmakeia**, which likely means sorcery or magic spells. Sorcery, prostitution, and idolatry are linked together in the way Jezebel is described in 2 Kings 9.22.[423] Aune suggests that it was thought that the incredible success of Rome could only be attributed to magic or sorcery.[424] **Vs. 24** reveals the typical way apocalyptic works. It is said that in Rome all the slain of the world could be found. This is not mere hyperbole. John is telling us that Rome is a type of all the oppressive cities everywhere. But it was true that the blood of prophets and saints could be found in her. This may be seen as the primary cause of her demise. She would be treated as she treated Peter, Paul, and others.

Rev. 19 has several sections, but our concern here is only with its first ten verses. This one is set apart from what precedes it by the now-familiar phrase, "after these things," which always indicates a new vision or audition (cf. 4.1; 7.1, 9; 15.5; 18.1).[425] We have contrasted in this section the fate of Babylon, the harlot (vv. 1–5), and the future of the New Jerusalem, the bride (vv. 6–9). The prostitute will die and be burned by her lovers (17.16–17), while the Lamb will welcome his bride.[426] Beasley-Murray has suggested that in vv. 1–4 we have the praises of heaven, while in vv. 6–7 we have the praises of the saints, apostles, and prophets.[427] Reddish points to the ever widening series of concentric circles of praisers – at the center of things is the throne from which the voice comes, then the twenty-four elders and living creatures, then the myriad angels who

---

[422] G. B. Caird, *Revelation* (1998), pp. 228–29.

[423] See C. Keener, *Revelation* (2002), p. 433.

[424] D. E. Aune, *Revelation 7–22* (1998), p. 1010.

[425] As M. G. Reddish, *Revelation* (2001), p. 359, points out, only here does it introduce an audition with the phrase, "I heard . . ."

[426] C. Keener, *Revelation* (2002), p. 449.

[427] G. R. Beasley-Murray, *Book of Revelation* (1978), pp. 271–76.

surround the throne, and then the inhabitants of earth who sing the praises (19.1–8).[428]

First, we hear the shout of Alleluia/Hallelujah from the myriad in heaven. This group was mentioned at 5.11. The term Hallelujah, literally "praise Yahweh," is found nowhere else in the NT other than in this book (indeed in this chapter alone), another telltale sign the author is surely a Jewish Christian. It has been suggested that this is a sort of Christian Hallel psalm, rather like one finds in Pss. 113–118. The Hallel was sung in praise of God's deliverance at Exodus Sinai.[429] It is thus appropriate here since we have just heard of the deliverance of God's people from their oppressors. Vv. 1–8 could then be taken as a liturgy of Hallelujahs. Salvation and judgment are juxtaposed in vv. 1–2 because they are seen as two sides of the same coin. Not only has justice been done and the oppressor punished, but the blood of the martyrs has been avenged. Vengeance or justice is left to God, and rejoicing is not over some human action but over the all-wise God's just actions. The elders and the four creatures all affirm this with an Amen and rejoice with an Alleluia.

Vs. 3 speaks of the smoke of the city's destruction rising forever, which may be a nice ironic touch, as Beale suggests, for "eternal judgment may be a partial polemic against the mythical *Roma aeterna* ('eternal Rome') which was one of the names for the Roman Empire."[430] **Vs. 5** is an exhortation for all God's people to praise him. This prevents us from relating this group to the martyrs only. It is both the little and the large, the socio-economically well-off and the poor, who are called upon to praise.

In **vv. 6 ff.** the saints respond to this exhortation and do praise God.[431] A vast throng praises, that it sounds like the rolling of many waters or the peals of great thunder. God is praised for reigning. There is rejoicing and giving him glory for something very special – namely, the marriage of the Lamb and his bride, and she has made herself ready. This is the first occurrence of this idea in Revelation, and it is a clear sign that we are rapidly moving toward the climax of the book. John draws on a variety of images such as the OT texts where Israel is said to be God's bride, though notably all of these refer to her as a faithless bride (cf. Hos. 2; Ezek. 16). The various traditions that refer to a messianic banquet are likely echoed here as well (cf. 1 En. 62.14; 3 En. 48.10). God was faithful and looked forward to a new and better marriage relationship (cf. Hos. 2.1, 19 ff.; Ezek. 16.59 ff., which is here depicted as being fulfilled). One must also compare the various sayings of Jesus about bride and bridegroom (cf. Matt. 22.1 ff. and Matt. 25.1 ff.). It should be kept in view that, when the woman was betrothed

---

[428] M. G. Reddish, *Revelation* (2001), p. 360.
[429] The term occurs some twenty-three times in the LXX version of these Psalms.
[430] G. K. Beale, *The Book of Revelation* (Grand Rapids, Mich.: Eerdmans, 1999), p. 929.
[431] Possibly there is a counterpolemic against Domitian's claims to be Lord and God. See Suetonius, *Dom.* 13.2, and Dio Cassius, *Hist. Rom.* 67.4.7.

in early Judaism, she was already called the bride, because she was already in a binding contract. Thus it is probable that the image of the marriage between Christ and his bride is seen as having an eschatological consummation. This relationship can only be seen as betrothal at this point.

It is said that the bride made herself ready, and she is given to wear the clean, gleaming white wedding dress, reflecting her purity and righteousness (cf. Eph. 5.22 ff.).[432] This indicates that the process leading up to the marriage is synergistic, requiring action by God to make his people clean but also on the believer's part to be prepared through repentance and faith. The flexibility of this image is quite clear, for, by **vs. 8**, the believers are no longer the bride but the wedding guests at the feast. Perhaps there is a distinction being made here between the church as a corporate entity being the bride, and individual Christians being wedding guests. The marriage supper of the Lamb may be contrasted with the supper of God in which carrion birds feast on the carcasses of the wicked (19.9, 17–18). Here also we hear a beatitude – "Blessed are those invited to the wedding dinner." It is a by-invitation-only affair. We are reminded of Jesus calling the great eschatological reunion a great feast, and probably our author has drawn on the Jesus tradition in this material. We should contrast the bride of Christ with the earlier image of the harlot.

In view of what follows this passage, it is clear that John foresaw this taking place once the bridegroom returns for his bride. This feast does not precede the return, either in heaven or on earth. The author is prophesying about the future. At **vs. 10** we learn an important lesson. No one and nothing other than God should be worshiped, but John himself makes the same mistake many have made. The angel had given the prophet the word of God, but the messenger must not be mistaken for the sender of the message.[433] Thus John is exhorted not to worship the angel. The angel is but John's fellow servant of God, and the brother of those having the witness of Christ. This verse may reflect John's awareness that there was a problem in Asia, even among syncretistic Jews, with the worship of angels (though Col. 2.18 may mean worship with rather than of angels).[434]

The appearance of this phrase here and in **vs. 10b** raises once again the question of whether we are dealing with an objective or a subjective genitive. Is this the witness that Christ bears or the witness about Christ? Either idea is possible.

---

[432] Wedding apparel could include white linen, bracelets, and even costly inscribed ornaments (Jos. and Asen. 3.6, 9–11; 4.1–2).

[433] On inspired angels, see Ezek. 1.12, 20–21; 10.17; 1 En. 68.2. When angels are messengers, they serve a prophetic function. See Zech. 1.14; Jub. 2.1; and C. Keener, *Revelation* (2002), p. 451.

[434] On the cult of angel worship, see R. A. Kearsley, "Angels in Asia Minor: The Cult of Hosios and Dikaios," in *New Documents Illustrating Early Christianity*, ed. S. R. Llewelyn and R. A. Kearsley, vol. 6 (Grand Rapids, Mich.: Eerdmans, 1992), pp. 206–9. C. Keener, *Revelation* (2002), pp. 451–52, suggests there may be an implicit critique of an angelomorphic Christology. See R. Bauckham, *Climax of Prophecy* (1993), pp. 142–49.

If an objective genitive is in view, then this verse must mean that the testimony about Christ is the very gist of Christian prophecy. It is what the Spirit inspires true Christian messengers to speak of. Or possibly, the spirit of true prophecy manifests itself always in testifying about and exalting Jesus.[435] Against Caird then, the objective genitive reading would not require that John thought the source of his inspiration was his own testimony to Christ.[436] The author says nothing of source, only of the spirit of prophecy. Nevertheless, it is not impossible that a subjective genitive is in view, in which case the gist of prophecy is the testimony Christ bore about himself. Why does this material appear here? Perhaps it reminds us that this revelation is all about Jesus, not about esoteric topics, not even about Rome or the church, except as they have bearing on the redemptive-judgment of the Lamb. Koester puts the matter this way: "the criterion of true prophecy is whether it moves people to worship the true God and to be faithful to Jesus."[437]

A CLOSER LOOK – JOHN'S ESCHATOLOGY

As Caird points out, John has a sort of double eschatology.[438] There has already been recounted the judgment on the harlot and the appearance of the bride at the wedding feast, and now John describes the last battle. Various of these events, including the fall of Rome, precede the millennium. After the millennium we have another battle, this time with Gog and Magog, and the final judgment of the dead transpires, and the New Jerusalem descends from heaven adorned as a bride for her husband. This can only mean, as Caird stresses, that John did not think the absolute end of the world was at hand, for the millennium and its sequel had to come first. In fact, if one includes the millennium, John believed the world would continue for a long but indeterminate amount of time before the real end, which entailed the new heaven and the new earth. This means that all this language about the time being short refers to the time being short before the preliminary eschatological events leading up to the millennium. We will deal with the various theories about the millennium shortly, but here an important conclusion must be drawn. The author did not believe he was living in the shadow of the final judgment or the battle of Gog and Magog, though he could conceive of how the events leading up to the millennium could transpire in his own era. The end in view at the end of each of the series of seven judgments is the end of John's extant world, the known Roman world, not the end of the entire world or of human history, much less the end of the material

[435] 1 Cor. 12.3 indicates that one can only say Jesus is Lord truly and authentically if one has the Holy Spirit, and conversely one cannot say "Jesus be cursed" if one has the Spirit.
[436] G. B. Caird, *Revelation* (1998), p. 238.
[437] C. Koester, *Revelation and the End* (2001), p. 170.
[438] Ibid.

universe. John, as we shall see, doesn't believe the material universe will come to an end. He believes it will be renewed into a new creation at some point after the millennium. At that juncture, God will dwell permanently on earth with his people, there will be the final merger of heaven and earth, of the eternal and temporal, and the "kingdoms of this become the kingdoms of our God and of his Christ."

BRIDGING THE HORIZONS

Seeing ourselves as others see us is a necessary, though difficult, task. It has been recently asked why the terrorists would target New York and Washington for their attacks in the fall of 2001. The reason is actually theological in part. To many such people, these large cities are the great symbols of the Evil Empire. It is no accident that Osama bin Laden said in one of his press releases after 11 September that what happened in those cities was a judgment of God on the wickedness of American culture. It appears that he saw these cities much the same as John saw Rome in his own day – as purveyors of idolatry and immorality. It is in some measure understandable why such a person would view things this way. The major visual exports of America to other parts of the world are films and television programs that glorify sexual immorality, greed, violence, and the like. There is the news media, which major in tales of woe and violence and seem, to foreigners, to always put a pro-American spin on their reporting. There is American business and industry, which is seen as self-serving and where benefits are doled out, it is perceived, to help only the rich few and to exploit the poor many. The recent scandals over Nike's use of Asian workers to make its shoes come to mind. In other words, while nothing can justify the actions of the terrorists in September 2001, there is some justice in their critique of American culture, especially as it is exported to the world. To give but one other example, at one point in the 1990s, *Baywatch* was the most-watched TV program in the entire world. What sort of messages about America would this product be sending to very conservative and highly religious peoples in other parts of the world? Whatever else one may say about comparisons between Rome/Babylon and New York/Gotham, we do indeed need to do a better job of seeing ourselves as others see us. As Keener remarks, "The sins hardest to see are those where our culture shares the same blind spots we have."[439]

In Rev. 17.14 we hear of war against the Lamb. It raises the important question of how Christians could help to stop the cycle of violence or violence's glorification. There is a story from the fourth century A.D. about a monk named Telemachus who once paid a visit to Rome and attended a gladiatorial fight held in the Roman Colosseum. Disgusted and horrified by what he observed, he

---

[439] C. Keener, *Revelation* (2002), p. 435.

hurled himself into the arena and stood between the gladiators seeking to prevent either of them from being killed. But, in the process, he himself was killed. This repulsed various of the observers of the contest, who one after another got up and left the Colosseum. It is said that this action precipitated the end of the gladiatorial games in that venue.[440]

Boesak encourages us to compare and contrast the woman in Rev. 12 with the woman in Rev. 17–19. Some feminist interpreters have quite naturally protested the extremes of these images of women, portrayed as either a saint or a harlot, but the very nature of apocalyptic rhetoric and its visual imagery is to use dramatic hyperbole to make a point. Boesak has summed up his comparison of these two extremes as follows:

They are both women, they are both called "mother" but the differences cannot be more fundamental. In chapter 12, we meet the "Messianic" mother, the giver of life. Here [in Rev. 17–19] we are confronted with the mother of whores, the very personification of the evil she is associated with. She does not understand or give life. This woman is the mother of death, who does not nurture or protect but destroys. The Messianic mother brings forth a child who promises life to the world. The mother of death is "drunk with the blood of the saints and the blood of the martyrs of Jesus" (17.6).[441]

Nations and empires rise and fall, as any student of history knows, but it is interesting to consider the psychology of shock as it applies to nations that suddenly have to deal with a major reversal. The lament in Rev. 18 raises this point as the various parties were not prepared for Rome's demise. Doubtless the shock would be no less great if suddenly Americans were faced by an invading army that took the capital city and burned it to the ground. And, in fact, our memory is so short that we forget this actually happened in the War of 1812! It is well for any nation, however powerful, to bear in mind that it is not invincible and might one day face a funeral lament like that in Rev. 18. Among other functions, this lament should serve as a wake-up call reminding us that we need to place our ultimate trust in God, not in our economic or military prowess.

I agree with the wise words of J. N. Kraybill in regard to providing an overall assessment of how applicable John's comments are to our own situation in the democratic nations of the world. He says,

Particularly in democratic societies, in which governments fulfill a range of productive and healthy roles, Christians cannot simply adopt John's stance of categorical condemnation. Sectarian withdrawal from society is not a valid option if the church can actively "engage the powers" so to speak or act for justice and truth. Yet John's keen insight into spiritual dimensions of political power might help us see that even the best of governments sometimes make choices or demands that followers of Jesus must challenge.

---

[440] See ibid., p. 418.
[441] A. Boesak, *Comfort and Protest* (1986), p. 110.

Christians in economically and politically powerful nations, in the terminology of Revelation, live more in Babylon than on Patmos. From our position of relative security and comfort it may be difficult to hear or accept John's radical critique of imperial power, a critique that seems logical to many people in the two-thirds world.[442]

But hear John's critique we must. As Kraybill suggests, we must ask today where and in what way governments and economic institutions demand allegiance that borders on idolatry. Which are the modern commercial empires that derive their own prosperity at the expense of poor and defenseless people? "What should Christians do when governments seek our personal or financial support for acts of violence or nationalistic self-interest? What ideology or pseudo-religion do political and economic powers use to justify their deeds? How are Christians tempted to take part or benefit?"[443]

Boesak points out that at Rev. 18.13 John may be critiquing the use of slaves by listing them last and then calling them not merely slaves but "souls."[444] In other words he qualifies their status as property by correcting the usual terminology with a reference to human souls. He has a point for the terminology here is not bodies (from *soma*) but souls (from *psuche*), a term presumably reserved in John's vocabulary for human beings. Boesak points out that to treat someone in a subhuman way, you must first envision them as less than human. The slave status is justified on the basis of seeing someone as subhuman or inferior in order to exploit such a person.[445]

The hymns in Revelation have various functions, both spiritual and political, and they provide important commentary on the action, reminding that God is still sovereign and will work all things together for the good of those who love God. They also give an opportunity for the audience to exercise their faith by joining in the singing, even in the face of adversity. It has also been suggested that some of these hymns function rather like the resistance song of the Civil Rights movement, "We Shall Overcome." I believe these observations are correct and helpful.[446]

The cry of Hallelujah in Rev. 19.6 (cf. 19.16 and 11.15) provided part of the inspiration for Handel's "Hallelujah Chorus" in his masterwork *Messiah*. The story of that work's composition bears repeating. Once Handel had been given the libretto, which amounted chiefly to a stringing together of important prophetic texts and some NT material from Revelation and elsewhere (in a fashion not too dissimilar to what we find John doing in Revelation), he secluded himself in his flat and began composing. The inspiration came quickly, and in only a matter of a fortnight or so, Handel had roughed out the whole score to his

---

[442] J. N. Kraybill, *Imperial Cult and Commerce* (1996), p. 10.
[443] Ibid., p. 22.
[444] A. Boesak, *Comfort and Protest* (1986), p. 120.
[445] Ibid., p. 121.
[446] See further, M. G. Reddish, *Revelation* (2001), pp. 372–73.

masterpiece. Working day and night, he had asked his housekeeper simply to leave a tray of food outside the door from time to time. When he reached the point of composing the Hallelujah Chorus, Handel is said to have remarked, "I did think I saw heaven opened and heard the angelic choir singing." He fell down and wept over the great gift of music God had given him. Something similar seems to have happened to John of Patmos while secluded on that island.

The image of the harlot, coupled with the image of the bride, raises for us the issues of our humanity and in particular our sexuality. Peterson's insights on these matters need to be reflected on at this juncture:

Whoredom is the use of good to do evil; the use of a good body to demean the person, the use of the means of realizing our identity to depersonalize identities. . . . Worship under the aspect of the Great Whore is the commercialization of our great need and deep desire for meaning, love and salvation, for the completion of ourselves from beyond ourselves. . . . The exploration and development of our unique human identity, of which sex is the physical means, is replaced by elaborate and deceiving fantasies. . . . Whoredom uses sex to lie about life: the truth of life is that love is a gift, that relationships are commitments, that sexuality is the sacrament of spirituality. The whore's lie is that love is purchased, that relationships are "deals," that sexuality is an appetite. For the Whore, sex is in the service of commerce; with the Bride, sex is devoted to love. For the Whore, sex is a contract; for the Bride, sex is a life commitment. For the Whore, sex is a calculation; for the Bride, sex is an offering.[447]

There is indeed a fine line between our spirituality and our sexuality. Passion for the latter can be masked as passion for the former. And when spiritual things are used to obtain sexual things, both spiritual and sexual prostitution has happened. We are inescapably embodied beings who are psychosomatic wholes. The spirit affects the body and vice versa. It is my thesis that if the human spirit is properly aligned with God in worship and service, it is much easier for the body to follow that lead. But if one is not in love and fellowship with God and God's people, human fallenness, especially fallenness of the body, becomes the dominant and dominating force in a person's life.

In the NT the body is regularly portrayed as the weak link in the Christian's armor, not because the body is inherently evil or sex is something dirty, but because this is the one part of who we are that is not currently being renewed by God. The renewal of the body must await the resurrection. The mind, the heart, the emotions, and the human will are being renewed now. Inwardly we are being renewed day after day, but outwardly our fallen bodies are wasting away. To this Rev. 21–22 adds the insight that even the internal renewal will not be completed before the New Jerusalem comes into view. There will be need for healing of memories and emotions even in that peaceable kingdom.

[447] E. Peterson, *Reversed Thunder* (1988), pp. 146–47.

Peterson goes on to talk about the seductiveness of Whore worship rather than Bride worship. He is referring to self-indulgent, self-centered worship that focuses on human beings and their needs rather than on God. Rather than inculcate a religion of giving, it inculcates a congregation of consumers. Rather than focus on grace, it urges reciprocity. Peterson calls this a form of worship that focuses on salvation by checkbook, meaning by money, religion as feeling, and self as god.[448] There is indeed far too much worship like this in the Western church, especially in North America, where the Gospel of health and wealth is often preached. Christian spirituality is closely aligned with the fulfillment of the materialistic American dream. The cure for this disease, however, is not mere criticism of the problem. It is to offer a positive alternative – namely true worship that focuses on God, as do all the worship scenes in Revelation. When a worshiper becomes lost in wonder, love, and praise of the great Someone outside of themselves, they become at least for a moment self-forgetful. They lose for an instance the self-consciousness that came with fallenness in the garden. They become more concerned about truly praising God from the bottom of their hearts than about how they will look to others around them if they do so.

True worship does not necessarily lead persons to feel good about themselves. Indeed, as Isa. 6 suggests, it may lead them to be profoundly uncomfortable about their uncleanness and unholiness. This is one of the reasons some people have such difficulty coming forward and taking communion. True worship leads a person to know and encounter God, and in that there is joy – joy in the Other rather than about the self. This is a joy that does not come from ordinary human experience, however exciting or enchanting. It often comes in spite of great suffering in the human experience. It comes from that close encounter with God and from the resultant indwelling presence of God's Spirit.

REVELATION 19.11–21.8 – THE RIDER ON THE WHITE HORSE, REDEMPTIVE-JUDGMENT, AND THE MESSIANIC MILLENNIUM

NRSV Revelation 19.11 Then I saw heaven opened, and there was a white horse! Its rider is called Faithful and True, and in righteousness he judges and makes war.

12 His eyes are like a flame of fire, and on his head are many diadems; and he has a name inscribed that no one knows but himself.

13 He is clothed in a robe dipped in blood, and his name is called The Word of God.

14 And the armies of heaven, wearing fine linen, white and pure, were following him on white horses.

---

[448] Ibid., p. 148.

15 From his mouth comes a sharp sword with which to strike down the nations, and he will rule them with a rod of iron; he will tread the winepress of the fury of the wrath of God the Almighty.

16 On his robe and on his thigh he has a name inscribed, "King of Kings and Lord of Lords."

17 Then I saw an angel standing in the sun, and with a loud voice he called to all the birds that fly in midheaven, "Come, gather for the great supper of God,

18 to eat the flesh of kings, the flesh of captains, the flesh of the mighty, the flesh of horses and their riders – flesh of all, both free and slave, both small and great."

19 Then I saw the Beast and the kings of the earth with their armies gathered to make war against the rider on the horse and against his army.

20 And the Beast was captured, and with it the false prophet who had performed in its presence the signs by which he deceived those who had received the mark of the Beast and those who worshiped its image. These two were thrown alive into the lake of fire that burns with sulphur.

21 And the rest were killed by the sword of the rider on the horse, the sword that came from his mouth; and all the birds were gorged with their flesh.

NRSV Revelation 20.1 Then I saw an angel coming down from heaven, holding in his hand the key to the bottomless pit and a great chain.

2 He seized the dragon, that ancient serpent, who is the Devil and Satan, and bound him for a thousand years,

3 and threw him into the pit, and locked and sealed it over him, so that he would deceive the nations no more, until the thousand years were ended. After that he must be let out for a little while.

4 Then I saw thrones, and those seated on them were given authority to judge. I also saw the souls of those who had been beheaded for their testimony to Jesus and for the word of God. They had not worshiped the Beast or its image and had not received its mark on their foreheads or their hands. They came to life and reigned with Christ a thousand years.

5 (The rest of the dead did not come to life until the thousand years were ended.) This is the first resurrection.

6 Blessed and holy are those who share in the first resurrection. Over these the second death has no power, but they will be priests of God and of Christ, and they will reign with him a thousand years.

7 When the thousand years are ended, Satan will be released from his prison

8 and will come out to deceive the nations at the four corners of the earth, Gog and Magog, in order to gather them for battle; they are as numerous as the sands of the sea.

9 They marched up over the breadth of the earth and surrounded the camp of the saints and the beloved city. And fire came down from heaven and consumed them.

10 And the Devil who had deceived them was thrown into the lake of fire and sulphur, where the Beast and the false prophet were, and they will be tormented day and night forever and ever.

11 Then I saw a great white throne and the one who sat on it; the earth and the heaven fled from his presence, and no place was found for them.

12 And I saw the dead, great and small, standing before the throne, and books were opened. Also another book was opened, the book of life. And the dead were judged according to their works, as recorded in the books.

13 And the sea gave up the dead that were in it, Death and Hades gave up the dead that were in them, and all were judged according to what they had done.

14 Then Death and Hades were thrown into the lake of fire. This is the second death, the lake of fire;

15 and anyone whose name was not found written in the book of life was thrown into the lake of fire.

NRSV Revelation 21.1 Then I saw a new heaven and a new earth; for the first heaven and the first earth had passed away, and the sea was no more.

2 And I saw the holy city, the new Jerusalem, coming down out of heaven from God, prepared as a bride adorned for her husband.

3 And I heard a loud voice from the throne saying, "See, the home of God is among mortals. He will dwell with them; they will be his peoples, and God himself will be with them;

4 he will wipe every tear from their eyes. Death will be no more; mourning and crying and pain will be no more, for the first things have passed away."

5 And the one who was seated on the throne said, "See, I am making all things new." Also he said, "Write this, for these words are trustworthy and true."

6 Then he said to me, "It is done! I am the Alpha and the Omega, the beginning and the end. To the thirsty I will give water as a gift from the spring of the water of life.

7 Those who conquer will inherit these things, and I will be their God and they will be my children.

8 But as for the cowardly, the faithless, the polluted, the murderers, the fornicators, the sorcerers, the idolaters, and all liars, their place will be in the lake that burns with fire and sulfur, which is the second death."

*B*etween the tale of the two great cities, one (Rome) that is destroyed and whose smoke rises up to the heavens and the other (New Jerusalem) that comes down from heaven, is the story of final judgment and the messianic millennium. The parallels between the two sections make clear that Rev. 19.11–21.8 must be taken together as a literary or rhetorical unit. Furthermore it appears that we must take this material as a chronological sequence in broad strokes. Judgment and tribulation leading up to the millennium are followed by that millennium, which in turn is followed by the final judgment on the world, the flesh, and the Devil (or better said in this case, the judgment on the Beast, the false prophet, and the Devil), and then finally we hear of the new heaven and the new earth. This is a perfectly plausible scenario for someone who grew up in early Judaism and was cognizant of Jewish speculations about the messianic age at the close of human history.

At the beginning of this section, we hear of heaven itself being opened, and more comes forth than a mere vision. Not merely a door in heaven opens, but heaven itself bursts forth on the scene. We must hark back to the material in 16.12 ff., the judgment of the sixth cup. There we heard of the armies assembling for Armaggedon (cf. 17.14). Rev. 16.15 refers to the coming of the Son like a thief in the night. Here is the expansion of that comment, and the battle described should not be distinguished from the one mentioned in Rev. 16 and 17.14.

The figure on the white horse is identified almost immediately by the allusion back to the beginning where we heard of the witness who was faithful and true (3.14 cf. 1.5). To understand this image, several pieces of background information are important. First, in early Jewish literature like 2 Bar. 72, we hear of a warrior Messiah who slays some of the nations and spares others. More crucial is the material in Ps. Sol. 17.23–27, and Ps. Sol. 19.[449] In the former text we hear of one with an iron rod who will break into pieces the nations' substance and with the word of his mouth will destroy the nations. Ps. Sol. 19 describes this more fully. Second, the image of Christ with an accompanying horde coming forth from heaven is found in 2 Thess. 1.7–8. Notice also in that text the use of the image of flaming fire. In addition one must compare the portrait of the royal figure in Isa. 11.3 ff. Again John has drawn on a variety of resources for his images.

When we hear about the eyes of this rider flaming like fire, we are to recall Rev. 1.14 and 2.18, identifying this figure as the Son of Man, not the figure on the white horse mentioned in Rev. 6.2.[450] This figure has many diadems, in contrast to the seven the dragon had and the ten shared by the ten kings. This rider is King of kings and Lord of lords. None can approach his royalty, royal power, or righteous judgment. Yet, even in this striking vision of disclosure, the figure has a name that no one knows but himself. Swete says that only the Son can understand the full mystery of his own being (cf. Matt. 11.27).[451] It was widely believed in antiquity that gods had secret names. If one knew the name of the god, one had some power or control over him.[452]

Vs. 13 says that the rider's garment is dipped in blood. Because of the sequence of the material, Caird argues that this can only refer to the blood of the martyrs,

---

[449] There are, of course, Jewish texts that depict God as the warrior, cf. Isa. 42.13; Hab. 3.11–14; Zeph. 3.17; 1 QM 18.1–3.

[450] See M. G. Reddish, *Revelation* (2001), p. 366.

[451] H. B. Swete, *Commentary on Revelation* (1977), pp. 251–52.

[452] See M. G. Reddish, *Revelation* (2001), p. 367.

since Armaggedon has not yet been fought.[453] Yet his view is virtually unique and requires ignoring Isa. 63.1–6, where the image of the garment dipped in blood and stained from walking in the winepress is the image of God judging, not of God suffering.[454] In a book where there is recapitulation and overlap, where judgments are discussed and exact chronological order is not always followed, it is strange that Caird should insist on it here to interpret this image. Yet Reddish points out that since the robe is bloodstained before the warrior engages in battle, another interpretation may be in order.[455] The two dominant interpretations are (1) the blood is that of Christ's enemies, and (2) the blood is Jesus' own blood. The combination of the warrior image that echoes Isaiah and the Word image, as we shall see, does not favor the interpretation of the blood being Christ's own.

We are told that the name of this figure is the Logos of God. This is reminiscent of John 1, and yet in Revelation this phrase seems to have a different field of focus. As Mounce suggests, here it refers to God's decisive oral judging of the nations, not to the revelation of God's being or his creative will.[456] Various scholars have noticed the striking parallel to Wisd. of Sol. 18.15–16, where we hear of the all-powerful Word of God leaping from the royal throne in heaven to execute judgment on Egypt. This suggests again that the subject matter of these verses is not the redemptive work of Christ (through his shed blood), but rather his work as final judge of all the earth.[457]

At **vs. 14** an army on white horses follows the initial rider. The army is said to be in heaven. Who then composes this army? It could be the angelic hosts, which would comport with what we find in 2 Thess. 1.7 ff. and Mark 13.27. Alternatively it could refer to the saints as in Rev. 17.14. There are several other parallels between our text and 17.14 that may favor the latter interpretation. In any event they wear fine, gleaming, pure white linen, a description applied to the bride of Christ in Rev. 19. This army, however, is never said to fight. In fact, they are wearing ceremonial garments, not armor or battle gear. Christ does whatever fighting is required, and that by his word.[458]

---

[453] G. B. Caird, *Revelation* (1998), pp. 242–43.

[454] In addition the Targum on Gen. 49.11 is along the same line.

[455] M. G. Reddish, *Revelation* (2001), p. 367. This is also the suggestion of C. Koester, *Revelation and the End* (2001), p. 176. It is not clear that he is right that the bloodstains are there before Christ engages in conflict. Rev. 19.11 has already mentioned that he wages war, before the description of the bloodstained robe in 19.13. He is right, however, that the image of Christ as a warrior is meant to disturb those who look at the world through rose-colored glasses (p. 178).

[456] R. H. Mounce, *Book of Revelation* (1977), p. 354.

[457] On the Word of God as a two-edged sword, see Heb. 4.12.

[458] See C. H. Giblin, *Book of Revelation* (1991), p. 181: "It is most unlikely that we are to understand the heavenly army as saints themselves. For, elsewhere in Revelation, it is the angels who militantly execute God's decrees or who figure in belligerent engagements (e.g., that of Michael and his angels in 12:7–9)."

Vs. 15 is a statement about judgment, the sharp sword of the word issuing from the mouth of the rider and falling upon the nations. There are echoes here of Ps. 2.8–9 and perhaps of Isa. 11.3–4. He will rule with an iron hand. This suggests strong control, not annihilation, and given that various of those he will rule must appear later for final judgment, this seems the correct interpretation.[459] In **vs. 15b** the rider treads the winepress of the wine of the fury of the wrath of the almighty God. This is just a further or alternative image to the one already conjured up in this chapter. Isa. 63.1–4 stands behind this presentation. The army is but a witness, for only the Son treads the winepress. Only he has the power and authority to execute judgment. He alone is King of kings and Lord of lords.[460] The rider also has his name inscribed on his robe and on his thigh, or perhaps what is meant is on the part of his garment where the bare thigh can be seen.[461] The inscription is surely King of kings and Lord of lords. This title not only expresses Jesus' universal sovereignty, but also when it is put back into Aramaic (leaving out the word "and") and its number is reckoned the result is 777, the victorious counterpart and antidote to 666.[462]

At **vs. 17** we have a different image – that of an angel standing in the sun and thus blindingly brilliant in appearance. We are told of a gruesome parallel to the marriage feast of the Lamb, namely the dinner of God served up for birds of prey such as vultures. The description progresses to what happens after the rider smites the nations. There is a great slaughter, and so the carrion birds are seen circling high overhead. Here too we have an invitation to dinner but of a more grizzly sort. It will entail eating the flesh of kings, tribunes, slaves, free, the little and the large, the great and the small. Ezek. 39.17 lies in the background.[463] There is, as Beasley-Murray says, an ironic reversal here. The sacrificial feast, normally an occasion when humans feast on animals, has been reversed. The triumph of God's kingdom involves a nightmare feast for the wicked and a joyful marriage feast for the saints.[464]

The great battle of Armaggedon proves to be a one-sided affair. The rider simply seizes the Beast and the false prophet and casts them into the lake of fire. Though the armies had assembled for a battle, it turned out to be an execution.

---

[459] It is possible that John sees the millennium rather like the description in 1 Cor. 15 about Christ gradually putting all things under his feet until the last enemy is conquered.

[460] It is interesting that the title King of kings was also used by Parthian kings. See C. Keener, *Revelation* (2002), p. 453.

[461] M. G. Reddish, *Revelation* (2001), p. 369, suggests that it might be an allusion to the practice of ancient sculptors to place the name of the deity on the thigh of one of the legs of the statue.

[462] See C. H. Giblin, *Book of Revelation* (1991), p. 182; M. Rissi, "Die Erscheinung Christi nach Off. 19, 11–16," *TZ* 21 (1965), pp. 81–95.

[463] C. Keener, *Revelation* (2002), p. 455, reminds us that in the Greco-Roman world it was believed that one's image survived into the afterlife, and so burial was important. To be left unburied and devoured by animals called in question one's status into the underworld.

[464] G. R. Beasley-Murray, *Book of Revelation* (1978), pp. 283–84.

It may be that we are to think of judgment falling on supernatural evil here, whereas it falls on human evil after the millennium, for we are not told that the evil armies are thrown into the lake of fire at this juncture. In "chapter 19 the actual eschatological battle is never depicted. John employs the traditional language and imagery of eschatological warfare for forensic rhetorical purposes. The Beast and its pseudo-prophet, who represent the destructive political power and imperial cult of Rome, are not killed but taken captive and thrown into a malodorous and fiery lake."[465] The rhetoric is clearly judicial in character, and what we see is a symbolic depiction of a judicial process. Christ merely speaks the judgment against these opponents. There is no real struggle here perhaps because the victory has already been won through the death and resurrection of Jesus, and perhaps also because John is emphasizing the power and sovereignty of Christ.[466]

We must always bear in mind the distinction between Hades, the place of the ungodly dead until the final judgment, and Hell, which corresponds here to the lake of fire. The former corresponds with Sheol, the latter with Gehenna. Hell is viewed as a place of torment by fire, as in other early Jewish literature. For example, 1 En. 54.1 speaks of a deep valley burning with fire, while 2 En. 10, of a fiery river, a place of various torments (cf. Mark 9.43; Matt. 5.22). The lake burns with sulphur. It was thus both incredibly hot but also odoriferous. Later, we will hear that the Devil, death, Hades itself, and all evil humans will be cast there (cf. 20.10, 14; 21.8). Of course, this image cannot be taken literally, but it should be taken seriously. Hell is viewed as a place of torment, not of comfort for the lost. It is a place where one experiences the absence of the presence of God forever, with no remedy. No literal lake of fire could approximate that horror. It appears that John views hell as a place of eternal punishment, not annihilation.

Certainly **Rev. 20** is the most controverted portion of the book of Revelation. Two contextual issues need to be considered before we look in depth at the first six verses. First, this material must be viewed in light of its immediate context in Revelation itself. The sequence of preliminary judgment, millennium, final judgment, new heaven and new earth in Rev. 19–22 must be taken seriously. Second, the larger context of Jewish literature, including intertestamental literature, which has to do with the fate of fallen angels and the Devil, needs to be kept in view. We begin by considering briefly some possible background material found in three different texts in the OT: (1) Isa. 24.21 ff.; (2) Dan. 7; and (3) Ezek. 36–39. Elsewhere I have shown at some length that Isa. 24.21 ff. is simply the first text of several that reflect on the fate of fallen angels or the demonic. These texts usually have to do with reflections on Gen. 6.1–4 and the punishment on those angels who mated with the daughters of humankind and so precipitated the flood (cf. Isa. 24.21–22; 1 En. 10.4–6;

---

[465] E. Fiorenza, *Revelation* (1991), p. 106.
[466] See P. Barnett, *Apocalypse Now and Then* (1989), p. 143.

2 Bar. 40, 56.13; Test. of Lev. 18.12; Jub. 5.6, 10.4–14; Jude vs. 6; 2 Pet. 2.4; 1 Pet. 3.19–20).[467]

In Dan. 7 we find a judgment scene involving the Ancient of Days and the one like a son of man. It is said in that text that judgment is given either *for* or *to* the saints of the Most High. The Aramaic text here at 7.14 could be translated "to the saints," a reading that seems supported by the LXX translation of Daniel at this juncture. Mounce compares Dan. 7.27, where the *lu* indicates an indirect object rather than a translation such as "on behalf of."[468]

It is important to keep the entire flow of Ezek. 36–39 in view. Ezekiel's vision of "death valley" has to do with the corporate revival of a spiritually dead people, using the concept of bodily resurrection, and the hope is for a restoration of Israel to the holy land with a new David ruling over them. After an unspecified amount of time, the rebellion of Gog from Magog (apparently a region in Ezekiel) is followed by the promise of the New Jerusalem with a new temple under paradisiacal-like conditions. There is little reason to doubt that the flow of events recounted in Ezek. 36–39 is being followed to some degree in Rev. 20–21, though the imagery and details are freely modified.[469]

Early Jewish speculation about the messianic age is also of relevance (cf. 2 Bar. 40.3; Sib. Or. 3.741–59, 767–95).[470] There were, for example, rabbis, such as Eliezer b. Jose, who reckoned the messianic age would last 1,000 years. One view of world history in both Jewish and Christian literature before and after the time Revelation was written is the notion that history follows the pattern of the creation week with the messianic age being an age of sabbatical rest from evil and other things. This would be followed by a timeless age, the eighth day of which would be the eternal kingdom (cf. 2 En. 32–33; Ep. Barnabas 15). In this sort of speculation, one of the main figures used was 1,000 years for each age of history. It is possible that John stands in this tradition of thought and envisions the millennium will be the sabbath age of history, when Satan is not allowed to create havoc and chaos among the nations, and thus there is a period of peace.[471] Since we know that John has earlier drawn on the Babylonian legends either directly or indirectly (see pp. 43–45 and 151–53), it is of some relevance that Tiamat, the chaos monster, was imprisoned and then released again at the end of time, where it is defeated once and for all by Marduk, the god of light.

---

[467] See the discussion on pp. 247–48.

[468] R. H. Mounce, *Book of Revelation* (1977), pp. 360–63.

[469] For example, in Rev. 20 we hear of Gog and Magog as if they were two differing entities.

[470] C. Koester, *Revelation and the End* (2001), p. 184, argues that while John makes abundant use of the OT in his description of the new heaven and new earth in Rev. 21–22, he describes the millennium in sparse prose without allusion to the OT. This is a helpful point, but it overlooks that John draws on a wider corpus of early Jewish literature, some of which is apparently echoed in this passage in Rev. 20.

[471] This may be related to what we find in Heb. 4, where God's sabbath rest is seen as a type of the kingdom.

Rev. 20.1–3 is transitional. In a sense 20.1–3 is the climax of the material in Rev. 19, for here the third member of the unholy trinity, the Devil, is finally dealt with, as the false prophet and the Beast were in Rev. 19. Like both of them, Satan is seized and cast somewhere. This must mean that we have to take Rev. 19.1–20.3 as some sort of sequence. Rev. 20.1 simply cannot be seen as a new beginning.[472]

Notice first in **Rev. 20.1** that the angel descends *out of heaven* with the key to the abyss (cf. 9.1).[473] Since what follows in vv. 4–6 is consequent upon this introduction in vs. 1, it appears to describe events that happen somewhere other than in heaven. The word translated as abyss originally had the meaning "bottomless," hence "bottomless pit." It is a place from which there can be no escape. In **vs. 7** this place of confinement is called a prison. The flow of the text makes it clear that Satan is not loosed from this location until after the millennium,[474] and the Jewish background of this material suggests that John saw this millennial age as coming at the end of human history, not immediately after the death and resurrection of Jesus.

At **vs. 3** Satan is chained with a heavy chain and his abode is sealed over so he will not be able to deceive the nations. There could hardly be a more complete description of putting Satan out of commission so far as his influence on human beings and human history is concerned. He is bound, chained, and sealed off.[475] Beasley-Murray notes how the various names of Satan relate to his various roles. As the Dragon, he is the primeval foe of heaven (remember the echo of the Tiamat story). As the Serpent, he is the deceiver of humanity from the beginning. He is called Ha Satan or the Devil because he has been the accuser of believers ever since the fall.[476]

In John's theology Christ has now paid the price on the cross. Since that event, Satan no longer has a legitimate place in the heavenly council. He will be cast into the abyss once the Parousia transpires, and he will be cast into the lake of fire once the millennium is over. His fall is threefold. But we are also told that

---

[472] This counts against any amillennial interpretation. Amillennialists tend to accept that Rev. 19 is about the Parousia but then want to argue that Rev. 20 is not about events subsequent to it. Also against the amillennialist view is that the role of the martyrs in Rev. 20 is very different from that in Rev. 6.9–11. There they are told to wait and receive robes. Here they reign with Christ. In Rev. 6 Satan is still engineering persecution and death for the witnesses still on earth. Here Satan is shut up and sealed off from them.

[473] As L. Thompson, *The Book of Revelation: Apocalypse and Empire* (Oxford: Oxford University Press, 1990), p. 177, points out, this is the reverse of what we saw in Rev. 9.1.

[474] The idea of Satan being imprisoned or bound during the church age makes little sense of texts such as Eph. 6.11; 1 Tim. 1.20; 2 Tim. 2.26; and 1 Pet. 5.8, which suggest that Satan was viewed as being alive and well and active in the world during the time of early Christianity.

[475] St. Augustine, the most influential amillennial interpreter of this material, interpreted the binding of Satan in light of Matt. 12.29 (see his *Civ. Dei.* 20.8). However, that is a reference to Satan being bound so that individual captives might be liberated from his clutches. Here we are told that there is a global effect to this binding of Satan. He can no longer deceive the nations, writ large.

[476] G. R. Beasley-Murray, *Revelation* (1978), pp. 284–85.

he will be released for a short while after the millennium. As Caird says, we are hereby warned about the resiliency of evil in this world. It will never be entirely eliminated before the new heaven and new earth.[477] Even then, it is said in this book that Satan will not be eliminated. Rather he will undergo eternal torment. Thus evil is never entirely eliminated. It is simply put in its place once and for all, once the new heaven and new earth transpires.

Vs. 4 reads literally, "and I saw thrones, and they were seated upon them, and judgment was given to them, and the ***psuche*** (life ?) of the beheaded because of the witness for Jesus and because of the Word of God. . . ." The big controversy about this verse is whether the "they" is synonymous with the beheaded, which had not yet been mentioned. Normally, one would expect an antecedent subject to be in view, but here the nearest one is the nations, which is impossible. In view of John's unorthodox grammar elsewhere in this work, a following subject is not beyond the realm of likelihood. One can point to **vs. 5b** where we have a reference to the first resurrection but not until after the subject has already been discussed.[478] The question must really be pressed about the degree of influence of Dan. 7 on this text. As Beasley-Murray notes, the judgment scene introduced in vs. 4 is not amplified on until vv. 11 ff., but in any case Dan. 7.9–14 stands in the background here.[479] There also we hear about thrones (plural) being put in place, but who is sitting on them? Daniel does not tell us directly, but 7.10 implies that they are those who assist the judge, the Ancient of Days. Presumably the heavenly council is in view in Daniel, which could be the case in our text as well. If so, then these angels or "elders" are given ***krima***, which seems to mean the power to pass judgment or pronounce the sentence. But then it is added, not necessarily as an afterthought (the ***kai*** may be translated as "also"), that the beheaded are also given this function.[480] Why?

First, we must bear in mind that beheading was the normal Roman means of execution, especially of Roman citizens who would be spared the humiliation of crucifixion. What is in view here is likely to be the martyrs that Rome executed, perhaps especially the higher-status ones like Paul who was a Roman citizen. What the martyrs had been waiting for in Rev. 6 comes to fruition. Second, why does John use the word ***psuche***? It seems that John is talking about these saints prior to their being raised, and so he refers to them as lives or "souls."[481] Because

---

[477] See G. B. Caird, *Revelation* (1998), p. 256.

[478] The suggestion of C. H. Giblin in "The Millenium (Rev. 20.4–6) as Heaven," *NTS* 45 (1999), pp. 553–70, that the millennium is a reference to heaven or a heavenly reign founders on several things, not the least of which are the references to resurrection and the Jewish traditions, including the Jesus tradition, about the thrones being set on earth for an earthly reign by the saints.

[479] G. R. Beasley-Murray, *Book of Revelation* (1978), pp. 292–93.

[480] It may be the case that John has only one group of persons in mind who sit on the thrones, namely the beheaded martyrs. See D. E. Aune, *Revelation 17–22* (1998), p. 1088.

[481] The white garment in 6.9–10 is only a temporary expedient apparently.

these martyrs were earlier said to be in heaven, it is plausible to argue that this scene transpires in heaven. In view of what follows, however, while the scene begins in heaven, it ends on earth. Of course, in John's view, in one sense the martyrs were already alive, as their protest in heaven in Rev. 6 shows. John did not hold to a view of the death of the person's self when the body died, nor did he affirm soul sleep.

Thus when it says in **vs. 4b** that "they came to life," this would be an inappropriate way of talking about the saints going to heaven.[482] The complaint in Rev. 6.9 seems to relate to their being without a body. The garment given them is a temporary expedient until this event – when the martyrs get to participate in the first resurrection. But who are those referred to as the ***oitines***? Is this a different group from the martyrs or the same as the beheaded? Probably a larger group is in view, but at Rev. 13.15 it was said that *all* those who do not worship the Beast are killed. This may suggest that John thought that all those Christians who lived just prior to the Parousia would be killed, some by beheading.[483] Perhaps John means all those already martyred, and those martyred in the last days will have the privilege of reigning with Christ. John simply does not tell us what happens to those not martyred who are true believers until they die a natural death. Nor does he speak of what happens to the OT saints. This passage is to offer comfort to those who are suffering and to indicate a great reward is in view if they persevere even to the point of death. Nevertheless, in view of what is said elsewhere in Revelation about those who were faithful and were in the Lamb's book of life, one may assume John thought such persons would also participate in the millennium in a positive way, though not in a judging role. This is especially likely in view of the echo of Dan. 7.9–14 in this text.[484]

Much of the argument about **vs. 4c** depends on whether we translate ***ezesan*** as "live" or as "come to life." The most important parallel is Rev. 2.8, where it is said that Christ died and came to life. The parallel suggests that we should see the reference to be to bodily resurrection in both cases. The saints are to reign with, while being in the same condition as, Christ for 1,000 years. It may be worthwhile to point to the original Gospel tradition about the twelve sitting

---

[482] Various texts suggest it is an acceptable synonym for resurrection. Cf. John 5.25; Rom. 6.10; 2 Cor. 13.4; 1 En. 103.4; Sib. Or. 4.187–90.

[483] M. G. Reddish, *Revelation* (2001), pp. 394–95, says aptly, "This is a scene of role reversals. The martyrs have had to stand before the imperial throne (at least figuratively) and receive the sentence of death. Now they are the ones who are seated on thrones and deliver judgment. . . . The millennium is John's way of offering encouragement to the martyrs. Those who have paid the greatest price receive the greatest reward."

[484] This seems a far more likely conclusion than that of M. G. Reddish, *Revelation* (2001), p. 383, who suggests that the resurrection of the rest of the righteous (the nonmartyrs) waits until after the millennium when they are raised with the unrighteous. This does not comport with what texts like 1 Cor. 15 suggest was early Christian thinking about such matters. It is because of John's concern about and focus on preparation for martyrdom in Revelation that he has stressed their role in the millennium.

on twelve thrones judging the tribes of Israel (Matt. 19.28; Luke 22.30). It is also profitable to consider the various Jewish traditions about a messianic age of limited duration that is followed by the final state of affairs (cf. 2 Esd. 7.26–44, 12.31–34; 1 En. 91.11–17; 2 Bar. 29.1–30.5, 40.1–4, 72.2–74.3). There is even a tradition that Rome would endure 6,000 years, which would be followed by 1,000 years of peace.[485] In the first of these texts, it is said that the messianic kingdom lasts 400 years, also a round number.

At **vs. 5** we hear what happens to the rest of the dead, those who did not come to life until the completion of the 1,000-year reign. As S. Llewelyn says, **protos** here is equivalent to **proteros** (as it is in 21.1), and it refers to the "first of two."[486] The "rest" must be distinguished from the other group of the dead, and thus our author believed in two resurrections. This comports with the belief of some early Jews in a resurrection of the righteous (cf. John 5.21, 29), a view also referred to by Paul in 1 Cor. 15 when he speaks about a resurrection of those who are "in Christ." It also comports with the literal meaning of the phrase **anastasis ex nekron** – resurrection from out of the realm of the dead ones (cf. Acts 17.31–32), suggesting a selective resurrection.

Those who participate in the first resurrection are blessed, for they avoid the second one leading to eternal death. Rather, they will be priests of God, and Christ will reign with them in the millennium.[487] While it is not clearly stated, it seems to imply that those who partake of the second resurrection will go on to partake of the second death. If true, then "the rest" refers not to the rest of the believers (i.e., the nonmartyrs perhaps) but rather to the rest of humanity. The word "resurrection" is used several times in this section without attempts to distinguish meanings. Just as the two deaths mentioned in this text involve the physical body (the second death happens to those who have been raised in bodies, and their bodies are cast into the lake of fire), so also do the two resurrections. There are no hints that one should be seen as a spiritual resurrection and the other as a physical one.[488]

Beginning at **vs. 7**, evil is taking its last shot at humankind. Satan is released, and immediately bad things happen. Gog and Magog are symbols of evil in the nations of the earth, and this evil comes from all directions. As Reddish says, "Clearly they do not represent two specific nations or peoples, for John locates them 'at the four corners of the earth' and says 'they are as numerous

---

485 See D. E. Aune, *Revelation 17–22* (1998), pp. 830–31.
486 S. R. Llewelyn and R. A. Kearsley, *New Docs* (1992), vol. 6, p. 131.
487 The English word millennium comes from the Latin *mille annum*, one thousand years.
488 Here again the amillennial view requires special pleading. See R. H. Mounce, *Book of Revelation* (1977), pp. 364–70. There is the further difficulty with that view if one argues that the millennium is the church age, then it becomes next to impossible to explain how Paul and other early Christians could have truly believed that Christ might return in their own lifetimes. A belief in a long messianic age leading up to the Parousia would seem to rule out such imminent expectation.

as the sands of the sea.' "[489] Evil traipses over the breadth of the earth looking for believers to combat. Continuing the battle metaphor, John says these evil ones surround the army camp of the saints and the city of the Beloved.[490] Is this a reference to Jerusalem? Elsewhere in this book that city is called Sodom and Gomorrah. Accordingly, some have urged that the Beloved city is the city of God, the New Jerusalem, which apparently is thought of as having descended during the millennium or immediately at the end of the millennium. This is not impossible, but there are no clear textual markers that John blends together the millennium with the new heaven and the new earth. That the believers are in a camp conjures up images of the wilderness wandering period of God's people. The essence of that description, however, is to make clear that God's people are a pilgrim people upon the earth until the end. Thus the Beloved city would seem to be another way of speaking about the society or the saints who are attacked. There is probably no reference to either Jerusalem or Rome here. Just when things look bleak, God sends down fire from heaven to consume the evil ones (cf. Ezek. 39.6). This amounts to taking the Devil and his minions and throwing them into the lake of fire to be tormented forever (**vs. 10**).[491]

After the millennium we hear of a judgment scene where all of humanity, both the great and the small, both the saved and the lost, stand before the great white throne of the holy Father. "No one is so important as to be immune from judgment, and no one is so unimportant as to make judgment inappropriate."[492] The prospect of judgment causes the earth metaphorically to shrink or even flee in fear. But fleeing is of no use. There is nowhere to run and nowhere to hide. There are two books that settle the issue – the book of deeds and the book of life. We have an image of God fairly reviewing all the deeds of a person's life. God will not be unjust in his judgment, for he will take everything into account.

The dead from the sea are likely mentioned separately because of ancient beliefs that those not properly buried did not make it into Sheol or the land of the dead called Hades (see Achilles Tatius 5.16.2). Thus all the dead, the dead from all parts of the earth, are judged according to their works. At **vs. 14** even death and Hades are cast into the lake of fire, making clear that neither of these two entities is identified with Hell. Those humans not found in the book of life and faith are cast into the lake, for all fall short when measured by deeds. Presumably the book of life is opened because believers are also present on this occasion, and though their deeds may fall short, they are not

---

[489] M. G. Reddish, *Revelation* (2001), p. 386.

[490] Encampment signifies a military formation and the embattled state of the saints under persecution. Cf. Heb. 11.34; 13.11, 13; Acts 21.34, 37 on the terminology.

[491] C. Koester, *Revelation and the End* (2001), p. 185, makes the helpful point that John's focus is on the saints reigning with Christ, not on where they do it. John is far more interested in theology than in geography.

[492] R. H. Mounce, *Book of Revelation* (1977), p. 376.

cast into the lake of fire because they have believed in the Lamb and the life he gives.[493]

Here, as in 1 Cor. 15, death is not viewed as a natural part of and ending to life. It is not seen as a part of God's original intent for his creation. It is viewed as the enemy that must be destroyed. It is also seen as the last enemy to be destroyed, for resurrection is God's final answer – the last and permanent provision of life for his people. It appears that our author believes in eternal punishment rather than annihilation of the wicked in view of Rev. 14.10–11.

In the concluding segment (21.1–8) of this rhetorical unit, there is one significant textual issue. At **vs. 3** one must decide whether *laos* or *laoi* is the proper reading here. The textual evidence is finally balanced. The following considerations seem germane: (1) Elsewhere in this book *laos* is not a technical term for Israel, the OT people of God. Indeed the term is even used of Gentile nations. (2) In this chapter John is going to go on to speak of "outsiders" – nations and kings outside the city of God who are being allowed into it. Our author believes there will be those saved from every tribe, tongue, people, and nation.[494] In light of these considerations, *laoi* is likely the proper and original reading. John's vision goes beyond the OT's one of a people of God. Here we are introduced to the peoples of God (i.e., Jews and various Gentile ethnic groups as well).

Of course, there are other ways that John goes beyond OT models in his final and climactic vision. In the New Jerusalem there is no temple, which proves that John did not feel obligated to follow Ezekiel's blueprint jot and tittle, but rather picked and chose what he would adopt and adapt. This also makes it clear that John knew he was dealing with symbols and metaphors, not a literal blueprint in the OT prophecies. Thus he could use the images flexibly and freely. Furthermore, as a text like Gal. 4.26 makes evident, John is drawing on a trajectory of early Christian thought about these matters. What he is trying to convey is the *character* of the final state, its nature, and what it might mean to a people of God weary of suffering. He is not interested in offering a geographically precise description of the new heaven and new earth.

A question to be raised about this material is, Is the author talking about a new heaven and a new earth that replaces the old one, or is he discussing the old heaven and earth being renewed? The first point is that John contrasts the new with the first heaven and earth. In view of what John has already said about the two resurrections, this sounds like replacement language. The second key point is that the verb **apelthan** means "to go away" or "to leave" or perhaps even

---

[493] P. Barnett, *Apocalypse Now and Then* (1989), p. 149, helpfully reminds us, "The language here and elsewhere in the Revelation is symbolic and pictorial, but that in no way lessens the underlying reality. Nor should the logistics in gathering and judging so many provoke doubts about the truth of the judgment of God (John Wesley thought the judgment would last one thousand years!). We must not reduce God to our own calculations."

[494] See the discussion on pp. 168–70 and cf. R. Bauckham, *Climax of Prophecy* (1993), pp. 238–337.

"to disappear." We also hear that the sea no longer exists. This latter suggests elimination of a particular part of the earthly terrain, but one cannot be sure of this since the sea is John's symbol for the chaos waters, the point of origin for evil and the demonic. Thus by saying the sea is no more, John may just mean that evil has finally been removed from the world.

Jewish background in regard to the replacement versus renewal notions was rather evenly divided. Isa. 65–66 was usually the point of departure, with texts like 2 Bar. 3.4 ff. using the material to speak of renewal while 2 Esd. 7.29 ff. or 1 En. 83.3 ff. speak about replacement. There is really only one NT text, 2 Pet. 3.6–7, that seems to address this issue, and it probably comes from the same period of time as Revelation. In the 2 Peter text, an analogy is drawn between what happened during the flood and what will happen – a great conflagration will burn up the earth and presumably the material heavens. The author talks about earth's elements dissolving and the heavens disappearing in some sort of big bang. But when he goes on to talk about a new heaven and new earth (2 Pet. 3.13), the author does not tell us whether it will be composed of the burned elements of the old or whether it will be *de novo*. The New Jerusalem that Paul says is from above is no rebuilt human city but rather a gift of God that he alone created. Since John also envisions this city coming down from above, he too must think of replacement in regard to the city, but that still would not rule out renewal of the material universe itself. In any event the symbolic nature of this material prevents one from pressing the issue.

Nevertheless Boesak is right when he stresses about John's use of Isa. 65–66 that

Isaiah's imagery is profoundly earthly, and such also is John's intention. There is no reason for us to believe that John is intentionally transporting Isaiah's vision into another world to come. The concern of the Apocalypse is not so much the creation of another world (a "next world") into which the church is called to escape. The whole point of John's writing is that it is in this world, in this human history, that the power of the Lord will be seen. It is for this reason that the triumphant church is not transported into the new Jerusalem, transported into the next world, but that the new Jerusalem comes down *out of heaven*.[495]

In **vs. 2** we have another of John's interesting mixed metaphors. A city is also a bride. This city comes from God, and it is prepared like a bride adorned for her husband. The idea of a New Jerusalem is not uncommon in early Jewish apocalyptic prophecy. For instance, Test. of Dan. 5.12 pictures the New Jerusalem as a place where the saints enjoy God forever. 2 Esd. 7.26 speaks of the city as being now invisible, but it will appear. This Jewish speculation seemed to envision a real city located on the spot of the present Jerusalem, whether a renewal of it or a replacement for it. There are some NT passages on the heavenly city that should

---

[495] A. Boesak, *Comfort and Protest* (1986), p. 129.

be consulted (Heb. 11.10, 12.22, 13.14; Phil. 3.20; Gal. 4.26). We have already noted Rev. 3.12, which speaks of the faithful being inscribed with the name of the New Jerusalem. It is thus possible that John is thinking along the lines of a real city located where the present Jerusalem lies. Another interesting suggestion is that the New Jerusalem is envisioned as already existing in heaven as the dwelling place of the departed saints and that it will descend at the end of time to be the dwelling of all true believers.[496]

One view that should likely be ruled out is that of Caird. Clearly John does not see the coming down of the New Jerusalem as a symbol for the continued coming down of God to be with his people, condescending to us. Rather John is narrating the final and unique coming that is in view. God is to dwell forever with his people, or what might be called Immanuel theology.[497] The very ways John modifies Ezekiel's vision at various points suggests he sees all of this as a glorious symbol of the final fellowship of God with believers, and also their fellowship with each other as the community of God. In short, we should not take this passage any more literally than we did that of the Beast with seven heads. We must ask what it symbolizes. What reality does it represent? We have a sort of *objet de art*–type description of how beautiful that final fellowship will be. Because this is a symbol of the character and quality of life in the final state, some of the details, such as one finds in vs. 27 ff., do not need to be pressed.[498]

The final state is represented as transpiring not when believers go up to heaven but when God and heaven come down permanently. The future for believers is bound up with the earth and its future, for they are raised out of that earth (cf. Rom. 8). In John's theology, creation and redemption should not be seen as two different categories. Creation has a place in the final order of redemption. There is a sort of *Urzeit-Endzeit* pattern here. The end will be as the beginning. It is not accidental that John, like what we find in Isa. 65–66, depicts the final state as like the first state in the garden of Eden. There is a certain amount of recapitulation of ideas though on a much grander scale in the new order. It is after all the creation order that is being redeemed, and that redemption means the completion of God's original plans for creation. "The future intended world of God's salvation is not envisioned as an island but as encompassing all of creation."[499]

The understanding of the text is helped by considering related ideas in early Jewish literature: (1) in Test. of Levi 4.1 (cf. Sib. Or. 5.447), the waters dry up at judgment; (2) in Sib. Or. 5.158–59, a great star falls from the sky and burns up the ocean. In both cases John is drawing on a traditional idea and set of images;

---

[496]   G. E. See Ladd, *Commentary* (1972), pp. 275–79.
[497]   G. B. Caird, *Revelation* (1998), pp. 261–65.
[498]   For example, how the unclean could even be around after the final judgment is the wrong question to ask. John's point is simply that all evil is excluded.
[499]   E. Fiorenza, *Revelation* (1991), p. 110.

(3) the bride image is carried forward from Rev. 19 and 20, and we should not be surprised to hear of a bride who already has a husband, in view of the binding nature of betrothal in Jewish society there is a clear analogy in 2 Esd. 10.25 ff. where bride and city images are combined, and there too the city is a heavenly Zion, not an earthly one.

Vs. 3 is striking in several respects. It reads literally, "Behold the tent of God is with humanity, and he will tent with us and we will be his peoples." The Greek word *skene* is the regular Greek word to render the Hebrew *mishkan*, which means tent (it is a derivative of *shakan*, 'to dwell', from which the word *Shekinah*, referring to God's glorious presence, comes).[500] Our text is a paraphrase of such texts as Lev. 26.11 ff. and Ezek. 37.27. By a stroke of sheer luck, the Greek and Hebrew words for tent have the same consonants, so the allusions to Hebrew are more obvious, and the similar sound would conjure up various things for Jewish Christians listening to this being read. They would be gathering from this that God's glorious presence will be with his people forever, and so certain things follow. First, humanity will finally see God and his glorious presence and live. This has traditionally been called the beatific vision, but it happens in the midst of the peoples of God, not as an isolated, mystical experience, like those of Hildegaard of Bingen. Second, there is a stress on this being the peoples (plural) of God who are ethnically, racially, culturally diverse, and permanently so. There is no room for any sort of racism in the final Dominion of God. Third, there will be no more death, not least because we will be in the very presence of life, and believers will experience God's eternal life directly. Fourth, the wiping away of tears from every eye alludes to Isa. 65.6–8, as does the dismissal of mourning, and pain. All the things that were a result of the fall will be wiped out. These conditions were promised to the martyrs in Rev. 7.17, and here they are seen as realized. The new order will be a place for endless life, joy, celebration, and love.

When we come to **vs. 5**, we hear the one sitting on the throne say, "Behold I make all things new." This cry suggests renewal of the burned-out old order. Various commentators have made much of the fact that this is the first place in the whole book that God has spoken. But this is not quite true in a couple of respects. Rev. 1.8 also involves God speaking, and so God speaks as Alpha and Omega, appropriately enough at the beginning and end of the book. But, furthermore, John sees Jesus as speaking as God in various places in the book. John is commanded at vs. 5 to write down these trustworthy and true words, a command already heard at 14.13 and 19.9, where it is an angel that gives it. It appears that here it is God who gives the command, although the change in verb tenses may suggest it is an angel here as well. Here we also have the statement "it is finished" or "it is done, or has come to pass." Not merely the completed work of Christ on the cross is in view, as in John 19, but the completion of the entire

---

[500] See the material in Pirke *Aboth* 3.9.

historical and redemptive process. Yet this ending is but a new beginning. It is only the old order of things that has passed away.

In view of the subject of vs. 5, most commentators see **vs. 6** as a case of God calling himself Alpha and Omega. The Creator or Author of Life is now seen as the Finisher or Completer of Life. And so, we will hear of creation renewed, restored, and re-created in the new heaven and new earth. God is not merely *at* the beginning and end of things, God *is* the beginner and ender of things. God is both the source and the goal of human life. The divine plan is for humans to go forward and dwell with God in the divine presence forever in an eternal, loving relationship.[501]

Since God is the source of life, it is only appropriate that God offers freely the water of life for the thirsty to drink. Humanity has been made so that we thirst for life that only God can give. John 4.14 or Jer. 2.13 may be compared at this juncture. In a dry and weary land like Israel, water was the difference between life and death. In **vs. 7** this blessed state of eternal life is only for those who conquer, those who overcome and become sons and daughters of God, a part of the family and so able to inherit all these things. Beasley-Murray notes that John here does not call God Father, but rather the overcomers are called sons.[502] Could this be because John reserved the use of the title Father for the relationship of Jesus to God? This could make sense in light of the OT usage where the Father–Son language characterized the special relationship between God and the king (2 Sam. 7.14; Ps. 2.7; Ps. 89.26–27). Believers are only sons and daughters of God in a derivative sense.

Scholars have often pondered over the reason for the list in **vs. 8**, but when one remembers that John's audience is Christians under pressure and threat of persecution, cowardice and faithlessness to the Lord, either spiritually or ethically, must be censured. Thus the cowardly, the unfaithful, the polluted (i.e., presumably those who participate in idol worship),[503] murderers, fornicators, idolators, magicians, and liars have been thrown into the lake of fire and so experienced the second death. This is evidence that John is no universalist, but we also should not minimize his hope for the conversion of many in all nations. The intended rhetorical effect of this verse was not to castigate the lost or gloat over their demise, but rather to warn the faithful of the dangers of spiritual or moral apostasy.[504] As Caird notes, all of these censured activities could in one way or another be linked to pagan rites. The most fundamental

---

[501] The goal is not the deification of humans or their absorption into the deity, but rather a permanent relationship that preserves the Creator–creature distinction.

[502] G. R. Beasley-Murray, *Book of Revelation* (1978), pp. 313–14.

[503] On which see pp. 281–82.

[504] See M. G. Reddish, *Revelation* (2001), pp. 404–5. P. Barnett, *Apocalypse Now and Then* (1989), p. 155, suggests that the list be bifurcated into two groups, with the cowardly, unbelieving, and polluted referring to lapsed Christians, and the the rest referring to non-Christians.

problem of humanity is whom they serve or worship, all other problems flow from that.[505] But, it is well to add with Koester that this warning indicates no one is immune from potential judgment, not even Christ's followers. "Nevertheless, the warning does not mean that anyone who has ever committed one of these sins will be excluded from the New Jerusalem. God's city is not reserved for those who have never sinned, but for those who are cleansed by the blood of Christ (7.14; 22.14).[506]

A CLOSER LOOK – JOHN AND RADICAL EVIL

It seems that much of the way John views government and God's solution to the human dilemma is grounded in his belief that evil has a radical hold on the world, including the world of human beings. From "John's point of view, the most significant thing Christians can do to change the world is to worship God and pray. Why? It is because just and lasting change in the world is ultimately God's doing."[507] This sheds new light on the worship scenes in the book of Revelation. They are no mere interludes, they are the prime actions Christians can take if they want to change the world they live in. Remember the silence in heaven when the offering is made at the incense altar, and the prayers go up to God before the seven judgments begin to fall. John is saying faithful witness, faithful worship, and faithful prayer can help change the world because they place matters in the hands of the only wise God who intends to work things out.

But this working out of things cannot involve a mere patching up of a fallen world.

Because of the evil in creation, judgment is coming. Because evil is so deep-seated and radical, however, it cannot be dealt with by a this-worldly judgment. Rather judgment takes the form of the end of the world. God wipes the slate clean. He will not allow evil to have immortality, so He brings the whole historical process to an end. . . . The human solution [to evil] is so fraught with evil that the very solution to evil itself breeds evil. Here evil is a mystery that only God can ultimately resolve. In such a frame of reference, prayer seems like the most important thing the people of God can do for the world. Evil is rampant; God needs to act; so pray![508]

John, in other words, does not believe in the myth of progress and would never be caught intoning, "Every day and in every way things are getting better and better." Lest this seem like fatalism of an extreme form, John does believe human beings play an important role in their own futures. In the first place, he believes that a particular human being, the Son of Man, totally changed the history of the world and dealt the decisive blow against evil in the midst

[505] G. B. Caird, *Revelation* (1998), pp. 266–67.
[506] C. Koester, *Revelation and the End* (2001), p. 194.
[507] C. H. Talbert, *Apocalypse* (1994), p. 70.
[508] Ibid., p. 71.

of space and time. In the second place, we have seen earlier in this work that John believes that prayer is taken into account as the divine plan of judgment and redemption is enacted. In the third place, John believes that at least some of the saints will help Christ in the millennium as justice is finally done and as the "kingdoms of this world become the kingdoms of our God and of his Christ." In short, it is the interaction between God and his people that is seen to change the world, and furthermore it is the response of humans to God's divine saving actions that determines their own roles in the world to come. John is no fatalist, but he does believe firmly in the sovereignty of God and the need for divine action if radical evil is to be dealt a death blow. He also believes in the importance of human response, enabled by grace, for Revelation is a hortatory work that warns against apostasy and urges believers on to great Christ-likeness. If either of these things were inevitable, there would be no need for such exhortations.

John is clearly an apocalyptic thinker and, as such, would see most modern theodicies as incredibly naive, not taking into account the depth of human and supernatural evil. His optimism would be grounded in grace, not in human nature, unlike most modern secular philosophies and self-help programs. The heart of the matter for John is the divine human encounter, not innate human ability or the nobility of human struggle. It is no accident that his work ends with the consummation of the divine human encounter, now without evil present any longer. The solution to the problem of evil, according to John, involves neither the dissolution of the Creator–creature distinction (or the absorption of the human into the divine) nor the denial of the reality of radical evil. Rather, it entails the transformation of the world and God's people into all that they were meant to be, which is to say into the likeness of Christ in the latter and the pre-fallen garden in the former. Until such time the most important things a believer is urged by John to do are (1) worship; (2) pray; (3) trust/believe; (4) witness, even by giving up one's life if need be; and (5) obey.

BRIDGING THE HORIZONS

In an insightful analysis of the material on the final judgment in Rev. 19–20, Giblin makes the following remarks:

In terms of clock-and-calendar time, of course, the end of Babylon and all other adversaries will take place simultaneously in an instant. Apocalyptic, however, requires sequences of particular visions in order adequately to present its theology. For it has no alternative to spelling out its relatively "pre-conceptual" theology in images, especially such as will move its readers to religious awe and a keenly felt hope for salvation.[509]

This is not to say that there isn't, broadly speaking, some chronological aspects to Rev. 19–20, but we have seen how John presents the same events in several

[509] C. H. Giblin, *Book of Revelation* (1991), p. 183.

different images on some occasions and recapitulates and expands on a particular image or idea for rhetorical effect on other occasions – creating emphasis. However, John does not see Evil as totally eradicated in an instant or even in the messianic millennium. Even Evil endures to the end. Thus Giblin has overstated things by stressing that judgment falls on all in an instant. Still he is right about John's visionary theology and how it requires a variety of pictures to tell one and the same story.

Biblical texts can and often have been misused to justify all sorts of illegitimate causes. Rev. 19, with the vision of the rider on the white horse, was used to justify, among other things, the Crusades against the infidels. But this text has nothing to say in support of human actions of violence that we initiate ourselves. The story is about the return of the Judge of all the earth, and his army is composed not of those currently on earth but those who come with him from heaven, whether angels, martyrs, saints, or all three. Furthermore judgment, so far as it involves human beings in this scene, is carried out by a judicial word, not by physical violence. Sacred texts in the wrong hands can be dangerous things, especially apocalyptic texts. Wainwright tells the amazing story of the Anabaptist leaders Matthys and Boeckelson, who sought to establish the new Jerusalem in Münster, Germany. They drove out any Catholics and Lutherans who wouldn't accept rebaptism. Upon the death of Matthys, Boeckelson proclaimed himself the king of the city, indeed as the new messiah, and as such entitled to multiple wives, forcing women to enter into polygamous relationships upon pain of death. Fortunately his reign in this "new Jerusalem" only lasted two years.[510]

The debate about the millennium has been waged for centuries in the Christian church and shows no sign of abating in our time. Indeed, the very popular Left Behind series of books by Tim LaHaye has only fueled the fires of controversy. The earliest Christian commentators on Revelation – those who were most nearly in touch with the original Christian thinking about John's apocalyptic work – were almost all convinced that John was speaking about a real messianic millennium at the end of human history that would transpire after the final return of Christ. This is how various second-, third-, and fourth-century interpreters such as Papias (a contemporary of John of Patmos), Justin Martyr, Irenaeus, Tertullian, Hippolytus, Lactantius, and others all understood the material.[511] Eusebius, in his famous work on church history, recognized that "chiliasm" was the dominant belief of the early church about these matters, even though he himself had his doubts and noted that Revelation was (and presumably should be) a disputed book in part because of this very matter (see *Hist. Eccl.* 3.39; 7.24). The first real commentary on Revelation was written by Victorinus, the bishop of Pettau (died 304). He was quite clear about Babylon symbolizing

---

[510] A. W. Wainwright, *Mysterious Apocalypse* (1993), pp. 91–93.
[511] See the discussion in ibid., pp. 21–31.

Rome, and this took on a personal significance for him because he died during the last great Roman persecution of Christians by Diocletian. Victorinus also saw correctly that there were Nero-like features in the description of the Beast. He believed fervently that Rev. 20 was describing an earthly kingdom in which nations would be placed under the rule of the saints. He reiterated the observation that there seemed to be recapitulation in the trumpets and bowls sequences.

Perhaps the earliest known real proponent of amillennialism was Tyconius, who wrote around A.D. 400. He is credited with persuading Augustine of this new alternative interpretation of the matter. Augustine maintained that the "first resurrection" refers to the dying and rising that happens to the individual at baptism. Furthermore Augustine pursued the individualistic interpretation of Rev. 20 to such an extent that he argued that when it was said Satan was confined to the abyss, this meant the abyss of the human heart, where wickedness would remain until Christ destroyed it.[512] This hermeneutical shift from premillennialism to amillennialism, however, was to have ominous effects for it suggested that the church age was the age when believers with Christ's aid could build an empire and put evil under their own feet.[513] This interpretation of Rev. 20 was in part the rationale used for the expansionist politics of the Holy Roman Empire and of various popes. They sought to be kingdom builders and the spreaders of millennial blessings. It was also a theology that helped undergird the Crusades. It is a theology, however, that John would probably have found entirely foreign to his own intentions. His work involves a devastating critique of political maneuvering and Christian participation in such activities. Furthermore he seems to have shared the early Jewish beliefs in a messianic kingdom initiated at the end of human history and inaugurated by the Messiah. If we are to speak anachronistically, John held a historic premillennialist view of such matters. It needs to be made clear, however, that when one reads John and his earliest Christian interpreters, they had something rather different in mind than what we find in modern dispensational premillennial interpretation.

Dispensational premillennialism did not arise before the nineteenth century but became very popular through the evangelistic work of John Darby, at the turn of the twentieth century, through the reference Bible containing the notes of C. I. Scofield. In the latter half of the twentieth century and in the early twenty-first century it has been the popular writings of Hal Lindsey, John Walvoord, and now Tim LaHaye that have propagated and popularized this way of interpreting

---

[512] See C. Koester, *Revelation and the End* (2001), p. 8.
[513] Jerome was something of a precursor to Tyconius because he argued in a postscript to Victorinus' commentary that Revelation, including Rev. 20, should be understood spiritually not materially. For example, he said that Satan is bound wherever and whenever a Christian obeys and remains chaste. See ibid., p. 6.

Revelation.[514] There are many problems with this whole approach to biblical prophecy in general and to the book of Revelation in particular. But I mention only a few here. (1) All of the prophecies in the OT were believed by their Jewish human authors to be referring to God's original chosen people – the Jews. A parsing out of prophecies so that some applied to Jews and some to non-Jewish peoples simply does not comport with the character and intent of such OT prophecies. Jews could conceive of Gentiles getting in on the blessing through them (à la Abraham traditions) but not separately. (2) Dispensational theology ignores that the people of God in the NT are not bifurcated into two groups – Israel on the one hand and Christians on the other. To the contrary, the people of God are viewed as Jew and Gentile united in Christ. In texts like Rom. 9–11, Paul makes clear that it is a matter of Gentiles being grafted into the original people of God, Israel, by faith in Christ, and Jews being regrafted into that same entity through faith in their own messiah. (3) No NT author looks for a fulfillment of prophecies to Jews in regard to the land of Israel or any other such thing that does not come through or from Jesus Christ. Indeed, such texts as Mark 13 and Rev. 20 suggest that such hopes for Jerusalem and the retaking of the Holy Land and the rebuilding of the Temple are not to transpire before Christ comes and the messianic age begins. Before the return of Christ, there can be no New Jerusalem, and there will be no need for a new temple when he does come (see Rev. 21–22). (4) Just as the Bible does not envision two peoples of God, though Revelation can talk about many ethnic groups as peoples of God,[515] so also the NT knows nothing about two second comings of Christ, one invisible and one visible. The Parousia is always portrayed in the NT as a visible event (cf. Mark 14.62 to 1 Thess. 4.16–17). (5) The classic texts thought to refer to the rapture, especially 1 Thess. 4.16–17, say nothing about saints being taken up suddenly into heaven. Rather, they go forth to meet Christ in the sky when he is returning, and then they return with him to the earth to reign.[516] (6) The exposition of Revelation offered in this commentary should make clear that John does not envision Christians avoiding the final tribulation by some sort of rapture. He does envision the church being protected from extinction during that time, though it remains an earthly entity.[517] (7) Perhaps most important, Revelation was written in the first instance for first-century Christians, and whatever the original author intended it to mean for them, that is still what the text means today. When John spoke of the future, he did so in general ways using universal symbols that could be apt in any and every age of church history. The attempt to derive more specificity from this metaphorical literature than it intends to convey is a mistake, as

---

[514] See A. W. Wainwright, *Mysterious Apocalypse* (1993), pp. 81–87.

[515] See pp. 251–53.

[516] See my treatment of all these matters in *Jesus, Paul and the End of the World* (Downers Grove, Ill.: InterVarsity Press, 1992).

[517] See pp. 169–72.

shown by how the 100 percent failure rate to identify one particular human referent, for example, for the anti-Christ figure.[518] Only when John deals with the final state of affairs in Rev. 19–22 is his language not apt as descriptions of various events in the battle of good versus evil in various ages of Christian history.[519]

In Rev. 20.7–10 we find a classic test case where the flexibility of apocalyptic ideas and images becomes clear. In Ezekiel, Gog is a person and Magog is a place (Ezek. 38.14–16), but not in Revelation. Already in Jewish tradition there was the notion that Gog and Magog could refer to two rulers or kingdoms (see Sib. Or. 3.319, 512). It does not follow from the plasticity of the images that John is speaking in a nonreferential manner. It simply means he is using various malleable metaphors to describe something he believes will be a future reality. As Reddish also points out, in Ezekiel Gog is a localized threat, but not in Revelation.[520] John is not interested in describing a "literal" fulfillment of OT apocalyptic images, for he alters them in various cases. Yet, on the other hand, he is interested in the fulfillment of God's promises and prophecies in the broader sense and in that fulfillment transpiring in space and time. For John, one should not expect metaphorical, apocalyptic symbols to be fulfilled literally! This ignores the nature of the genre of apocalyptic prophecy and the type of symbols both Ezekiel and John were using.

Another useful cautionary word comes from Koester, who stresses,

Revelation does depict warfare but of a different sort. An important discipline in reading these texts is to ask what they say and what they do not say.... Here the most important point is that his account of the great battle in 19.11–21 explicitly mentions

---

[518] As C. Koester, *Revelation and the End* (2001), pp. 24–25, points out, the original exposition by Darby and then Scofield of Daniel leaves much to be desired. For example, Darby argued that God continued fulfilling prophecies up through Dan. 9.26 but then mysteriously stopped for over 2,000 years without fulfilling Dan. 9.27. Yet read in context, these two verses seem to be talking about things within the same time frame. In addition Darby's calculations depended on following the punctuation found in the KJV of Dan. 9.25, but that form of reckoning collapses if one follows the punctuation found in the NRSV or the TEV or other translations. That is, Dan. 9.25 if punctuated one way takes the 49 years and the 434 years as all transpiring between the command to rebuild the walls of Jerusalem and the coming of the anointed one, Jesus. The NRSV punctuation suggests that the anointed one will come after only the 49-year segment after the exile. In other words, this anointed one would have to be Joshua or Zerubbabel (Ezek. 3.2; Zech. 4.14) or perhaps Cyrus (Isa. 45.1), but not Jesus. Calculations involving symbolic numbers are precarious under any circumstances but especially when they are based on the punctuations of a particular English translation, when the original Hebrew or Aramaic had no such punctuations!

[519] On the various views of the millennium held by conservative or Evangelical Christians, cf. R. G. Clouse, ed., *The Meaning of the Millennium: Four Views* (Downers Grove, Ill.: InterVarsity Press, 1977), and S. J. Grenz, *The Millennial Maze: Sorting Out Evangelical Options* (Downers Grove, Ill.: InterVarsity Press, 1992).

[520] M. G. Reddish, *Revelation* (2001), p. 386.

only one weapon: the word of God. No mention is made of missiles, aircraft, and tanks. All attention concentrates on the sword that comes from the mouth of Christ the warrior, the sword of his word (19.5, 21). By describing a battle that is waged and won by a word that is visualized as a sword, John shows that he is not describing an ordinary conflict, but using picture language to speak of the ultimate triumph of god over evil.[521]

In other words, there can be no justification for the use of this material to support wars or attacks one nation may wage on its own against another using conventional weapons. It would be far closer to the spirit of what John says to talk about evangelists going into foreign countries and proclaiming judgment unless there is repentance, in the fashion that Jonah is reported in the OT to have done.

The book of life and the book of deeds are both referred to in Rev. 20, and they remind us of the two poles of truth about the Gospel. On the one hand, salvation is a free gift of God that is received through faith. This is how one's name comes to be inscribed in the Lamb's book of life. On the other hand, all persons, even Christians, will be held responsible for the deeds they have done in the body.[522] Paul conjures up the image in 1 Cor. 3.10–15 of ministry work that is done well or poorly, and how even apostles will be held responsible for the quality of such work. If they have built in shabby fashion, they may be saved but as through fire. Their work will not stand the final scrutiny of God's judgment of deeds. While it costs nothing to come to God, it costs everything to serve God properly. Christians are held to a higher standard of scrutiny in regard to their actions, for to those to whom more is given, more is required. George Buttrick once said in a famous sermon that a talent is a two-sided coin. On one side it says ability, but on the other side it says responsibility.

The images in Rev. 21 about the New Jerusalem, which is synonymous with the bride of Christ, remind us that John is not so much talking about a place but a community. Rather like our concept when we say that wherever our family is, there is home, John is suggesting that community creates place rather than the reverse. It's not a matter of geography but rather of ***koinonia***. This may also help explain why it is that there is no temple in the midst of this community. The separation between God and his people has been totally removed, and now they dwell together in harmony and fellowship. Christians are meant to be a pilgrim people until they finally find their rest in the everlasting arms of God in the everlasting city of the New Jerusalem. Even the journey to heaven after death is part of the pilgrimage, not its final destination.

---

[521] C. Koester, *Revelation and the End* (2001), p. 174.

[522] C. Koester (ibid., pp. 190–91) stresses that John in the end does not suggest that salvation is ultimately based on good deeds by humans, but on God's grace. The mention of the book of life is meant to encourage faith, not cause despair or fatalism.

But when God does finally dwell with humankind, what must be the condition of the realm for that to be an enduring reality? Boesak says,

The God who longs to teach the nations how to "beat their swords into plough shares, and their spears into pruning hooks" cannot be at home in a land "filled with horses [where] there is no end to their chariots" (Isa. 2:4, 7). A God who passionately wants the nations to stop learning war can never be at home in a world where livings are made from war and destruction, where those who murder children made in God's own image are decorated, and where violence and death are glorified. A God who wishes fervently that the people would understand what it means to walk in the light of the Lord cannot be at home in a world whose people have filled their lands with idols, where they bow down to the work of their hands and to what their fingers have made. A God who has made human beings in God's own image cannot be at home in a world where these human beings are humbled and brought low. . . . John longs passionately for another day, another world.[523]

In other words, unless there is truly a new heaven and a new earth, God could never permanently dwell with us.

REVELATION 21.9–22.5 – THE TOUR OF THE NEW JERUSALEM

NRSV Revelation 21.9 Then one of the seven angels who had the seven bowls full of the seven last plagues came and said to me, "Come, I will show you the bride, the wife of the Lamb."
10 And in the spirit he carried me away to a great, high mountain and showed me the holy city Jerusalem coming down out of heaven from God.
11 It has the glory of God and a radiance like a very rare jewel, like jasper, clear as crystal.
12 It has a great, high wall with twelve gates, and at the gates twelve angels, and on the gates are inscribed the names of the twelve tribes of the Israelites;
13 on the east three gates, on the north three gates, on the south three gates, and on the west three gates.
14 And the wall of the city has twelve foundations, and on them are the twelve names of the twelve apostles of the Lamb.
15 The angel who talked to me had a measuring rod of gold to measure the city and its gates and walls.
16 The city lies foursquare, its length the same as its width; and he measured the city with his rod, fifteen hundred miles; its length and width and height are equal.
17 He also measured its wall, one hundred forty-four cubits by human measurement, which the angel was using.

---

[523]   A. Boesak, *Comfort and Protest* (1986), pp. 130–31.

18 The wall is built of jasper, while the city is pure gold, clear as glass.
19 The foundations of the wall of the city are adorned with every jewel; the first
was jasper, the second sapphire, the third agate, the fourth emerald,
20 the fifth onyx, the sixth carnelian, the seventh chrysolite, the eighth beryl, the
ninth topaz, the tenth chrysoprase, the eleventh jacinth, the twelfth amethyst.
21 And the twelve gates are twelve pearls, each of the gates is a single pearl, and
the street of the city is pure gold, transparent as glass.
22 I saw no temple in the city, for its temple is the Lord God the Almighty and
the Lamb.
23 And the city has no need of sun or moon to shine on it, for the glory of God is
its light, and its lamp is the Lamb.
24 The nations will walk by its light, and the kings of the earth will bring their
glory into it.
25 Its gates will never be shut by day – and there will be no night there.
26 People will bring into it the glory and the honor of the nations
27 But nothing unclean will enter it, nor anyone who practices abomination or
falsehood, but only those who are written in the Lamb's book of life.

NRSV Revelation 22.1 Then the angel showed me the river of the water of life,
bright as crystal, flowing from the throne of God and of the Lamb
2 through the middle of the street of the city. On either side of the river is the tree
of life with its twelve kinds of fruit, producing its fruit each month; and the leaves
of the tree are for the healing of the nations.
3 Nothing accursed will be found there any more. But the throne of God and of
the Lamb will be in it, and his servants will worship him;
4 they will see his face, and his name will be on their foreheads.
5 And there will be no more night; they need no light of lamp or sun, for the Lord
God will be their light, and they will reign forever and ever.

Though the majority of the book of Revelation after the opening letters
involves forensic rhetoric, with occasional epideictic interludes, once one
gets past the final judgment scene, one is dealing with the rhetoric of praise and
blame, the rhetoric of encomiums, and John cannot wax eloquently enough in
praise of the New Jerusalem. But the praising of a city involves the praising of
a people for whom that city is their chief cultural expression. Hence John has
used the personal image of the bride as well as the impersonal image of the city
to present the final state of affairs. But, unlike most Greco-Roman encomiums,
John is mainly praising God not a group of people or its cultural expressions.
The goal of a speech praising a city was to make it possible for the hearers to
picture the city in their mind in vivid detail (see Theon, *Progymn.* 7.53–55).
D. Balch has shown how it was common enough to praise cities as if they were

people.[524] The very nature of encomiums is that they strive to be hyperbolic to make an enduring and endearing impression on the mind of the listener.[525] Quintilian says that in praising a city one should praise its magnificence, utility, beauty "and the architect or artisan must be given due consideration. Temples, for instance, will be praised for their magnificence, walls for their utility, and both for their beauty or the skill of the architect" (Inst. Or. 3.7.27). It seems clear that John is cognizant of what sort of praise would be rhetorically appropriate for the New Jerusalem, and he offers such praise effusively, not neglecting to stress the praise of the architect – God.

For our purposes, it is important to remember that John's vision is not merely about salvation from the world and its injustices. It is also about salvation *of* the world, including the redemption of the earth and the material cosmos itself. John, like other early Christians such as Paul, was not interested in propagating an otherworldly or world-negating religion. To the contrary, John believes this is still God's world, and God intends to remedy the human dilemma, ultimately within space and time.[526]

We are told at **Rev. 21.9** that the angel who will give John the tour of the New Jerusalem is one of the seven who poured out the cups of wrath on the earth that resulted in the seven last plagues. We are meant to identify this angel with the one referred to in 17.1, who summoned John to view the harlot city Babylon. The Greek of 21.9 is nearly identical to 17.1, signaling a clear parallel. John wants to imply a direct contrast between the two great cities – harlot versus bride, gaudy versus beautiful, full of disease and death versus full of new life. Basically the material in v. 9 ff. is an expansion of what was first mentioned in 21.2. John is using his interlocking rhetorical technique, first introducing a subject, then concluding the former subject, then continuing with the new subject.[527]

A CLOSER LOOK – NUPTIAL AND CITY IMAGERY AND JOHN'S INTERTEXTUALITY

One of the great imponderables about John's work is whether it is a work of careful scribal activity as a result of laboring over numerous texts and composing a rich tapestry of material that is indebted to many sources, or whether it is just that John's mind is saturated with early Jewish ideas and images and so the

---

[524] D. Balch, "Two Apologetic *Encomia*. Dionysius on Rome and Josephus on the Jews," *JSJ* 13 (1982), pp. 102–22. The lament in Rev. 19 for Rome is a form of funeral oratory, but it is not an encomium. The good aspects of the city are not being laid before the audience.

[525] See C. Keener, *Revelation* (2002), p. 491.

[526] See E. Fiorenza, *Revelation* (1991), p. 128.

[527] See the discussion by B. W. Longenecker, " 'Linked like a Chain': Rev. 22.6–9 in Light of Ancient Transition Technique," *NTS* 47 (2001), pp. 105–17. See the discussion on pp. 17–18.

combinations and permutations come quite spontaneously without profound reflection or careful literary art. Whichever may be the case, J. Fekkes has shown that John is indebted to a variety of ideas and sources in his portrayal of the New Jerusalem as both city and bride, with probably Isaiah, in particular Isa. 54 and 61, being the predominant influences or sources.[528]

One of the most fascinating aspects of the use of the bridal imagery is how John develops the imagery over the course of three chapters, 19.7–9, 21.2, and 21.18–21. The first of these texts depends on Christian tradition (cf. 2 Cor. 11.2; Eph. 5.22–33), the latter two more on strictly Jewish texts. The choice of items to include in the description of the bride's apparel suggests this is a royal wedding or the wedding of an affluent person (white linen, precious stones, gold, pearls). One may compare the description in Jos. and Asen. 18.5–6: "And Aseneth . . . brought out her first robe, (the one) of wedding, like lightning in appearance, and dressed in it. And she girded a golden girdle around (herself) which was made of precious stones. And she put bracelets on her fingers . . . and precious ornaments she put around her neck in which innumerable costly and precious stones were fastened, and a golden crown she put on her head, and on that crown . . . was a big sapphire stone, and around the big stone were six costly stones." This reference, coupled with the indebtedness of the city imagery to a text or source like Tob. 13.16–18, indicates that John is familiar with not just the OT but also other early Jewish sources. But he combines them and edits them in a way that makes clear he is not simply trying to represent or exegete these texts, but rather to use them to describe a somewhat different matter.

Fekkes is also correct to note that while John may have held out hope for an eschatological restoration of the city of Jerusalem in the eschatological era, his main concern is with the people of God being a city/temple where God dwells. The preparation of the bride for the bridegroom must happen before the Parousia, and so it is no accident that this is mentioned in Rev. 19.7–9 just before the Parousia material. The wedding, however, cannot transpire until the arrival of the bridegroom, hence the further use of nuptial imagery in Rev. 21. Fekkes is also right that the precious stones and the like are apparently meant to reflect the spiritual purity and beauty of the bride when she finally reaches the eschatological state.

In the use of this material we are not so much dealing with issues simply of intertextual echo, for it is not so much that John wants his audience to go back and examine the context of allusions to the OT as he wants them to go forward to an understanding of the New Jerusalem that is yet to come. He is not trying to revive hopes of the restoration of the literal city of Jerusalem but rather hopes

---

[528] J. Fekkes, " 'His Bride Has Prepared Herself': Revelation 12–21 and Isaian Nuptial Imagery," *JBL* 109 (1990), pp. 269–87.

for the revival of the people of God as bride/city at the consummation of all things.[529]

⚜

Here we have a more detailed look at the city. Once again, we hear of John being carried away by or in the Spirit to a great and high mountain. From this vantage point, John sees the city coming down out of heaven, like some sort of enormous spacecraft. It is not clear whether we are to think of the city landing on the mountain or whether that is just the vantage point from which John sees the city. It is probably the former, in which case there may be an allusion to the mythological notion of the world mountain. In view of the parallel in Ezek. 40.2, where the structure is on a high mountain, this seems likely here as well. This being the case, we should also compare Ezek. 28.13–14.

There were various other early Jewish texts about mountains on which one had visions (1 En. 17.2; 18.6–8; 24.1–3, and in the OT, Exod. 3.1, 12; 19.1–34.35; 1 Kings 19.1–18), but of more relevance are the traditions about Mount Zion as a holy mountain (cf. Rev. 14.1; Isa. 2.2–3; Joel 2.1; Ps. 2.6; 3.4; 48.1). Keener says John is contrasting this setting with the seven mountains on which Babylon/Rome sits.[530] It would appear that John is aware of the range of early Jewish speculations about the New Jerusalem (cf. Zech. 12.–13.6; Tob. 14.4–7; 4 Ezek. 8.52; 10.2–7; 44.54–55; Ap. Dan. 5.4–13; 1 En. 85–90; Sib. Or. 3.552–731; 5.361–433).[531]

Caird carefully points out the parallels to the descriptions of great cities in Ezek. 28.12–14 of Tyre and in Isa. 14.12–14 of Babylon.[532] The Ezek. 28 passage is crucial as there too we have the holy mountain identified with the garden of Eden.[533] The idea of a world mountain where the gods live in a sort of paradisaical state was widespread in the ANE, but in Revelation, even humans get to dwell there with God. Ps. 48.2 seems to draw on this tradition of the great northern, mythical mountain. Against Caird, John does not claim to see the city come down twice. This is but the close-up of the more distant shot when the city was introduced earlier in the chapter.[534] The city is said to radiate or reflect the very glory of God. Just as God's Shekinah glory rested on the Tabernacle in the wilderness, here it permeates the whole city. Therefore there is no more division of secular and sacred. The whole city is a holy temple, for God is with his people throughout the city and they are his temple. This

---

[529] I also agree with Fekkes that Ezek. 16 should not be seen as background here, as it entails a negative portrayal of unfaithful earthly Jerusalem.

[530] C. Keener, *Revelation* (2002), p. 492. On Jerusalem being set on a mountain, cf. Ep. Arist. 83–84, 105–106; Jub. 4.26.

[531] See E. Fiorenza, *Revelation* (1991), p. 111.

[532] G. B. Caird, *Revelation* (1998), p. 270.

[533] John derives his list of precious stones from that chapter as well. Cf. 1 En. 18.8.

[534] G. B. Caird, *Revelation* (1998), p. 270.

explains the significant departure from Ezekiel's vision that climaxes with the description of the Temple. John's vision is no mere recapitulation of Ezekiel's vision. This becomes clear when analyzing the measurements. Ezekiel's vision involves a temple area that is 18,000 cubits around, but John's is 2,000 times larger! "The dimensions of the city are 12,000 stadia on each side, a number that corresponds to the numbers of people brought into the redeemed community (7.4–8; 21.16)."[535] In other words, the city is just the right size. If John had been a universalist, the city would have been described as being even larger!

We are told that the city's brilliance is like jasper, like that of precious stones. God's own presence is described in these very terms at Rev. 4.3 when his appearance on the throne is approximated. John is saying that the city partakes of the very character of God, and of God's brilliance. This city is, however, a striking sight for reasons besides its brilliance. It appeals to the hopes of Greco-Roman people who longed to live in the ideal or perfect city.[536] More to the point, this vision gives the lie to the notion that Rome is the Eternal City. No, the Eternal City is not built up by humans but rather is sent down from God. True human community can only be created by God and with God at its center. "Revelation's final visions imagine heaven as world, world as city, and the New City as open inclusive place of citizenship and well-being for all."[537]

This city is a perfect cube – the same in width, height, and length. It does have a wall around it, but, as we shall see, compared to the height of the city it is minuscule. The wall is 72 yards high (or possibly thick),[538] but it is dwarfed by a city that is 1,500 miles high! This suggests that God's city needs little or no protection, for God the Almighty one dwells therein.[539] Since the city is a cube, we might envision it as taking up the whole space between London and Athens, or more appropriately the whole of the Mediterranean crescent from Jerusalem to Spain. John perhaps may see it as coterminous with his known or extant world.[540] John then would be suggesting that the new creation is coterminous with the new people of God or their new community. The city has twelve gates, three on each side of the city, and at each gate there is a guardian angel, like the angel guarding the garden of Eden presumably. The twelve tribes' names are written on the twelve gates, which are pure pearl.[541] In view of the vision

---

[535] C. Koester, *Revelation and the End* (2001), p. 195.

[536] See E. Fiorenza, *Revelation* (1991), p. 113.

[537] Ibid., p. 114, which also includes the insight that "in short, the narrative symbolization of God's eschatological city integrates heaven and earth, city and nation, culture and nature, sacred and profane, Israel (twelve tribes) and Christianity (twelve apostles)."

[538] See M. G. Reddish, *Revelation* (1985), p. 407; D. E. Aune, *Revelation 17–22* (1998), p. 1162.

[539] As C. Keener, *Revelation* (2002), pp. 494–95, suggests from a functional point of view you have to have walls to have city gates!

[540] See P. Barnett, *Apocalypse Now and Then* (1989), pp. 156–57.

[541] The Temple Scroll from the Qumran community also has the names of the twelve tribes inscribed on the temple's twelve gates.

in Rev. 7, which refers to the twelve tribes, it is hard to know whether John is stressing the continuity between the old and new peoples of God, or whether he thinks Jew and Gentile united in Christ is the true Israel. The latter seems to be suggested by the combination of twelve gates with tribal names and the foundations with the apostles' names.[542] It is hard to know why John mentions the gates in the order that he does, or the stones for that matter. The twelve foundation stones seem to be envisioned as sticking out somewhat at the base of the walls of the city. On them are the twelve names of the apostles of the Lamb. Beasley-Murray says they are especially mentioned because they represent the testimony of the church of Jesus, so that whoever builds on their testimony has a sure foundation in Christ (cf. Eph. 2.19 ff.).[543]

The angel has a golden measuring rod, very appropriate for a golden city. He is to measure the city, its gates, and walls. In contrast to Ezekiel, here the city is being measured to show its magnitude. In Ezekiel the measuring is for the sake of showing how much needs protection. Sometimes such measuring exercises are for sizing something up for judgment, but clearly that is not the case in Rev. 21. The width, length, and height of the city is said to be 12,000 stadia (1,500 miles). By contrast, the wall is only 144 cubits (about 72–75 yards) in height or possibly width. Both sets of numbers are multiples of twelve, which likely means these numbers are symbolic of a measurement that is completely adequate to surround and include the whole of the vast numbers of the peoples of God, while the small number as applied to the wall suggests little or no need for protection for this city, unlike any other city in antiquity. Furthermore the gates are always open in all directions for those who will come, and the city is alive all the time. The New Jerusalem is an inviting and safe place for all comers.[544]

The main thing to be said about the precious stones, other than that there are as many conjectures as commentaries about their symbolic significance, is that Ezek. 28.13 is in the background, where the precious stones are linked to God's own dwelling in Paradise. It is possible that the stones are connected to the signs of the zodiac.[545] Caird suggests that John is using the reverse order to that used in astrological speculations to try and discourage such speculations among his audience.[546] T. F. Glasson, however, seems to have disproved that theory.[547] More probable is that John has remembered what was said about the stones in the breastplate of the high priest (cf. Exod. 28.17 ff.; 39.10 ff.). The point would be how beautiful, precious, and holy the city is. But on closer inspection,

---

[542] M. G. Reddish, *Revelation* (2001), p. 406.
[543] G. R. Beasley-Murray, *Book of Revelation* (1978), p. 321.
[544] M. G. Reddish, *Revelation* (2001), p. 411.
[545] See R. H. Mounce, *Book of Revelation* (1977), pp. 393–94.
[546] G. B. Caird, *Revelation* (1998), pp. 276–77. This might also explain the reference to sorcerers at 21.8.
[547] T. F. Glasson, "The Order of the Jewels in Revelation xxi.19–20: A Theory Eliminated," *JTS* (1975), pp. 95–100.

it appears that John has derived his stone list in part from Exod. 28.17–20 and in part from Ezek. 28.16, including nine stones that appear in both lists. No one stone list corresponds with John's.[548] The mention of such stones suggests a holy city but also a city of unlimited resources. The list has rhetorical and aural dimensions. In particular, when read in the Greek, nine of the stone names end with the siblant *s* sound, and three with the nasal *n* sound. The idea of pure pearl gates may come from Isa. 54.11–12, if the author thought carbuncle is the same as pearl. One may contrast this to the inferior description of Babylon at Rev. 17.4 and 18.12, 16. The streets are said to be made up of translucent, pure gold,[549] which is hard to imagine or visualize. It appears that John has one great and wide main street down the center of the city paved in gold. The word *plateia* is singular here, and there is no clear reason to think it is collective.

At **vs. 22** we hear of the absence of the temple. The major difference between the New Jerusalem and the old one, or between the New Jerusalem and a description of any major ancient city, is that there is no temple in the New Jerusalem, which is to say there is no more separation of secular and sacred zones, no more separation between God and God's people. This contrasts strongly with OT and early Jewish expectations about the eschatological Jerusalem (see Jub. 1.27–29; 1 En. 90.28–29; Sib. Or. 3.7. 2–6). John expects a degree of intimacy between God and his people not ever dreamed of by other early non-Christian Jewish writers (cf. 1 Cor. 13.12). This can only be put down to John's Christology, for he believes the Lamb has truly made a full and final atonement for sin, and thus there is no more need for temple sacrifices. He believes the Lamb has ushered his followers into the very presence of God. But he does not believe that believers will be able to have that sort of intimacy with God prior to the resurrection and the final state of affairs. Only in the latter will they be in a truly holy condition so as to come directly into the presence of God.

The association of the Lamb and God in one breath implies their unity.[550] This explains why both Christ and God can be called the Alpha and Omega, and why earlier in Revelation we heard of Christ sharing the Father's throne. This has clear implication for John's doctrine of God, as discussed in the Introduction. At **vs. 23** we hear that no sun or moon were needed since God and the Lamb light up the city with their brilliance. The Lamb is the lamp (cf. John. 8.12). The nations will be able to see to walk because of his light.

---

548 See the careful study of W.W. Reader, "The Twelve Jewels of Revelation 21.19–20: Tradition History and Modern Interpretations," *JBL* 100 (1981), p. 455: "The enumeration of the stones in the Johannine Apocalypse does not correspond to any known list of stones in late Judaism, neither to a Hebrew, nor a Greek, nor an Aramaic list. In addition to this, the stones of the Apocalypse cannot be correlated with specific tribes, apostles, zodiac signs or geographical directions. Furthermore, nothing can be derived from the colors, names, or sequence of the stones."

549 On the basis of texts like Exod. 24.10, Ezek. 1.22, and C. Keener, *Revelation* (2002), p. 495, proposes that the clarity suggests God's glory and perhaps also his purity.

550 See G. R. Beasley-Murray, *Book of Revelation* (1978), p. 327.

Then we hear of the kings of the earth bringing their treasure into the city (cf. Ps. 72.9–16; Is. 45.14, 60.5–16, 61.6). Keener aptly sums up what is happening here: "In Revelation the gifts that the nations bring are not simply wealth but 'glory' (21.24 . . . 26); they offer their glory to God in light of God's greater glory (21.23), forsaking idolatry."[551] In this city there is no night, so the gates are always open.

Who are these kings of the earth? As mentioned in earlier discussion, John hopes for the conversion of many in the various nations. While John is no universalist, as his comments of the destruction of the wicked show, he believes a very large number of people will be saved, from all walks of life, from all nations, from all social classes. The image of the kings may come from the OT idea that the Gentiles upon the earth would give tribute to God after the messianic reign had begun, but if so, John has modified the idea to apply not to a temporary messianic age but to the final state. In Rev. 13.14 the nations were said to have been deceived by Satan, and the kings of the earth were his vassals (17.2). At the end of history, however, John believes they can be reclaimed since the deceiver has been finally and permanently removed. The song of the redeemed in 15.4 said that all the nations would come and worship the true God. John believes even this will be fulfilled one day. This text is not speaking of pagans doing homage to a mightier God but of representative conversions from all the nations at or near the end of human history. John's is a far more optimisitic vision than many commentators have thought.

Why are these individuals outside the city? At the time John wrote, perhaps they were not yet within the believers' camp, but John foresees them coming into the city of God in the future. The evil having all been removed, the peoples of the nations left are viewed as converted, so finally the whole earth worships the one true God and walks in his light. No one got in by chance, only those whose name was written in the Lamb's book of life. Thus **vs. 27** served to reassure the audience that the coming in of the pagan nations did not mean the entrance of uncleanness or sin into the holy city.

Finally, John sees a river like crystal flowing from the throne of God and of the Lamb (one shared throne). A combination of Ezekiel and Genesis 1–2 is in the background. The river being crystal clear and pure is a perfect symbol of life flowing from God to God's people. This river apparently goes down the middle of the golden street, and on either side of its banks are trees of life (or is there only one tree?),[552] which bear twelve different kinds of fruit year-round, some each month. The leaves of the trees are said to be a cure for the nations. Again Ezek. 47 is in view. But why would healing be needed in the New Jerusalem? Presumably the healing of memories and minds goes on. While resurrection

---

[551] C. Keener, *Revelation* (2002), p. 498.
[552] The singular may suggest only one tree.

could instantly provide a whole body, the healing of the hearts and minds of people is seen to take much longer.

All that was formerly under the curse of God will be no more. The reference to the curse alludes to Zech. 14.3, but in light of the paradisiacal imagery here, Gen. 3.14, 17 must be in the background as well. Giblin reminds us that the presence of healing is one thing, but the absence of the curse is another. Together the images suggest not only cures for what ails us but also no further prospects of judgment, no further residual effects of the original curse on sin.[553] God's face will finally be seen (cf. 1 Cor. 13), which is to say God's people will have direct and unmediated access to God. They will bear God's name; that is, God's character will be indelibly stamped upon them and reflected by them in the New Jerusalem. We may contrast this with the brand of the Beast on those who serve him (13.6; 14.9; 17.5; 20.4).[554] There may be a contrast between the brand, for branding is something done to animals, and the name engraved, which is something done for humans. God treats his people as special people, while the Beast dehumanizes his followers. There will be no more night, and people will reign with him forever. All that causes human beings to fear, represented by sea and night, has been removed. The New Jerusalem is a picture of perfect and eternally abiding good.

A CLOSER LOOK – HEAVENLY JERUSALEM OR SKY CITY?

In his interesting study entitled *The New Jerusalem in the Revelation of John: The City as Symbol of Life with God*,[555] B. Malina applies his typical socio-cultural analysis of the Mediterranean world to the study of Rev. 21–22, with mixed results. As in some of his previous studies there is still too much of the following. (1) He over-relies on Greco-Roman sources as if they provide the ultimate matrix for understanding this highly Jewish work. (2) As in the commentary on Revelation he undertook with Pilch, there is the serious error of equating Jewish or Jewish Christian prophecy with Greco-Roman astral prophecy. This is not to say that early Jews were not interested in astrological matters, for clearly they were, but their focus was almost exclusively on things of the earth and in human history, not celestial events. (3) While certainly John mentions some celestial events, such as the falling of the star called Wormwood, when it comes to his discussion, for example of the Lamb, John is certainly not drawing on astral speculation about the constellation Aries; rather his depiction of the heavenly Lamb is grounded in OT Passover rituals and in early Christian thought about the death of Jesus. Nor is John talking about some astral conjunction between Aries and some

---

[553] C. H. Giblin, *Book of Revelation* (1991), p. 212.
[554] Ibid. Giblin thinks John has in mind the headband worn by the high priest, which reads, "Holy to the Lord."
[555] Collegeville, Minn.: Liturgical Press, 2000.

sky city. The marriage of the Lamb takes place on earth and comports with the other Jewish and NT traditions about the eschatological marriage feast transpiring at the end of human history on earth. Malina is simply wrong that John is primarily interested in certain sky segments and events rather than in the eschatological story line already shared by this author and his audience. (4) To make his interpretation work, which entails seeing this as an esoteric work that only certain kinds of initiated astral prophets might understand, Malina must argue that John is simply writing to his fellow prophets in Asia, not to the churches. This makes little sense of Rev. 2–3. While prophets are an issue for John, they are not his primary audience, and Rev. 22.9 does not suggest otherwise. (5) Malina seems to operate with a paradigm that does not recognize that early Jews did not simply identify the sky with heaven. For them, the sky was at most the lowest level of heaven, but God's dwelling place was far above that, either in the third or seventh level above it. When John describes heavenly events, it cannot be assumed he is simply describing events in the sky, though clearly he does sometimes refer to the latter. (6) The Lamb that John is concerned with is a symbolic portrayal of a historical person – Jesus of Nazareth, now resident in heaven, not a star sign that John has loaded with other significance. (7) The city John is concerned with is the dwelling place of the saints in heaven that then descends and becomes a part of the new earth. In no case is John simply drawing on Mesopotamian or other sorts of speculations about cities thought to have been seen in the sky. (8) John's book is about visions he saw while on Patmos, not about his being transported into the sky by the Spirit where he saw astral events. John's visions are not to be equated with those of apocalyptic figures who do tours of heaven or hell; in particular they are not to be equated with Enoch. The biblical story of Enoch included the notion that he was taken up into heaven never more to return. This is a different matter to being given a vision of heaven and the other world while remaining a person on earth. For example, John sees the temple in heaven (11.19), and the city coming down from heaven (Rev. 21–22), but he sees this in a vision from afar. He does not claim to be there. He is on earth envisioning what those things are or will be like.

Despite these criticisms, there is some helpful material in Malina's study. For one thing, he has pointed out the dangers of anachronism in envisioning ancient cities as if they were the same as modern ones. But there is also a danger in using phrases like "ruralized peasant society" when, in fact, John is addressing city dwellers of some kind, not ruralized peasants. But Malina is right that the dangers of projection of modern concepts into ancient settings are considerable. Technologically, for instance, ancients were limited to energy provided by animals, humans, and things like simple ovens and water-driven devices. He is also right that large estate owners as part of the elite often ran both the cities and the rural areas. But it would be wrong to call such elite persons farmers or ranchers.[556] If one actually reads the story of the lives of elite Roman citizens (e.g., some of the senators of Rome, or someone like Seneca, or Tacitus' father-in-law Agricola), one realizes that these people lived in the city most of the time and dealt largely with the problems of city life. They would retreat to their country villas in the heat of the summer. Those villas would often be run by freedmen or slaves or extended family members.[557] Malina is, however, right that there were no nation states or free market economies as we know them, and this affected the shape of ancient cities and what made them run. The existence of slaves as the basis of so much manual labor in the Roman economy should make clear what a different socio-economic situation John's audience lived in from ours. Obviously sanitation, comfort, and safety were all more difficult issues to tackle in a premodern city like Ephesus or any of the seven cities John addresses. I agree with Malina that the New Jerusalem that John envisions is much more like an ANE rather than a Greco-Roman city, not least because ANE cities had a temple at the heart of them.[558] This observation should, however, have warned him against assuming that John's dominant paradigm for thinking about his subject matter is Greco-Roman in character. In fact, it is Jewish and Scriptural in character. For John the persons in heaven, including God and Jesus and the saints, not celestial bodies, are the controlling forces in the universe, and his attention focuses on their interaction with earthly persons and affairs. Furthermore the references to the twelve tribes and twelve apostles in connection with the New Jerusalem have no connections with the twelve signs of the zodiac. They are grounded in the historical realities of Israel and the earliest followers of Jesus.

BRIDGING THE HORIZONS

There must be a new earth. This earth – raped, robbed, torn, filled with anger and revenge, with hurt and pain – cannot and should not remain. This earth had been the dwelling place of the Beast, the false prophet of the Beast who came out of the sea. It was the throne of Babylon, the great harlot. This earth had given refuge to the murderers of the saints of God but became, by the same token, the arena of the suffering and death of God's children. It was never "home" for them. . . . Indeed, in the experience of the little people of God, the earth belonged to the mighty and the powerful who claimed it for themselves, and they were the enemies, the killers of those who sought to remain faithful to Jesus Christ. So this earth should be no more. . . . Normal is no longer hiding in the night, leaving loved ones behind and fighting with wild Beasts for the enjoyment of the Beast. What is normal now is walking in the light of God and living from the fruits of the tree of life.[559]

---

[556] Ibid., p. 31.
[557] Against Malina (ibid., p. 32), who tries to argue the city residence was usually secondary.
[558] See ibid., pp. 46–47.
[559] A. Boesak, *Comfort and Protest* (1986), pp. 126–27, 136.

These words of Allan Boesak remind us that this is literature written for the oppressed and persecuted, who have despaired of any merely human solutions to the human dilemma. This is literature that believes that God must intervene if the world is truly to change and if there is to be enduring, loving human community on the earth. It is not that John didn't know that there were some good aspects to the present world; it is just that he believed, with Paul, that the form of this world was passing away, including governmental structures among other things. Everything had been relativized by the Christ event, but the Christ event does not immediately heal all of Jesus' followers. The evil in the world was so great that there needed to be a further intervention and redemptive-judgment by Christ. Thus the new heaven and new earth must include not merely a replacement for the old world but healing from the old world, a wiping away of tears left over from the suffering. There will be pathos as well as joy in the life to come.

The final vision in Revelation is, of course, about heaven and its holiness, or, better said, about the invasion of earth by heaven, thereby finally entirely sanctifying the earthly realm. Many people's vision of this final destination for believers is either too narrow or simply wrong. Peterson points out,

> many people want to go to heaven the way they want to go to Florida – they think the weather will be an improvement and the people decent. But the biblical heaven is not a nice environment far removed from the stress of hard city life. It is the invasion of the city by the City. We enter heaven not by escaping what we don't like, but by the sanctification of the place in which God has placed us. There is not so much as a hint of escapism in St. John's heaven. This is not a long (eternal) weekend away from the responsibilities of employment and citizenship, but the intensification and healing of them.[560]

Peterson goes on to stress that the holiness that the heavenly Jerusalem possesses is expressed in its beauty, and symmetry, its light, and life giving fruit, and its fertility: "holiness is perfectly proportioned wholeness."[561] It is that which sustains us and enlivens us. It is "a holiness that is neither cramped, or distorted, but spacious; an illumination that goes beyond the minimum of showing what is true by showing it extravagantly beautiful; a nourishment that is the healthy feeding of our lives, not the frivolous adornment of them. . . . There is an implicit rejection in the visions of versions of holiness that are squinty and contorted, versions of truth that are dull and drab, and versions of growth that are decorative or effete."[562] The holiness of the holy city has to do with love and community and the best family reunion ever. It is the opposite of a tourniquet menta-lity that, rather than giving joy, kills joy, by stressing what must be given up rather than what can be had, what must be avoided rather than what we must

---

[560] E. Peterson, *Reversed Thunder* (1988), p. 174.
[561] Ibid., p. 177.
[562] Ibid., p. 183.

immerse ourselves in a positive way. Holiness is about completion, about "the hopes and fears of all the years" being met in Christ in our final eternal fellowship with Him. While evil starves us of what we truly need, this holiness and wholeness are fed on the basics that actually sustain life, and by this I mean embodied life.

Just as John's vision of heaven does not amount to our exchanging earthly excitement and pleasure for heavenly boredom and asceticism, so also it does not entail a disembodied shadowy existence. The new creation is just that: a new creation involving persons in resurrected bodies and an earth that has been renewed. "The two words, *heaven* and *earth*, together tie us to a material creation that, as far as our senses report it to us, never ends. We are immersed in materiality from start to finish. . . . The great invisibles, God and the soul, are incomprehensible apart from the great visibles, heaven and earth."[563] God is indeed the ultimate ecologist.

Frankly I would not care much for a Creator God who chose in the end to abandon his material creation in exchange for a purely spiritual state of affairs. Fortunately this is not the God of the Bible. The God of the Bible desires fellowship so badly with his creatures that he becomes one of them to redeem them, and the second person of the Trinity remains one of us – the God–human being forever. This being so, it is not godly spirituality that denigrates, negates, or tries to escape our material condition. Rather, it is a matter of the transformation of that condition. "Our unregenerate nature has a way of slipping the leash of the physical and running away like a disobedient dog into all kinds of lush spiritualities. But all dematerialized spiritualities are vacant lots."[564] John would have been very concerned indeed about those who pursue a spirituality that negates, withdraws from, ignores the world for the sake of otherworldliness. He would not be any happier with certain forms of a rapture theology that allows people to neglect their job as caretakers of the earth, since it is seen as inevitable that this world is going to hell eventually anyway. John would have problems with modern spiritualities based in certain forms of medieval mysticism that ignore the cries in Revelation for justice and redemption within space and time and not outside of it.

And finally, John would be frustrated with the way that Revelation has often been used, particularly his heavenly worship scenes, to inculcate a theology of Christian life and worship that justifies a dematerialized, dehistoricized spirituality. For John, salvation must happen in space and time or not at all, precisely because sin and evil are historical problems that plague human history. The atonement must be made on earth, and the resurrection must come forth from earth. Eternal life begins here and now, not then and later in heaven. Otherwise God's sovereignty, justice, and redemption are not demonstrated in the realm

---

[563] Ibid., p. 170.
[564] Ibid., p. 171.

where they need to be demonstrated – on earth. No such demonstrations are required in heaven. John, with other early Christians, prayed, "thy kingdom come on earth" and assures his audience that, at the end, "the kingdoms of this world will become the kingdoms of our God and of his Christ."

REVELATION 22.6–22.21 – THE EPILOGUE

NRSV Revelation 22.6 And he said to me, "These words are trustworthy and true, for the Lord, the God of the spirits of the prophets, has sent his angel to show his servants what must soon take place."

7 "See, I am coming soon! Blessed is the one who keeps the words of the prophecy of this book."

8 I, John, am the one who heard and saw these things. And when I heard and saw them, I fell down to worship at the feet of the angel who showed them to me;

9 but he said to me, "You must not do that! I am a fellow servant with you and your comrades the prophets, and with those who keep the words of this book. Worship God!"

10 And he said to me, "Do not seal up the words of the prophecy of this book, for the time is near.

11 Let the evildoer still do evil, and the filthy still be filthy, and the righteous still do right, and the holy still be holy."

12 "See, I am coming soon; my reward is with me, to repay according to everyone's work.

13 I am the Alpha and the Omega, the first and the last, the beginning and the end."

14 Blessed are those who wash their robes, so that they will have the right to the tree of life and may enter the city by the gates.

15 Outside are the dogs and sorcerers and fornicators and murderers and idolaters, and everyone who loves and practices falsehood.

16 "It is I, Jesus, who sent my angel to you with this testimony for the churches. I am the root and the descendant of David, the bright morning star."

17 The Spirit and the bride say, "Come." And let everyone who hears say, "Come." And let everyone who is thirsty come. Let anyone who wishes take the water of life as a gift.

18 I warn everyone who hears the words of the prophecy of this book: if anyone adds to them, God will add to that person the plagues described in this book;

19 if anyone takes away from the words of the book of this prophecy, God will take away that person's share in the tree of life and in the holy city, which are described in this book.

20 The one who testifies to these things says, "Surely I am coming soon." Amen. Come, Lord Jesus!
21 The grace of the Lord Jesus be with all the saints. Amen.

*T*his section concludes the book, offering final testimonies from God, the Lamb, the Spirit, the bride, and the prophets who speak to the bride for the Spirit."[565] The Epilogue to the great work should be compared to the Prologue, and it shares numerous of its elements. It has appeared to most, however, to be a bit more disjointed than the Prologue. Perhaps the major difficulty is determining who is speaking at what juncture. Most scholars argue vv. 6–7 have Jesus speaking, vv. 8–9 an angel, vv. 10–16 again Jesus. Beasley-Murray urges that the angel is certainly the speaker in vs. 6, and that the sayings that follow are from Jesus but mediated through the angel. He argues that all of vv. 6–15, which make up the Epilogue proper, are mediated through the angel, whoever they are from.[566]

The parallels between Prologue and Epilogue include that (1) the book is genuine prophecy (cf. 1.3; 22.6, 9–10); (2) they are by a duly commissioned prophet (cf. 1.1, 9–10; 22.8–10); (3) they are to be read in churches (1.3, 11; 22.18); and (4) they encourage the faithful (1.3; 22.7, 12, 14). Furthermore, at 22.8, John mentions his name for the first time since the first chapter, and there is reference in both the beginning and the end of the work to an angel being the means by which this revelation comes to John. There is also an echo in 22.7 of 1.3 in reference to the blessing that falls on the obedient.[567] This may suggest that the Prologue was written after the rest of the work and on the basis of the Epilogue.

In **vs. 6** we hear the by-now-familiar affirmation about the truthfulness of the words in this book, coupled with the statement that God is the God of the spirits (plural) of the prophets. This likely means that God is the source of the prophet's inspiration because God is the ruler over human spirits (cf. Num. 16.22; 27.16; Heb. 12.9), in this case specifically the spirits of the prophets (1 Cor. 14.32).[568] John then has in mind not the Holy Spirit but human spirits of the prophets. In regard to these words being trustworthy and true, Reddish is correct that we have here an echo of the description of Christ in Rev. 19.11, which implies that he is the ultimate source of the trustworthy and true words of this book, as Rev. 1 suggested at the outset.[569]

Vs. 6 stresses that an angel shows God's servants what must happen shortly (*en taxei* here probably means "soon" rather than "quickly," but on whose clock?

---

[565] C. Keener, *Revelation* (2002), p. 513.
[566] G. R. Beasley-Murray, *Revelation* (1978), pp. 334–35.
[567] See C. Keener, *Revelation* (2002), p. 513.
[568] D. E. Aune, *Revelation 17–22* (1998), p. 1182, notes that the "spirit" was viewed as the highest human faculty.
[569] See M. G. Reddish, *Revelation* (2001), p. 424.

Cf. 2.16; 3.11, 22; 22.7, 12, 20). Caird is likely wrong to interpret this to mean that Christ meets people at their deaths or in a crisis or in the Eucharist.[570] Jesus says that he is coming, and **taxu** could be adverbial in sense here and mean "quickly." But the question is, in part, how such language is meant to function in a work of apocalyptic prophecy. Does it function so as to dictate that the thief in the night must appear within a certain time frame or to warn that He *could* be coming soon and thus one must always be prepared?[571] The latter seems more probable as John is not interested in date setting, unlike some writers of apocalyptic material, and as the hortatory and rhetorical function of the work as a whole points us in this direction.[572] Furthermore, as we have seen, John operates with a double eschatology. One set of things can be said about the period leading up to the millennium, another about the things that follow the return of Christ and the millennium. Koester's reminder is apt:

Revelation declares that "the time is near" (Rev. 22.10), only to confound the readers' sense of timing with a kaleidoscopic spiral of visions that periodically repeats similar messages through different images and interrupts its forward movement with suspended judgments and heavenly interludes. Revelation can tell readers that the marriage feast of the Lamb "has come" and that the bride "is ready." Yet, it does not allow readers to see the bride until more than a thousand years have passed in its visionary world (19.7–8; 21.2, 9). Readers are left with the assurance *that* the End will come, but without knowing *when* it will come.[573]

In **vs. 7b** we have the sixth of seven beatitudes in this work. "Blessing comes to those who live by the words of this book."

In **vs. 8** John has heard and seen these things. Thus this book is meant for both the ears as well as the eyes of both John and his audience. Once again we have John falling at the angel's feet to worship, and once again the angel prohibits this (see 19.10). Perhaps John is identifying with his audience to tend to worship something less than God as God.[574] The angel is a fellow servant of God, and he also must keep the words of this book. This implies that God's people are raised to equal status, at least with the angels.

---

[570] But see G. B. Caird, *Revelation* (1998), pp. 282–83.

[571] See C. Keener, *Revelation* (2002), p. 519: "Rhetorically, this functions especially as a call to perseverance for the book's primary audience, but it also functions as a warning to shake Sardian and Laodicean Christianity for their complacency."

[572] See E. Fiorenza, *Revelation* (1991), p. 115: "The urgency of Revelation's imminent expectation clearly serves rhetorical functions." She adds that the intent is to offer prophetic exhortation and motivation.

[573] C. Koester, *Revelation and the End* (2001), p. 203.

[574] On the issue of angelomorphic Christology, see L. T. Stuckenbruck, *Angel Veneration and Christology* (Tübingen, Ger.: Mohr, 1995). I do not find his arguments that we have an angelomorphic Christology persuasive, not least because of the verses being considered.

In contrast to other apocalyptic works, including Daniel, John is told *not* to seal up the words of this book because its contents will come to pass in the near future (*eggus*). This contrasts with the command given in Dan. 12.4, 9–10 and in 1 En. 1.2. Some have seen the sealing-up command as a literary device that goes along with pseudonymous authorship, but we do not have that in this work, and so there is no command to seal it up. John believed that at least some of the events leading up to the material in Rev. 19–22 were on the near horizon or, as in the case of Rev. 12.5–6, had already transpired.[575] The question to be asked about **vs. 10** is, The time is near for what? For some of the preliminary judgments to begin? For the return of Christ to happen? In vs. 6 the preliminary events are in view, but in vs. 12 it is the coming of Christ of God that is in view. **Vv. 11–12** indicate that, when that "near" time comes, there will be no more opportunity for repentance. The unrighteous and filthy will remain like that, and the righteous and holy will remain just that. Perhaps a more helpful reading of vs. 11 is offered by Reddish, who paraphrases, "Let those who are wicked continue in their wickedness if that is what they choose; but they must pay the consequences. On the other hand, let those who are righteous continue to do what is right because that is what God expects and demands from them."[576]

In **vs. 12** we learn that the coming One arrives with a reward in hand. The concept of salvation by grace, which John is well familiar with, does not rule out rewards for good behavior in the kingdom. Each will be repaid according to what he or she has done on earth (cf. Rom. 2.6; 1 Pet. 1.17). We are not told in vs. 12 whether God or Christ is the subject. In light of Rev. 1.8, it may be God, especially in view of what we heard in Rev. 21 about God coming down with the New Jerusalem. However, as Bauckham has shown, both God and Christ are called Alpha and Omega in this work (in 1.8 and 21.6, it is God; but in 1.17 and probably here at 22.13, it is Christ).[577] This does not make Christ a second God, but rather includes him in the being of the one God of Israel who is Alpha and Omega. The use of the reward language, like the use of Alpha and Omega language, is derived from Isaiah (cf. 40.11; 62.11 on the former; 41.4; 44.6; 48.12 on the latter). It implies that John sees Christ as included within the godhead, for only God is the truly eternal one who will at the last day dispense rewards.

The seventh and last beatitude is found at **vs. 14**. Blessed are those washing their robes[578] so that they may have the right to partake from the tree of life and enter into the gates of the heavenly city.[579] At Rev. 7.14 we have similar

---

[575] See C. Keener, *Revelation* (2002), p. 514.

[576] M. G. Reddish, *Revelation* (2001), p. 426.

[577] R. Bauckham, *Theology of the Book of Revelation* (1993), pp. 57–58.

[578] There is an alternate reading here blessing those who do the commandments, which is favored by S. Goranson, "The Text of Revelation 22.14," *NTS* 43 (1997), pp. 154–57. In view of Rev. 3.4 and 7.14, this seems less likely to be the original reading.

[579] C. Keener, *Revelation* (2002), p. 515, is likely right that those Christians from Sardis may have seen this as a stern warning in light of what is said of them at Rev. 3.4. This then is another way the beginning and the end of the book are linked.

words though there the verb "wash" is in the aorist. To partake of the tree and to eat of the tree are just two alternative ways of speaking of the same blessing – partaking of eternal life. Caird insists that marytrdom is in view in the metaphor of washing, as if the martyr's own death cleansed and atoned for them.[580] But "wash" here is in the continual present tense and is more likely to refer to an ongoing activity or benefit than to a one-time death of a saint. Most likely those who wash are those who live a righteous life. Those who are outside the bounds of the city are called the usual list of things associated with wickedness (cf. 21.8). But here also the term "dogs" appears. This term in Semitic circles always had negative and pejorative senses, usually referring to Gentiles and their various forms of uncleanness. Here an impious or immoral person seems likely to be in view rather than the more specific sense the word sometimes has of male prostitute (but cf. Deut. 23.18).[581] Dogs in the Greco-Roman world were viewed as sexually immoral (Aelian, *Animals* 7.19).

In **vs. 16** we learn that it is Jesus who sent the interpreting angel to John. He is the ultimate source of this revelation. This revelation was not meant to be private property but was rather for the churches (plural). Jesus is of the root and of the lineage of David. The reference to his being the root may present Jesus as the very source of the Davidic line.[582] He is, in any case, viewed as the long-sought-for Jewish Messiah. He is the fulfillment of Isa. 11.1 and, as we learn next, the fulfillment of Num. 24.17, which speaks of the early shining star.[583] He is not seen as the morning star but rather as the Davidic king that would arise from the line of Jacob. The prophecy from Num. 24.17 was the one shortly after John's time that Simon bar Kosiba used to make messianic claims for himself (calling himself Bar Kokhba, "son of the star") and to lead an ill-fated revolt against Rome in A.D. 132–35. But there is also another tradition of interest. Martial, a contemporary of John's, wrote a poem for Domitian, praying for his return from the northern part of the Empire, that included the lines, "Thou morning star / Bring on the day! Come and expel our fears, Rome begs that Caesar / may soon appear."[584] It is thus quite possible that we have more anti-imperial rhetoric from John here.

It is somewhat of a surprise to hear both the bride and the Holy Spirit beckon Jesus to come, but one must remember that the Spirit and church bear a joint witness to Christ, and the Spirit is in a sense resident on earth with the church. We hear in Rom. 8.36–37 of the Spirit as offering intercessory prayer, so this may

---

[580] G. B. Caird, *Revelation* (1998), pp. 284–85.
[581] For a comparison with the similar use of the term at Qumran, see M. Philonenko, " 'Dehors les Chiens' (Apocalypse 22.16 et 4QMMT B 58–62)," *NTS* 43 (1997), pp. 445–50.
[582] See C. Keener, *Revelation* (2002), p. 516. This would comport with the notion that he is Alpha as well as Omega.
[583] For a messianic interpretation of that star passage during John's general era, see 1 QM 11.6–7; CD 7.18–21; 4 QTest 9–13; Test. of Lev. 18.3; Test. of Jud. 24.1.
[584] See A. Boesak, *Comfort and Protest* (1986), p. 137.

be the case here as well. Is Jesus being beckoned here, or rather the people of the world? In light of **vs. 20** and that the verb "come" (*erchou*) is in the singular, it is likely the former. Jesus is the one who offers freely the water of life (echoing Isa. 55.1 and possibly John 7.37–38), and God's people are beckoned to partake but they, in turn, beckon Christ to come so they may partake in the heavenly city. As Swete says, "The end is not an event but a person, from whom the world devolves and to whom it moves; he has shared his throne and his title with Jesus."[585]

At **vs. 18** we hear that the words of this book are prophecy. Vs. 18b–c must be seen for what it is. We have a traditional formula meant not to establish the canonical status of this book or to set it alongside the OT, but rather to insist on its inspired and authoritative character. Being the Word of God and of true prophecy, it should not be altered either by addition or subtraction. It is simply fortuitous that this occurs at the end of the book that was later to become the last book of the NT canon. The author draws on a similar warning in Deut. 4.2 (cf. Deut. 12.32).[586] If one seeks to alter the book, one will endure some of the plagues or have one's portion in the tree of life taken away.[587] It is hard to deny, in light of this last comment, that the author believed that a person could commit apostasy by some action and so have the privilege of eternal salvation taken away from him. John was not an advocate of "once saved, always saved" theology.

In **vs. 20** the author offers the same prayer we have from Paul at 1 Cor. 16.22 – *marana tha*. This is not a curse formula but rather a prayer for Christ to come, and early Aramaic Jewish Christian people did not pray for a deceased rabbi to come. They prayed to God in Christ to return. Some have thought the original setting of the *marana tha* prayer may be eucharistic, inviting Christ to spiritually come with the eucharist. But the *Didache*'s use of the anathema/marana tha (*Did.* 10.16) seems to be of little relevance, and, as Reddish says, the context in both Revelation and 1 Corinthians favors seeing it as an eschatologically focused prayer.[588] John is simply offering a straightforward prayer for Christ to return, which is the event that provides the climax of the book and its blessed aftermath.

This prayer and also the benediction invoking grace shows two more pieces of evidence that our author knew Paul's letters, or at least some of them. Of

---

[585] H. B. Swete, *Commentary on Revelation* (1977), p. 316.

[586] One can also compare the similar warning about not revising the LXX in Ep. Arist. 310–11, or not revising 1 Enoch in 1 En. 108.6. These warnings can be compared to the history of the transmission of the text of the NT, which reminds us that there was a scribal tendency to polish and emend documents when they were copied. Josephus says that no one dares or ought to dare to change or emend the Scriptures (*Apion* 1.42).

[587] This warning has nothing to do with John's belief in the cessation of prophecy! Pace R. L. Thomas, "The Spiritual Gift of Prophecy in Rev. 22.18," *JETS* 32 (1989), pp. 201–16. To the contrary, he is a part of that living and ongoing tradition, and he seems in part to be responding to other prophets in this work, though he sees them as false prophets.

[588] M. G. Reddish, *Revelation* (2001), p. 431.

course, the benediction is also understandable as an epistolary closing element. The book ends as it began – as a letter to the churches. But note that it also ends as it began (1.4), with the word grace. In fact, these are the only two places in the book where that word occurs, but the theology of grace undergirds John's whole understanding of God in Christ's work of redemption.[589] The work ends not so much on a Pauline note as on a Christian note.

BRIDGING THE HORIZONS

Reinhold Niebuhr is credited with once saying, "It is unwise for Christians to claim any knowledge of either the furniture of heaven or the temperature of hell, or to be too certain about any details of the Kingdom of God in which history is consummated."[590] I take it that his point in the main is that an overly literal interpretation of the last few chapters of Revelation is a serious mistake. It is also a mistake to assume that these hyperbolic and metaphorical images are not referential in the broad sense. John certainly believes in the reality of heaven and hell, of bodily resurrection and judgment. The apocalyptic clothing in which he embodies his discussion of these realities must not obscure this. For example, while John may not believe in literal flames in hell, he believes that image accurately sums up the misery and painfulness of being in a place where one experiences the absence of the presence of God forever. It is wrong to caricature the material in the book of Revelation or the beliefs of its author. Reducing the book to mere fantastic nonreferential pictures is just as reductionistic and unfaithful to the author's intent as is a wooden literalism. The very way John uses his source material flexibly, not simply repeating the images or ideas he derives from Ezekiel or elsewhere, shows that he himself is no literalist. But, he also does not believe he is writing a fantasy or a record of mere subjective dreams. Somewhere in between these extremes is the truth about John's Revelation. Once we have correctly assessed what John is claiming, then it is up to us to decide if we can imaginatively enter into and believe in John's vision.

Though John is not warning against adding books to the NT canon at the end of his work, it is worth reflecting on the function of a canon. The word **kanon** refers to a measuring rod by which other things can be judged. The earliest Christians did not believe that the Hebrew Scriptures were the only revelation God had given. Some were given orally and never recorded (cf., e.g., 1 Kings 18.13). Nor did they believe that the inspired works of John and Paul and others ruled out other prophets and prophetic oracles in the NT period. They did believe that the canon of inscripturated revelation should be the measuring rod to judge the truth or falsity of other prophecies and prophetic works. "The

---

589 Ibid.
590 R. Niebuhr, *The Nature and Destiny of Man*, vol 2: Human Destiny (New York: Scribner's Sons, 1964), p. 294.

Bible itself teaches us that it is not all that God ever spoke, but it remained wholly God's Word and therefore the standard and criterion for measuring other claims."[591]

Yet while John had no idea of a canon of the NT in mind when he wrote, providentially God did intend for Revelation to be the last book in the canon. As such, its final warnings remind the later generations of Christians that there is a standard of measurement by which all claims to prophetic inspiration should be evaluated – the Holy Scriptures. God's word is sufficient and should not be emended (see Prov. 30.5–6). This, however, does not mean that God cannot continue to speak to his church by other means as well.

One of the major emphases in homiletics these days is on storytelling. John is most certainly a storyteller par excellence. But he does not make up the story as he goes along. As many sources as he uses and as flexibly as he uses various OT, early Jewish, early Christian, and even pagan images, he still recognizably believes in and bases what he says on the common story he shares with other Christians that focuses particularly on the role of Christ in history. There is a lot to be said for a dramatic reading of the book of Revelation. Such a way of dealing with the text is by no means a recent phenomenon. One of the famous circuit riders of the early nineteenth century who helped generate the camp meeting movement, James McGready, was a compelling storyteller. He "would so describe Heaven, that you would almost see its glories."[592] In an age of TVs, computers, and the cinema, that is, in an age of increasingly visual learners, it makes good sense that a work like Revelation could and should be used to reach a postmodern audience. Just as retelling the parables has become a popular homiletical move, so also Revelation's retelling could be profitable. But this presupposes that the proclaimer understands at least a good deal of what is proclaimed, for he or she will also be called upon to explain things.

As apartheid was coming to an end, A. Boesak wrote the following amplified version of John's ***marana tha*** prayer:

> For the pain and the tears and the anguish must end.... Come, Lord Jesus.
> For the comfort of this world is no comfort at all.... Come, Lord Jesus.
> For there must be an end to the struggle when the unnecessary dying is over....
>   Come, Lord Jesus.
> For the patterns of this world must change.... Come, Lord Jesus.
> For hate must turn to love; fear must turn to joy.... Come, Lord Jesus.[593]

---

[591] C. Keener, *Revelation* (2002), p. 520.
[592] T. K. Beougher, "Did You Know?" *Christian History* 45 (1995), p. 2.
[593] A. Boesak, *Comfort and Protest* (1986), p. 138.

IV. APPENDIX: A Millennial Problem

*W*ithout question, one of the most problematic of passages not only in the book of Revelation but in the entire New Testament is Rev. 20.4–6. Elaborate eschatological schemas have been generated using this text as the linchpin of their arguments, whether one takes an amillennial, premillennial, or postmillennial view of John's argument. It therefore behooves us to give some more detailed consideration to the grammar, syntax, and meaning of these verses. Until the twentieth century, hardly any commentator denied that Rev. 20.4–6 referred to a historical period, whether past, present, or future, and even today most commentators believe that John was intending to be historically referential when he presented this material.[1]

The two major millennial viewpoints within the Christian community are the amillennial (traditionally held by most Catholics, mainline Protestants, and conservative Reformed denominations) and the premillennial (traditionally held by most Evangelicals and today, in its dispensational form, overwhelmingly the most popular form of eschatology for conservative Protestants, charismatics, and messianic Jews). This issue has been brought to the fore again recently by the best-selling series of novels by Timothy LaHaye and others, entitled the Left Behind series, which to a large extent is based on a certain kind of dispensational interpretation of the book of Revelation.[2] The amillennial view differs from that of the premillennial (whether historic premillennial or the dispensational form) in believing that the church age is the millennium and that there will be one general resurrection of the dead after Christ returns, followed by final judgment and the new heaven and the new earth.

In Rev. 20.1–3 there are two events that are important to what follows in Rev. 20.4–6: (1) the descent of the angel from heaven and (2) the binding of Satan and sealing him in the abyss for a thousand years "in order that he not

---

[1] It is of course another matter as to whether one believes John was right in taking such a view of history.

[2] See my article "What the Left Behind Series Left Out," *Bible Review* 18 (2002), pp. 10, 52.

deceive the nations any more." One must ask where John envisions this activity taking place. We are told that the binding takes place "out of heaven," for that is where the angel comes from to bind Satan. Earlier in Revelation it was said that Satan had been cast down upon the earth from the heavens (see Rev. 12.8–9). It is then logical to conclude that this binding happens not in heaven. This is important because when one gets to Rev. 20.4–6 John merely repeats the visionary phrase "and I saw," and there is no marker in the text to suggest that the locale of the events described in Rev. 20.4–6 is any different from that of the ones immediately preceding in 20.3. This suggests that what is being described in Rev. 20.4–6 is viewed as happening outside heaven. Indeed it is most naturally taken to refer to something happening on earth. Can we be more specific?

Whatever group or groups of persons are involved in the event described in Rev. 20.4, there is no dispute that the text says that *they reigned* with Christ (vs. 4c) or that they shall be priests of God and Christ (vs. 6b). This too is quite important for determining how John views the setting of these events. There are some parallels from earlier in his book – Rev. 1.6, 3.21, and 5.10. In the first of these texts it is said that Christ is the firstborn of the dead and the ruler of the kingdoms *of the earth*. In Rev. 3.21 Christ speaks to those believers who conquer, that is, those who triumph over worldly evil and are faithful unto death. Christ promises to such martyrs that they will sit with him upon his throne. Finally we read in Rev. 5.10, "You have made them to be a kingdom and priests to serve our God, and *they will reign upon the earth*." Doubtless John is in part drawing on material in Dan. 7.27. He seems to envision these saints having dominion with the Son of Man over the nations. There can be no a priori reason then why John could not also have envisioned them judging the nations with Christ, perhaps along the lines envisioned for the twelve in Luke 22.30.

The upshot of the three earlier passages in Revelation seems to be (1) that the saints will reign with Christ upon the earth (cf. 1.6–5.10); (2) that the reference to their being priests of God further demonstrates the interrelatedness of 5.10 with 20.4; and (3) that 3.21 should be connected with 20.4–6, which speaks of sitting with Christ and reigning with him. All of this is rather compelling evidence that the setting of the events described in 20.4–6 is envisioned to be outside of heaven and upon the earth. Perhaps the clinching fact comes to the fore when one examines Rev. 11.15–17. There we are told that the kingdoms of this world have become the kingdom of God and Christ and that this will be followed by a forever reign upon the earth. In 11.18 this reigning is linked with the final judging of the nations as well as with the rewarding of the servants, just as the millennium is said in Rev. 20.1–4 to be preceded by the imprisonment of Satan so he can no longer deceive the nations. There can be no excuses for the nations during or after the millennium. John believes that there will be a point in the future when the kingdoms of the world become the kingdom of God. This implies an earlier time when this was in some sense not the case, which would seem to rule out the idea that the kingdom is always and everywhere to be identified with the church until the new heaven and new earth exist. It seems that John is emphasizing that the world becomes the kingdom of God in a special sense at some juncture in the future. The angels are praising in 11.15–18 some event that is close to the time of final judgment and final reward as well.

Another important point about Rev. 20.1–3 needs to be stressed: the strong verbs used to describe the angel's action in relationship to Satan – he seized him, he bound him for 1,000 years, he threw him in the abyss, and he locked the abyss and sealed it over so he could no longer deceive the nations. A more complete removal of Satan from the earthly scene could hardly be imagined. The purpose of this action is not punitive but preventative, so Satan will no longer deceive anyone.[3] This further emphasizes that it will be Christ and the saints, not Satan, who will be ruling over the nations during the millennium.

The usual amillennial interpretation of these three verses is that Satan's binding is only partial and that it transpires during the church age between the ascension of Jesus and the Parousia. The difficulties with such an interpretation are great. Not only elsewhere in the Johannine corpus but elsewhere in the New Testament, Satan is depicted as being a roaring lion during the Christian era (1 Pet. 5.8), the prince of this world (John 16.11), or the one whom Christians are exhorted to give no opportunity to (Eph. 4.27) or told to avoid the wiles of (Eph. 5.11–12) or told to be careful not to fall into the Devil's snares (cf. 1 Tim. 3.7; 1 John 3.10; Jude vs. 9; 2 Cor. 2.11). This hardly sounds like a Satan hermetically sealed off from the earthly sphere. None of these Scriptures are apt if early Christians like John thought of Satan as already bound and unable to deceive persons. Indeed John has gone out of his way in Rev. 12.7–12 to depict Satan as alive and well on planet earth, busily deceiving all sorts of people and nations during the era in which John lived.

But it is not just the wider early Christian witness that speaks strongly against an amillennial interpretation of Rev. 20. John is also drawing on Dan. 7 here. The parallels between Rev. 20 and Dan. 7 include (1) that thrones (plural) set up for judgment are mentioned in both texts, and (2) that both the Son of Man and the saints or holy ones are to have dominion over the earth (cf. Dan. 7.14, 27 to Rev. 20.4–6). It could be argued that the "saints" in Dan. 7 are the angels, or the heavenly court, and this could be correlated with John's idea of the twenty-four elders sitting on thrones in heaven around the throne of the Most High God (cf. Rev. 4.4–11.16). But the elders are never described by John as judging, only as singing, whereas of the saints it is said they will reign with an iron rod like and with Christ.

While the "elder" interpretation is not an impossible reading of Rev. 20.4–6, it is unlikely because John makes clear that the people who will be helping in

---

3 Incarceration in the Greco-Roman world was generally not seen as a form of punishment but rather as a holding pattern until the judicial process had run its course and a verdict had been rendered.

the reigning "come to life" (see later in Appendix) to do so. It seems clear that John has martyrs being at least part of the group of those who reign with Christ on thrones. This is what those who conquer are promised in Rev. 3.21, and this may be compared to the promise to Jesus' followers in Matt. 19.28, Luke 22.30, and 1 Cor. 6.2, which says believers will even judge angels! John's Revelation is a book meant in part to comfort Christians under pressure and being persecuted, and it makes good sense that he would want to stress that those who are faithful even unto death have a special reward when the kingdom comes on earth. With these things in view we can now consider Rev. 20.4–6 in some detail.

After John has removed Satan from the scene, which is a way of setting up the positive scene found in Rev. 20.4–6, he proceeds to draw on Dan. 7 to present his millennial vision. It appears that John at least interpreted Dan. 7.22, which is alluded to in Rev. 20.4 to mean that judgment was given "to" rather than "for" the saints. Rev. 20.4a then seems to refer to saints sitting on thrones and judging. But after his initial statement about enthronement John goes on to add, "and the souls of those who were beheaded because of the witness/testimony of Jesus and because of the Word of God and whoever had not worshiped the beast nor his image and had not received the mark upon their foreheads and upon their hands." Is John just referring to martyrs here or also to other faithful believers who had not engaged in emperor worship? It seems likely that John has in view both the beheaded and those who had been faithful without being martyred. This comports with the tenor and nature of John's exhortations in his letters to the seven churches.[4] Augustine's interpretation that John is referring to regeneration here is clearly ruled out by the Greek word rendered as "having been beheaded." There are to be sure discussions in the New Testament about people being spiritually dead but not about their being spiritually beheaded! Could John have had in mind the martyrs and saints reigning with Christ in heaven during the time of the so-called intermediate state? This is not impossible, but the overall impression left by Rev. 20.4–6 likely rules out this idea. I would judge it likely that John in Rev. 20.4a refers to the general group of saints reigning with Christ and that vs. 4b specifies one subset of that group, namely the beheaded martyrs.

A brief consideration of John's use of the term *psuche* is in order. In all but perhaps two cases John uses this term to refer to the principle of life in living creatures who have physical bodies. This is the case in Rev. 8.9, 12.11, 16.3, and 18.13, and perhaps also in 18.4. On the one hand, Rev. 12.11 is very clear and refers to martyrs – "they loved not their lives (*psuche*) unto death." Obviously John is using *psuche* not to refer to the Greco-Roman notion of the immortal soul but rather to refer to the life principle that animates a living person, a more Jewish use of the term. On the other hand, Rev. 6.9 could be taken as a reference to disembodied souls. Thus we must ask, Which way is John using the term in

---

4   On which see pp. 102–8.

Rev. 20.4? The answer is in part determined by the setting in Rev. 20 seeming to be the same as the setting in Rev. 5.10, namely upon the earth. Even if one were to argue that John initially sees the souls of the beheaded as being in heaven, he goes on to mention that they "came to life," which seems far more likely to refer to resurrection than to the transition from earthly existence into heaven. There are, however, other reasons to see Rev. 20.4–6 as not referring to the intermediate state in heaven.

In the first place, Rev. 20.6 says blessed is the one who attains to the first resurrection, not to disembodied life in heaven. In the second place, the verb ***zao*** here is an important one for John. In Rev. 1.18 Christ identifies himself as the living one and identifies true life as life back from the dead – resurrection life (cf. the parallel to 2.18). In fact Christ in that text says, "look, I am alive forever." Christ being alive is closely linked to his glorified state, more particularly with his being in a glorified body that can be seen. The hope that Christ holds out to John in the vision is the same one he wants John to hold out to his audience of pressured and persecuted Christians – the promise of new life in the form of a resurrection body. With the possible exception of Rev. 6.9, nowhere in Revelation are there any references to "living" without them being references to life in some sort of body (cf. 4.9–10; 16.3).

There is a contextual reason as well why "they came to life" likely refers to life in a resurrection body. Notice the reference to "the rest of the dead" coming to life at the end of the millennium. Whatever "come to life" means in vs. 5, it surely also means in vs. 4. Otherwise there would need to be some kind of indication in the text that John was talking a purely spiritual matter in the first instance, but a physical and bodily one in the second reference to "they came to life." Here in Rev. 20.4 as in Rev. 13.14 we probably have an ingressive aorist that should be translated "came to life." (cf. TEV, NIV, NEB, NRSV, and JB, which all have this translation).

In addition we are told that those who make the first resurrection avoid the second death. The inference is that they live forever. For John, as for other early Christians, true blessedness involves existence in a resurrection body (cf. 1 Cor. 15). As the saints under the altar in Rev. 6 make evident, life without a body and prior to the final resolution of all matters is an interim condition, not the final blessedness. It is a time of waiting, and in Rev. 6 those saints are impatient. There is no good evidence in Revelation or elsewhere in the NT that "resurrection" or "coming to life" ever refers to entering the intermediate state in heaven at death.

There is another relevant observation in comparing Rev. 6.9 and Rev. 20.4–6. In Rev. 6.9 while the saints are in heaven they are under the altar, not on thrones, and instead of judging, ruling, or reigning with Christ they are asking how long before judgment will take place. By contrast in Rev. 20.4–6 those mentioned are said to be reigning. More specifically John says in vs. 6b they "will reign," clarifying that the reigning he has in mind is still in the future. The aorist tense used in vs. 4b conveyed the sense of certainty that this would transpire for the martyrs and others who had resisted emperor worship, where as the future tense in vs. 6 indicates that this will transpire on the earth in a time yet to come.

There is no dispute that John refers to two resurrections in this passage. It has been the view of premillennialists that in both cases a physical resurrection is in view. The former is viewed as the resurrection of the saints to reign with Christ; the latter is viewed as the resurrection of the wicked for judgment (cf. 20.11–15). That John speaks of a first resurrection and a second death strongly suggests that he has a sequence of resurrections as well as deaths in mind. This view is also supported by John speaking of "the rest of the dead," which means he has in mind some of the dead coming to life at one point and the rest coming later. If there is only one group called "the dead" here, then it follows that resurrection means the same sort of coming to life for each group, otherwise "the rest" never would come to life in the manner the others had come to life. Furthermore, "the rest" cannot refer to all the dead brought to life at the end of some sort of millennial period. Only a view that holds to two bodily resurrection events can account for the phrase "the rest." In short John affirms two resurrections of the dead: one is blessed, the other not blessed; one is before the millennium, the other after it.[5]

It is then proper to conclude that John believes in a future millennial reign upon the earth of Christ with at least some of the saints. This will transpire after the series of seven judgments but prior to the final judgment and the new heaven and new earth. John is what Eusebius was later to call a "chiliast," a believer in a thousand-year reign. This was one of the reasons why there was debate as to whether Revelation should be included in the canon. Of course, since Revelation is a book of many symbolic numbers, it would appear likely that John is not specifying a particular length of time for this millennial reign, other than to suggest it will last for a long time and then will be terminated. Historic premillennial belief based on this passage and others never affirmed a pretribulation rapture of the believers so that they might avoid the final tribulation. This was a much later notion that surfaced with the rise of dispensational theology in the nineteenth and twentieth centuries.

---

5   It would appear that Paul also affirms the notion of a particular blessed resurrection for those who are in Christ in 1 Cor. 15. He says that when Christ returns, those who are in Christ or belong to him will be raised (vs. 23). He does not say everyone will be raised on that occasion. See my discussion of this matter in *Conflict and Community in Corinth* (Grand Rapids, Mich.: Eerdmans, 1994). The phrase "resurrection from out of the dead ones" is the phrase Paul chooses to use, not "resurrection from death or from the realm of death."

Author Index

Extra-Biblical Texts Index

Scriptural Index

Note: Excludes Revelation references.

Subject Index